HARVARD HISTORICAL STUDIES • 170

Published under the auspices
of the Department of History
from the income of the
Paul Revere Frothingham Bequest
Robert Louis Stroock Fund
Henry Warren Torrey Fund

CHARLES B. LANSING

From Nazism to Communism

GERMAN SCHOOLTEACHERS UNDER TWO DICTATORSHIPS

HARVARD UNIVERSITY PRESS

Cambridge, Massachusetts, and London, England

2010

Library of Congress Cataloging-in-Publication Data
Lansing, Charles B.
   From Nazism to Communism: German schoolteachers under two dictatorships / Charles B.
Lansing.
     p. cm.
   Includes bibliographical references and index.
   ISBN 978-0-674-05053-2 (alk. paper)
   1. Education—Germany—History—20th century. 2. Education—Germany (East)—History.
3. Teachers—Germany—History—20th century. 4. Teachers—Germany (East)—History.
5. Education and state—Germany—History—20th century. 6. Education and state—Germany
(East)—History. 7. National socialism and education—Germany. 8. Communism and
education—Germany (East) I. Title.
   LA721.8.L29 2010
   370.943'0904—dc22   2009036538

To Amy

Contents

Abbreviations

BAB	Bundesarchiv, Berlin
BGL	Betriebsgewerkschaftsleitung, city-wide union leadership in the case of Brandenburg an der Havel
BLHA	Brandenburgisches Landeshauptarchiv, Brandenburg State Archive
CDU	Christlich Demokratische Union, Christian Democratic Union
DEG	Deutsche Erziehergemeinschaft, German Educators' Community
DSF	Gesellschaft für Deutsch-sowjetische Freundschaft, Society for German-Soviet Friendship
DstA	Domstiftarchiv, Cathedral Foundation Archive, Brandenburg (Havel)
DVfV	Deutsche Zentralverwaltung für Volksbildung, German Central Administration for Education
FDGB	Freie Deutsche Gewerkschaftsbund, Free German Trade Union Association
FDJ	Freie Deutsche Jugend, Free German Youth
GARF	Gosudarstvennyi Arkhiv Rossiiskoi Federatsii, State Archives of the Russian Federation in Moscow
GDR	German Democratic Republic
GLE	Gewerkschaft Lehrer und Erzieher, Union of Teachers and Educators
GUE	Gewerkschaft Unterricht u Erziehung, Union of Teaching and Education (formerly GLE, name changed in 1951)
KPD	Kommunistische Partei Deutschlands, Communist Party
LDPD	Liberal Demokratische Partei Deutschlands, Liberal Democratic Party
NSDAP	Nationalsozialistische Deutsche Arbeiterpartei, National Socialist German Workers' Party or Nazi Party
NSLB	Nationalsozialistische Lehrerbund, National Socialist Teachers' League

NSV	NS Volkswohlfahrt, National Socialist People's Welfare
PG	Parteigenosse, member of the Nazi Party
RGVA	Rossiiskii Gosudarstvennyi Voennyi Arkhiv, Russian State Military Archive
SAPMO	Stiftung Archiv Parteien und Massenorganisationen der DDR im Bundesarchiv, Foundation for the Archives of the GDR's Parties and Mass Organizations in the Bundesarchiv
SED	Sozialistische Einheitspartei Deutschlands, Socialist Unity Party
SMA	Sowjetische Militäradministration, Soviet Military Administration
SPD	Sozialdemokratische Partei Deutschlands, Social Democratic Party
SS	Schutzstaffel, StadtA Brandenburg, Stadtarchiv Brandenburg an der Havel, City Archive, Brandenburg (Havel)

FROM NAZISM TO COMMUNISM

Introduction

Almost five years after the collapse of the Third Reich and the Soviet occupation of eastern Germany and less than one year after the creation of the socialist German Democratic Republic (GDR), a representative of the regional chapter of the teachers' union reported on the recent union leadership election for Brandenburg an der Havel, a small historic city 50 kilometers west of Berlin. The functionary noted in the spring of 1950 that the so-called reactionary forces of the "petit bourgeoisie" had retained control by decisively defeating the small group of Communist teachers. The delegates—men and women who had only recently been chosen by the teaching staffs of individual schools—had elected a local leadership that consisted almost exclusively of non-Communist teachers; only two of the 22 individuals belonged to the ruling Communist party, the Socialist Unity Party (SED) of Germany. Since the local union leadership was expected to play a number of important roles in the nascent GDR, not least of which was the economic and ideological mobilization of the teachers on behalf of the Communist state and party, officials were deeply disappointed with and angered by the teachers' rejection of the Communist slate of candidates. Cause for additional alarm was the fact that a large majority of the delegates had selected as the city's new union chairman not the candidate endorsed by the SED but the respected teacher Johannes S., a member of the Liberal Democratic Party (LDPD) who had been teaching in Brandenburg since 1912 and had been a thorn in the side of the Communist authorities for some time.[1] Although the functionary refrained from saying as much in the report to his superiors, the spring 1950 elections represented

1

a clear rejection of the ruling party's increasingly radical policies of the past several years.

That the city's teachers turned to Johannes S. for leadership is not surprising. A physically imposing figure born in 1884 in the Pomeranian city of Greifswald, he had had as of the spring of 1950 a distinguished career in Brandenburg, having worked in a number of its schools in a variety of capacities over the course of more than 30 years. In addition to teaching, he had served as an elementary school principal and even as Brandenburg's school superintendent. During the Second World War, he had continued to teach in the city's schools until the final months of the war, when he was conscripted into the Nazi militia, the Volkssturm, and ultimately wounded as a consequence of his efforts to help defend the city from the advancing Red Army. Over the course of his career, he had belonged to a number of professional organizations, including the Prussian Teachers' Association and the National Socialist Teachers' League (NSLB). A committed democrat, he was before 1933 a member of the bourgeois progressive German Democratic Party. Although approximately 23 percent of German teachers had joined the Nazi Party (NSDAP) by 1939, Johannes S. never became a National Socialist.[2]

Nonetheless, elements of Johannes S.'s career as a teacher in Brandenburg an der Havel are quite surprising. Although he had served in the late Weimar Republic as the deputy principal of Brandenburg's pedagogically and politically progressive Secular School (Weltliche Schule or Sammelschule), an institution despised by local and regional Nazis, Johannes S.— unlike many others affiliated with the school—was not demoted, transferred out of the city, or dismissed when Nazi officials closed the school in the early months of the Third Reich. Moreover, he had been a Freemason from 1928 to 1935, a fact that had exposed him to potential dismissal by the Nazis during their purge of political and racial "undesirables" in the first years of the Nazi regime. Finally, if one were to take seriously the postwar statements of Communist party and state officials regarding the necessity of a complete purge of those teachers who had taught during the Third Reich and their replacement with a new generation of "untainted" pedagogues, then Johannes S. should have fallen victim to the second major wave of political purges that swept over Brandenburg's teachers: the denazification campaigns that began in 1945 and ended in 1948. Yet Johannes S. not only continued to teach in the city's schools, just as he had since 1912, but was appointed by officials in August 1945 to serve as Brandenburg's superintendent of schools and in this capacity oversaw the first centrally coordinated denazification purge of the city's teachers.[3]

Also surprising is Johannes S.'s ability to lead the teaching staff at a time when the Communist state and party were transforming the school system, its pedagogues, and their professional organization into a highly centralized, ideologically conformist system of indoctrination. Beginning in 1947, education officials in the Soviet occupation zone overhauled the purpose and philosophy of German education. The much more indigenous and heterogeneous immediate postwar reforms of the German education system were now being replaced by a more rigid and less adulterated import model from the Soviet Union. Whereas the education system had traditionally sought to instill in pupils the ideals of classical humanism, which since 1945 had been used to help build an "antifascist" and "democratic" Germany, the new education model aimed to convey to the young students the values of a "socialist humanism," one that glorified the "active" support of the socialist collective rather than "bourgeois" individualism. Officials ceased promoting classics such as G. E. Lessing's *Nathan the Wise* or Friedrich Schiller's *William Tell* and called instead for a new literary canon of German and Soviet socialist works. Rejecting the rich German pedagogical tradition embodied in the theories of Wilhelm von Humboldt and Georg Kerschensteiner, officials formally adopted the theory and practice of Soviet pedagogues such as Anton Makarenko. Increasingly, all "Western" pedagogical traditions, including the previously tolerated progressive German models of teaching, were actively opposed by education officials. Nor were the reforms limited to curricular issues. In late 1947, Soviet occupation officials called for the indoctrination of eastern German teachers in Marxism-Leninism and the "accomplishments and successes" of the Soviet Union. This point was underscored at the Third Pedagogical Congress held in July 1948, at which teachers were told to think of themselves as "political teachers" as well as pedagogues and state functionaries.[4] Similarly, the SED at this time began a process of increasing its control over the schools. The SED Politburo announced: "Now begins a new phase in the internal development of our school system: the raising of standards in the classroom and the anchoring of democratic content . . . thus the further expansion of our school system is not possible without conflict between reactionary and progressive concepts or without a struggle between the enemies and the friends of the new school."[5] Communist teachers were organized into party school groups, and positions in the education bureaucracy, which was now beginning to displace the regional governments as the highest authority on education, were increasingly filled with loyal Communists. The SED's campaign to transform East German society along Soviet lines also affected the teachers' union. In early 1948, the SED began its effort to politicize and control the Union of Teachers and Educators (GLE), designating it the "main instrument for the political training of teachers."[6]

As a consequence of these efforts, local Communist officials had increasingly voiced their dissatisfaction with Johannes S., the GLE leadership, and Brandenburg's teachers in general. In 1949, Johannes S. earned the enmity of local state and party officials by interfering with their efforts to replace older, non-Communist members of the local union leadership with younger, pro-SED teachers. Faced with three party members selected by the Communist school superintendent for appointment to the leadership, he instead nominated three Liberal Democrats, all of whom the city teaching staff elected at a meeting in May. In a scathing attack, the Communist school superintendent denounced the elderly pedagogue for his "bourgeois" attitudes and "unprogressive" (*fortschritthemmend*) policies, such as working to reemploy purged Nazis and obstructing the hiring of Communist principals.[7]

That Johannes S. continued to teach in Brandenburg's schools and that he assumed formal control of the union in the spring of 1950 represented the clear failure of the authorities to create a new education system in which a teaching corps consisting exclusively of politically and ideologically conformist pedagogues organized in an institutionally subservient teachers' union instructed pupils according to a new Communist curriculum. His significance is magnified by the fact that his personal and professional biography from 1933 to 1953 is shared in part by a significant portion of Brandenburg's teaching staff. For example, the city's first teacher training course set up in 1945 with the goal of very quickly producing a new crop of pedagogically suitable teachers "uncontaminated" by Nazism and German militarism was run by the elementary schoolteacher Johanna M., a woman who had begun her career in Brandenburg before the First World War and had been, in the words of a local journalist writing in February 1933, "a known personality in nationalist circles."[8] Her notoriety stemmed from an exceptional degree of involvement in rightist political activities that included, in the late Weimar Republic and early Third Reich, lecturing on nationalist topics, serving as the local chairwoman of both the Women's Committee of the rightist German National People's Party and the nationalist, conservative Queen Louise League, and even running for a seat in the provincial legislature on the German National People's Party ticket. During the Third Reich, while belonging to the NSLB and the National Socialist People's Welfare (NSV), the Nazi welfare agency, Johanna M. taught uninterruptedly in the city's schools. In addition to organizing and running the city's first teacher training course in the immediate postwar period, Johanna M. also served as deputy principal of Brandenburg's Görden Elementary School for Girls. To take another example, Otto S., a secondary schoolteacher who began teaching in Brandenburg in 1906 and had once also belonged to the German National People's Party, nevertheless weathered the postwar denazification purges, joined the Christian Democratic Union (CDU), and went on to serve in school leadership positions in the late 1940s.[9]

In fact, many of the men and women who chose Johannes S. as their union leader in 1950 had also been educated in the German Empire, had begun working in the classroom during the Weimar Republic or Third Reich, had joined a variety of political and professional organizations that were affiliated with the Nazi Party, and had in the postwar era failed to embrace the SED and its efforts to transform the East German state, society, and economy. Moreover, elements of his story are shared by a younger group of teachers whose biographies differed significantly from his: the men and women who were schooled in the Third Reich and received their professional training after 1945. They, too, were confronted with state and party efforts to instrumentalize education for political and ideological ends. Like their more experienced and usually older colleagues, they rallied to the nascent teachers' union as a vehicle for the defense of their professional, legal, and material interests. Although officials had trained these men and women in the hope that they would wholeheartedly support the postwar "democratic" reforms of eastern German society, many of these *Neulehrer,* as they were called, stood apart from the actions of the increasingly dominant SED.

*　　*　　*

This book examines the experience of Johannes S., Johanna M., Otto S., and their Brandenburg colleagues in the period 1933–1953, focusing on how they interpreted, reacted, and ultimately adapted to the Nazi dictatorship, the Second World War, the Soviet occupation, and the establishment of the GDR. Drawing on German and Russian archival collections as well as oral histories, this study seeks to answer, in part, one of the most central questions of this period in German history: To what extent and in what ways did twelve years of fascism and six years of war influence the creation of the East German Communist state? Assessing the legacies of the Third Reich requires that the multifaceted experiences of hundreds of teachers be framed in a way that permits relevant commonalities to be identified and measured; to this end, this study focuses on the complex but fundamental relationships among the state, the city's pedagogues, and their professional organization during the Nazi and Communist periods. The book establishes, for instance, the means by and the extent to which the Nazi and East German dictatorships co-opted Brandenburg's teachers, and to what extent the official policies were resisted, obstructed, or evaded. It does so by examining previously ignored or misunderstood processes and institutions like the purges of the German teaching staff in the periods 1933–1938 and 1945–1948 and the actions of the NSLB and the postwar GLE.[10] This book argues that National Socialist policies such as the 1933 Law for the Restoration of the Professional Civil Service and the "reeducating" of pedagogues in NSLB training camps, for example, failed to change substantially the physical and ideological composition of the city's teaching staff. Much the same can be said for the effects of Soviet and German Communist exclusionary policies after 1945. As a result, the men and women charged in the postwar era with educating a new "antifascist" generation were, to a surprising degree, the same individuals who had dutifully worked to nazify Germany's pupils in the Third Reich. These men and women brought to their designated role in the postwar reconstruction of eastern Germany many of the same attitudes and skills—not least of which was a remarkable ability to adapt to different political and ideological circumstances—they had developed in the late Weimar Republic and the Third Reich.

The experience of Brandenburg's teachers was also marked by significant discontinuities. The book makes the case that the Nazis' evisceration of the traditional teachers' professional organizations and replacement of them with the NSLB, which failed to mobilize ideologically and politically pedagogues on behalf of the Third Reich, had a significant impact on teachers' attitudes toward their postwar union and thus toward the nascent East German state. That pedagogues rallied to the GLE, and thereby tolerated many of the educational reforms in eastern Germany, was due in large part to the stark contrast created between the welcome activities of the GLE and teachers' memories of the (non)actions of the NSLB. The teachers' embrace of the postwar union was also a consequence of wartime developments. This study situates the experience of the Second World War, with its related broad and deep impact on the German state and society, in the larger story of Germans' experiences of both the Nazi and the early East German dictatorships. The role of the war in at first hindering and then ultimately reversing, sometimes only partially, certain Nazi social and educational policies is evaluated. The book maintains that efforts to indoctrinate teachers were redirected or sharply curtailed over the course of the war. Similarly, Brandenburg's teaching staff underwent at this time a process of "deprofessionalization," characterized by, among other things, a sharp drop in their material and social standing and the loss of their exclusive claims on teaching Germany's youth. As a result, Soviet officials and East German Communists found on their arrival in Brandenburg a group of men and women less wracked by the class, social, and organizational tensions that had fragmented the city's community of teachers as of January 1933.

The relationship between the pedagogues and the postwar state and party reveals that the experience of living through the Third Reich and the Second World War predisposed Brandenburg's teachers neither against nor for a "democratic" postwar society and polity as defined by the Communists. Men and women like Johannes S. and Johanna M. neither actively resisted nor enthusiastically supported the nascent "antifascist" order. Nevertheless, as is argued here, the mixture of continuities and discontinuities—in the composition of the teaching staff, for example, in the relationships between the city's teachers and the state, party, and union, and in attitudes and professional practices—that defined the collective biography of Brandenburg's teachers in the period 1933–1953 helped to stabilize the GDR in its formative years, including during its first major crisis, the Uprising of 17 June 1953.

One central narrative and interpretive axis of this book is the efforts of both the Nazis and the Communists to create a unified corps of politically reliable teachers charged by the state with the indoctrination of German youth. Both leading National Socialists and East German Communists believed education was central to their planned transformations of German society, politics, and economy. Illustrating the initial seriousness with which many Nazi officials held education reform, Adolf Hitler stated to assembled Stormtroopers (Sturmabteilung) and Schutzstaffel (SS) leaders on 1 July 1933:

Revolutions can only be considered successful if they stamp their spirit and insights not only on the supporters but also on the era itself. The new state is a work of fantasy if the state does not create a new kind of man. For two thousand five hundred years, almost all revolutions, with only very few exceptions, have failed because their leaders did not recognize that what is essential in a revolution is not the seizure of power but the indoctrination of mankind.[11]

Although not the only means of indoctrination, the school system was to play a decisive role in creating this "new kind of man." Similarly, postwar officials planned to make wide-ranging education reform a foundation of the "new" Germany. Amid the ruins of the Second World War, for instance, leading Communist and Socialist officials in eastern Germany called in October 1945 for a "new type of democratic, responsible and capable teacher" who alone would be able to transform pupils into "agents" of a peaceful, "antifascist," and democratic reconstruction.[12] Otto Grotewohl, leading German Communist and future first minister-president of the GDR, made clear the importance of teachers for the Communist postwar project at a July 1946 SED conference:

> The central issue related to the creation of a democratic school system is and remains that of the teaching staff. . . . Our party has proposed to the responsible agencies solutions . . . [addressing teachers' material living and working conditions] because we see a real and close relationship with the teaching staff as the decisive precondition for the reeducation of the German people along the lines of peaceful thinking in the spirit of genuine and true humanity.[13]

And a necessary cornerstone of any reform of the education systems for men like Hitler or postwar education minister Paul Wandel was presumably the thorough transformation of the teaching staff. Accordingly, as will be shown, both regimes implemented a wide array of measures to replace the current and largely suspect pool of teachers with a newly formed, ideologically and, in the case of the Nazis, racially homogenous, pliant teaching staff able to teach a new politicized curriculum to Germany's future citizens. Both regimes, for example, carried out purges of "undesirable" pedagogues from classrooms throughout Germany, though they used differing criteria. In addition, both regimes sought to indoctrinate teachers to make them willing to instill the new ideological values in the youth. Through a variety of formal and informal institutions, programs, and experiences, especially the

NSLB, the Nazi state schooled Germany's teachers in the racist, violent, and social Darwinistic worldview that lay at the heart of the Third Reich. And for the Soviet and German Communist officials, the postwar inculcation in German teachers of "antifascist," "democratic," and, eventually, socialist values by similar means was also a very important policy goal.

Yet no account of the experience of one group of Germans under both regimes should limit itself to an analysis of the state's actions. An equally important, if less immediately apparent, element of the story—and a second axis of this book—is the actions of the teachers themselves as they confronted a mixture of intended and unintended radical changes in their workplace. During the period 1933 to 1953, for example, the composition of the school day and calendar were altered, the very structure of the school system was changed more than once, the nature and actions of teacher organizations were overhauled, and pedagogues were repeatedly required to teach protean and heavily politicized curricula. Such changes were part of revolutionary programs that sought to instrumentalize teachers and their classrooms for ideological ends. Yet there were clear limits to the efficacy of both these National Socialist and East German Communist efforts. To the clear disappointment of both regimes' officials, a person's willingness to teach a new curriculum or to become a member of a politicized teachers' union did not necessarily involve a willingness to fight tirelessly and with complete conviction on behalf of either the Third Reich or the GDR. Long after the Nazi dictatorship had been set up and much of German society "coordinated," one ardent Nazi school principal in Brandenburg complained that only a few of his teachers had joined the Nazi Party or an affiliated organization and, more seriously, "sadly, simply belonging to one of these formations does not guarantee activism, not even honest conviction. . . . What is lacking is a teaching staff that can offer mainly on the basis of its attitude the prerequisites to develop the National Socialist spirit in the school."[14] On the eve of the Second World War, another ardent Nazi principal similarly criticized the city's teaching staff; in a pamphlet celebrating the 350th anniversary of the Von Saldern secondary school, Walter Holöhr called for new teachers who were more "youthful"—who, as he defined it, would not "race through the lessons they are duty-bound to give but for which they lack inner conviction and genuine engagement."[15] Mirroring this was the complaint of an SED official in May 1949 that of Brandenburg's more than 400 teachers, only "80 belong to the SED, though one can describe only a few of these as activists. There exists here a firmly built bourgeois teachers' organization."[16] A year later, Brandenburg's superintendent of schools voiced similar concerns in his political and pedagogical evaluation of the Goethe secondary school for girls and its principal:

> All these things contribute to . . . [the principal's] coolness [*Reserviertheit*] toward Marxism. The entire teaching staff is similarly oriented. One joins a "democratic" organization but not the largest workers' party (the SED is the strongest party in the city and in the city council in Brandenburg) and declares that it is quite enough if one has joined a democratic organization since one is then in the National Front and that is the main thing. The teaching staff must be led, with skill and a certain carefulness, from the position "it is enough just to be a member" to that of political activism. That will not be easy work, since the teaching staff consists almost entirely of older academically trained teachers who will not be replaced in the near future.[17]

In other words, pedagogues were teaching the redesigned postwar curriculum, but a great majority refused to join the SED or get involved in any party. From the point of view of their overseers, they were following the letter of the new program but not its spirit. Such statements do not reflect a proclivity of Communist officials seeking to motivate the party members by means of constantly criticizing the pace and scope of their work on postwar transformation, but instead illustrate the genuine frustration and disappointment that both National Socialist and Communist officials felt regarding the teachers' very limited participation in these dictatorships' ideological projects. Note, also, however, that such reluctance to support the regime fully or even to the degree officials desired was not a form of explicit opposition or resistance. As the story of the Brandenburg teachers' role in the Uprising of 17 June illustrates, an unwillingness to embrace the regime to the extent it desired did not translate into organized resistance to the state and party. Instead, the teachers behaved collectively more like the supposedly apolitical civil servants of Germany's fabled *Berufsbeamtentum* (tenured civil service) than like either defenders or opponents of the new order. This study uses an analysis of the relationships among the state, the pedagogues, and their professional associations to identify the methods teachers used to defend their political and professional autonomy and to assess their efficacy.

The same analysis enables this book to compare concretely the Third

Reich and the early GDR, thereby illuminating many of the important similarities and differences between the two regimes. Whereas the majority of recent studies in this area compare National Socialism and Communism in terms of programmatic affinities or theoretical distinctions, this study compares the two regimes' intent, means, and overall impact as experienced by ordinary men and women like Johannes S. I will analyze the Nazis and the Communists' planned and realized uses of the schools, the ways they co-opted institutions and practices, and their defeats and successes. The experiences of one professional group under both regimes serve as a lens that clarifies the similar and different aspects of the two systems, thereby making the case that a perspective that focuses on the actions and attitudes of ordinary Germans is a necessary and particularly fruitful approach to understanding Germany's two dictatorships, as well as the complex, protean, and historically contingent processes of state formation and state-society development in twentieth-century Europe.[18] Such an approach should also help to legitimize the notion of comparing the Third Reich and the GDR. What has led me to do so is neither my political convictions nor my methodological training but the fact that millions of Germans, including a great many of Brandenburg's teachers, lived and worked in both regimes. It is their story this book seeks to excavate.

The study of Brandenburg's teachers in this period also makes it possible to address in an unique and very illuminating way the important but often slippery issue of continuities and discontinuities between National Socialist Germany and the allegedly "antifascist" East Germany. This book first identifies and then evaluates some of the significant political, professional, cultural, and social continuities and discontinuities. The continuities of personnel are particularly important. Chronicling the makeup of Brandenburg's hundreds of pedagogues from 1933 to 1953 makes it possible to determine the extent of these continuities. These pedagogues' stories tell much about both the principal factors that shaped these continuities—from deliberate state policies, such as the purges, to unintended consequences of the war—and their significance. This study will assess, for example, whether the fact that a teacher was active professionally in the Third Reich sheds light on his or her postwar career—and if so in what ways.

Continuities of attitudes and practices are also a fundamental part of this story. Many more teachers than has been previously acknowledged weathered the denazification programs and the Second World War and continued to teach in eastern German schools after 1945, so it needs to be established that long-held beliefs and traditional ways of doing things could have also survived into the postwar era, and the effect this could have had on the emerging postwar order needs to be analyzed. It is important that a large number of teachers showed a sustained, pronounced unwillingness to involve themselves substantially in the Nazi and Communist revolutions, an attitude and set of practices that originated in their professional self-identifications with Germany's long-established, supposedly apolitical civil service. Widespread apathy among teachers often served as a stabilizing force in the Third Reich and the GDR, despite the repeated complaints and fears of state and party officials. As for the cluster of practices and attitudes associated with the relationship between teachers and their professional organizations, it is important that over the course of the late Weimar Republic, Third Reich, and early GDR, most German teachers became members of at least three unions. Each of these differed significantly in form and function from its predecessor; the history of the postwar union reveals that these differences often had far-reaching influences on larger social, political, and economic developments.

The significance of the story of Johannes S. and his fellow teachers does not end here; it also shows that historians need to reconceptualize their periodization of postwar German history, pushing its beginning back much earlier than 1945. Casting the notion of the *Stunde Null* (zero hour) into the dustbin of history enables us to understand for the first time the fundamental, multifaceted impact that fascism and war had on the postwar order, in this case the creation of the East German Communist state and society. Brandenburg's teaching staff contributed to the creation of the East German dictatorship as a consequence both of specific Soviet and East German Communist actions after 1945 and, equally important, of their experiences with the Nazi state and party in the period 1933–1945. As this study makes clear, histories of postwar Germany, and more broadly of postwar Europe, cannot exclude this formative earlier period. This book, anchoring the history of East Germany in that of the Third Reich, is the first English-language study in the nascent body of scholarship that extends the interpretive horizon regarding the GDR back to before 1945.[19] The history of East Germany must be regarded as beginning much earlier than the final collapse of the Nazi state, for the simple but important reason that the overwhelming majority of the people who supported, resisted, or simply lived through the efforts of the Soviets and German Communists to transform society did not suddenly materialize in the summer of 1945 but had in fact lived through the Third Reich and the Second World War.

Brandenburg an der Havel : A German Community

Just as the biographies of Johannes S. and Johanna M. represent in important ways the story of Brandenburg's pedagogues, the major social, economic, and political developments in Brandenburg since Napoleon's defeat have some important commonalities with those of the larger German society. Brandenburg's history also has some exceptional qualities: some aspects of its people's experiences were intensifications or extrapolations of developments elsewhere in Germany, and some were entirely new. For example, Brandenburg both was a traditional bastion of Prussian militarism and was known as a highly industrialized stronghold of socialism. Whereas the immediate background to the story of Brandenburg's teachers under the Nazi and early Communist dictatorships was political paralysis and economic collapse, as existed throughout Germany in the late 1920s and early 1930s, this study ends by analyzing an especially dramatic and destructive manifestation of popular discontent with the East German regime, the uprising in June 1953.

Finally, whereas officials nazified street names and cultural organizations in every community in the period 1933–1945, the Third Reich did more in Brandenburg. The city not only established itself as a center of Nazi terror, in that it was the site of Germany's largest and most modern prison, which housed political prisoners such as Erich Honecker, the future head of the GDR, but also was one of the few communities to participate in the T4 program, which murdered the handicapped and others allegedly "unfit for life," an important prolegomenon to the Holocaust. This special mixture of the typical and the exceptional justifies centering this study of Germans living under two dictatorships on the men and women of Brandenburg.

*   *   *

In the decades preceding 1933, Brandenburg emerged as one of the most important communities in the vital region of Prussia, largely as a consequence of the interrelated forces of industrialization and demographic expansion. Originally settled in the tenth century on the banks of the bending Havel River, Brandenburg in 1900 was a small city that had three districts, each separated from the other by a network of canals and rivers; the streetscape was a mélange of architectural monuments to both the city's storied medieval past and its more recent Wilhelmine prosperity. In the first district, the Altstadt, the city's iconic statue of the medieval knight Roland, created in the fifteenth century and more than 5 meters tall, stood in front of the red-brick Gothic city hall, which anchored the neighborhood on the northern bank of the Havel. The Neustadt district, on the Havel's southern bank, contained a dense collection of noteworthy structures, including the late medieval St. Catherine Church and the city's functioning city hall, local district court, and large, imposing main post office. The third district, the cathedral island (Dominsel), was bordered by the Havel River to the east and the large Lake Beetz to the northwest; the Cathedral of Saint Peter and Saint Paul, begun in the Romanesque style in the twelfth century, and the Ritterakademie—an elite secondary school—were located there.[20] Whereas slightly more than 12,000 people lived in Brandenburg in 1819, the number increased to more than 28,000 in 1880 and had grown to approximately 45,000 by 1900. Proximity to Berlin, affordable real estate, and an excellent transportation network consisting of the Havel River, the Magdeburg-Brandenburg-Berlin rail line, and good intercity roadways enabled the city and its businessmen to take advantage of nineteenth-century German industrial development. Whereas Brandenburg had become by the 1850s a center of textile production, with more than 105 cloth manufacturers, 40 weavers, and two silk goods factories, by the final quarter of the nineteenth century, as in a great number of other cities and towns throughout the recently created German Empire, the city's manufacturing base had shifted to more modern industrial ventures such as machine construction and metalworking.[21] In 1871 the brothers Carl, Adolf, and Hermann Reichstein, for example, opened a factory to build baskets and baby carriages, and soon became Europe's largest manufacturer of the latter. A decade later the brothers expanded their product line to include the new English sensation, bicycles. By the end of the century the factory, named the Brennabor Works, employed 2,000 workers and sold its annual production of 20,000 bicycles and 120,000 baby carriages to customers in Europe, Asia, Africa, and South America. In 1881 Ernst Paul Lehmann started a factory that produced toys made out of sheet metal and soon established an international reputation for his mechanical windup playthings and figures. Because of these firms and many others, Brandenburg had become by the turn of the century a center for both bicycle and toy production, though other traditional industrial enterprises such as iron foundries also flourished at this time. On the eve of the First World War, the industrialist Rudolf Weber founded the area's first steel manufacturing plant, the Brandenburg Steel and Rolling Mill. During that war, Brandenburg's industrial production shifted to making war materiel such as grenades.[22]

The men who moved to Brandenburg to work in its factories began in the second half of the nineteenth century to organize themselves in political parties in order to promote their interests. In 1865 the city's first workers' association was founded, and three years later the first local group of the General German Worker's Association (Allgemeiner Deutscher Arbeiterverein) was organized. Both socialism and trade unionism took root early and flourished among the city's industrial workers, despite repressive government actions between 1878 and 1890. In municipal elections held in 1897, five socialist candidates were elected to the city council. Two years later, two-thirds of all candidates elected by the lower class of Prussia's three-class suffrage system were members of the Social Democratic Party (Sozialdemokratische Partei Deutschlands, SPD), and by 1901, all. Joining the SPD on the political landscape in this period were the Conservative, National Liberal, and Progressive People's parties. Despite this variety of political organizations, the local SPD's activities in the final decades of the nineteenth century earned the city a reputation as a stronghold of German socialism, a designation that remained in the minds of many Germans well into the mid–twentieth century.[23]

Whereas official political life during the First World War consisted largely of increasingly less successful efforts to secure food for the almost exclusively urban population, the revolutionary developments spreading through Germany in November 1918 transformed Brandenburg's political landscape. Following the abdication of Emperor Wilhelm II, the bulk of the city's political establishment threw its support behind the nascent republican government. Large segments of the population, however, rallied around the city's more radical Workers' and Soldiers' Council. This potentially explosive division of power resolved itself peacefully in the winter of 1918–1919, and Brandenburg was spared the violence and destruction of the Spartacist uprising in Berlin in January 1919.[24]

Beginning in the spring of 1919, Social Democracy (both the movement and the party) established itself as the most powerful political force in the city. In the municipal elections held on 19 February 1919, the SPD secured a majority by winning 27 of the city council's 48 seats. Support for the SPD decreased in the elections of May 1924 as the United Bourgeois List, which represented broad elements of the middle and upper classes and was created, according to later party officials, to fight "tirelessly" the "Red Majority" in Brandenburg, captured a plurality of council seats. The Social Democrats remained nonetheless a powerful block within the city council and succeeded in November 1926 in appointing as mayor one of their own, Dr. Ernst Fresdorf. The political climate in this period continued to be characterized by intense factionalism and, as Brandenburg's archivist wrote in 1936, by "bitter class struggle." Social Democratic initiatives like the municipal welfare agency encountered fierce opposition from other political parties. Tensions came to a head in 1927 after a councilman from the Communist Party (Kommunistische Partei Deutschlands, KPD) defected to the Bourgeois Working Group (Bürgerliche Arbeitsgemeinschaft), the successor to the United Bourgeois List, creating an exactly even division of seats in the council between the two leftist parties, the SPD and the KPD, on the one side and the Bourgeois Working Group on the other, and thus forcing the government to hold new elections. Brandenburg's city government was suffering from the same political volatility that characterized the national situation. In May 1927 the SPD regained its position as the city's strongest party, winning 22 of the council's 44 seats. Although a local chapter of the National Socialist German Workers' Party (Nationalsozialistische Deutsche Arbeiterpartei, NSDAP) had existed since 30 April 1925, it did not participate in the 1927 elections.[25]

The economic depression and political radicalization that overtook Germany in the late Weimar Republic hit Brandenburg particularly hard. A very large part of the city's production consisted of luxury goods like bicycles, toys, and piano boards, which were among the first items to suffer from the dramatic shrinkage of consumer demand. A subsequent wave of bankruptcies idled businesses and factories, resulting in massive layoffs that swelled the city's unemployment numbers. A market share secured in the mid-1920s by record production levels failed to save the internationally renowned Brennabor Works from bankruptcy in 1931. The closing of the Elisabeth Works iron foundry and the collapse of the Brandenburg Bank Association revealed that the city's economic troubles extended far beyond the industries that produced luxury goods. Consequently, an unprecedented number of Brandenburgers—approximately 50 percent of the population— were by January 1932 living partially or exclusively on some form of state welfare. Twelve months later, the city remained mired in economic misery; the number of unemployed had not decreased appreciably since the beginning of the previous year.[26]

The economic crisis mirrored and contributed to the city's political radicalization and paralysis in the Weimer Republic's final years. In the public sphere, the city's politicized newspapers viciously denounced their opponents and uncompromisingly advocated their solutions to the community's crises. The strongly pro-Nazi *Brandenburger Warte* illustrates this phenomenon particularly well. On the eve of Hitler's assumption of power, this newspaper regularly accused the city's leading or governing "Marxists" of corruption and also vituperatively decried progressive institutions such as the city cooperative *(Konsumverein)*. For the conservative newspapers like the *Brandenburger Warte* and their readers, the Social Democrats' efforts to introduce the pedagogically progressive and secular "unitary school" into Brandenburg were especially threatening, illustrating the seriousness with which Germans debated and discussed education issues in this period. The sharp disagreements regarding education that had come to a head with the creation in 1927 of a progressive Secular School—a coeducational elementary school that, among other things, did not teach religion or use corporal punishment—had not settled down five years later; in various elections held in the spring of 1933, for example, the existence of the Secular School and the more general topic of schools and school reforms continued to be fiercely debated.[27] A member of the Brandenburg provincial legislature, campaigning in the city on behalf of the Bourgeois Working Group, decried in March at a rally that

> instead of showing the pupils that we have become an impoverished people and conveying to them, by means of examples from Prussian-German and Brandenburg history, how a people and a community in times of emergency can work their way up again to prosperity as long as the inner strength of the bourgeoisie and the unity of the community exist—instead of such a valuable history lesson, one has blathered about international reconciliation in the schools of the red communities and contaminated the brains of the kids with pacifist thoughts. By dividing the denominational and the secular schools, Marxism has ripped apart the children's souls and put them at the mercy of its politically selfish efforts.[28]

The reporter concluded approvingly: "The speaker proved the deleterious effects of the curriculum in the secular schools with several very apposite examples. Such conditions must be cleared up as quickly as possible."[29] For broad sections of the conservative and antirepublican population, the Secular School served as a lightning rod for their deep-seated anger. Social

Democratic and liberal Brandenburgers, for their part, saw the Secular School and other educational changes as benchmarks of the progress that had been made since 1918 in reforming the traditional authoritarian school system. As the Brandenburg chapter of the League of Free School Societies (Bund der Freien Schulgesellschaften) celebrated—just days before Adolf Hitler's appointment—recent enrollment increases in the Secular School, the group also sought to rally its supporters against current and future "reactionary" efforts to undo the reforms:

> The forces of reaction pounce on the schools with desperate bitterness. . . . The proven protector of the ruling class is considered the most suitable to bring the reactionary spirit into the schools. Children should learn to see the world only through the lens of nationalist and religious ideas. Against this the League of Free School Societies struggles. Away with phrases that cloud the minds! Away with the anachronistic tendencies that only serve the narrow ruling class! Our children should learn to see the world without prejudices. The entire class period should be used to enable workers' kids too to cope with life. The League has the mission to ward off pernicious tendencies, to clear the way for a free education.[30]

As will be discussed shortly, one of the earliest Nazi measures that affected the city's schools was the closing of the Secular School.

The Nazi "Machtergreifung" (takeover) in 1933 and its attendant reforms did little to deescalate the highly charged public political discourse. Although the "coordination" of the city government was preceeded by a purge of nonrightists from the local administration, papers like the *Brandenburger Warte* nonetheless kept the politicized atmosphere alive by covering in great detail the "Red Terror" in Brandenburg during the 1920s and at the same time continued to attack the city's "Marxists"; such public abuse often took the form of articles gleefully reporting on the loss of power, arrest, and ultimate imprisonment in concentration camps of the city's leading "Marxists." A regular target of vitriol were a handful of "Marxist" teachers. The paper either demanded their immediate dismissal following detailed accounts of their "misdeeds" or, in some cases, celebrated their punishments as signs that the "Iron Broom" was sweeping clean the city's schools.[31]

Nor was the picture much different within the municipal government. Following the disputed election of the SPD candidate, Paul Szillat, as mayor in the spring of 1932, all non-SPD and non-KPD council members resigned, leaving those two parties to try to govern via a rump city parliament. This situation fueled the growth and popularity of radical antirepublican parties such as the KPD and the NSDAP. At an election rally held in the summer of 1932, 32,000 Brandenburgers—approximately half of the city's total population—turned out to hear Hitler give a speech. Whereas the NSDAP had garnered fewer than 600 votes in the 1928 Reichstag elections, over 7,000 and more than 16,000 Brandenburgers voted for the Nazis in the 1930 and 1932 Reichstag elections, respectively. The national parliamentary elections held in November 1932 resulted in slight losses for both the SPD and NSDAP, while at the same time increasing the number of KPD votes by approximately 50 percent. When Reich president Paul von Hindenburg appointed Hitler chancellor at the end of January 1933, National Socialism had already established itself as one of the most powerful and popular political movements in Brandenburg. Nazism had, however, failed to unseat the SPD city government, and in January 1933 the city was divided bitterly and almost evenly between two political camps: one consisting of the SPD, the KPD, and smaller, liberal parties such as the German State Party, the other represented by the NSDAP and the German National People's party.[32]

Following Hitler's assumption of the chancellorship, Brandenburgers experienced the Third Reich in many of the same ways the rest of Germany did. Both before and during the Second World War, rearmament programs drove the city's economy and brought more and more people to the city. New factories and industries were set up in Brandenburg; the airplane manufacturer Arado, for example, was building airplanes in the city by 1938. Similarly, the car manufacturer Adam Opel AG moved its truck production facilities to Brandenburg in 1935–1936, making the city the site of Germany's largest and most modern truck manufacture plant and the primary supplier of the trucks to the Wehrmacht in the war. Already existing industrial plant and enterprises were expanded and/or converted to support the country's rearmament. The Brennabor Works shifted from producing bicycles and baby carriages to hand grenades and artillery gun carriages. To take another example, the well-known Brothers Wiemann shipyard continued to build ships, but its products were now vessels with military uses such as landing craft. In order to meet the seemingly inexhaustible demand for workers, more than 35,000 people moved to Brandenburg between 1933 and 1944. Of these, more than 15,000 were forced laborers and prisoners of war housed in more than 40 camps throughout the city. The Nazi rearmament also brought thousands of soldiers back to Brandenburg, thereby reestablishing the city as one of Germany's largest, most important, and most storied military towns, a status that had originated in the seventeenth century and helped make Brandenburg a birthplace (*Ursprungsort*) of the Prussian army. Beginning in 1935, several regiments consisting primarily of infantry, artillery, and antiaircraft troops moved back into the many barracks scattered throughout the city that had been empty since the early Weimar Republic.[33]

Nor can one describe the major political, social, and cultural developments in Brandenburg after 1933 as exceptional. As in communities throughout Germany, local Nazi officials dismantled the politically diverse and democratic municipal government, replacing it with an authoritarian form of government staffed largely by Nazis and run along the Nazi principle of *Führerprinzip*. Opponents such as Social Democrats, Communists, Jews, and pacifists were harassed, assaulted, forced out of their jobs, and arrested. Early in the Third Reich, such men and women were placed in "protective custody" in the city's concentration camp, one of the first of its type in Prussia; its population grew from 24 to 1,200 inmates in fewer than nine months. Although officials closed the camp in January 1934, those who ran afoul of the Nazi state and party, many for political reasons like future GDR head Erich Honecker, were imprisoned in Brandenburg-Görden, Germany's largest and most modern prison; beginning in 1940, the facility, located on the outskirts of the city, also doubled as an official execution site, where more than 1,700 people were killed by the Nazi state. The city was acquiring at this time a reputation as, in the words of one historian, "a center of political terror and murder."[34] In the social and cultural spheres, the nazification of the city progressed in the standard fashion. The Franz Zielger School became the Hermann Löns School and St. Anna Street became Adolf Hitler Street, for example, and National Socialist festivals like the Day of Work and the Heimat Week reconfigured the rhythm of life in the city. Non-Nazi media such as the local Social Democratic *Brandenburger Zeitung* were shut down. Organizations like clubs and unions were either formally absorbed by Nazi institutions or banned the way the leftist cooperative had been. The "coordination" of society included eventually forcing the city's youth into Nazi organizations such as the Hitler Youth and the League of German Girls and channeling people's leisure into activities and pursuits organized by state programs such as Strength Through Joy.[35]

Postwar developments in Brandenburg also mirrored those in other parts of eastern Germany. Having suffered substantial physical damage in the final weeks of the war as a result first of bombing raids and then of the Red Army conquest of the city, Brandenburg ended the war under Soviet occupation. Under the watchful eye of the local Soviet Military Administration (SMA) and the thousands of Red Army troops stationed in the barracks that had once housed Prussian and Wehrmacht units, a new "antifascist" administration was set up, led by Max Herm, a Communist who had been active in city affairs in the Weimar Republic before being imprisoned in a series of concentration camps for much of the Third Reich, and staffed by fellow Communists and Social Democrats. The total reconstruction of Brandenburg—from clearing the streets of rubble and corpses to purging Nazis from positions in government, business, and schools to restarting trade and industrial production—was the order of the day. Remnants of Nazism and militarism were effaced from public and private life; Adolf Hitler Street was renamed, for example, the portraits and coats of arms of the Prussian monarchy and aristocracy were removed from the walls of the Ritterakademie secondary school, and National Socialist materials like books, flags, clothing, and paraphernalia were confiscated. An important element of the "denazification" process, one that began in the summer of 1945 and continued until early 1948, consisted of several rounds of investigations and evaluations of the Nazi activities of many Brandenburgers by specially appointed commissions; as a result of their work, not a few men and women received punishments ranging from loss of a job, prohibition from practicing a specific profession, the denial of voting rights, fines, and even imprisonment. Similarly, city officials confiscated approximately 70 businesses—including the Ernst Paul Lehmann toy factory, local bank branches, and restaurants—that belonged to former Nazis and "war criminals." The corollary of neutralizing Nazism's legacies was the reconstitution of political life in the city along democratic and "antifascist" lines; local chapters of the KPD and SPD were founded again in the summer of 1945, and the new "bourgeois" LDPD and Christian Democratic Union (CDU) were created several months later. As was occurring throughout eastern Germany, local KPD and SPD organizations in the spring of 1946 joined to form a new SED. The first postwar communal elections, held in September 1946, resulted in a city parliament in which the SED held 30 of the seats, followed by the CDU and the LDPD with 11 and 9, respectively. Despite their best efforts to clean up and rebuild the city, officials had to struggle to feed, to find sufficient housing for, and keep healthy the city's swollen population. Similarly, efforts to restart the economy were severely compromised by, especially, the widespread Soviet dismantling of many of the city's storied factories; the Opel truck plant, the Brennabor Works, and the Brandenburg Steel and Rolling Mill, for example, were disassembled and shipped to the Soviet Union.[36]

The founding of the GDR in October 1949 changed very little in Brandenburg; life in the city continued to marked by the war's legacies. The war's physical devastation was still visible throughout the city. Although the principal bridges linking the various city sections had been rebuilt by 1949, much of the rest of the city's infrastructure remained damaged. Moreover, the population continued to suffer from too little to eat and insufficient housing; the city's teachers, for example, continued to depend on municipal handouts of basic necessities such as shoes and housing. The SED's dominance of city politics developed and expanded, a manifestation of the increasingly radical course being followed by the SED across the GDR. Beginning in 1947, the SED began to push former Social Democrats out of influential positions in the party and state. The adoption of the unitary list in the communal elections in the fall of 1951 ensured that the SED increased its control of the city's parliament. Having transformed itself into a "party of the new type," the SED pursued in the early 1950s a series of radical political, economic, cultural, and social policies; important elements of "building socialism" included the development of heavy industries at the expense of consumer goods production, the collectivization of agriculture, the elimination of private enterprise, the building up of the GDR's armed forces, and the persecution of churches and their organizations. The widespread discontent that resulted from the rise in political oppression and the decline in living standards eventually erupted in the Uprising of 17 June. Although communities across the GDR participated in the uprising, events in Brandenburg were distinguished by the fact that more than 15,000 men, women, and youth took to the city's streets in a day-long orgy of violence and destruction directed at manifestations of the state and party.[37]

As this historical overview illustrates, the history of Brandenburg in the nineteenth and twentieth centuries mirrored that of many other German communities. Yet there were unique or exceptional qualities to the city and its inhabitants that also justify focusing this study of Germans from 1933 to

1953 on those living and working in Brandenburg. The city and its population found itself more than once at the center of important historical developments in Germany, for example. An SS division from the city participated in June 1934 in the centrally directed and retroactively sanctioned murder of Hitler's political opponents known as the Night of Long Knives. The city also played a central role in what many scholars consider the prolegomenon to the Holocaust. Beginning in 1940, a small group of doctors, nurses, SS men, and other officials in Brandenburg began killing Germans who were physically handicapped and/or had hereditary illnesses by pumping carbon monoxide into a former garage of the old prison. Brandenburg was the site of the first experimental gassing in Germany, conducted in January 1940 by Christian Wirth, who designed for the occasion a gas chamber and fake showers and who later played an important role in the "Final Solution" as the first commandant of the Belzec death camp. Before the euthanasia program Aktion T4 was closed down in 1941, almost 10,000 individuals were exterminated in the city.[38] Most important, the city's reputation as a "Red Bastion" makes it an especially suitable case study for examining the Nazi purge of political "undesirables," since the Nazi state and party presumably implemented policies that sought to restructure the city's administration, including its teaching staff, along National Socialist lines at least as vigorously and thoroughly in Brandenburg as in other communities. The degree to which the Nazi state transformed the teaching staff is examined more fully in Chapters 1 and 2. Similarly, the city's traditional reputation as a bastion of workers and their culture, including their traditional support for socialism, raises the question whether segments of the population were possibly ideologically predisposed to support, actively or passively, the postwar efforts of German Communists and the Soviets to create an "antifascist" Communist state. Can one, for example, speak of a continuity of pro-Socialist attitudes among large numbers of the city's population from the pre-1933 period to the postwar era? Did such a possible dynamic affect the attitudes and actions of the city's teachers? Such questions are explored in Chapters 4 and 5. The relationship between long-term continuities and the postwar actions of Brandenburg's teachers is also examined in the book's final chapter, a detailed exploration of the teachers' nonparticipation in the unusually large and destructive disturbances on 17 June 1953.

＊　　＊　　＊

In Brandenburg and throughout the GDR, the suppression of the Uprising of 17 June led immediately to a relative stabilization of the East German state and society because a short-term amelioration of some of the regime's unpopular policies associated with its "building socialism" program was instituted and measures such as increased housing construction and consumer goods production were introduced as part of what was called the New Course, with which authorities placated the public. For teachers like Johannes S., Johanna M., and Otto S., the "softening" of state and party education policies following the uprising, however incomplete and brief, nonetheless marked the end of an extraordinary period in the lives of Germany's teachers. Over a 20-year period, they had lived through two German dictatorships and one world war. They had raised in the schoolyard first the swastika of the Third Reich and later the hammer and compass flag of the GDR. They were at one time members of the NSLB and at another the GLE; the earlier lectures on racial science were eventually replaced by exhortations to support the Five-Year Plan. They had endured the Nazi and Communist campaigns to transform teaching staff, in terms of both their composition and their members' attitudes and actions. Johannes S. and his colleagues had also weathered the unplanned assault on their professional lives that resulted from the radical demands of the Second World War and the ephemeral but nonetheless extensive disruptions that accompanied the destructive Uprising of June 17 in Brandenburg. Although some pedagogues actively contributed to the nazification and/or the sovietization of German schools and society, the majority of teachers did not, choosing instead to comply with these regimes' demands of them only to a certain, rather limited degree. It is this remarkable story—of continuities and discontinuities, of resistance, support, and accommodation, and of the fundamental relevance of the experiences of Germans during the Third Reich for the history of the creation of a postwar "antifascist" state and society—that is told in the following pages.

CHAPTER 1

National Socialism's Assault on German Teachers

The National Socialist acquisition of power initiated a process of radical change in the lives of German teachers such as Johannes S. and Johanna M. By March 1933, the triumphant accounts of Nazi political successes on the national level that began with Hitler's appointment to chancellor had given way in newspapers like the *Brandenburger Anzeiger* and *Brandenburger Warte* to gleeful stories about the implementation of the "national revolution" in the municipal administration of Brandenburg an der Havel. Social Democratic, Communist, Jewish, and "pacifist" civil servants in the city were harassed, arrested, or punished in the workplace. On the orders of Nazi minister of the interior Wilhelm Frick, for example, Potsdam officials in the spring of 1933 suspended, replaced, or dismissed the chief of police, the mayor, the assistant mayor, and numerous city councilmen. The purge reached down into the middle and lower levels of the city's administration. Local and regional Nazis also took the "Iron Broom of the National Front" to the city's labor office and welfare bureau, as well as to the leadership of the trade unions. Nor did these Nazis limit themselves to bringing about the dismissal of political opponents. Prominent leftists such as Friedrich Ebert, son of the Weimar Republic's first president, were beaten and arrested; in July Ebert was imprisoned, joining several other prominent Brandenburgers, for example, former mayor Paul Szillat, in the Oranienburg concentration camp.[1]

Few Brandenburgers expected the purges to end there, least of all the city's teachers. That they as civil servants would be specifically targeted by the new regime as it transformed German society was made clear in a speech delivered in late February 1933 in Brandenburg by Hermann Neef, Nazi Old Fighter and soon-to-be *Führer* of the German League of Civil Servants. Saving Germany from the "materialism" of the Weimar Republic, Neef argued, required a "far-reaching cleansing" of the professional civil service. Nazi officials over the course of the past several weeks had begun the process, and they planned to broaden its scope significantly:

> But this cleansing is not yet finished; it must be energetically implemented not only among the high-ranking and most senior positions but also among the mid- and low-level civil servant groups. The German civil servant is the trustee of the interests of the German nation. It is therefore absolutely necessary that this civil servant also thinks, feels, and acts German. But one cannot believe a Marxist perspective can meet this requirement. Thus in this regard much must be fundamentally changed. One cannot hold it against National Socialism if it in the course of this rights earlier wrongs (disciplinary acts, punisment transfers, promotion discrimination). National Socialism approves of a strong civil service in the traditional sense because Nazism knows that the implementation of National Socialist goals is simply not possible without a clean professional civil service.[2]

Similar sentiments were expressed more crudely and frequently by the far-right *Brandenburger Warte*. With articles and editorials like "Goodbye, You Red Comrades" (March 4), "Red Pedagogues" (March 11), and "Cleansing of the School System" (May 13), dripping with a searing mixture of sarcasm and hatred, that paper kept alive the issue of the alleged unsuitability of certain teachers—those who belonged to the SPD, for example—and singled out specific individuals teaching in Brandenburg's schools. Clearly seeking to pressure Nazi officials to act, the paper even published the names of teachers and other civil servants who had recently belonged to the SPD and other Social Democratic organizations. "The new momentum, which will also stimulate the Prussian schools by means of the creation of a nationalist Reich government," a *Brandenburger Warte* author prophesied in early February 1933, "will result in the disappearance of many more party-book bigwigs from Prussian schools."[3]

The wishes of the reporters and editors of the *Brandenburger Warte* and their supporters were soon answered; effectively beginning with the Law for the Restoration of the Professional Civil Service enacted on 7 April 1933, state and Nazi Party officials drafted and implemented over the next six years a series of laws, decrees, and regulations aimed at "cleansing" the

German state by transforming civil servants, including teachers, into a politically and racially homogenous professional group. National and state ministries of education required teachers to account for their past political affiliations and to prove their so-called Aryan racial status. State and party agencies investigated teachers' ties to organizations such as Masonic lodges, while at the same time implementing broad anti-Semitic measures such as the Reich Citizenship Law of 1935. According to the new laws, those deemed unfit for educating Germany's youth in keeping with National Socialist principles were to be removed from the classroom. School principals, senior administrators, and pedagogues who had been active in the Social Democratic or Communist parties, as well as all Jewish public school instructors, were ultimately to be dismissed. Still others were to be punished by being demoted to lesser positions and/or transferred to different and often less prestigious institutions. Nor were the laws solely deployed as a means to redress past wrongs, enabling Nazi officials to purge the teaching staff of those whose transgressions had taken place before the Nazi "seizure of power." They were also, in theory, powerful tools with which to police the attitudes and actions of Germany's teachers on a daily basis. Even if an employee weathered the purges associated with the Restoration Law, for example, the state could at any time determine that he or she did not have the requisite qualifications or was not acting "at all times and without reservation in the interests of the national state" and demote, transfer, or dismiss the employee. Similarly, skirting immediate punishment did not offer those identified by the state in 1935 as former Freemasons substantial relief or peace of mind; fear that the authorities could reassess their past leniency likely lingered in many teachers' minds. In a confidential Education Ministry circular following the promulgation of the revised Civil Servant Law of 1938, for example, the ministry ominously claimed the right to intervene in situations when "a civil servant does not consciously or intentionally reject the National Socialist ideology, but through his official duties—especially through the decisions he makes—or through his official or private behavior allows it to be seen that he emotionally and intellectually stands apart from the National Socialist ideology."[4] By 1938 the Nazi state possessed not only the legal and institutional means to purge civil servants who, in its eyes, rejected National Socialism but also the tools to ensure that remaining teachers complied with state and party wishes.

Like their colleagues throughout the country, the teachers of Brandenburg experienced in its entirety the lengthy and multifaceted Nazi assault on Germany's educators. State and party officials at every level evaluated the city's teaching staff according to National Socialist criteria; they then worked to remove from the classroom those deemed politically or racially "unsuitable." This chapter investigates the means by which the Nazi state sought to transform the city's pedagogues, focusing on three especially important campaigns to "cleanse" the teaching staff through a series of laws and decrees: the Restoration Law (1933–1934), the anti-Masonic decrees (1935–1937), and the Nuremberg Laws (1935–1937). How did each purge originate, what forms did it take, and how did it apply to men and women like Johannes S. and Johanna M.? Close attention to the implementation of laws and measures in the city's schools illuminates the dynamics of each purge as well as the individuals and institutions most actively involved. Having made the ideological conformity of the civil service a priority, the Nazis had, by the time the Second World War began, successfully implemented a series of sweeping changes in Brandenburg's schools, including the erection of a seemingly powerful legal framework for purging the teaching staff along racial and political lines.

Despite the intensity of calls for action from the Nazi Party and local press, we must also ask whether, on closer inspection, these measures in fact resulted in a thoroughgoing transformation of the city's teaching staff. How successful were the Nazis in remaking the teaching staff through each law or decree? Were there factors that significantly hindered the Nazis' efforts? In order to answer this fundamental question, this chapter will analyze the purge campaigns, establishing and evaluating to the fullest extent possible how many, what kinds of, and in what ways teachers suffered as a consequence of state and party efforts to remake the teaching staff. This scrutiny will reveal a very different picture from the one created by a study of the means alone. Here, the focus on a single city and its teachers permits a uniquely comprehensive and long-term analysis of the fates of specific individuals in the early Third Reich. The story of Brandenburg's teachers tests the assumption, long held by scholars of Nazi Germany, that the purge of Germany's teachers was thorough and complete. Introduced into the discussion for the first time here will be the effect of a select constellation of personal, political, ideological, and economic factors on the scope and intensity of the purge.[5] For example, what was the impact of the shortage of qualified teachers that plagued Brandenburg and other communities throughout the Third Reich? Did the paucity of teachers disrupt the everyday running of the schools, and by extension impede Nazi purge efforts? Faced with staffing inadequacies, were local education officials compelled to defend their subordinates in the face of external demands for reform—from the NSDAP, from regional and national state organs, or from concerned private citizens and groups? Similarly, what role did the issue of the pay and social status associated with the teaching profession play in Nazi officials' efforts to alleviate the shortage and, with it, any obstacles to the implementation of the Restoration Law, the anti-Masonic decrees, and the Nuremberg Laws? It is in this context that other relevant factors, such as the more traditional notions of Nazi state and party dysfunctionality—bureaucratic infighting, for example, or the lack of clear planning in many policy areas—need to be acknowledged and understood. This close examination of the purges will establish that as a result of the incomplete "cleansing" of the schools along National Socialist lines, the great majority of pedagogues in Brandenburg in 1938 had been teaching there since before 1933, consequently shedding light on the possibilities and limitations of the Nazi "revolution" in the German school.

Brandenburg's Schools and Teachers

As of 30 January 1933 Brandenburg's school system consisted of 18 institutions, ranging from selective secondary schools (*Gymnasia*) to public elementary schools (*Volksschulen*).[6] At the top of the city's educational hierarchy were its three academic secondary schools, the Knight's Academy of the Cathedral (Ritterakademie zu Dom), the Upper Lyceum (Oberlyzeum), and the Von Saldern Secondary and Upper Immediate School (von Saldern'sches Realgymnasium und Oberrealschule). The Ritterakademie, established in 1705, offered a classical curriculum for the male children of the urban elite and the landed gentry. The Upper Lyceum instructed the city's girls in home economics as well as in modern languages and the natural sciences, striving to balance the practical and the intellectual elements of a girl's education. The Von Saldern pupils learned from a more modern curriculum, one that emphasized mathematics and the natural sciences as well as modern languages. Only a small fraction of the city's pupils attended these academic secondary schools, but they had a disproportionate social significance and status, since all three conferred on their graduates the diploma—known as the *Reifezeugnis*—necessary for admission to German universities.[7]

Brandenburg's two middle schools, the Municipal Intermediate School and the Augusta Intermediate School, enabled boys and girls, respectively, to continue beyond the elementary school level and thereby obtain an intermediate diploma *(Mittlere Reife)* that would permit further study at an academic secondary school or provide qualification for employment in the civil service's intermediate levels.[8] The great majority of the pupils attended one of the city's eight elementary schools, which included by 1945 the Jahn School, the Franz Ziegler School, the Rochow School, the Roland School, the Nicholas School, the Fontane School, the Werner Mölders School, and the Hans Schemm School. The city also made available a nontraditional, purely secular education at the Secular School, its single progressive school. All students were required to study at one of these elementary schools until at least the age of 10, and those not transferring to a higher type of school had to continue until the age of 14. Occupational training was provided at the city's two vocational schools, the Trade Vocational School (Gewerbliche Berufsschule) and the Municipal Trade Institute (Städtische Handelsanstalt). Finally, Brandenburg catered to the special needs of its pupils with, for instance, the Catholic Community School (Katholische Gemeindeschule) and the Pestalozzi School for the Developmentally Disabled (Pestalozzi Hilfsschule). At these 18 schools, more than 6,000 pupils were enrolled each year.[9]

In order to teach its youths, Brandenburg employed at any one time more than 200 pedagogues.[10] Despite not insignificant lacunae in the surviving archival record, historians have sufficient information to delineate some of the teaching staff's professional, political, and social characteristics as of January 1933. A large number of teachers, for instance, had begun their careers in the imperial period. Almost 50 percent of the Augusta School's instructors had been teaching since before the First World War. Approximately 20 percent of the Franz Ziegler School's and 25 percent of the Roland School's teachers entered the profession during the reign of Emperor William II. In January 1933, the average age of the city's pedagogues was approximately 40. Although there were slight variations in average age among the teaching staffs at individual schools, neither the school type nor the individual school itself produced significant discrepancies. The city's middle or elementary school teachers were no older on average than its *Gymnasia* instructors.[11]

Just as the majority of pedagogues in Germany were male, men dominated the teaching profession in Brandenburg.[12] They filled more than 66 percent of the positions, and the gender imbalance was especially pronounced in the middle and high schools. At the Ritterakademie and the Von Saldern secondary school, for example, the entire teaching staff was male.[13] Even at the girls' Upper Lyceum, female teachers constituted only a slight majority. In fact, men made up approximately 80 percent of all secondary school teachers. Women were concentrated mainly in the elementary and specialty schools. Only at the Secular School and the Pestalozzi School was the teaching staff divided evenly along gender lines.[14]

Brandenburg's teaching staff in January 1933 was also fragmented politically. Here extant sources offer only partial insight into the situation, identifying individuals' party affiliations in a small number of cases (representing approximately 15 percent of the teaching staff) and revealing even less comprehensively nonparty manifestations of political mobilization. There was strong support by teachers for liberal-bourgeois parties, in particular the German Democratic Party and the German People's Party (Deutsche Volkspartei), though a not insignificant number had joined the Social Democratic Party and the German National People's Party (Deutschnationale Volkspartei). Although the Communist Party had established its political strength in industrial centers like Brandenburg in the early 1930s, it found little support among the city's teachers. Similarly, teachers' membership in the Nazi Party was quite low; no more than 10 teachers—less than 5 percent of the total—were NSDAP members as of 30 January 1933, a percentage that corresponds to the membership data for all German teachers.[15] Membership figures alone, of course, are far from perfect indicators of political commitment. Although the city's teaching staff had produced relatively few registered supporters of the NSDAP in early 1933, one of the most active and prominent members of the local Nazi Party chapter was the pedagogue Dr. Ludwig Z. of the Ritterakademie. Having founded the far right Socialist-Nationalist Union in Brandenburg in 1922, he and his followers merged with the NSDAP in 1932. He worked to convert his fellow Brandenburgers to National Socialism by many means, especially the many lectures and public talks he gave on topics such as "Deliverance Will Happen Only through Us" and "Brandenburg's Liberation," which in this particular case bookended the Nazi "seizure of power."[16] Brandenburg's teachers also belonged to a diverse collection of associations that although they were not political parties or even necessarily formally affiliated with them were nonetheless active in a broad political sense in the public sphere. On the left of the spectrum were more profession-specific organizations like the Working Group of Social

Democratic Teachers and the League of Free School Societies; the more conservative members of the teaching staff congregated in the Reich Colonial League, the Stahlhelm, the Queen Louise League, or the Kyffhauser League.[17]

Sometimes corresponding to the political fault lines within it, the teaching staff were also sharply divided in terms of their professional organizations. The number of pedagogues who had joined the NSLB as of January 1933 was quite small, though a slightly greater number had joined the NSLB than the NSDAP. The vast majority, however, were affiliated with one of the major teachers' organizations such as the German Philologist Association or the Prussian Teachers' Association—two of a multitude of organizations that represented Germany's pedagogues, who lacked a unified professional voice. The existence of these organizations exemplified and reinforced significant and long-standing social, professional, and religious divisions among the country's pedagogues. For example, high school philologists ensconced themselves in the German Philologists' Association in order to promote the study of Greek and Latin, thereby defending their social and professional elitism. Of the 19 philologists at the Von Saldern secondary school for whom we have personnel files, for example, 15 belonged to this organization. An even greater percentage of Ritterakademie pedagogues belonged. As will be seen in Chapter 2, most of the teachers retained these memberships for years, relinquishing them in 1937 only under great pressure from Nazi officials. Many middle school instructors joined an organization that emphasized their particular needs, the Intermediate School Teachers' Association. Various issues, especially those touching on status, prevented serious cooperation between the philologists and the intermediate school teachers, and similar forces created chasms of understanding and attitude between the middle and elementary school teachers. Shunned by their socially and professionally acknowledged superiors, elementary school instructors nursed their collective feelings of inferiority in the Prussian Teachers' Association. Even German middle and elementary school principals had their own organization, the Principals' Association, and at least some of Brandenburg's principals were members. Finally, most German female teachers belonged to their own organization, the All-German Female Teachers' Association. Nominally an umbrella institution that served female teachers' needs, it was in reality a collection of largely autonomous subassociations, such as the German Female Philologists' Association, which promoted its members' specific professional needs and desires. City records indicate that more than a few female teachers, working at various types of schools, were members of this organization. As a professional group, Brandenburg's teaching staff was highly fragmented organizationally in January 1933.[18]

Initial Measures and the Law for the Restoration of the Professional Civil Service

Adolf Hitler's ascension to power at the end of January 1933, while making itself felt at once in Brandenburg's streets and newspapers, had little immediate impact on the teachers' professional lives. As a systematic purge of the teaching staff was being considered and drafted in Berlin, the nazification of local teaching staffs occurred in a decentralized, piecemeal fashion. Whereas regional Prussian education authorities began the slow process of overhauling elements of the education system—issuing a decree in early February, for example, that made corporal punishment permissible—the lead in the attack on Brandenburg's teachers was taken by the local pro-Nazi *Brandenburger Warte*. In the article "Subverting the Patriotic School—The Guilty Caught," published on 6 February 1933, the paper first celebrated the initial "cleaning up" that had presumably taken place on the national and regional levels and then, after denouncing the Brandenburg chapter of the Free School Societies, prophesied future purges:

> Comrade Bergemann and his red school society can rest assured that the previous elimination of the red party-book civil servants [*Parteibuchbeamten*] in the Prussian schools has only been a child's game [*ein Dorfspiel*]! The new momentum, which will also stimulate the Prussian schools by means of the creation of a nationalist Reich government, will result in the disappearance of many more party-book bigwigs from Prussian schools, even those who previously thought their situation seemingly secure![19]

After such purges failed to take place in Brandenburg over the course of the next couple of weeks, the newspaper stepped up its campaign with a series of articles that called attention to specific Brandenburg teachers and their allegedly "traitorous" deeds. For example, in a 25 February article, the *Brandenburger Warte* denounced the "pornographer" Otto W., head of the "anti-Christian Secular School that supports the class struggle," as part of its larger attack on school superintendent Paul Strauch. One week later, the paper broadened its campaign to include Von Saldern teacher Julius S., accused of "dictatorially" forcing pupils to honor visiting French students and promoting "liberalism and pacifism." Throughout March, the *Brandenburger Warte* mockingly and brutally maligned a small number of pedagogues; secondary school teacher Dr. Heinrich M. was denounced as an atheist, a Social Democrat, and an "irresponsible demagogue," for example, while the paper demanded that Erich B. be punished for having ordered his pupils to sing the Marseillaise in 1929 in honor of a French guest. Entire schools were even pilloried; the Roland School, according to the paper, sinned on one occasion by disciplining some girls who sang the National Socialist "Horst Wessel Song."[20]

This campaign to cleanse the teaching staff was part of a larger call for, and at times celebration of, the political and ideological settling of scores with various men and women who were active in local public life. By the end of March 1933, the *Brandenburger Warte* gleefully reported on the purge of the city's administration, as the mayor, numerous city council members, the chief of police, and even the director of sanitation were removed from their positions for political reasons.[21] The so-called "Iron Broom" had not yet swept the schools clean of "unsuitable" elements, however, so the paper's campaign continued. Although the "throwing out" of Secular School director Otto W. and the dismissal of superintendent Strauch in early April were brazenly celebrated, as was educational officials' decision to shut down the Secular School, the rightists of the *Brandenburger Warte* nevertheless demanded that much more be done:

> Finally! Brandenburg has waited for this event. Brandenburg is finally free of Comrade School Superintendent Strauch. He has been thrown out of his position. A request of School Superintendent [Paul] Schmidt, Potsdam: now make good where Strauch's "Marxist" overzealousness resulted in serious damage. Loyal, blameless men with great pedagogical talents, teachers who are the real schoolmasters with the best beliefs suffered under Strauch, were not promoted, were bullied, were in some cases punitively transferred. Eliminating Strauch's influence is a task for his successor.[22]

For Brandenburg's Nazis and other conservatives, Strauch's firing represented the culmination of more than eight weeks of public agitation. They did not intend to stop here, however. His termination was not to conclude a chapter in the city's recent history; it instead demonstrated the growing momentum behind the "national revolution," one that was now, finally, to be implemented in the city's schools.

The significance of Strauch's dismissal goes well beyond revealing the ascendancy of Nazis in local government or possibly heralding further personnel changes: he was the first city educator to fall victim to a new mechanism for transforming Germany's civil service, replacing the previous approach—characterized by informal, piecemeal, and local efforts—with something more formal, centralized, comprehensive, and, theoretically, far more effective. On 7 April 1933 the Nazi minister of the interior, Wilhelm Frick, issued the Law for the Restoration of the Professional Civil Service, a far-reaching measure aimed at legally purging Germany's civil servants—including primary and secondary school teachers—according to National Socialist racial and political criteria.[23] Frick, echoing the sentiments of Hitler, intended to use the measure to create an ethnically pure, ideologically homogenous, and politically conformist civil servant corps. By doing so, Nazi leaders hoped to strengthen the bonds of loyalty between the civil servants *(Beamte)* and the state and to efface what they regarded as the pernicious legacy of the Weimar Republic regarding the state bureaucracy: the alleged staffing of the civil service with unqualified political appointees. Senior career bureaucrats hoped to use the law to restore order to the "wild," decentralized wave of firings and purges within the bureaucracy that local and regional Nazi Party leaders had carried out since 30 January 1933. Ostensibly a measure to identify and purge unqualified civil servants hired during the Weimar Republic, the Restoration Law gave the Nazi state unprecedented control over the lives of *Beamte* by providing it with the legal mechanism to remove those they regarded as unfit for civil service.[24]

Article 1 of the Restoration Law both symbolized the measure's extrajudicial nature and defined its scope. Rather than initiate a lengthier process of formally revising or repealing current statutes, Nazi leaders drafted an extraordinary law empowering them to punish *Beamte* "even when the necessary conditions under the relevant law do not exist." Although the Restoration Law failed to specify what the state meant by the term *Beamte,* a subsequent decree established a comprehensive definition. Regular, irregular, probationary, dismissed, retired, and trainee civil servants—in fact, every conceivable type—fell under the law's purview. Along with judges and notaries, for example, public school teachers were now explicitly included in the list of state employees subject to the law.[25]

The law's pernicious nature became clear in article 2; it targeted civil servants hired after 9 November 1918 if, in the Nazi state's eyes, they lacked the "requisite or usual training or other qualifications." Such individuals were to be dismissed and denied traditional rights such as receiving a pension and the continued use of official titles. Implementation decrees issued over the next five weeks dramatically expanded the article's scope to include current and former members of the KPD or a related organization as well as individuals who had previously been active "in a communist sense," regardless of formal membership in a Marxist organization. Furthermore, the measure created a formal and artificial distinction between "political" and "nonpolitical" *Beamte*. A "political" civil servant could only be considered "suitable" for retention in the state's service if "on the basis of his position and activity in public service, on the basis of his experiences and the honorableness of his attitudes and deeds, he appears suitable for entrustment with the office and has proven by an exemplary execution of the office that he is suitable."[26] Raising the professional standards required of so-called political *Beamte* and couching these standards in especially broad and imprecise terms left ample room for unscrupulous or ideologically driven officials to find pretexts for terminating their colleagues.

The measure's anti-Semitic nature was revealed in article 3's blanket dismissal of Jewish civil servants. Here questions of qualifications and training were irrelevant, since all *Beamte* "of non-Aryan descent" were to be purged. Exceptions were to be made only for individuals who had entered the civil service before 1 August 1914 or fought in the First World War for the Central Powers.[27] A subsequent decree specified that it sufficed to be categorized as "non-Aryan" if at least one grandparent qualified as "non-Aryan," by which was meant Jewish. Even marriage to a so-called non-Aryan, according to guidelines issued on 6 May 1933, provided grounds for dismissal.[28]

Exceeding article 3 in scope, subjectivity, and malleability, article 4 targeted the regime's political opponents. Officials "who because of their previous political activity do not offer security that they will act at all times and without reservation in the interests of the national state" could now be dismissed from government employment.[29] The definition of political activity was initially left unclear. Implementation decrees instructed authorities to scrutinize the "total political engagement" (*gesamte politische Betätigung*) of state employees in order to determine their suitability and also shifted article 4's emphasis from proscribing the continuance of past political activity to prescribing current and future political engagement. Simply belonging to a "national" party, regardless of whether one paid dues and attended its meetings, no longer demonstrated one's "national reliability." According to the new standard, the conduct of civil servants—what they said, wrote, and did—revealed their true political conviction. The decree made clear that simply joining the NSDAP, for example, would not shield one from punishment if one defamed in word or deed the state, its leaders, or other "nationalists."[30]

The implementation decrees failed to resolve completely the Restoration Law's essential vagueness, thus adding to its impact. Free from stringent limitations, the Nazi state would judge the past political actions of its teachers by standards of its own and decide who had acted and was acting in support of a "national" Germany and who was not. Even though a supplemental law removed some of the imprecision by explicitly identifying as a "terminable" offense any formal membership in political organizations that supported Marxism, Communism or Social Democracy, article 4 remained a broad and very powerful weapon in the state's hands.[31]

Such far-reaching state empowerment can also be found in articles 5 and 6. Government officials, for example, could now transfer any civil servant to another position, regardless of adverse effects on salary or professional standing, so long as the new position was in the "same or equivalent career track [*Laufbahn*]" as the previous one. Although this small caveat may have prevented the Education Ministry from officially transforming university-trained secondary school teachers into lowly postal employees, it did nothing to prevent the Ministry from demoting them to inferior positions in one-room rural elementary schools. Similarly, article 6 entitled state agencies to retire prematurely any civil servant "for the purpose of rationalizing the administration."[32]

The Restoration Law stipulated that this comprehensive suspension of teachers' professional rights was to last only until 30 September 1933.[33] The law's framers believed six months would be sufficient in order to purge the German civil service of Jews, Social Democrats, Marxists, and other political and racial undesirables. The Revision to the Law for the Restoration of the Professional Civil Service of 23 June 1933 upheld the six-month deadline for the state's racial and political purges, permitting an extension only for those cases involving articles 5 and 6.

How was such a broad and seemingly powerful law to be implemented in Brandenburg and elsewhere? Before the Nazi state could begin the process of dismissing teachers and other civil servants, it first had to identify the political and racial undesirables within the teaching staff and administration. To this end, the Education Ministry collected official personnel files from local school superintendents and distributed questionnaires to all active and retired teachers. Entitled the "Questionnaire for the Implementation of the Law for the Restoration of the Professional Civil Service," the form was a tool designed to determine the *Beamte*'s basic professional history. There were questions regarding, among other items, one's official rank and title, one's professional training, and whether one's promotion to full civil servant status took place before 1 August 1914. More ominous were the questions regarding political activity and racial background. Teachers were asked whether they had belonged to Weimar political parties or activist organizations that included the SPD-affiliated paramilitary organization Reichsbanner and the recently banned League for Human Rights. In order to classify teachers according to racial criteria, the Nazi state required all pedagogues to provide detailed information regarding not only their own "Aryan" origins but also that of their parents and grandparents.[34] That the government threatened to dismiss any teacher who provided false or misleading information only underscored the questionnaire's importance. Brief, seemingly innocuous, but yielding potentially damaging information, it provided the basis for the first step in purging Germany's teachers as envisioned in the Restoration Law.

Another necessary step was the establishment of an institutional framework for evaluating, identifying, and punishing "unsuitable" teachers. Following the Restoration Law's promulgation, Prussian education minister Bernhard Rust quickly asked the Nazi Party in every Prussian administrative district to assemble special three-man commissions—known as Personnel Committees for the Cleansing of the Civil Service (*Personalausschuss zur Säuberung der Beamtenschaft*)—to assist the regional governments' school bureaus in evaluating the questionnaires and personnel files.[35] The NSDAP and the NSLB contributed to the process further by providing to the commissions material regarding individual teachers' political attitudes and activities. Should doubts be raised about the reliability of accusations formulated on the basis of such additional material, commissions were to seek the opinion of the state government, the district's chief administrative officer, and the school superintendent. Serving in an advisory capacity only, the commissions and state school bureaus forwarded their reports to the regional governmental heads, who in turn passed them on to the Education Ministry. The final decision regarding suspension, retirement, transfer, or dismissal lay exclusively with Minister Rust.[36]

In the Potsdam Governmental District, which included Brandenburg, the commission began to evaluate teachers on 29 April 1933. According to the one extant report, Potsdam's Personnel Committee for the Cleansing of the Civil Service was responsible for evaluating the district's 3,700 teachers. After a review of more than three weeks, the Committee reported in late May that it had so far temporarily suspended 85 teachers and that it expected to finish its activities in approximately three more weeks.[37] The Committee failed to make its self-imposed deadline. Cases were considered and evaluation reports drafted throughout the summer and into the early fall. Only in late September, months after the originally anticipated conclusion date, did Potsdam's *Regierungspräsident*, Dr. Ernst Fromm, inform the Education Ministry that the Committee had completed its task.[38]

As the Committee's tardiness suggests, the first stage of the purge of the civil service was not without problems. The volume of the questionnaires and personnel files to be examined overwhelmed the committees and protracted the entire process. Over the course of the summer, the Prussian Education Ministry repeatedly admonished the committees and the local authorities to expedite the processing of the questionnaires and the evaluating of the teachers. The delays were also partly the result of the committees' not infrequent difficulties in collecting the information needed to evaluate teachers; education officials scolded individual school principals such as Von Saldern's Ferdinand G. for failing to pass along either entire teachers' files or important elements thereof.[39] The Prussian Education Ministry acknowledged in early October that the Restoration Law's original deadline for evaluating cases involving articles 2–4 would not be met as a consequence of the significant backlog of unresolved cases, and the ministry and the committees would continue to work until a decision had been reached on all the outstanding cases.[40]

Tensions between state authorities and the committees were another hindrance to efficient and speedy purging of teachers. In early August the Interior Ministry criticized the personnel committees for sloppy work. Especially in cases pertaining to article 4, local authorities were accused of abdicating their sense of responsibility by rubber-stamping the committees' often incomplete or unsubstantiated evaluations. According to the Ministry's circular, time and energy were being wasted, as the Ministry was forced to examine individual cases directly in order to verify or complete the reports. The Education Ministry repeated these admonishments in a circular dated 12 August 1933. Rust demanded of the local authorities and the committees a "most careful" drafting of reports and an "exhaustive" handling of the individual cases. Furthermore, the Education Ministry explicitly proscribed authorities from reaching unofficial deals with teachers that would allow them to volunteer for transfer to different schools in the district in order to avoid more serious penalties.[41]

Despite these logistical difficulties, state ministries did implement the Restoration Law. In the Potsdam District, almost 4,000 teachers filled out the questionnaires. They submitted attestations declaring that their parents and grandparents were neither "racially" Jewish nor of the Jewish faith. Former Social Democrats swore under oath that they no longer belonged to the SPD and had severed all connections to it. Local NSDAP and NSLB chapters provided the Committee with additional information regarding the political background and behavior of individual teachers. Committee members and local school officials spent more than five months reviewing this large collection of information and drafted reports that were sent to the regional and national education authorities. In late November, Minister Rust formally thanked the Committees for their work. As the result of their efforts, Rust claimed: "based on reports currently in my possession, all teachers who are openly resisting or secretly working against the successful construction of the National Socialist state have been removed from the schools or will soon be. A secure foundation for a healthy renewal of the education system in Prussia has thus been created."[42] Unsatisfied with merely demoting, transferring, retiring, impoverishing, and dismissing politically and racially "unsuitable" teachers, the Nazi state symbolically ended the purge with one final act of humiliation and degradation. In a circular dated 27 December 1933, Minister Rust forbade local authorities to organize formal farewell parties or ceremonies for the purged and demoted teachers, since in the minds of the Nazi leaders, they did not deserve the state's customary thanks and recognition of faithful service.[43]

How many teachers suffered the indignity of a ceremony-less termination or demotion? Contrary to the expectations of Nazi officials such as Minister Rust and the later judgments of historians, the Restoration Law, arguably the Nazis' most powerful weapon against political, ideological, and racial enemies, did not result in a large-scale purge of teachers. Extant records indicate that only a very small group of Brandenburg teachers were terminated. The Potsdam *Regierungspräsident* informed the Education Ministry that 47 of the approximately 3,700 teachers in Potsdam District had been fired in accordance with article 4. Only two of the 47 were from

Brandenburg: elementary school principals Otto H. and Otto W. That Otto W. was purged is not particularly surprising; as the "pornographer," according to local Nazis and conservatives, in charge of the "anti-Christian" and "class-struggle" Secular School and as a Social Democrat very active in local politics, Otto W. was the most prominent, and possibly the most despised, "Marxist" teacher in the city. The *Brandenburger Warte* so hated him that it demanded in July that he also be put in a concentration camp! Moreover, Otto W. had already been dismissed in late March as a result of a decree of the Potsdam *Regierungspräsident;* the committee's implementation of article 4 of the Restoration Law merely made this permanent. Like Otto W., Otto H. was also especially active in Social Democratic politics: in the town of Putlitz, where he lived before moving to Brandenburg in 1932, he founded a local chapter of the Reichsbanner and was also in charge of the local SPD chapter. Moreover, conservatives accused Otto H. of moral degeneracy and of politicizing the school, summed up by an anonymous author in the *Brandenburger Warte* as his having overseen "a terror that had no equal."[44] By facilitating the firing of both men, the Restoration Law removed permanently from the classroom two of the most notorious "Marxist" educators in Brandenburg, something celebrated at the time in print and presumably in the minds of not a few Brandenburgers. What such supporters of the "national revolution" did not realize at the time was that Otto W. and Otto H. would be two of only four from Brandenburg to be forever prevented from corrupting Germany's youth.

Instead, Brandenburg's other politically "unsuitable" pedagogues were either simply shipped off to different classrooms, where they could theoretically poison the minds of new groups of German boys and girls, or were not materially affected at all by the Restoration Law. Although Otto H. belonged to a group of five elementary and middle school teachers who had been suspended pending the Education Minister's final decision, two of the other four individuals, also principals, were ultimately only demoted and transferred out of Brandenburg, while elementary school teacher and assistant principal Paul S. was transferred to a school located about 80 kilometers to the east, and Willy S., an elementary school teacher at the Nicholas School, apparently suffered no lasting punishment at all. And even when punishment was meted out, it was not necessarily permanent; despite his 1933 demotion from middle school principal to elementary school teacher, Karl P. was back in the classroom in Brandenburg's Municipal Intermediate School by May 1940.[45] In addition to these pedagogues, most of the teaching staff of the Secular School were punished in accordance with the Restoration Law. Although extant records indicate that at least most of these men and women were Social Democrats, Nazi officials nonetheless transferred four, Werner B., Bruno J., Gertrud Z., and Fritz N., out of Brandenburg and fired two, Käthe B. and Erna F. Although available sources do not explain why the two were dismissed, it is possible that they were fired in part or largely as a consequence of early Nazi efforts to remove women from the workplace; it is less likely that either was terminated because of her political activities. Fritz N., whose punishment consisted only in being transferred, was a prominent Social Democrat who, like the fired Otto W., was active in local politics, including running for city council in March 1933 on the SPD ticket. Moreover, at least five teachers who had been affiliated with the Secular School, including the Social Democrats Thea N. and Karl H., continued to teach in the city's schools.[46]

That approximately 10 of the city's elementary and middle school teachers suffered as a result of the Restoration Law should not be minimized; at least as important, however, is the fact that many other potential victims—including those who had belonged to the SPD or other leftist organizations—escaped the purge unscathed. Of the ten teachers (excluding those discussed above) identified in May and June 1933 in the pages of the *Brandenburger Warte* as currently or formerly, often until very recently, belonging to the SPD and teaching at that time in Brandenburg schools, only one was punished—in this case, transferred in August 1933; the rest were not dismissed, demoted, or transferred. Included in this group was Hermann H. of the Pestalozzi School, who as both a known member of the SPD and, more important, a school principal qualified as exactly the type of person the Nazis intended to remove from the school. He remained in charge of the school until at least the fall of 1944. Similarly, following the publication of the names of nine teachers who belonged to the Republican Club—denounced in the paper as a "kitchen [*Garküche*] of Marxism. Here was decided and discussed, here were the blows against the National Front planned, here the string-pullers of the leftist parties amused themselves"—only one elementary school teacher, in addition to Karl P., whose demotion was discussed above, was eventually punished, in this case by being transferred out of the city. Although the Restoration Law specifically sought to rid Germany of these kinds of civil servants, was conducted in a thorough manner, and had the full force of the state behind it, most Social Democratic teachers were not removed from Brandenburg's classrooms in 1933.

The city's vocational schools were the scene of an especially bitter campaign to purge "Marxist" and other "unworthy" pedagogues, though its final results were not that different from the process under way in the elementary and middle schools. The primary driving force behind this attempted purge was the efforts of two vocational school teachers to use the current political climate to settle old scores. With the *Brandenburger Warte* largely sparing the vocational schools its vitriol, state and NSDAP investigations commenced only after Friedrich R. and Walter R. enlisted the district NSLB in the summer of 1933 to pressure the city government to punish 10 vocational school teachers. In a report titled "The Boss-ocratic Conditions at the Brandenburg Municipal Trade Institute," Walter R. accused his principal and two colleagues of unpatriotic activities. Principal Wilhelm K. was, he argued, guilty of favoritism toward Social Democratic teachers, and men like Alfred H. were unfit for public service as a consequence of their memberships in and actions on behalf of the Republican Teachers' Association and the Republican Club.[47] Friedrich R. authored a report titled "The Boss-ocratic Conditions at the Brandenburg Trade Vocational School," in which he accused seven of his colleagues of an array of alleged political and ideological misdeeds. These actions had resulted, he claimed, in the Marxist contamination *(marxistische Verseuchung)* of the pupils and the teaching staff.[48]

Having decided to transfer two and fire the rest of the accused vocational school teachers, Brandenburg's city government forwarded its decisions and the necessary documentation to Potsdam for review and execution. The *Regierungspräsident* concluded, however, that there was sufficient cause for dismissal or transfer of only two of the 10 individuals. Moreover, the officials reported to their Berlin superiors that the entire case was an elaborate act of revenge by Friedrich R. and Walter R. and their accomplice, vocational school principal Otto H. Their grievances extended back as far as the late 1920s and centered on alleged hindrances to their professional advancement at the hands of the "Marxist" teachers running and staffing the schools.[49] Potsdam officials nonetheless decided to act on some of the teachers' complaints and punish two pedagogues in August 1933. Despite recognizing his good teaching performance and his minimal involvement in "Marxist" activities, state authorities retired deputy principal Karl L. as a consequence of his former membership in the Republican Teachers' Association and the Republican Club and his "unpolitical" articles published earlier in the local Social Democratic newspaper the

Brandenburger Zeitung.[50] Similarly, officials demoted and transferred deputy principal Alfred H. because they believed he did "not offer security that he will act at all times and without reservation in the interests of the national state," even though they conceded that he was a talented teacher, that there was no proof of his alleged "Marxist" agitation in the classroom, and that they were not certain he was even supportive of "Marxism."[51] This limited purge of the vocational schools not only illustrates the roles individuals, the press, Nazi organs, and different state agencies played in implementing the Restoration Law but also highlights the paradox that despite the potentially low standards necessary for punishment, very few teachers were purged.

The Restoration Law had even less of an impact on the city's university-educated pedagogues. At the Ritterakademie, for instance, the initial wave of evaluations and punitive measures did not affect a single teacher. Once authorities closed the Ritterakademie in 1937, however, two pedagogues were retired through invocation of article 6. The Von Saldern secondary school also weathered the purge largely unscathed. Beginning in March 1933, the *Brandenburger Warte* singled out three of its pedagogues for vitriolic attacks, repeatedly calling attention to such political sins as forcing pupils to participate in "party-political Social Democratic" events, indoctrinating the city's youth in "liberalism" and pacifism, and defaming Germany's past. Over the course of the late spring and summer, the newspaper kept up the pressure on state and party officials by voicing its dissatisfaction that the "Iron Broom" had not yet cleansed the city's secondary schools. Such efforts seemed to have succeeded in September regarding the pedagogue Julius S., who, after the paper condemned him for alleged antinationalist statements and actions, was eventually fired for his Social Democratic affiliations. However, he appealed his termination. Von Saldern director Ferdinand G. wrote to Prussian education authorities and successfully argued for his subordinate's reinstatement, citing S.'s professionalism. Despite the very public and malicious nature of his case, S. weathered the Restoration Law's implementation and continued to teach at the Von Saldern secondary school until his death in September 1940.[52]

The cases of Heinrich M. and Paul G. illustrate especially well the imperfect implementation of the Restoration Law. A teacher at the Von Saldern secondary school since 1928, the 39-year-old Heinrich M. admitted in his questionnaire to having belonged until recently to the SPD, the Reichsbanner, the Republican Teachers' Association, the Iron Front, and the Working Group of Socialist Teachers. Brandenburg's provisional school superintendent concluded in August 1933 that Heinrich M., who taught at Von Saldern, was "in attitude and actions a staunch and determined [entschiedenen und entschlossenen] SPD man" and thus recommended that the Brandenburg Province *Oberpräsident* fire him, despite his wartime service, according to article 4. The report of the personnel committee advising the *Oberpräsident* seconded the superintendent's conclusion. Moreover, the *Brandenburger Warte* had singled him out for abuse, having denounced Heinrich M. in March for his allegedly "treasonous" past behavior. In mid-August, the *Oberpräsident* informed Brandenburg's mayor that an application to dismiss Heinrich M. was before the Prussian minister of education and therefore recommended that city officials prepare to find a replacement. Yet no state disciplinary action was taken. On 14 September 1933 the Prussian Education Ministry informed the Brandenburg Province *Oberpräsident* that Heinrich M. was to continue teaching, which he did for the rest of the Third Reich. The fate of his Von Saldern colleague Paul G. followed a very similar path. Brandenburg's provisional school superintendent recommended the *Oberpräsident* fire Paul G. on the basis of past political activities identified on his questionnaire, a course of action approved by the Committee. City officials began the process of replacing this 55-year-old former Social Democrat, calculating, for example, the pension to which he was entitled. Nevertheless, the Prussian Education Ministry ordered that he was to remain in the classroom, which he did until he retired for health reasons in September 1944.[53] Then again, the Prussian Education Ministry used the Restoration Law to demote and transfer the Upper Lyceum's Elisabeth W. to an elementary school. Although her case seems to exemplify the law's successful application, later developments belie its efficacy. She resumed teaching at the Upper Lyceum soon after the war's outbreak and continued to do so into the postwar era. Her colleague Erich B. was not so lucky. Hounded by the rightist press for allegedly unpatriotic actions like having once had his pupils sing the Marseillaise and having once assigned Erich Maria Remarque's *All Quiet on the Western Front,* this 38-year-old former German State Party member hanged himself in June 1933 as a result of, in the words of the Upper Lyceum's principal, "overstraining of the nerves, brought about by the uncertainty he felt regarding his future."[54]

Although Minister Rust hoped to use the Restoration Law as a means to apply "stricter" standards "to teachers and educators of youth than to other officials," he failed.[55] Whereas the municipal government was "swept clean"—replaced by a Nazi mayor, a Nazi-dominated city council, and a "coordinated" bureaucracy—the law's implementation did not significantly transform the city's teaching staff, as no more than 5 percent of the teaching staff were dismissed, demoted, or transferred.

The Nazi State's Campaign against Freemasons

Beginning in July 1935 and lasting for more than a year, persecution of Freemasons represented another important step in the National Socialist plan to establish a politically homogenous and ideologically loyal corps of teachers. Harassment of and discrimination against Freemasons by Nazi activists had taken place since the Third Reich's creation. In the spring of 1933 there were widespread attacks against Masonic lodge members by Stormtroopers and NSDAP thugs, and state police placed their activities under surveillance. Nazi opposition to Freemasonry resulted not from a realistic understanding of its principles and activities but grew out of a worldview that linked international Freemasonry with a supposed drive for global domination by "World Jewry." Although the Prussian Freemasons were overwhelmingly nationalistic, Protestant, and politically conservative, Nazi ideologues like Alfred Rosenberg believed that their institutions and values were fundamentally antithetical to National Socialism. Instead of espousing a *Weltanschauung* based on racial struggle in defense of the *Volk*, Freemasonry stood for humanistic ideals and a Christian sense of brotherly love. Nazi theorists rejected the Masonic notion of democracy as "race-corrupting" because of what they regarded as its misguided and utopian sense of universalism. The attacks on Freemasonry were part of the Third Reich's broader rejection of the republican liberal order. To rid the country of this "un-German" spirit, the Nazi state targeted both the Masonic lodges and those members who were active in politics, state administration, the arts, and the economy.[56]

In response to Nazi actions and propaganda, Prussian Freemasons tried to accommodate the new regime by adopting desperate measures, including the voluntary exclusion of Jews from membership, even going so far as to rename themselves "German Christian Orders" in order to suggest a *völkisch* identity. These measures failed to placate the government. A Gestapo report from April 1934 expressed the government's dissatisfaction:

The individual Freemason Lodges and Orders have clearly tried to demonstrate their allegedly progovernment efforts following the National Socialist Revolution by means of name changes, coordination [*Gleichschaltung*], [and] introduction of the Aryan and Führer Principles. These superficialities have, however, not altered their true attitudes. . . . Even the voluntary dissolution of individual Lodges and Orders does not mean that the organizations thereby wish to demonstrate their positive attitude toward the National Socialist state. The reason has more to do with the fact that the dissolved organizations themselves realized that they would have been banned after a thorough examination for being incompatible with state interests.[57]

Official public denunciations and state repression continued.[58]

In 1935 Nazi persecution of Freemasons entered a new and more serious phase as state ministries replaced the uncoordinated, piecemeal harassments, arrests, and confiscations with a comprehensive, centrally directed program aimed at destroying German Freemasonry once and for all. In meetings between the Reich Interior Ministry and the Prussian Masonic organizations in late spring and summer 1935, the Ministry sought to persuade the lodges to dissolve themselves before the state forcefully broke them up and confiscated their property. The Prussian Freemasons conveyed their agreement in a letter to the Interior Ministry in May 1935 and quickly set about dismantling the system of regional and local lodges. They completed their work in less than eight weeks and in July 1935 held final ceremonies to mark the end of more than two centuries of cultural, social, and political engagement. For those lodges unwilling to dissolve themselves, the consequences were more severe. On 17 August 1935 the Interior Ministry ordered the immediate forced dissolution (*Zwangsauflösung*) of all lodges and "lodge-like" organizations and the confiscation of their property.[59]

Yet simply disbanding Freemasonry did not end Nazi persecution. The regime continued to regard former Masons as enemies of Nazism, and state agencies shifted the focus of their attacks from the organizations to the individuals. In the summer and fall of 1935, state leaders like Frick and Rust turned to identifying Freemasons among Germany's civil servants and then curtailing their possible influence in state and society. In a published decree dated 10 July 1935, the Interior Ministry required that all civil servants, including teachers, declare formally and in writing all previous or current ties to Freemasonry. The authorities maintained publicly that no one would be punished for the information provided. In a confidential memo accompanying the July decree, however, Frick ordered that no former Mason be hired for, or promoted to, a leadership position in the civil service. Although these measures nominally targeted principals or school administrators who were former members, regular teachers who were Freemasons had little reason to feel secure in their jobs. Their statements were placed in their personnel files, thereby joining incriminating material regarding political activities and racial background as potential justifications for future punitive action.[60]

Regional and local authorities quickly acted on Frick's directives. The Brandenburg Province *Oberpräsident* and the Potsdam *Regierungspräsident* collected the declarations, drafted reports that provided the names of former Masons and their membership dates, and sent the materials to the Education Ministry.[61] At the same time, state ministries worked to strengthen the anti-Masonic measures. In September and October, the Education Ministry sent out hiring and advancement guidelines for teachers who had been members. Moreover, Rust instructed authorities to include in their evaluations of former Masons the important criterion of the date the individual had resigned from the lodge. Men who quit only after 30 January 1933 were to be subject to the full range of discriminatory measures, including in certain cases transfer to another position according to article 5 of the Restoration Law. Finally, the areas of prohibited work were expanded beyond "leadership" positions to include any post involving personnel administration.[62]

For Brandenburg's teachers who were or recently had been Freemasons, the Nazi campaign had no discernible short- or long-term effects. Masonic lodges had existed in Brandenburg since at least the late eighteenth century, and a small number of pedagogues had been members in the Weimar Republic. For example, extant records indicate that approximately 14 percent of secondary school teachers had been Freemasons. In August 1935, the city's teachers submitted to Potsdam officials signed statements regarding current or former membership in a Masonic lodge. Fontane School teacher Margaret H., for example, provided education officials with two sets of declarations, the first containing her attestation that she had never been a Freemason. As a result of such statements, *Oberpräsident* Kube informed the Education Ministry on 27 August 1935, for instance, that five of the Von Saldern's teachers were former Freemasons and that four of them had been long-standing members.[63] Nevertheless, the authorities took no disciplinary action against any of them. In a report sent in late September to the Education Ministry, *Regierungspräsident* Dr. Ernst Fromm identified a total of 92 additional Freemasons teaching in the Potsdam District. Eight of these men worked in Brandenburg. Included in this small group were two principals and one vice principal; the rest were elementary or intermediate school teachers. Whereas principal Karl P. had resigned from his lodge before 30 January 1933, the rest had maintained their memberships well into the Nazi period. Intermediate school teacher Dr. Fritz R. quit only in September 1935.[64] All eight men continued to teach, regardless of Masonic membership tenure or school leadership position. This is especially surprising in light of the explicit intention of state authorities at the outset of the anti-Masonic campaign to terminate all those *Beamte* who were involved in "personnel matters," a broad designation that could be construed to include teachers. If former Freemasons were proscribed from training junior civil servants, one would think that state and party leaders would have prevented such individuals from training the next generation of National Socialists, Germany's schoolchildren.

State and party officials were aware of and continued to be disappointed with such shortcomings. In February 1937 the Education Ministry voiced its displeasure with the results of the anti-Masonic campaign. Despite the measures' intent, officials argued, former Masons continued to hold positions of influence, especially regarding personnel matters.[65] Party officials were just as vigilant as government leaders. In a meeting that took place in June 1937, NSDAP and NSLB officials demanded that Potsdam *Regierungspräsident* and former German National People's Party supporter Count Gottfried von Bismarck-Schönhausen remove a small group of principals and senior teachers from the classroom. Although Bismarck-Schönhausen resisted dismissing the pedagogues solely on the grounds of their former Masonic affiliations, he responded by proposing to demote and, if necessary, transfer them to positions of lesser influence and status.[66] For Brandenburg's teachers, such lingering unhappiness—and the half measures devised to deal with the situation—changed very little; none of the pedagogues earlier identified as current or former Freemasons, including those occupying a leadership position in the school, were dismissed, demoted, or transferred in the period before the Second World War. The experience of Brandenburg's teachers lends credence to historian Thomas Neuberger's claims that despite police harassment, the vast majority of former Freemasons "led a fully normal life professionally and socially, undisturbed by the state and Party, and, loyal to the fundamentals of Freemasonry, strove to be loyal citizens of the state, even now of the Third Reich."[67]

The Reich Citizenship Law and the Persecution of Jewish Teachers

Following a wave of increased anti-Semitic violence in Germany that began in early 1935, the Nazi state moved in the late summer of that year to harness the growing discontent of party radicals regarding the so-called Jewish question by considering comprehensive discriminatory legislation. In a high-level conference held on 20 August 1935 in Berlin, interior minister Wilhelm Frick, economics minister Hjalmar Schacht, justice minister Franz Gürtner, and Gestapo central office head Reinhard Heydrich, among others, discussed the importance of reconciling the Nazi Party and Stormtrooper dissatisfaction with the state's imperative of maintaining a sense of legality and order. Instead of "wild," local measures such as banning Jews from public swimming pools or smashing windows of Jewish-owned businesses, the ministers concluded that the government needed to come up with a legal framework that would implement much, if not all, of the NSDAP's anti-Semitic program.[68] During the NSDAP's so-called Party Congress of Freedom held weeks later in Nuremberg, Interior Ministry officials drew up laws that addressed the sensational topic of Jewish-"Aryan" relations and the equally important issue of German Jews' citizenship status. The Party Congress closed on 15 September 1935 with the formal presentation of three anti-Semitic laws to a special session of the Reichstag for adoption: the Reich Flag Law, the Reich Citizenship Law, and the Law for the Defense of German Blood and Honor.[69]

Whereas all three of these together disenfranchised and demoted German Jews to an inferior status equivalent to that of foreigners, the Reich Citizenship Law directly threatened the livelihoods of Jewish teachers and other state employees. The law clearly established that only those who were "of German or kindred blood" were citizens with all the traditional political rights and obligations. Having failed to define "non-Aryan" or to specify whether such newly disenfranchised Germans could continue to be civil servants, the state tried to address both these problems in the First Supplemental Decree of 14 November 1935. This measure both provided detailed, if still confusing, criteria for the definition of a Jew—full and part (*Mischlinge*)—and authorized the removal of the Jews' fundamental civil rights. Foremost among these was the proscription of voting or holding office by Jews. The Second Implementation Decree of 21 December 1935 ordered the dismissal of all Jewish state employees—including teachers—who had previously been exempted from the anti-Jewish clauses of the Restoration Law.[70]

Wasting little time after the laws' promulgation, the Education Ministry set about purging Jewish teachers from Germany's classrooms. On 30 September 1935, Minister Rust ordered school authorities to suspend immediately any teacher who had at least one Jewish grandparent or who was a member of a Jewish religious community. The fates of these suspended teachers would be determined after the publication of the Citizenship Laws' implementation decrees.[71] From the outset, this purge contained important similarities with the Restoration Law's punitive administrative measures instituted in 1933 and 1934. Since local authorities had asked teachers to include in the "Questionnaire for the Implementation of the Law for the Restoration of the Professional Civil Service" information about their racial lineage and religious affiliation, officials used this questionnaire beginning in late 1935 to identify those who were to be dismissed.[72]

On 12 December 1935 the Education Ministry ordered local authorities to dismiss all Jewish *Beamte* by the month's end. Officials could dispense with the traditional formalities for "firing" civil servants. Certificates of dismissal, for example, were unnecessary, and local authorities were to prepare and issue simple termination notices without seeking the Education Ministry's approval.[73] The persecution of Jewish pedagogues, meanwhile, continued. On 7 September 1936 Rust ordered all civil servants to provide information again about their spouses' lineages. At this time simply being married to a Jewish spouse (*jüdisch versippt*) did not automatically result in immediate dismissal. The Ministry instructed local authorities to determine whether such *Beamte* qualified for punishment and if so, to recommend whether the minister should retire them in accordance with article 6 of the Restoration Law.[74] In early 1937 the Interior Ministry entered the fray with the requirement that all teachers must pledge that neither they nor their spouses had Jewish parents or grandparents.[75]

In March 1937 the Potsdam District *Regierungspräsident* notified the Education Ministry that the decree of 7 September 1936 regarding *jüdisch versippt* civil servants had been carried out in Brandenburg and other cities within the district. Local authorities had completed their identification of such teachers and had pronounced judgment on their current indispensability and future usefulness.[76] Punitive measures soon followed as state agencies lost little time in acting on the newly gained information about teachers' ancestries. In April 1937 a confidential Interior Ministry circular ordered the retirement of male civil servants married to Jewish women unless special circumstances necessitated their retention. Identical instructions were extended in mid-August 1937 to civil servants who were either "*Mischlinge* of the first degree," that is, someone with two Jewish grandparents, or were married to such persons.[77] For teachers, the anti-Semitic legislative campaign culminated in a simply worded but sweeping decree dated 2 July 1937 that stated: "Jews cannot be the teachers or educators of German youths."[78] Using information proffered by the individuals themselves, education authorities had by late 1937 dismissed all Jewish and *jüdisch versippt* teachers in Germany.[79]

Although the Nuremberg racial laws and the decrees implementing them provided fewer loopholes for individual teachers or local authorities to exploit, dismissal of the probably small number of Jewish teachers in Brandenburg had only a minimal impact on the city teaching staff's composition. Prussian Education Ministry records indicate that one teacher, the Municipal Intermediate School's Norbert E., was fired because he was Jewish.[80] In response to inquiries as to the fate of *jüdisch versippt* teachers, local school authorities informed the Education Ministry in August 1937 that Waldemar D. of the Augusta Intermediate School had been retired in accordance with article 6 of the Restoration Law.[81] In June 1937 the Prussian Ministry of Economics and Labor retired vocational teacher Frans S. because his wife was Jewish; his subsequent divorce and remarriage to a so-called Aryan woman facilitated his later wartime reemployment in the city's schools.[82] The extant records, while possibly incomplete, mention no other anti-Jewish discriminatory actions regarding the city's teachers. This does not seem incongruous in light of the more accurate statistical record regarding the overall Jewish population in the city and region. As of June 1933, 401 Jews lived in Brandenburg, and Jews constituted only 0.28 percent of Brandenburg Province's population.[83] Implemented much more rigorously than the Restoration Law or the anti-Masonic decrees, the purge of Jewish pedagogues, though devastating for men such as Waldemar D. and Norbert E., nevertheless directly affected only a very small number of Brandenburg teachers.

Understanding the Incomplete Transformation

By 1938 the Nazi state possessed not only the legal and institutional means to purge civil servants who consciously rejected National Socialism but also the tools to ensure that remaining teachers complied with state and party wishes. Crucial to accomplishing this was the broadly conceived and open-ended nature of the new laws and practices. The Restoration Law empowered officials to continue to watch over Germany's teachers and, if the need arose, to punish them in a number of ways. Were a former SPD member like director Hermann H. to fail to demonstrate his "national reliability," education officials, drawing on information collected as a result of the April 1933 law and its subsequent implementation decrees, could use the same legal measures to remove him from the classrooms of Brandenburg or any other German community. Attestations regarding previous political or even not explicitly political, as in the case of Freemasonry, affiliations could serve as swords of Damocles hanging over individual teachers, possibly influencing their actions in the Third Reich. That the information submitted to the state could harm one was demonstrated clearly in the anti-Semitic purge of the teaching staff begun in 1935. Having submitted detailed information regarding their racial lineages first in 1933 and then again in 1935, teachers designated "Jewish" or *jüdisch versippt* were removed from the classroom. Clearly, under the right conditions, the Nazi state could rigorously purge the teaching staff. On the eve of the Second World War, the revised Civil Servant Law of 1938, in which the Education Ministry sought to ensure that no teacher "emotionally and intellectually stands apart from the National Socialist ideology" in any aspect of his or her professional or personal life, represented the culmination of a process, begun in 1933, in which the de jure and de facto reach of the state penetrated the classroom to a far greater degree than ever before.[84]

Although it is difficult to evaluate whether the Nazi state successfully rid the classrooms of teachers who "emotionally and intellectually [stood] apart from the National Socialist ideology," it is possible to determine the degree to which Nazi state and party leaders overhauled the group of men and women teaching in Brandenburg's schools. Undisputed is the official position that state and party leaders sought to transform Germany's teachers. Although Hitler made few public statements about teachers and their potential role in the Third Reich, men such as NSLB leader and *Gauleiter*

Hans Schemm, *Oberpräsident* Kube, Interior Minister Frick, and Education Minister Rust did. The Restoration Law and the Reich Citizenship Law were part of a panoply of measures and decrees intended to create, as Nazi educational theorist Dr. Wilhelm Hartnacke expressed it, "a new generation of teachers who can put educational values in their correct order of worth."[85] These teachers, Hartnacke argued, "must learn that they are agents of the State and, if they do not conform, must take the consequences."[86] In order to attain and then preserve this desired conformity, Nazi leaders used available legal and political mechanisms.

Yet, as we have seen, instruments such as the Restoration Law, the anti-Masonic measures, and the racial decrees did not result in a wide-scale transformation of the city's teaching staff. That fewer than 5 percent of the teachers, consisting mostly of those who worked at the Secular School, were purged in the summer and fall of 1933 as a result of the Restoration Law reveals the failure of Nazi state and party leaders to change substantially the composition of Brandenburg's teaching staff. Similarly, the failure to transfer or dismiss a single Brandenburg pedagogue who had, at least in some cases, been a member of the Freemasons as late as 1935 also belies the stated intentions and early pronouncements of state and party leaders. A comprehensive analysis of the effects of Nazi purges from 1933 to 1938 reveals that the vast majority of pedagogues who were teaching in 1933 in Brandenburg continued to do so as of 1938. At the Augusta Intermediate School, for example, no more than a couple of teachers left the school during this period. To take another example, at least 85 percent of the Franz Ziegler School's teaching staff had been teaching since before Hitler's ascension to power. A similarly high percentage can be found among the Nicholas School's teachers. At the Pestalozzi School, there was no turnover at all in the first several years of the Third Reich; moreover, the single teacher to depart before 1939 did so most likely as a consequence of having reached the mandatory retirement age. As this case illustrates, much of the turnover within Brandenburg's teaching staff did not result from punitive state actions but rather from illnesses, voluntary transfers, changes of careers, and even deaths. Maria S., for instance, quit her job at the Catholic Community School because of health problems.[87] Illness also forced the retirement of Municipal Intermediate School teacher Richard E. Men such as Ritterakademie philologists Kurt B. and Ernst G. joined the military, sometimes serving as instructors in military schools. Others such as Von Saldern's Adolf S., Augusta School's Ernst G., and Rochow School's

August E. left the city's service having reached the mandatory retirement age. Ardent Nazi and Ritterakademie principal Dr. Ludwig Z. quit the school administration to enter the nascent Nazi city government. The departure of Fritz E., Christian K., and Erich B. may have been involuntary but not as a result of Nazi policies: all three died in this period.[88] Nazi Germany's first and most extensive attempt to transform the country's teaching staff, represented here in the experiences of the men and women teaching in Brandenburg, was anything but an unqualified success.

The Nazi state's failure to use measures such as the Restoration Law and the anti-Masonic decrees to transform Brandenburg's teaching staff was the result of a constellation of personal, political, ideological, and economic factors. One important explanation as to why known Freemasons or SPD members were not punished to the law's full extent was that it was not uncommon for local school authorities to intervene on their behalf. Some directors or school administrators, more familiar with the individuals in question and more aware of their past actions and current capabilities than regional or national state and party leaders, petitioned for exemptions from punitive or discriminatory measures. For example, Ritterakademie principal Dr. Ludwig Z. wrote in July 1933 to the Prussian school authorities in an attempt to convince them that his teachers did not need to fill out the Restoration Law's questionnaire. Submitting his own questionnaire and a list of the teachers, he argued that he "was convinced that an application of Paragraphs 2 to 4 of the 7.4.33 Law or something similar was invalid for these teachers, . . . thus it is unnecessary for them to fill out the questionnaires. I would like to note that the Ritterakademie's character requires that only such teachers and *Beamte* be hired about whose nationalist reliability there can be no doubt."[89] To take another example, the Upper Lyceum's principal, Gustav S., wrote to Brandenburg Province's *Oberpräsident* to make the case that four teachers, presumably previously targeted by the state in connection with the Restoration Law's implementation, were in fact not guilty of previous "deleterious" political activity. Possibly worried that published accusations in the *Brandenburger Warte* could compel the state to punish secondary school teacher Erich B., Gustav S. defended his employee in letters sent both to education officials in Berlin and to the rightist newspaper. Similarly, Von Saldern director Ferdinand G. not only appealed directly to Prussian school officials in Berlin in an effort to counter public accusations made against two of his teachers by the *Brandenburger Warte* but also forwarded numerous testaments, some written by pupils, to the political reliability of both men. Regarding the Nazi campaign against Freemasons, Thomas Neuberger writes that such protective intervention was very common. By informing the responsible ministry that an incriminated *Beamte* was neither in a leadership position nor in charge of personnel matters, immediate superiors often successfully removed individuals from the state's scrutiny.[90]

School principals were able to protect many of their teachers from the state's purges because by the mid-1930s Germany was suffering a shortage of teachers. Originating in the late Weimar Republic and continuing into the early Third Reich, hiring freezes, wage cuts, and restrictions on access to higher education had resulted in a "drastic instructor deficit." The closing of more than half of the Prussian pedagogical academies in 1931 sharply limited the state's capacity to train new teachers.[91] Searching for ways to cut state expenses, the Prussian Education Ministry in 1932 went so far as admit not a single new student for teacher training for the following year, although the remaining seven academies were eventually compelled to admit a total of 350 students in 1933. Such policies left cities like Brandenburg struggling by the mid-1930s to ensure that enough teachers stood in front of the classrooms. In response, Reich education authorities in April 1935 lifted the permanent hiring freeze for teachers and soon afterward resumed normal hiring activities. Such measures were limited in their short- or medium-term efficacy. Nazi officials failed to implement the broad reforms necessary for Germany to produce enough pedagogues. The Prussian academies were renamed colleges for teacher training *(Hochschulen für Lehrerbildung)* and in some cases moved out of cities and into the countryside. Such reforms did little to solve the immediate problem. Only one new college was opened in Prussia during the prewar years. Moreover, since the length of study at a college remained two years, newly minted teachers would enter the classroom in 1936 at the earliest.[92] As a result of these limited measures, the situation failed to improve. In 1936, officials were unable to fill more than 1,300 vacant elementary school positions in Germany. Moreover, the dearth of teachers increased during the second half of the 1930s. By 1938, the teacher training colleges were graduating a total of 2,500 pedagogues per year, but German schools needed to fill 8,000 positions.[93] The failure to expand teacher training institutes in the early 1930s meant that by the time the Nazi state had reversed its hiring policies, there were still too few formally trained men and women to begin teaching.

In Brandenburg, such problems were exacerbated by a population explosion that consisted not only of new workers in the growing industrial sector but also additional children in the schools. By 1936 more than 1,000 new pupils had enrolled in the city's vocational schools. In the period 1933–1938, more than 20,000 people moved to Brandenburg; this population increase of 33 percent seriously worsened the city's shortage of teachers. In response to this growing demand for teachers and classroom seats, Brandenburg officials created new positions at extant schools and, as time went on and the situation worsened, eventually built an entirely new school, one staffed by a newly assembled teaching staff. Two new positions were created in 1934 at the Augusta Intermediate School, for example, filled by women who had worked for years as elementary school teachers but were now promoted to middle school positions since the city did not have enough qualified middle school pedagogues to meet the demand. Two years later, local education authorities sought to fill at least six new teaching positions, in both elementary and middle schools, and in 1937 an additional three positions were created. Nevertheless, the shortage of qualified teachers in Brandenburg continued. In 1938, the Von Saldern secondary school, for instance, exceeded its usual capacity by more than 600 pupils. Local officials had already concluded by March 1936 that adding teaching positions alone would not solve the problem and that a more radical solution, building at least one new school with a new teaching staff, was necessary. In 1938, city officials urgently—and ultimately successfully—sought permission from regional authorities to open a new school, which would require a new teaching staff. The opening in April 1938 of the Herbert Norkus School, soon renamed the Hans Schemm School in honor of the deceased founder of the NSLB, certainly helped to alleviate the overcrowding in the classroom but failed to solve the problem fully. On the eve of the Second World War, Potsdam education officials were forced to appeal to the Reich Education Ministry for supplemental funds so that the city could educate the "rapid increase" in school-age youth that had resulted from the "filling [up of the city] with the armaments industry." The persistent shortage of sufficient teachers and classroom space to educate all of the city's youth during the war ultimately forced Brandenburg's municipal government to open another school, the Werner Mölders School.[94]

Further contributing to the increasingly serious situation was the persistence of low wages for pedagogues and feelings of embitterment among them. In March 1934, Nazi officials extended indefinitely the severe reductions of civil servant wages that began with Chancellor Heinrich Brüning's emergency austerity decrees issued in 1930 and 1931. As a result of the pay cuts, teachers continued to draw in 1934 a salary that was 30 to 40 percent lower than it had been in 1928.[95] Nor did the situation improve significantly over the next several years. Although some of the reductions were reversed in 1939 and 1941, others remained in effect well into the postwar era. Such low wages represented a strong disincentive to secondary school graduates deciding on a profession.[96] A similar effect resulted from the low social prestige of teaching and teachers in the Third Reich. Ridicule of teachers in the press and popular culture, as well as occasionally in prominent Nazi Party leaders' public statements, convinced both current and potential teachers that they were not or would not be sufficiently appreciated for their contributions to the transformation of Germany. Many chose to escape the low pay and "the continual defaming of the profession and the work" by changing careers or decided never to become teachers.[97]

Faced with these difficulties in gaining new pedagogues and retaining those already teaching, education authorities adopted reforms and, at times, worked to minimize the effects of state and party purges. State agencies increased their recruitment efforts and eased restrictions against women studying pedagogy. Some principals and school administrators also took this status quo into account when deciding how to implement punitive measures such as the Restoration Law and the anti-Masonic decrees. In addition to enhancing their power, the laws' vagueness made possible a maneuverability that could be exploited when school administrators applied them. When pressured by NSLB and NSDAP leaders in June 1937 to punish a small group of former Freemasons, Potsdam's *Regierungspräsident* and former German National People's Party supporter Count Gottfried von Bismarck-Schönhausen used this flexibility to spare several teachers serious consequences. In reporting his discussion with the Nazi Party leaders, Bismarck-Schönhausen noted:

> they mentioned first, that it is the Party District Leadership's wish that these principals and senior teachers be dismissed according to the Restoration Law. In the course of the discussion agreement was reached that the list would be first checked by the School Department for its completeness and then requests would be made according to article 5 of the Restoration

Law—due to the great teacher shortage—regarding the principals and the senior teachers.[98]

Since article 5 stipulated transfer, not termination, the teacher shortage thus played an important role in shielding these pedagogues from outright dismissal. Although transfers certainly qualified as a form of punishment, one that probably adversely affected the teacher, it clearly undermined the Nazi goal of removing "unsuitable elements" from the classroom. Teachers thus shielded could move to a new locale and, by the standards of the Nazi state, there potentially corrupt the minds of a different set of young Germans.[99]

The absence of a comprehensive plan for the transformation of Germany's teaching force also explains why the Nazis failed to take advantage of legal and administrative purge mechanisms. Provided by the regime with only platitudes and vague notions about the ideal Nazi pedagogue, state and party authorities lacked a precise set of principles and procedures necessary for effective reform. Measures were instead conceived and implemented in an ad hoc fashion, and this absence of systematic clarity and foresight limited their efficacy. The string of qualifications in the form of decrees that characterized the Restoration Law's implementation contributed to confusion and delay in identifying, evaluating, and disciplining Brandenburg's pedagogues. Similarly, the campaign against Freemasonry and its former members was hampered by state-party and center-periphery disagreements over the policy's intent and scope. These divisions within the Nazi state over education policy were also exploited by the shifting concentrations of power in the Nazi polycracy. As in the case of the conflicts taking place throughout the economy and the administration, men like Rust, Frick, Hans Schemm, Baldur von Schirach, Alfred Rosenberg, Martin Bormann, and Joseph Goebbels battled each other for control over individual education programs. Institutional rivalries such as those between the Interior Ministry and the NSLB often obstructed unified and coherent policymaking, in this case preventing the creation of a single Nazi organization for teachers.[100]

Finally, another explanation for the flawed implementation of the purge was the authorities' implicit acknowledgment that purging pedagogues was neither the sole nor the most effective means of shaping the teaching staff. As the next chapter will show, NSDAP, NSLB, and state leaders envisioned a far-reaching series of measures and institutions that would ideologically transform the teachers into committed Nazi pedagogues. Confronted with the necessity of keeping as many qualified men and women in the class-room as possible, state and party leaders placed their bets on radically re-training the remaining teachers as to how and what they thought and taught. The main vehicle for this professional, social, political, and peda-gogical indoctrination was intended to be the teachers' professional organi-zation, the NSLB.

CHAPTER 2

The Incomplete Revolution of the National Socialist Teachers' League

While state and party officials were implementing the Restoration Law campaign to purge the teaching staff of Brandenburg and other communities, a new threat to teachers and their traditional professional lives emerged. In June 1933, more than four months after Hitler's assumption of power, Brandenburg's main newspaper, the *Brandenburger Anzeiger*, ran for the first time an article about the local chapter of the NSLB. Signed by elementary school teacher and local NSLB chapter leader Willi Sülz, the notice presented basic information such as the procedure for joining the organization and the amount of membership dues and chapter fees. A day later, a second newspaper article announced the date and agenda of the NSLB's next meeting. Additional notices about the chapter and its scheduled activities followed at regular intervals.[1] The newspaper articles heralded the NSLB's arrival in Brandenburg; they did not, however, shed much light on the nature of the organization itself, and most likely left their readers with a number of questions. What exactly was the organization, its nature, and its mission? What did membership in it entail? Did every pedagogue have to join or could one remain a member of one of the many teacher organizations that had existed to serve the city's teaching staff for decades?

By the eve of the Second World War, such questions had long been answered; over the course of the 12 years since its founding in 1927, the NSLB had forced its way into the professional life of every teacher. Membership was now effectively compulsory, especially since all other teachers' organizations had been forcibly dissolved. Members were expected to at-

tend regular meetings and were "encouraged" to subscribe to NSLB publications. Teachers were in most cases expected to participate in Nazi public events like rallies as part of a single NSLB group. Moreover, the NSLB
administered benefits such as health care for the teachers and, most important, oversaw their ideological (re)training. This chapter explores the history and actions of the NSLB chapter in Brandenburg in order to analyze
the second major National Socialist effort to transform the teaching staff:
the ideological reeducation of Germany's teachers. Whereas the Restoration Law and other Nazi purge measures sought to change the makeup of
the teaching staff, the NSLB strove to remake ideologically the men and
women standing in the classroom. The NSLB's founder, Hans Schemm,
described its mission:

> So long as the entire German community of educators does not think and
> feel along National Socialist lines, education as we understand it cannot be
> organized in a sound manner. The sooner we succeed in creating the Na-
> tional Socialist teacher, the development of the one type of school that be-
> fits National Socialism will be even more a matter of course. The school
> reform can only be carried out by men who have become complete Na-
> tional Socialists.[2]

Despite the centrality of the NSLB in Nazi plans for the transformation of
German teachers and the education system, scholars either have largely
ignored it or have misunderstood its role in the "Nazi revolution" in the
schools. Providing the only detailed, English-language account of the NSLB
and its activities, this chapter first investigates the means by which the
NSLB sought to accomplish this goal and then assesses the impact of the
NSLB on Brandenburg's teachers. As will be shown, it implemented many
changes in the organizational lives of the city's teachers. Long-established
relationships between teachers like Johannes S. and non-Nazi teachers' organizations were forcibly dissolved, and the teachers were corralled into
the new Nazi professional association. In addition, NSLB officials introduced a lengthy and extensive program of political reeducation that consisted of a wide variety of indoctrination tools, from specialized periodicals
to regular lectures to training camps.

This chapter begins with a brief history of the NSLB, which has largely
been ignored in the English-language scholarship despite its central role in
teachers' lives. Against the backdrop of national developments, the early
history and development of the Brandenburg chapter is chronicled, includ-

ing a detailed analysis of the membership data. By focusing on the teaching staff of a single community, this study helps illuminate the pace and degree of the changes. Since the NSLB's raison d'être was ideological indoctrination, this chapter scrutinizes the NSLB's efforts to turn Germany's teachers into National Socialist pedagogues. Although the production and dissemination of propaganda was one important element of the NSLB program, the centerpiece of efforts to transform the teachers was the special training camps *(Schulungslager)*. Intended to be held during school breaks, especially in the summer, and to last at least a week, these indoctrination camps were designed to provide pedagogues with a "total immersion" in National Socialism, structuring the experience so that they absorbed Nazi values and ideas through both traditional formats such as lectures and discussions and more unusual means such as the "lived" experience of the camp. The wearing of identical clothing and dispensing with traditional forms of address, for example, was intended to ensure that teachers understood the *Volksgemeinschaft* (the National Socialist racial national community) on an immediate and personal basis. An analysis of this indoctrination program—its nature, scope, and impact on the teaching staff—lies at the heart of this chapter. Judging by the experiences of Brandenburg's teachers, were the intentions of NSLB leaders such as Hans Schemm fully realized? Can the program be considered a success by these officials' own standards and expectations? Which German pedagogues experienced the special training camps and how did factors such as number of participants and frequency of indoctrination affect the program's efficacy?

By examining these special training camps, this chapter assesses whether the far-reaching and comprehensive nature of this signature NSLB initiative, in the hands of zealous Nazi officials, enabled the NSLB to accomplish its central goal: the indoctrination of Germany's teachers. A close examination of the history of Brandenburg's NLSB chapter, including an analysis of the relationship between it and the city's teaching staff, will provide answers to the following important questions: Did NSLB efforts result in the "entire German community of educators," as Schemm prophesied, "think[ing] and feel[ing] along National Socialist lines"? Did years of meetings, lectures, propaganda, and special training camps "creat[e] the National Socialist teacher"?[3] Similarly, did the NSLB efface the traditional professional, social, and political divisions and thereby unify Germany's teachers in more than just a formal or organizational sense? That is, did it facilitate the integration of teachers into the racial national community that scholars like

Peter Fritzsche believe was the foundation of the Third Reich, a *Volks-gemeinschaft* that, according to Götz Aly and others, "level[ed] out" the class differences among Germans?[4] Or did a multitude of factors, ranging from nearly constant financial limitations to worsening staffing pressures, prevent the NSLB from carrying out the (re)training program on the scale originally conceived and presumably necessary to transform teachers' attitudes? And if that is the case, rather than developing into a local community of Nazi teachers unified in their political and professional outlook, did the city's teaching staff on the eve of the Second World War remain sharply divided along political, gender, social, religious, and professional lines? In addressing such questions, this chapter sheds light on larger themes about the Third Reich and the nature of National Socialist rule, including the means by which National Socialists mobilized Germans for the transformation of German society, as well as the efficacy of such policies.

The National Socialist Teachers' League

Although the local press first mentions a Brandenburg chapter of the NSLB in the late spring of 1933, membership records suggest the possibility of some kind of NSLB presence in the city well before then. At least nine local pedagogues joined the NSLB in the period before 1933. This group consisted almost exclusively of men, and its members came from nearly all levels of the city's educational system. One taught at a secondary school, two at middle schools, five at elementary schools, and one at the trade school. The lone female member taught at the Augusta Intermediate School. Almost all joined the NSLB in 1932. The single exception, elementary school teacher Richard P., had joined in 1929; with a membership number of 33, he was one of the first German teachers to join the nascent NSLB.[5] It would be a mistake, however, to assume the existence of a local chapter on the basis of the membership data alone. It is more likely that a small group of like-minded pedagogues had joined by 1933 a Bavaria-based organization that in 1930–1931 had only covertly established a foothold in the region. Supporting the notion that no local organization existed in Brandenburg before 1933 is the fact that subsequent attempts by the NSLB to expand in the province of Brandenburg were not particularly successful, and membership grew very slowly. More important, what little growth did occur took place not in large urban areas like Brandenburg and Frankfurt an der Oder but in the countryside and in the region's small towns.[6] Extant sources also do not indicate the existence in Brandenburg prior to the Third Reich of any established organization, complex or primitive, legal or illegal. Moreover, this loose collection of Nazi teachers lacked basic characteristics of political organization such as an established hierarchy and clearly defined and differentiated areas of responsibilities shared among various individuals. Finally, the absence of any public activity by the local NSLB group before June 1933 strongly suggests that a Brandenburg chapter became active only during that spring. That elementary school teacher Adolf Klauss, a committed Nazi who served as of June 1933 as local chapter treasurer of the NSLB, was active on behalf of National Socialism before then as the local chapter leader of the Civil Servant League confirms this conclusion.[7]

Just what kind of organization had teachers such as Richard P. and Adolf Klauss joined? A national organization that had been founded only recently, the NSLB by 1933 had grown at a remarkable rate in size and stature within the Nazi institutional universe. In January 1927 elementary school pedagogue Hans Schemm—a First World War veteran, former Free Corps member, and long-standing National Socialist—organized in Hof an der Saale in Bavaria the first official meeting of "national socialist-minded" teachers. Twenty-three teachers—from Saxony, Thuringia, and Bavaria—attended the gathering and elected Schemm *Führer* of the NSLB. Subsequent meetings and conferences followed over the course of the next two years, taking place in and around Hof, and the membership slowly rose from 23 to approximately 200.[8]

As membership grew, the NSLB's organizational structure and political-ideological role also developed. In the spring of 1929 Schemm invited a small group of Nazi pedagogues, including his future successor as both district leader *(Gauleiter)* of the Bavarian Ostmark and head of the NSLB, Fritz Wächtler, to join the recently formed Working Committee and thereby assist him in running the NSLB. Party officials at the Fourth Nazi Party Conference in August 1929 extended the NSLB's jurisdiction to cover the entire Reich and officially upgraded Schemm's title and position within the Nazi Party hierarchy to that of Reich Leader *(Reichsleiter)*, thereby elevating him to the same rank within the party as a powerful Old Fighter like Gregor Strasser.[9]

The NSLB's principal political and ideological activity, in addition to public speaking engagements by Schemm and his Working Committee members, consisted in this period of collecting those "articles and works from pedagogical, educational and cultural areas" that sought to conform teachers' professional training and activities "to the National Socialist idea in organizational and programmatic form."[10] In order to facilitate this, as well as to establish the NSLB's legitimacy as an affiliated organization of the Nazi Party and to attract new members, in 1930 the NSLB published its official platform. Consisting of seven brief points, the small document revealed the NSLB's mission of bringing National Socialism to Germany's schools, pupils, and teachers and at the same time uniting the teachers within a Nazi organization. Point 5, for example, called for the "ruthless struggle against the largely liberal, Marxist and democratic contaminated teachers' organizations in the states as well as nationally." The NSLB advocated seizing political power in Germany, fighting "cultural bolshevism," and, in a savvy attempt to appeal to elementary and middle school teachers by playing on their professional insecurities, establishing universal teacher training at the university level, thereby making available to all pedagogues the elite training traditionally reserved for secondary school teachers.[11]

Amid the political radicalization and economic turmoil of the Great Depression in Germany, the NSLB continued to grow in size, structure, and purpose. In an effort to improve its efficacy, as well as to coordinate better structurally with the Nazi Party, the NSLB was organized in 1931 into 33 districts *(Gaue)*, corresponding with those of the NSDAP. Recently created institutions such as district business offices *(Gau-Geschäftsstellen)* and officials such as district heads *(Gauobmänner)* oversaw the expansion of the bureaucracy necessary to support a national organization. At the regional and local levels, the NSLB diversified structurally into subdistricts, local groups, and even so-called school cells.[12]

Although this reorganization had been largely fueled by the NSLB's expansion into new regions in the early 1930s, it still could not officially agitate or propagandize in Germany's largest state, Prussia, because of a Prussian Interior Ministry decree of 30 July 1930 that forbade civil servants to join the Nazi Party or one of its affiliated organizations. Before the law was repealed in 1932, individual NSLB groups nevertheless worked surreptitiously to recruit new members in Prussia. A rally held in Bochum in 1931, for example, took place under the auspices of the *"Völkish* Pedagogical Working Group." Another Nazi Prussian group—calling itself the "League of National Teachers"—was formed in Potsdam in the winter of 1930–1931. These legal and illegal expansion efforts were aided by the recruitment of high-profile pedagogues and education theorists, for example Ernst Krieck, who publicly supported the NSLB and who often actively campaigned on its behalf. As a result of this push into new territory and of internal structural reorganization, membership grew tremendously. The NSLB's first Reich conference, held in April 1932 and operating under the motto "Pestalozzi, Fichte and Hitler," drew more than 5,000 men and women to Berlin to hear prominent speakers such as Krieck and Brandenburg Province *Oberpräsident* Kube. In the period of 1932 from early summer to October, the number of members doubled to approximately 10,000 German teachers.[13]

With Hitler's appointment as chancellor in January 1933, the NSLB stood poised to bring the Nazi revolution to Germany's schools and teachers. Headquartered in Bayreuth, the NSLB had built up since 1927 a core membership comprising approximately 4 percent of the teaching population, a leadership consisting of determined men such as Schemm and Wächtler, and a highly structured organization that reached from the national level to individual schools.[14] What the institution lacked in early 1933 was a clear understanding of how to go about achieving its goals. Schemm, Krieck, and others intended for it to transform Germany's teachers along National Socialist lines. German scholar Willi Feiten writes that "it was Schemm's idea to create a unified group of educators, active in everything from kindergartens to universities, whose existence and unity should be a testament to the National Socialist *Weltanschauung*."[15] The NSLB's leaders lacked, however, a coherent program for overhauling the educational system and retooling current pedagogical norms. The official platform established broad goals but provided little guidance on how specifically to achieve them. Furthermore, the leaders did not believe such a detailed vision was necessary. Rejecting the possibility that conventional education issues such as school organization, construction, and curricula ought to be addressed first, Schemm believed that "in the Third Reich the first and most important duty is not to create or invent new school types and curricula models. The duty of a true German education is to take the glorious, racially high-quality German body and the German soul . . . in caring, protecting and supporting hands."[16] Although the NSLB soon turned its full attention to winning over German teachers by eradicating all other teachers' organizations, uncertainty regarding the means with which to implement the "Nazi revolution" among teachers persisted for years.

Following Hitler's assumption of power in January 1933, membership in the Brandenburg chapter of the NSLB increased at first gradually and then, by midspring, dramatically. In February and March, at least nine teachers joined. Six—divided evenly between men and women—were elementary school teachers, and three, two men and a woman, were philologists. The stream of new members grew significantly larger in April and reached a climax in May. More than 15 pedagogues became members in April and 52 in May. Elementary school teachers again led the way, comprising a majority of the new members in this period. The number of middle school teachers in the NSLB more than doubled from four to ten. Summer's arrival brought an end to the rapid growth—in June local NSLB officials recorded only six new members, and a paltry eight joined in July and August.[17]

Symbolically marking an end to this significant recruitment period, the Brandenburg chapter publicly claimed on 17 August 1933 almost 200 members.[18] This number more closely reflects the NSLB's aspirations, as well as its proclivity for propaganda, than the actual situation within the Brandenburg teaching staff. In fact, the number of registered members as of August was much lower. Most of the city's male secondary school teachers, for instance, had not yet joined. These elitist pedagogues became members only in 1937, following the definitive success of the NSLB's four-year struggle against the German Philologists' Association. A large number of female secondary school teachers also failed to join in the spring of 1933, even though their main professional organization—the German Female Philologist Association—would soon complete its formal merger into the NSLB on 1 October 1933. Similarly, a large number of elementary school teachers had not joined by the late summer of 1933. Extant membership data indicates that more than 39 out of approximately 120 were still not members as of August 1933. Despite the lacunae in the membership records, it is clear that many pedagogues—representing men and women teaching at all types of schools—did not rush to enlist in the NSLB in the first six months of 1933. Combining the number of known, registered members with the small group of teachers whose membership dates cannot be established yields a total that falls short of 200. Nonetheless, Brandenburg chapter leaders had reason in August 1933 to feel optimistic and celebratory—in less than five months, chapter membership had grown by more than 600 percent.[19]

Even so, it was not until late 1933 that the Brandenburg chapter underwent a transformation that both conformed its structure to that of the national and regional organizations and laid the institutional foundation for an efficient implementation of the NSLB's expanding mission among the city's pedagogues. At the heart of this process lay a structural reform designed to enable the chapter to differentiate its role among teachers in line with the professional differences within the teaching staff. In November 1933 local leaders created and staffed chapter departments *(Fachschaften)* and sections *(Fachgruppen)* that mirrored the traditional school types. The chapter now included departments for secondary school, vocational school, middle and elementary school, as well as more specialized, individual sections for commercial subject teachers *(Handelslehrer)*, trade school teachers *(Gewerbelehrer)*, middle school teachers, and elementary school teachers. Heading up these departments were some of Brandenburg's most committed National Socialist teachers: Ritterakademie director Dr. Ludwig Z., one of the most prominent local Nazis, was put in charge of the *Fachschaft* for secondary schools, for example, and Walter R., who played an unusually active role in the purge of the teaching staff discussed in the previous chapter, oversaw the department for vocational schools. Previously a small, loosely organized collection of teachers who campaigned on behalf of National Socialist candidates, the Brandenburg chapter had evolved by early 1934 into an institution led by influential and fervent National Socialists and capable, in theory at least, of educating and efficiently "coordinating" the teaching staff by tailoring its message to appeal to the diverse traditional concerns and aspirations of German teachers.[20]

Strength through the Elimination of Rivals

Having formally and publicly established itself in the late spring and summer of 1933, the Brandenburg chapter began a lengthy and very difficult process of consolidating its control over the city's teachers by compelling them to sever fully their ties with professional groups such as the Prussian Teachers' Association, the Intermediate School Teachers' Association, and the All German Female Teachers' Association.[21] Such a naked power grab was neither limited to teachers' organizations nor particular to Brandenburg; throughout the country and in all realms of German society, Nazi leaders were at this time forcibly absorbing previously independent institutions such as labor unions into their National Socialist equivalents. In August the NSLB published guidelines regarding the membership obligations of the recently incorporated members. The notice declared that "as a result of the corporative admission of all old associations into the NSLB, all members of the associations, including retirees since 1 July, are to pay a monthly contribution of 1.30 RM or .65 RM (partial payee) to the NSLB, in so far as they are organized inside the Kurmark District (Government District of Potsdam, Frankfurt [Oder], Schneidemuhl)."[22] According to the announcement, association treasurers were to forward to the NSLB their membership lists and the back dues for July and August of those teachers who had not as of August 1933 directly applied to join the NSLB. All organized teachers, regardless of their individual actions or decisions, were not only now officially considered to belong to the NSLB but also expected to contribute financially to the local chapter.

The regulations issued in the late summer of 1933 represented only the latest in a series of moves by the NSLB in its campaign to become the sole teachers' professional association. Rather than joining the NSLB, some pedagogues continued to maintain membership in their non-Nazi professional organizations. At least 13 of the 22 men teaching at the Von Saldern secondary school remained members of their traditional non–National Socialist teachers' organization. Similarly, a majority of Ritterakademie teachers continued to belong to the German Philologists' Association. Moreover, an even greater number of teachers decided to join the NSLB while at the same time remaining members of their current professional associations, in effect hedging their bets against the longevity of the NSLB and of the Third Reich.[23] The decision to continue to belong to the German Philologists' Association, for instance, reflected far more than a sense of tradition or a reluctance to embrace a new organization.

Significant political, religious, and social factors were involved in the decision to join a professional association, as evidenced in the organizations' number and diversity. The more than 40 national organizations included the massive German Teachers' Association (Deutscher Lehrerverein) and the Catholic Teachers' Association of the German Reich, as well as the much smaller Reich Union of German Certified Teachers of Commerce (Reichsverband Deutscher Diplomhandelslehrer) and the Principals' Association. These entities served as advocates of teachers' various "collective interests" (Standesinteressen), promoters of pedagogical scholarship, and forums for debate and discussion.[24] Equally important were economic considerations. Each individual association maintained for its members a broad array of social services, including health care funds, death benefits, personal and legal insurance funds, and convalescence homes. With many of the details regarding the NSLB's assumption of other associations' social services still to be determined as of the summer of 1933, quitting a non-Nazi teachers' organization raised the possibility of losing these important benefits. As Feiten recognized, the "coordination" of the professional associations into the NSLB meant that "every independent educational and social-political activity of the teaching staff had to come to an end."[25]

In order to counter the inherent threat posed by the non-Nazi professional associations and to complete the integration of all teachers into the NSLB, party and NSLB leaders began in the late spring of 1933 the crucial process of eliminating Germany's traditional teachers' organizations. At the NSLB's second Reich conference, held on 8–9 April 1933 in Leipzig, Schemm announced to the more than 3,500 participants—including invited heads of most of the major teachers' associations—his intention of incorporating all current organizations and their members into a new "German educators' community" (Deutsche Erziehergemeinschaft, DEG) to be led and represented by the NSLB.[26] According to an NSLB pamphlet published shortly before the Reich conference, "the goal is the creation of a unified German educators' community on the basis of a true Christianity, a conscious national education, and a true national community." Under the sole leadership of the NSLB, the DEG would both root out "Marxist, liberal, and pure intellectual" forces and depoliticize teachers' organizations by prohibiting their involvement in political or cultural-political (kultur-politisch) activities. The guidelines clearly indicate the NSLB's grand ambition of representing every type of pedagogue in every conceivable capacity, including assuming the traditional "trade union" (gewerkschaftlich) role previously played by the associations.[27] Within weeks, Schemm's call for the dissolution of the existing organizations into a new, NSLB-led teachers' community began to bear fruit. In April and May NSLB officials conducted negotiations with individual associations. On 10 April 1933 the Saxon Teachers' Association agreed officially to transfer itself into the NSLB. The Saxons' Prussian colleagues followed suit a few days later when the Prussian Teachers' Association's representative assembly authorized its chairman, Heinrich Diekmann, to start a dialogue among itself, its parent organization, the German Teachers' Association, and the NSLB regarding dissolution into the DEG. On 22 April 1933 the regional chairmen of the German Teachers' Association—Germany's largest teachers' organization—met and agreed to carry out the NSLB's call for self-dissolution. More than six weeks later, the German Teachers' Association took the significant step of formally appointing Schemm its chairman, thereby handing over to the NSLB leader control of the largest single group of teachers. This initial momentum, however, quickly stalled. Despite various public announcements and loyalty declarations, many groups were unwilling to accede to Schemm's demands. Associations such as the powerful Philologenverband showed no signs of subsuming themselves organizationally under the NSLB and were instead actively resisting such measures.[28] The process was, with very few exceptions, completed at another conference, held in Magdeburg in early June. The representatives of 48 national organizations and approximately 111 regional or local associations signed an agreement legally dissolving their organizations into Schemm's educators' community.[29] Although a small number of not insignificant issues remained to be resolved, by the end of 1934 the NSLB had secured its right to represent exclusively Germany's teachers and to oversee their ideological transformation.[30]

Neither the guidelines published in Brandenburg in August 1933 nor the intricate maneuvering by Schemm and other NSLB leaders in 1933 and 1934 tell the entire story. The claim that all teachers' associations had dissolved themselves into the NSLB not only ignored the fact that powerful organizations such as the German Philologist Association were resisting "coordination" but also masked a fundamental uncertainty within the local NSLB chapter regarding its hold over the city's teachers. Published notices reveal a not insignificant amount of confusion and delay on the part of the Brandenburg chapter in compelling pedagogues to sever all ties with their former organizations. Confronted with examples of continued activity on the part of former associations despite their formal dissolution in the early summer, local NSLB officials decreed in early August that these organizations, now reconstituted as NSLB *Fachschaften,* could hold meetings and assemblies only with the approval of and direct supervision by local officials. Similarly, these officials reminded members to pay organization dues not to their non-Nazi professional associations but directly to the local NSLB treasurer. The issue was neither easily nor quickly resolved, however. At the end of the year, NSLB officials threatened to expel from the NSLB those teachers who still maintained their memberships in non-Nazi professional organizations and refused to pay their dues in full. Similarly, the NSLB reminded teachers in December that the NSLB was the sole Nazi professional organization for teachers and that attempts either to revive disbanded or to found new associations were prohibited. More than a year after the local chapter's founding, officials were still admonishing members to pay their dues in full and on time.[31]

Brandenburg NSLB leaders had additional reasons for concern. Although many pedagogues were formal members, they displayed a clear lack of enthusiasm for the NSLB and its events. Officials announced in the fall of 1933, for example, that they would begin immediately to take note of members' attendance at events such as the NSLB's regular meetings.[32] More worrisome than lackluster participation was the widespread discontent about the numerous financial burdens the NSLB placed on teachers. In addition to paying dues, members were expected to pay for a series of additional products and services, for example wall calendars. The NSLB's plans to construct a building—to be known as the House of German Education and to be funded principally by members' contributions—encountered resistance among Brandenburg's teachers. In September 1933, provincial leaders decreed that every pedagogue would contribute 5 reichsmarks for the project, an amount equal to slightly less than four months' membership dues. Less than eight weeks later, NSLB officials reminded members that this contribution was not a donation and that every teacher was obligated to pay the full amount. District leader Martin Müller noted in a letter to the Reich leadership that "in various local groups in Kurmark District the philologists are up in arms against the costs regarding the House of German Education."[33] Although funds were collected for the building, financial obligations to the central office of the NSLB continued to worry local and provincial officials.[34] As local chapter leader Sülz quickly discovered, membership in the NSLB did not transform Brandenburg's teaching staff into a community of active, zealous Nazi pedagogues.

The NSLB Mission—Transforming Germany's Teachers?

According to one contemporary writer, in order for the NSLB to educate Germany's pupils effectively, it first had to reeducate Germany's teachers: "Next naturally the German teacher must be made aware of this completely new task of training Germany's youth. To create the new German pedagogue in the spirit of National Socialism is the true mission of the National Socialist Teachers' League (NSLB). It occurs by the same means by which the [Nazi] movement has conquered the entire people: training [Schulung] and propaganda."[35] These two closely related tools—the focused, specialized, and primarily ideological (re)training of teachers and the creation and diffusion of National Socialist educational propaganda—lay at the heart of the NSLB's mission. This is not to say, however, that the NSLB fulfilled no other functions within the Nazi state; the NSLB performed a wide variety of services on behalf of state and party institutions. For instance, it served as a watchdog over Germany's teachers. Its officials collected sensitive and potentially damaging information on its members, including reports of political activities and connections between German teachers and foreigners. The NSLB also played an important role as one link in the party-state chain of political evaluations. The organization's reports on its members were sent to party and state education authorities for consideration in hiring and promoting decisions. On at least one occasion, NSLB members were called on to assist the party in campaigning for the Nazi version of an election.[36] Brandenburg's chapter performed a wide variety of services on behalf of the Nazi state and party. The NSLB trained individual members to serve as school air raid wardens, for example, and the local chapter worked to establish a closer relationship between the city's employment office and its pupils. More common were the efforts of the NSLB to compel teachers to participate in official events and activities. The Brandenburg chapter mobilized its members in support of state-sanctioned festivals such as Harvest Day and May Day, for example, and urged the teaching staff to attend events put on by the National Socialist Culture Community and the Strength Through Joy program.[37] Despite these diverse ancillary functions, NSLB activities nonetheless centered on propaganda and ideological reeducation as the primary tools with which to transform Germany's teaching staff and thereby strengthen National Socialism.

One of the NSLB's most important propaganda functions was the regulation of German publishing on all issues related to education. The NSLB's press officials monitored, commented on, and directly influenced what press organs—including those of the party, of the state, and, for a brief while, of the non-Nazi teachers' professional associations—wrote about teacher training, pedagogical theory, and the school system. The NSLB had at its disposal powerful tools with which to influence what these publications reported and published, including the full-scale "coordination" of the personnel of editorial boards and the ability to grant and rescind publishing licenses. In addition to its role as external editor and potential censor, the NSLB was also actively engaged in creating and publishing its own periodicals and books. Its weekly newspaper, originally known as the

Reichszeitung der deutschen Erzieher (Reich newspaper of the German educator) and later renamed *Der Deutsche Erzieher* (the German educator), appeared in national and regional editions. Originally free of charge, this paper reached a circulation of 320,000 in 1936. The NSLB also published a periodical for Germany's pupils, the student magazine *Hilf mit* (Join in), which had a circulation of two million in 1934 and more than four million in 1939. Within the Nazi regime's first two years, the NSLB's press and propaganda apparatus had developed 26 district periodicals focusing primarily on political and ideological themes, 29 journals examining pedagogical and education policy issues, 8 scholarly publications, and 6 youth magazines.[38] This comprehensive press policy included more than just journals and magazines. Officials reviewed outside book manuscripts that dealt with pedagogical topics and, on occasion, intervened to find publishers for the reviewed works. The NSLB also developed in 1938 its own line of books, the Bayreuther Books for Education and Teaching. League publications were intended for a broad audience that included teachers, school pupils, and the general public.[39]

Although officials took the NSLB's propaganda mission very seriously, they marshaled even greater resources for their second task, the ideological transformation of Germany's teachers. According to Hans Schemm, the success of Nazi education policies depended on the NSLB's reeducation efforts:

> So long as the entire German community of educators does not think and feel along National Socialist lines, education as we understand it cannot be organized in a sound manner. The sooner we succeed in creating the National Socialist teacher, the development of the one type of school that befits National Socialism will be even more a matter of course. The school reform can only be carried out by men who have become complete National Socialists. . . . I take the view that nothing is as important in a people as an organic, soundly developed teacher training program, because the national community [*Volksgemeinschaft*] will be completed only after the elementary school teacher has formed the German individual according to our wishes.[40]

In short, *Schulung* lay at the heart of the NSLB's program. This special training represented, as Feiten writes, "the conscious orientation of behavior as expressed in attitude, convictions, and performance to the idea of the Third Reich."[41] The NSLB's leaders intended this "behavior orientation" to

inculcate teachers with crucial Nazi concepts such as the leadership principle, race theory, and the centrality of the *Volk,* in effect transforming
Germany's teachers—most of them not NSDAP members—into Nazi pedagogues who would create loyal and fervent Nazis out of Germany's youth.
As organized and implemented by the NSLB, the training consisted of a
broad spectrum of activities intended to mold German teachers ideologically. Officials organized, for example, lectures, presentations, evening
gatherings *(Heimabende),* day conferences, and special congresses.[42]

In Brandenburg, the NSLB district meeting *(Kreisversammlung),* held
less frequently than every month, provided an opportunity for NSLB officials both to spread Nazi propaganda and to entertain and edify their members more generally. The centerpiece of the *Kreisversammlung* was a talk,
usually delivered by a local NSLB member. In August 1934, for example,
middle school director Johannes M. spoke about "racial history and history
as racial fate"; in this talk, he surveyed the history of racial thinking, argu-
ing that the ails of contemporary society—the low birth rate, licentious
culture, and the depopulating of the countryside—were the product of
miscegenation. The solution was for the teacher to expose the pupils to
these issues in the classroom. In August 1933, Brandenburg's school superintendent spoke to the members on "the intellectual foundations of National Socialism and the consequences of this for pedagogy." According to
Superintendent Wolff, teachers were to turn pupils into Germans who "are
prepared to serve and in whom the spirit of the people and the state lives;
the pedagogue should help, by means of this conscious connection between the individual and the people and the state, transform the people,
despite their differences, into a racial community that conceives of the
state as a community of struggle and fate [*Kampf- und Schicksalgemein-
schaft*]."[43] In January 1937, on the other hand, middle school pedagogue
Ernst R. gave a talk that accompanied a slide show presentation on his recent study trip to Algeria. Although elements of the talk—in particular the
racial composition of the Algerian people and the situation of Algerian
Jews—conveyed core Nazi values, the lecture was mostly free of ideological content, introducing the audience instead to Algerian culture, history,
and geography.[44] As these examples show, the district meeting lectures
could be explicitly and largely political, as in the case of Wolff's lecture on
the foundations of National Socialism, or mostly educational but with
shades of ideological indoctrination, as in the case of the slide show presentation.

Like the district meetings that all of Brandenburg's pedagogues were expected to attend, the NSLB department meetings were hardly sites of intense and exclusive political indoctrination; they took place even more irregularly than the *Kreisversammlungen* and were often concerned with issues that were only indirectly ideological. The Brandenburg NSLB department for elementary school teachers met only six times in 1934. Whereas three of the lectures—on the role of elementary schools in the Third Reich, on racialist thought and history instruction, and on paramilitary games in elementary schools—appear to have concerned conventionally political topics, the talks on the cultural significance of Brandenburg's Eastern March, on local geography, and on the pedagogical uses of scholarship on the Ice Age focused on general pedagogical or instructional issues. Similarly, in a 12-month period from November 1933 to November 1934, the department for middle schools, which met six times in this period, organized three talks, of which two foregrounded core National Socialist issues: the origins and development of the Nordic race and the significance of the subject of biology in Nazi pedagogical scholarship. The third lecture discussed the role of instruction in German "prehistory" in the middle schools.[45] Although the district and departmental meetings were not infrequently used as a means to instruct the teaching staff in various Nazi tenets, the fact that NSLB members came together only infrequently and that the centerpiece of more than a few meetings concerned topics that were possibly completely or at least largely devoid of ideological content raises questions about the efficacy of efforts to transform Brandenburg's teaching staff by means of local NSLB activities.

The NSLB's most important and effective indoctrination tool, however, was the training camp experience. According to interior minister Frick, these camps were to "create the political man, who in his thoughts and deeds is rooted in his *Volk* and who wholly and most deeply feels bound to the history and destiny of his *Volk*."[46] Beginning in 1934, the NSLB set up a nationwide system that included as of 1936 more than 50 camps. Located in primarily nonurban environments throughout Germany, the camps provided NSLB officials with an unique opportunity to compel teachers to experience National Socialist ideology by first removing them from their regular surroundings and then subjecting them to an intense political indoctrination process, typically lasting between 7 and 14 days. Often wearing uniforms or identical camp clothing and housed in barrack-like domiciles, the teachers followed a heavily prescribed daily routine that usually included roll call, raising and lowering of flags, sports, military drills, marching, physical work, and ideological-political lectures.[47] The officials of the NSLB believed that the pedagogues needed to "live" and "feel" National Socialism in order for them to incorporate its tenets into their teachings and everyday lives. This emphasis on experiencing Nazism, rather than simply learning about the leadership principle, the community's supremacy over the individual, or the importance of physical strength, meant that the transformative power of the *Schulungslager* was intended to far exceed that of more traditional means such as lectures and meetings held locally. The camps would facilitate the transmission of knowledge, certainly, but they would also play the more important role of transforming the attitude, instinct, and character of Germany's teachers.[48] Illustrating the ideals of the *Schulungslager,* one supposed participant describes his experience in the *Reichszeitung der deutschen Erzieher* (Reich newspaper of the German educator):

> The keeping-in-step when marching, when working, when feeling is accomplished. The lectures that are held in the mornings by the best experts take care of the spiritual keeping-in-step. We learn about our ancestors in an entirely new light, and we stand in amazement before their high culture. Entirely new perspectives regarding race and culture open up, we become aware of the enormous importance of the national character, we experience the violent struggle of our people for its unity, and we become more and more proud to be able to live in this era and to participate in its formation. More and more and deeper and deeper we penetrate into the spirit of National Socialism with all its effects and we are filled with wonder at the courage, the strength, and the assuredness with which all questions of everyday life, of politics, and of the economy are tackled and implemented.[49]

In addition to compelling pedagogues to experience National Socialism on a physical, emotional, and intellectual level, NSLB leaders also sought to use the training camp system in its campaign to integrate teachers more deeply into the larger Nazi racial community that state and party leaders sought to construct. "The *Schulungslager* facilitate the realization of the people's community [*Volksgemeinschaft*]," a Nazi propagandist wrote. "They set the individual in full possession of his physical, intellectual, and moral strengths and thus deepen the communal thinking [*Gemeinschaftsdenken*] in the context of the people." By collecting a group of teachers in one place at one time, officials worked to instill the notion that each person was not a completely free individual, independent of his or her surroundings and fellow humans, but a single component of a larger whole, the national community. Both the program's specific curricula and its extracurricular activities stressed the importance of community—from the feeling of camaraderie gained from "communal work" (*Gemeinschaftsarbeit*) performed at a communal camp (*Gemeinschaftslager*) to an understanding of the central National Socialist concept of the *Volksgemeinschaft*—in the lives of Germany's teachers. On completion of the training camp, the "reborn pedagogue" was to have, according to a Nazi writer, an entirely new relationship to his fellow Germans, especially his pupils:

> He has now become a leader [*Führer*], a leader of the German youth! Now he can better understand his HJ [Hitler Youth] comrades when they march and sing and camp, he understands their tempo and stands very close to the essence of the young Germany. He hears the heartbeats of National Socialism and knows he is one with the millions of young souls who have pledged themselves with body and soul to eternal Germany and its *Führer*.[50]

Such a teacher now could and would educate the next generation of Germans along National Socialist lines.

Equally significant and arguably more pressing for the NSLB was the camps' role in diminishing, if not completely removing, the significant professional, social, political, and religious divisions within Germany's teaching force. Participants were not divided according to their academic backgrounds or professional and social status. Lordly philologists and lowly elementary school teachers ate, worked, marched, played, and learned beside one another at the training camps. The sense of equality expressed itself in almost every facet of the camp experience, including the way the participants interacted with one another. The participants wore the same clothes, ate the same food, and performed the same physical work. More important, camp participants were to refrain from addressing one another with the formal second-person *Sie* and any academic or professional titles; they were instead to use the very informal *Du*, something then traditionally reserved for very close friends and family. Evening activities were especially designed to foster a sense of solidarity, and a typical "camaraderie evening" (*Kameradschaftsabend*) consisted of singing around a campfire, playing music, reciting folk and regional poetry, and telling jokes.[51] "No one notices what [kind of teacher] one is," one enthusiastic *Schulungslager* participant wrote, "where one comes from and no one asks. One is simply a comrade."[52] According to men like Hans Schemm and Fritz Wächtler, the training camp would play the decisive role in unifying and ideologically transforming Germany's teachers.

Whereas extant records provide a detailed overview of NSLB activities in Brandenburg, the situation is far less clear regarding the participation of Brandenburgers in the training camps. In an August 1937 article in the *Brandenburger Anzeiger,* a teacher reported on his experiences at a "border camp" (*Grenzlandlager*) organized by the Brandenburg NSLB under the direction of district leader Dr. Johannes Mahnkopf. This account makes clear, however, that this "camp" was not a *Schulungslager;* all elements of the experience—from bike trips to hikes to town tours to lectures— centered on introducing the participants to the culture, people, and geography of the part of eastern Brandenburg Province that shared a border with Poland. Absent were, for example, the prescribed activities such as military drills and ideological-political lectures designed to enable teachers to "live" and "feel" National Socialism. Moreover, this writer mentions spending time with members who were attending a *Schulungslager* in the vicinity of this *Grenzlandlager.*[53] This travelogue, though illuminating in its own right, sheds light neither on the structure and activities of a specific training camp nor on an individual teacher's attitudes toward the experience. Similarly, NSLB archival collections in Berlin and elsewhere have very little information regarding the participation of individual Brandenburg teachers in the *Schulungslager.* According to the personnel files of the city's secondary school teachers, for example, only a very small number of Brandenburgers attended a *Schulungslager.* For example, only two of the Von Saldern's roughly 23 pedagogues and only one of the Upper Lyceum's approximately 20 teachers attended a camp. Moreover, records indicate that at least one of these three was a zealous and especially active National Socialist; Heinrich M. was praised by his principal, in connection with the teacher's request to be transferred to a school in the newly conquered eastern territories, as "belonging to the few personalities whose impulse to be active and participate far exceeds the norm."[54] Such a person was already a committed Nazi and therefore most likely not in need of reeducation. A similar picture of the pedagogues' reeducation experiences emerges when we analyze the developments and institutions on the regional level. In the Kurmark District, which included Brandenburg, NSLB training efforts started slowly and only with great difficulty. Only 350, or 2.6 percent, of the region's teachers had received some extended training as of 1 January 1935; in contrast, the national average per district was 10.5 percent.[55] Following an Education Ministry decree calling for the "overhaul" *(Überholung)* of the teaching staff, regional officials began in early 1935 to organize a series of training sessions that would reach a greater number of pedagogues. In March district officials informed the national leadership of their plan to hold three training courses during the Easter vacation. Intended to serve as a trial run for the summer sessions, the Easter program sought to instruct 112 attendees in physical fitness, "ideological enhancement including practical-political enlightenment" *(weltanschaulich Befestigung einschl. realpolitische Aufklärung)*, and more specialized continuing education courses. Held in four locations throughout Brandenburg Province, the Easter camps, in the words of regional NSLB officials, "were partly carried out with great success": not only were the officials able to evaluate the instructors and other personnel the NSLB planned to use at the summer training camps but also they believed that a whole lot *(eine ganze Anzahl)* of the teachers who attended the camp at Lychen would help run future *Schulungslager.* Intent on building on this success, district *Schulung* leader Dr. Gerhard Hoppe two months later called for summer training camps to be held on a more massive scale and for a significantly longer period of time, an important precondition, according to NSLB theory, for ideologically reeducating the teachers. The NSLB's officials wanted to educate 47 groups, each with an average of 30 teachers, for approximately 11 days. Camp reeducation would again emphasize physical activity, a sense of camaraderie, and the "clarification" of ideological tenets.[56]

Regional enthusiasm, however, ran up against the Reich leadership's financial limitations and priorities. Hoppe's request that Bayreuth contribute 14,000 reichsmarks for the training sessions was flatly rejected. District NSLB leader Martin Müller then turned to the Reich Education Ministry for financial assistance, noting that the combination of NSLB Kurmark District funds and members' fees would not suffice to pay for the entire program. Although it is ultimately unclear how, if at all, the NSLB secured additional funding, in 1935 the regional officials nevertheless succeeded in organizing a number of summer *Schulungslager,* though on a slightly more modest scale than initially envisioned. Slightly more than 1,900 volunteers, out of the province's 12,500 pedagogues, participated in 25 camps.[57] Despite having to lower their expectations, regional NSLB officials did in the summer of 1935 reach slightly more than 15 percent of the region's pedagogues, a not unimpressive start to a program that all assumed would expand and develop into the centerpiece of NSLB indoctrination efforts.

These numbers alone do not tell the entire story; they fail to indicate, for example, what kind of teachers attended the *Schulungslager.* Not all types of teachers participated to the same extent. Whereas approximately 60 percent of Germany's elementary school pedagogues had attended a training camp by this time, less than 10 percent of the middle school instructors and only around 15 percent of the secondary and vocational school teachers had. Moreover, according to an internal NSLB report, the participants consisted of the region's most zealously pro-Nazi teachers. "Essentially the best and most active forces from the pedagogical circles made themselves available this summer," Hoppe wrote; "the story will already be more difficult next spring and summer when we will approach those who will not voluntarily attend."[58] Rather than introducing large numbers of teachers to National Socialism, in the summer of 1935 the NSLB subjected to ideological training the very small group of people—approximately 16 percent of the province's teaching force—who "needed" it least. If the NSLB's efforts at mass indoctrination were to continue at this pace, officials would need more than six years and a much more inclusive recruitment policy in order to reach every teacher in the district just once. As will be shown in Chapter 3, circumstances did not permit the NSLB to develop along this path; the Second World War, with its growing demands on state and party resources, ultimately severely disrupted the NSLB's indoctrination efforts.

Blissfully ignorant of what lay in store for the NSLB, its officials looked forward, at the very least, to replicating in 1936 the *Schulungslager* program on the same level as the previous summer. Financial shortcomings continued to handicap regional plans, however. In December 1935, Hoppe informed Reich *Schulung* leader Carl Wolf of the Kurmark District's "terrible money difficulties" and raised the possibility that regional authorities would lack sufficient funding for the next summer's training camps. In a related effort to avert the predicted financial shortcomings, Müller repeatedly sought approval from state and party agencies for his proposal to raise membership fees to cover the costs of *Schulung.* Having received no outside financial assistance and faced with the approach of the summer school recess, regional NSLB officials in April 1936 informed the subdistrict leaders *(Kreisamtsleiter)* that the lack of money prevented the NSLB from organizing summer training camps on the regional level. The *Kreisamtsleiter* were ordered to take responsibility for planning and executing NSLB training sessions, which could consist of such provisional and presumably more cost-effective elements as lengthy marching trips along Germany's eastern border, so long as sufficient attention—calculated at 50 percent of the entire endeavor—was paid to the teachers' ideological-political education. Such stopgap measures, while ensuring that some NSLB activities would take place that summer, would also have meant that many of the special, and even fundamental, features of the *Schulungslager* program would be omitted or at the very least heavily diluted. Removing pedagogues from their communities, subjecting them to ideologized routines, and breaking down professional and social barriers among teachers, for example, would take place only in modified, in most cases weakened, form, or not at all. Pedagogues would not, in short, "live" and "feel" National Socialism, at least not in the form and to the degree that Schemm and other Nazi leaders originally desired. Financial aid finally arrived in late April in the form of NSLB approval for an increase of all members' dues, to last for three months, in order to help pay for the coming summer training camps. A fairly desperate response, given officials' awareness of the deleterious impact earlier membership fee increases—to fund the construction of the NSLB's House of German Education in Munich, for example—had had on members' attitudes toward the NSLB. It was thus able on relatively short notice to organize a series of summer training camp sessions. According to statistics compiled on the national level, in 1936 it significantly expanded its camp indoctrination program, increasing the number of teachers it trained in its *Schulungslager* by approximately 26 percent.[59]

The summer of 1937 marked the apogee of these camp reeducation efforts. Approximately 45,000 German teachers were sent to the training sessions, an increase of about 1 percent from the previous year and the largest number to attend in a single year. Moreover, as of this date, approximately 50 percent of all the members had attended a camp.[60] An important factor behind this development was the decision to make permanent the membership fee increase levied the previous year.[61] Members now paid twice to attend the compulsory camps—in the form of a surcharge to the monthly dues and in the form of per diem charges while attending the camp. Although this arrangement freed most NSLB officials from having to struggle to fund the summer training camps, the Kurmark District NSLB continued to suffer from financial difficulties that affected its ability to hold the camps. Fiscal constraints, for example, forced the regional NSLB to depart from past practice and to cut out all camp sessions in the first quarter of 1938. When the NSLB's Training Department in the fall of 1938 analyzed participation statistics for the various districts for the period 1933–1938, it determined that the Kurmark District had only been able to train 30 percent of its teaching staff in *Schulungslager,* thereby distinguishing itself as one of the six districts with the lowest proportional attendance rates in Germany. In the districts of Pomerania, Württemberg, and Danzig, officials had succeeded in convincing large numbers of their members to attend more than one training camp session![62]

This lack of regular and sufficient funding played a large role in the inability of the Kurmark District NSLB to organize and execute a reeducation program designed to transform the district's entire teaching staff politically. Reporting to Bayreuth, regional *Schulung* officials noted that as of September 1939—four years after the NSLB's program began and after the outbreak of the Second World War—no more than 506 of the 706 members living and working in Brandenburg and its immediate environs had attended a *Schulungslager.* Years of state and party coercion and enticement had resulted in 70 percent of the members attending a camp, a remarkable statistic but one that still fell short of the goal of Nazi party and state leaders to instill core National Socialist values in every teacher by means of regularly attended training camps.[63] Although one should not overlook the social and political significance of the NSLB's success in subjecting hundreds of teachers to its basic indoctrination program, the statistic nonetheless illustrates the NSLB's failure to get all teachers, and not just members, to attend. This mixture of success and failure—of progress and incompleteness—also characterized the NSLB's efforts on the national level. As of late 1939 it had trained in *Schulungslager* more than 210,000 teachers, comprising approximately 60 percent of its membership.[64] Moreover, it was not possible for large numbers of members to attend more than one, given the somewhat small number of *Schulungslager,* the somewhat lengthy intended duration of each session, the difficulties of finding a sufficient block of time, during the school year or over a school break, to attend, and the large number of attendees at a camp. Finally, 40 percent of NSLB members, in addition to the thousands of teachers who had not joined the organization, had still not attended a *Schulungslager* and thus had not undergone what it considered its most important and effective political indoctrination process.

Despite Schemm's and Wächtler's grand designs and even grander rhetoric, the NSLB's plans for training Brandenburg's teachers encountered three significant obstacles: financial shortcomings, state competition for control of teacher training, and staffing pressures resulting from certain political and economic policies. Although many of the fiscal difficulties— along with their underlying causes—affected every region and district, the Kurmark's geography uniquely exacerbated its financial plight. District officials such as Müller and Hoppe were responsible for the largest district in Germany and thus the costs, especially those related to traveling, that the NSLB and its members were expected to bear for its standard activities were far greater than in other districts. According to Müller, the main source of the district's "powerful financial burden" was the necessity of funding teachers' travel to attend meetings, conferences, and training camps.[65]

Another impediment to this training camp program was the bureaucratic struggles between the NSLB and state agencies. Mirroring the acrimonious conflict over the German Educator Communities that took place in the first two years of the Third Reich, the Education Ministry and the NSLB fought from 1933 to 1936 for control over teacher training. Education Ministry officials wanted to maintain traditional control over teacher qualification and training, and Minister Rust planned to use the Central Institute for Education and Teaching as a means for ideological and technical supplemental education. Having organized lecture series and training courses in a small number of camps in 1933 and 1934, Rust hoped to expand this into a national system of *Schulung* sites and camps through which all elementary school teachers would pass every year. Schemm and NSLB officials, however, resisted vigorously. After more than three years of institutional clashes, NSLB leader Fritz Wächtler and Minister Rust reached a compromise in February 1936 that decisively resolved the issue of control over *Schulung*. According to this agreement, the NSLB exclusively oversaw the teachers' ideological reeducation, and state education authorities supervised the vocational supplemental training. Moreover, education authorities agreed to recognize the NSLB's claims for special treatment as an NSDAP "ancillary organization" and thus permit teachers to attend NSLB training courses throughout the year.[66] With the agreement concluded, the NSLB was now solely responsible for the Third Reich's political indoctrination of its teachers. Individual teachers no longer had to choose between attending an Education Ministry–sanctioned political education course and an NSLB-sponsored *Schulungslager.* Moreover, interested pedagogues no longer had the single option of sacrificing part of a school break in order to participate in the NSLB program; although many still attended summer training camp sessions, it was now also possible, though by no means necessarily easy, for pedagogues to go to a *Schulungslager* held during the school year. That year the NSLB enrolled a greater number of teachers in its camps than ever before in a single year, an increase of more than 25 percent from the previous year's total. This trend continued, and in the following year the NSLB ideologically schooled more than 45,000 pedagogues.[67] In addition to clearing up various legal and logistical problems, the resolution of the serious dispute with the Education Ministry helped the NSLB expand its *Schulung* program significantly to include more camps and more participants.

Finally, the NSLB's efforts to indoctrinate all German teachers were also hindered by economic and political developments that made it increasingly difficult for school principals to release pedagogues from their teaching duties in order to participate in its activities. The Nazi rearmament program contributed to a decrease in the number of men standing in the front of classrooms. Beginning in October 1935 and accelerating in the following years, the state increasingly called on able-bodied men—including young, freshly minted teachers and older, seasoned pedagogues—to submit to lengthy formal military service or short-term military training courses.[68] City and regional education administration documents indicate that by 1936 male teachers from Brandenburg were regularly called up to take part in short-term military training programs and exercises. A teacher at the Jahn School participated in 12 military exercises in the period 1935–1939. Another joined regular military units for three weeks' training in 1937. At least nine teachers underwent significant periods of military training in 1938. One from the Pestalozzi School served for 30 days in 1938, and others were away from the classroom for periods longer than two months. In the period August 1935–September 1938, more than 200,000 German men entered military service. Within the next nine months the armed forces grew by an additional 180,000 men.[69] Although the statistics do not indicate how many of the conscripted men were teachers, it is likely that the extensive scale and comprehensive scope of the military call-up included a not insignificant number of pedagogues.

The staffing pressures created by military policies might have been negligible had they not coincided with a teacher shortage that developed in the second half of 1930s. The instructor deficit resulting from Weimar-era and early Nazi policies such as hiring freezes, wage cuts, and re-strictions on access to higher education continued to handicap the schools.[70] As discussed in Chapter 1, these national developments com-bined with local changes—especially the flood of workers and their fami-lies moving to Brandenburg to work in its growing armaments industry—to make teachers a valuable labor commodity with which officials could not easily dispense.[71] By 1938 principals and school superintendents in Bran-denburg and throughout Germany had smaller pools of permanent and substitute teachers with which to free up NSLB members so that they could attend a training camp. The effect of both forces—conscription and scarcity—can be discerned in the marked decline in teacher participation in the *Schulungslager.* The NSLB in 1938 trained fewer than 36,000 peda-gogues, representing both a 20 percent decline from the year before and the beginning of a trend. In 1939 only 30,000 pedagogues attended, a de-crease of approximately 33 percent from the 1937 high-water mark and well below the total for 1935.[72] Despite having secured funding for the training camps and having established a working relationship with the Education Ministry, the NSLB in the years leading up to the war continued to struggle to realize fully its plans, due in part to a dearth of available manpower.

The NSLB's Failed Revolution

Despite years of NSLB propaganda and training camps, Brandenburg's teachers remained as of 1938 deeply divided along religious, professional, social, and political lines. Five years of NSLB activities had failed to create a community in which all German teachers would "march together, valued equally, with equal rights, each only carrying out his instructions in his part," toward the common goal of strengthening the National Socialist state.[73] Instead, long-standing fissures continued to fragment Branden-burg's teaching staff. The pedagogues in each school were divided politi-cally between those who had and had not joined either the NSDAP or a related organization such as the Stormtroopers or SS. By May 1939, 51 percent of the city's elementary school teachers had joined the NSDAP. The situation at the Jahn School was typical. Whereas 8 of the 16 teachers were ardent National Socialists, a number of whom chose not just to join the party but also to assume leadership positions in it or another Nazi organization, the other 8 displayed no particular degree of political engagement. The teaching staffs of the Roland and the Herman Löns schools were similarly divided, although in these cases the non-Nazis clearly outnumbered the party members: only 36 and 35 percent of the teachers, respectively, had joined the NSDAP. On the other hand, more than 63 percent of the teachers of the Hans Schemm and the Heinrich von Kleist schools were Nazi Party members. An even greater percentage— 71 percent—of teachers at the Boys' Intermediate School belonged to the NSDAP, whereas extant records indicate that the proportion of Nazi Party members (*Parteigenossen*) at the aristocratic and very conservative Ritterakademie remained at 36 percent until 1937, when the school was closed and its teaching staff dispersed. Similar percentages could be found among the teachers of the other two secondary schools; as of March 1938, 8 of the 23 Von Saldern pedagogues and 5 of the 14 Upper Lyceum teachers were NSDAP members. Moreover, the number of pedagogues in Brandenburg as of 1939 who belonged to the Stormtroopers or the SS was quite small. In the case of the Jahn, Nicholas, and Fontane schools, only one teacher at each school was a Stormtrooper; at least one teaching staff had no Stormtrooper members, and no elementary school had more than two. Brandenburg pedagogues who had joined the SS were even less common; there was no more than a handful of SS teachers in the period 1933–1939. According to a former pupil who became a postwar teacher trainee in Brandenburg, the Boys' Intermediate School teaching staff was divided between "convinced" Liberals, zealous Nazis, including an SS man, and even one closet Marxist, all of whom sought in little ways to shape the pupils' convictions.[74]

Membership statistics do not tell the entire story; as school officials, party radicals, and others observed, political divisions were especially evident in teachers' actions. The case of Von Saldern pedagogue Rudolf R. is particularly illuminating. A philologist who began teaching in Brandenburg in 1918 after being badly wounded in the First World War, he had joined the NSV in July 1934 and the NSLB in June 1937. Denounced in August 1935 by elementary school teacher and *Jungvolk* leader Max R., an exceptionally zealous Nazi, allegedly for having mocked the *Jungvolk* in class and for treating Jewish pupils preferentially, Rudolf R. defended his actions and attitudes:

I treat him [a particular Jewish student] in the same manner I try to treat the other pupils. I consider doing so my duty, which corresponds to my sense of justice. . . . I treat rather all pupils equally, regardless of whether they are Aryan or non-Aryan. Kindly disposed to all equally . . . Because I consider every young man who attends the school to be a full pupil of the school and as such to have equal rights. That means such a pupil has a right to be treated like his fellow pupils. That is also the position of the teaching staff, which I made clear to the pupils.[75]

A former member of the rightist German National People's Party and the right wing paramilitary veterans' association Stahlhelm and a cofounder of the local chapter of the nationalist Verband nationaler gesinnter Soldaten, he nevertheless refused to see his pupils through the lens of National Socialism. This resistance to adopting the National Socialist perspective on various political and social matters not only persisted but also continued to get him in trouble with the Nazi state and party. On 10 November 1938, as some Brandenburgers assaulted the city's Jews, ransacked their stores and homes, desecrated the Jewish cemetery, and burned the city's synagogue in connection with the Kristallnacht pogrom taking place all over Germany, Rudolf R. sought to prevent the mob from breaking into and plundering a store that belonged to a Jewish friend, someone he considered "a decent businessman" and a "genuine nationalist" *(immer deutschnational gewesen);* Rudolf R. scolded both those demolishing the store and the many bystanders and sought in vain to convince a policeman to intervene to protect the store. As a result, he was briefly suspended from teaching, vilified in the local press, and investigated by school officials and the police. Authorities labeled him an "inveterate" "arch-reactionary" who, it was suspected, "was the leader of his fellow teachers who believed as he did and who knew to hide skillfully their reactionary attitudes." "Rudolf R. is to be judged based on his full behavior," another official concluded, "as being indifferent to the creation of the Third Reich." Disappointing those who hoped, at the very least, his suspension would be made permanent, Rudolf R. returned to the classroom less than 10 weeks after his remarkable display of civil courage and personal loyalty; he continued to teach until his death in August 1942.[76]

Nor was Rudolf R. the only Brandenburg pedagogue whose behavior disappointed and, in some cases, angered state and party officials. For example, the experienced secondary school teacher Friedrich K., a member of the NSLB and NSV by 1939, was officially criticized for failing to demonstrate any "active participation in the Party or any of its organizations." Officials in 1936 forcibly retired Von Saldern's principal, Ferdinand G., for his alleged "coolness" toward National Socialism. Such evident lack of enthusiasm or commitment also extended to some who had even joined the NSDAP. Von Saldern pedagogue Conrad K. protested in mid-1942 against his forced six-month deployment to mentor children who had been evacuated from dangerous, most likely urban environments as part of the Nazi Kinderlandverschickung program. A public argument with a Nazi official visiting from the regional party leadership resulted in local and regional officials evaluating Conrad K.'s activities as a pedagogue and a National Socialist. Seconding the opinion of his principal that the 57-year-old teacher responded to "the demands of the day" in a way that was "anything but National Socialistic," party officials concluded that Conrad K. was a lousy Nazi: his participation consisted only in the payment of his dues, he was "one of the last" teachers to join the NSLB, and his "inner disposition" to the Nazi movement was far from perfect. A report from the personnel department of the regional NSDAP leadership concluded

> that he as a party member, as I have observed, has not once worn the NSDAP pin may also be proof. He has great deficiencies in questions of ideology and character, so that he is not to be judged reliable or exemplary. His position in the movement is now such that a single concrete incident will open a case before the party court in which at the same time his whole deplorable attitude would get what it deserves.[77]

As a consequence of such behavior, some Brandenburg teachers were expelled from local Nazi organizations. Following a serious episode in which the Gestapo and education authorities first investigated and then punished him for a public demonstration of support for the oppositional "Confessing Church," the former Ritterakademie and current Von Saldern pedagogue Dr. Karl G., for example, was thrown out of the NSLB in early 1938 for "antisocial behavior"; he had not only refused to buy lottery tickets to support a job creation program but also labeled the colleague selling the tickets a denunciant. A welcome development, Von Saldern principal Walter H. implied in a letter clearly intended to incite the *Oberpräsident* to increase his punishment, for someone who "not only is not a contributing [*aufbauendes*] member of the teaching staff but supports as a convinced reactionary [*Ewig-Gestriger*] the subterranean currents agitating against the National Socialist movement."[78]

If political affiliations and activities clearly continued to divide the city's teaching staff, Brandenburg's pedagogues as of May 1939 appeared at first glance to be united professionally, since approximately 93 percent of them had joined the NSLB, especially when compared with the sharply fractured organizational landscape during the Weimar Republic. This extremely high percentage, however, is deceiving. Whereas the great majority of teachers became NSLB members by the end of 1933, most philologists resisted joining for more than three years. Whereas 11 *Gymnasium* teachers joined the NSLB in 1933, only two did so in the period 1934–1936. Only after the Philologenverband's decisive defeat in 1937 did the great bulk of the remaining philologists—at least 17—become members.[79] Although the philologists no longer struggled against their alleged professional and social inferiors through their own professional association, they did not necessarily shed their ingrained sense of superiority and distinctiveness after they had finally joined the NSLB. For example, Von Saldern pedagogue Rudolf R. continued to administer the health insurance fund of the former Philologenverband chapter, an activity that some interpreted as an attempt to preserve the traditions of the Philologists' Association. Nor did the NSLB really compel secondary school teachers to work to efface their notions of professional and social preeminence and uniqueness. Although NSLB district meetings brought together all of Brandenburg's teachers, at least as important, possibly even more, were the equally regular department meetings. Secondary school pedagogues, for example, gathered every couple of months to discuss matters relevant to themselves and the upper schools. It was in these professionally segregated meetings in 1934 that Brandenburg's philologists listened to lectures on important topics such as Nazi racial science, population politics, the so-called Austrian problem, and genealogical research. Similarly, at least half of the time demanded of middle and elementary school teachers by the local NSLB was spent in exclusionary department activities.[80] This is not to say that the NSLB's officials failed in every respect to tear down the traditional social and professional barriers among the different kinds of teachers; what is clear, however, is that certain of its policies in fact worked at cross-purposes to this central goal. Although extant records do not permit a full assessment of the impact of the NSLB's apparently schizophrenic operations, the efficacy of its efforts to unify Germany's teachers must be called into question, since its activities permitted at the very least the continuation of traditional divisions.

Moreover, it was not uncommon for the existence and activities of the NSLB to divide individual school teaching staffs. After more than three years of Nazi rule, the Von Saldern teaching staff remained sharply split regarding participation in the NSLB. In a report to the provincial *Oberpräsident*, the leader of the school's NSLB school cell noted that "when Director [G.] retired in October of last year [1936] five of the Saldria's twenty-one teachers belonged to the NSLB. Among the teachers there sharp political conflicts existed that were so obvious that they were known even to the pupils."[81] Of the five teachers who were NSDAP members, two had joined as early as 1931, including the zealous and unusually active Nazi and Stormtrooper Artur K., who arrived in Brandenburg in late 1933. Teaching at the same school, however, were four former Freemasons and two former SPD members who had been the target of a vitriolic Nazi press campaign in the spring of 1933.[82] In charge of the school was Ferdinand G., a longtime and active member of the former German Democratic Party who had been teaching in Brandenburg since 1904 and who was pushed out of his job in October 1936 as a consequence of the machinations of a few of his Nazi subordinates and their allies in the education administration and the NSDAP. A history of clashes between the principal and Nazi organizations such as the *Jungvolk* and the NSLB, in which he rebuffed some of their efforts to intervene in school affairs, exploded in January 1936 with two events: his "failure" to end the 1936 celebration of Hitler's appointment to chancellor with the singing of the "Horst-Wessel Song" and the national anthem and the alleged "electoral sabotage" he carried out in connection with the March 1936 elections. That the episodes were ultimately brought to the attention of *Oberpräsident* Kube and other senior Nazi civil servants in the regional government was the result of two Nazi Von Saldern teachers denouncing Ferdinand G. to local NSDAP and NSLB leaders. Galvanized especially by the charge that he had impeded the efforts of the Nazi teachers to compel their colleagues to vote in the coming parliamentary elections, authorities quickly moved to retire the 60-year-old principal. His departure, and especially the way it was brought about, failed to calm the situation among his school's teachers, however; at least one non-Nazi teacher publicly expressed his disapproval.[83]

Partially in response to this situation—the existence of a teaching staff that, though divided, on balance displayed a "coolness" toward the NSDAP—state education authorities appointed an ardent Nazi and NSLB member to take over the school's directorship. In a letter explaining his selection of the technically unqualified Dr. Walter H. as principal, *Oberpräsident* Kube informed Education Minister Rust that "the new head of the Saldria will have to accomplish the difficult task of restoring to comradely cooperation a teaching staff that is divided and filled with mistrust on both sides and of building a relationship of trust with NSDAP and Hitler Youth offices."[84]

Yet both the proposed appointment and the desired unity among the Saldria's teachers proved more difficult than state and party officials anticipated. Almost two years later, Kube continued to plead with Rust to disregard state regulations and make the appointment of Walter H. official. Kube justified the 38-year-old secondary school teacher's candidacy by noting that he had made some—though not complete—progress in fulfilling his "special assignment," creating a sense of cooperation within the "not very unified" and "in many ways very distrustful" teaching staff. Since his arrival, three more pedagogues had joined the Nazi Party, and seven had become NSLB members, though the increase in League membership was most likely the result of the Philologenverband's final dissolution in 1937. Some teachers were quite active in the local NSLB: Latin teacher Hermann H. served as head of its secondary school department, for example, and biology and physical education instructor Artur K. led the NSLB school cell. The majority of the Saldria's teachers, however, had not joined the Nazi Party, and more than a few were not NSLB members.[85] According to the head of the Brandenburg NSLB, Rudolf R. joined the NSLB only because education officials ordered him to do so in 1937 and had not attended a single meeting as of December 1938. He not only was the leader of a group of reactionaries among the teachers, according to his principal, but also had ended a friendship with a colleague who had joined the NSDAP. To take another example, the accusations of one pedagogue in the winter of 1937–1938 that another was a Nazi "denunciant" did little to improve relations among the teaching staff. On the eve of the Second World War, state and party officials continued to fret about the divisions among the Von Saldern teachers, concerned especially about an alleged political "opposition group" that demonstrated clear "passive resistance" to the principal's efforts to transform the school and teaching staff along National Socialist

lines. Despite officials' efforts, the teaching staff remained largely as it had
been earlier in the Third Reich—"not a calm, homogenous body but one
full of political and personal reciprocal tensions."[86]

The teachers at the Ritterakademie were similarly divided. In a letter to
Oberpräsident Kube in 1935, the Ritterakademie's director wrote:

> of the 13 teachers, four are NSDAP members, of whom two belong also to
> the NSLB, another teacher is a member just of the NSLB, two are in the
> SA. Sadly, simply belonging to one of these organizations does not guaran-
> tee activism, not even honest conviction. . . . What is lacking is a teaching
> staff that can offer mainly on the basis of its attitude the prerequisites to de-
> velop the National Socialist spirit in the school.[87]

That only four Ritterakademie teachers had joined the NSDAP and only
three the NSLB is especially significant because the school was a bulwark
of German patriotism, nationalism, and tradition. For more than 200 years,
its graduates had distinguished themselves as military officers and states-
men.[88] Yet the Nazi Party and the NSLB still failed to convince more than
a few of its teachers to join either of them or to "develop the National Socialist spirit" among their colleagues and pupils. Many joined the NSLB
only in 1937, when membership was effectively compulsory and shortly before Nazi officials closed the Ritterakademie. In fact, the behavior of the
teaching staffs of the Saldria and the Ritterakademie demonstrate clearly
that the NSLB failed both to unite Brandenburg's teachers and to transform them into an ideologically homogenous group of active National Socialists.

This assertion does not mean that Brandenburg's teachers did not share
certain values with the Nazi state and party. Much of the recent scholarship
on the Third Reich emphasizes the high degree of consensus between most
Germans and many Nazi policies, identifying in particular "consensus-
building" issues such as the creation of a racial community, an important
element of which was the social, economic, and political exclusion of Germany's Jews, and Hitler's foreign policy successes in the 1930s.[89] For pedagogues like the Upper Lyceum's Felix S., who gave a February 1937 NSLB
lecture on "Raw Materials and Colonies," or middle school director Johannes M., who spoke in August 1934 on "Race and History," Nazi rearmament programs and anti-Semitic policies were most likely very attractive.
To take another example, classes were canceled one day in January 1935
so that the teachers as well as the pupils of the Upper Lyceum could listen

to and then celebrate the results of the plebiscite that returned the Saar to Germany.[90] However, the extent to which Nazis and Brandenburgers "shared cultural and political dispositions" is likely more complex than would appear at first glance. The example of Von Saldern pedagogue Rudolf R. is especially illustrative. State evaluations of his teaching reveal that he taught the new politicized curriculum; a June 1934 history lesson observed by education officials was a discussion of the relationship between North America and Japan from "geographical, racial, military-political, and political-economic" perspectives. Yet Rudolf R.'s actions—his outright refusal to participate in the NSLB, for example, his belief in the equal treatment of "Aryan" and "non-Aryan" pupils in his classroom, and his courageous actions during the Kristallnacht pogrom—demonstrate the limits of his willingness to go along with the Nazi state and party. His actions in and outside the classroom demonstrate that he could participate in certain of the regime's projects—including teaching a nazified curriculum—without fully embracing the Nazi state's ideological priorities, without changing his attitudes and behavior to conform to the tenets of National Socialism. Nor was Rudolf R. alone; the actions of his Brandenburg colleagues from 1933 to 1939 demonstrate that not a few shared his misgivings about important elements of the "National Socialist revolution." Teaching staffs were divided between zealous Nazis and those unwilling to participate in Nazi programs like the *Schulungslager* to the degree the state and party desired. The actions of Brandenburg pedagogues such as Rudolf R., Ferdinand G., and Paul G. reveal that if teachers sought to be part of a Nazi-defined national community, they—and not the National Socialists—determined the scope of their participation. Excluding Jews from this community would be permitted, for example, but these teachers, most of whom began their teaching careers before January 1933, were not willing to work to erase traditional social, professional, and cultural divisions among teaching staff.[91]

That Nazi leaders took this situation seriously is a point that needs to be acknowledged and appreciated; the repeated expressions of criticism were genuine and significant. For example, the principal Walter H. noted with alarm the "reactionary" teachers under him who made up an "opposition group" that ultimately turned the majority of Von Saldern pedagogues against him and his reform plans. His very appointment, in fact, was the result of serious political tensions among the school's teachers; his predecessor, Ferdinand G., had been driven out by two zealous Nazi teachers working with local NSLB and Nazi Party leaders. Similarly, Nazi officials closed the Ritterakademie in 1937 due to concerns that the school was a "bulwark of antistate subversion" whose teaching staff, pupils, and supporters were "reactionaries" threatening the Third Reich. The appointment in 1934 of a zealous Nazi to take charge of the school resulted not in its transformation along National Socialist lines but a series of scandalous "reactionary" episodes that ultimately compelled authorities to close down the 232-year old institution. Local NSDAP, NSLB, and education officials correctly discerned not only that most Brandenburg's teachers did not experience, to borrow historian Peter Fritzsche's phrase, a "brown revolution of the mind" in the period 1933–1939 but also that certain teachers' actions demonstrated instead the persistence of pre-Nazi attitudes and practices.[92]

Failing to turn every Brandenburg pedagogue into an ardent Nazi did not mean the "National Socialist revolution" did not leave its mark on Brandenburg and its schools. As of 1938, a multitude of reforms, including the requirement that teachers give the so-called German Greeting when entering the classroom, imparted a profoundly National Socialist tone to life inside the schools.[93] In Brandenburg, the girls at the Upper Lyceum beginning in the spring of 1933 were permitted to wear "nationalist" insignia and to recruit in school for Nazi organizations such as the League of German Girls. Hitler's portrait was hung in the school's main auditorium, and the teaching staff on 8 September swore an oath to Germany's *Führer* and Reich chancellor. During the Third Reich, the Upper Lyceum's pupils participated in Nazi-organized parades and rallies, sang the "Horst Wessel Song" to close school festivities, took school trips to Germany's border regions, watched National Socialist films like *Hitlerjunge Quex*, attended special lectures on Nazi topics, listened to radio broadcasts of speeches by Hitler and other Nazi leaders, and collected food and other goods as part of various NSV campaigns. Similarly, the boys and girls of the Von Saldern secondary school celebrated at school Hitler's birthday and appointment to chancellor, rallied and paraded in honor of German mothers and fallen "heroes," took field trips to the local cinema to view Leni Riefenstahl's propaganda films, and participated in Nazi collection drives. Even the routine of the elite Ritterakademie was nazified; the sons of *Junkers*, Prussian officers, and the upper bourgeoisie listened to Nazi radio broadcasts, for example, celebrated the return of the Saar and the annexation of Austria, and participated in Nazi programs to help local farmers with the harvest.[94]

The National Socialist revolution also transformed what students learned in the classroom. New subjects were introduced in Brandenburg and elsewhere, and old disciplines were recast along National Socialist lines. As early as the summer of 1933, regional education officials ordered principals and teachers to integrate core National Socialist subjects such as genetics *(Erbbiologie)* and racial studies *(Rassenkunde)* into the curricula. The probationary teacher Albert S. publicized the recasting of a traditional discipline like history along National Socialist lines. "The *Führer*," Albert S. wrote in a pamphlet celebrating the Von Saldern's 360th anniversary in 1939, "expects history class to be a political schooling of Germany's youth."[95] Education authorities redesigned the teaching plans, subordinating the content of the curricula to the Nazi state's larger ideological mission. According to the revised syllabi and teaching guidelines issued in the late 1930s, an important function of teaching elementary school pupils German was to instill in them a political consciousness and to lay "the foundations for pride in the homeland, community, *Volk*, and *Führer*."[96] Officials instructed pedagogues to use war literature and literary works depicting the National Socialist movement. Similarly, an important function of German instruction on the high school level was, in addition to developing pupils' patriotic and National Socialist consciousness, motivating them to act on behalf of the regime; the goal was to create not "the contemplative [*beschaulich*] but the active [*tätige*] individual."[97] Instead of developing an understanding of the past, elementary school history instruction was to impart crucial Nazi values like racialism and the necessity of *Lebensraum*. It was also "to be imbued with the heroic spirit and the concept of the *Führer* in Germanic-Teutonic form."[98] According to the revised high school geography syllabus, pupils were to focus on the political, cultural, and racial division of the world, paying particular attention to the threats to Germany's survival posed by other nations and races. To take another example, officials overhauled the Latin and Greek courses; the Education Ministry now expected pedagogues to stress the racial similarities between the Romans, Greeks, and Germans, all of whom were considered "Northern People of Culture."[99] Nazi education officials even politicized the art curriculum. According to the revised guidelines, pupils were to study "individual great art works of German heritage (for example the *Führer*'s buildings) and, when possible, examples of native arts and crafts."[100] Nowhere were the curricula changes more pronounced than in the girls' secondary schools. Instead of the traditional broad, academically rigorous course of study, German girls starting in 1937 focused on languages and on the "disciplines of feminine creativity" such as needlework, home economics, and hygiene.[101] By such means, Nazi education officials hoped to instill in pupils voluntaristic, martial, *völkisch,* and social Darwinist values.

A comparison of the graduation exam questions and their evaluation criteria at the Brandenburg secondary schools illustrates the nazification of the curriculum. An analysis of the subject of German at the Von Saldern secondary school from 1930 to 1937, for example, reveals a clear politicization of the curricula and of the exam process. In the late Weimar Republic and even into the early years of the Third Reich, students were examined on traditional themes found in classic works of German literature. The significance of Goethe's *Faust* to the student, the possible contemporary existence of a "human commandment" *(Gebot der Humanität),* and a comparison of Goethe's *Iphigenia* with modern dramatic works formed the heart of three questions on the 1932 exam. By 1939, examiners demanded that pupils discuss the political and cultural significance of radio in the National Socialist state, the supremacy of man over machine, and the relevance of older works such as Heinrich von Kleist's *Prince of Homburg* for young National Socialists. A similar change took place at the Ritterakademie. Whereas graduation exam questions in the subject of German focused in 1932 on the pupil's personal reaction to Henrik Ibsen's *Brand,* for example, and on an interpretation of Wilhelm von Humboldt's adage "One can accomplish much so long as one trusts oneself," the 1935 exam expected pupils to discuss the depiction of the German soldier in a First World War memoir, the realization of a racial community in National Socialist Germany, or the many possible manifestations of heroism.[102]

As part of the Nazi transformation of the education system, special pro-Nazi supplemental brochures *(Ergänzungsbroschüren)* were distributed, and schoolbooks were revised or, beginning in the late 1930s, completely replaced with new National Socialist textbooks. In addition to teaching pupils basic math skills, for example, the textbook *Rechenbuchs für Knaben- und Mädchen-Mittleschulen* disseminated core National Socialist concepts like militarism and racism by means of its arithmetic exercises. Using data on illiterate soldiers serving in various armies in the First World War, one math problem depicted the Germans as having had the best educated military and the Russians the worst. In another exercise, pupils practiced forming percentages by dividing the number of Jewish "foreign elements"

(*Fremdkörper*) in Germany by the number of "Aryans."[103] From the Nazi flag flying in the school courtyard to revised textbooks, manifestations of the Nazi dictatorship constituted the basic elements of the lives and work of Brandenburg's teachers.

Schemm, Wächtler, and other zealous NSLB members intended, however, to go far beyond curricula changes and political evaluations of teachers. It was not enough for them that the NSLB grew from a marginal organization with a very small number of members into a national institution representing more than 300,000 teachers or that it had established itself as an important partner of the state and NSDAP in supervising and controlling Germany's teaching staff. The goal of Schemm and his supporters was the transformation of all teachers into Nazis. In a collection of speeches and articles published posthumously, Schemm described the NSLB's mission:

> As with the NSDAP since its beginning . . . the NSLB has pursued one goal in all its activities: the creation of a group of educators girded by National Socialist ideology and spiritually unified who will tackle the great educational project regarding the German youth. . . . We all want German pedagogues who should educate our proud German youth to be steadfast Germans. We want to help them rediscover the German soul. Only for this reason did we create the great organization of the NSLB.[104]

Although the NSLB fulfilled some aspects of its broad and ambitious mission, it failed to develop fully the necessary network to reach effectively and to transform ideologically most teachers. Financial and political issues ultimately crippled the NSLB's attempts to create the system of training camps that lay at the heart of its reeducation project. Hindered significantly by bureaucratic infighting and insufficient financial support, the program developed very slowly and began only in 1936 to indoctrinate large numbers of teachers. After 1937, however, war preparations—including, most important, the conscription of many male teachers—resulted in the camp system's swift downsizing and set the stage for its eventual abolition during the Second World War.

The experience of Brandenburg's teachers conformed to this national pattern. Many NSLB members—though not all—did attend the training camps, but not in the numbers that would have been necessary to achieve its aims. Instead, the great majority of teachers who attended a camp did so only once and thus spent no more than two weeks receiving at best a very brief and superficial political "reeducation." Insufficient indoctrination also meant that the NSLB failed to erase many of the fundamental divisions among Brandenburg's teachers. Rather than developing into a local community of Nazi teachers unified in their political and professional outlook, the city's teaching staff remained sharply divided along political, gender, social, religious, and professional lines. The German invasion of Poland in September 1939 confirmed and made irreversible a gradual loss of stature and significance of the NSLB within the Nazi state that would culminate in its dissolution in 1943.[105]

CHAPTER 3

Keeping the Schools Running during the War

The German invasion of Poland in September 1939 unleashed forces that radically transformed almost every aspect of German society. This wave of changes, intended and accidental, did not spare Germany's schools and their teachers. Over the course of six years, the Nazi state and party placed incredible demands on Brandenburg's pedagogues: many were taken out of the classroom and sent to fight at the front, for example, while others were transferred to schools in Poland and other newly acquired territories in an effort to "Germanize" this *Lebensraum*. For those who remained in Brandenburg, Nazi and wartime encroachments into their professional lives were just as far-reaching. Keeping the schools running under "total war" conditions meant that teachers were required to work longer hours for no additional pay, a worsening situation that contributed to the decrease in their real wages. They were expected to work under increasingly arduous conditions as, for example, the number of available classrooms shrank and average class size spiked. Another consequence of Germany's deteriorating military position was the explosion of extracurricular demands on teachers and their pupils. Whereas before 1939 pedagogues had occasionally supervised boys and girls helping out with the harvest or participating in Nazi rallies and parades, they now deployed for long periods of time to provide some semblance of instruction to boys who had been ordered to serve as antiaircraft helpers or air raid wardens.

Although the impetus for some of the changes in Germany's school system originated in long-held Nazi plans for reform, many arose out of officials' efforts to respond to a rapidly developing wartime situation. A central question explored in this chapter is whether education policies after 1939—either the manifestation of long-held National Socialist desires or desperate efforts to maintain control over a chaotic situation—had unanticipated consequences that affected the teachers. The most serious challenge facing education authorities was the severe shortage of qualified pedagogues that only worsened over the course of the war. This chapter therefore focuses on the means with which the Nazi state responded to the deteriorating manpower situation and the effect of such efforts on Brandenburg's teachers. In order to do so, the analysis will address the following questions. First, what concrete measures did local and regional officials implement in the schools in order to ensure that a sufficient number of teachers stood at the front of German classrooms? Second, in what ways did these measures, especially the employment of untrained school helpers (*Schulhelfer*) in the classrooms—a program that began on a modest scale but quickly grew to become the primary means by which the authorities tried to keep the schools functioning—change the composition of the teaching staff? Third, did the panoply of state responses include putting back in the classroom individuals who had previously retired from teaching as well as, more significantly, those who had been punished for political reasons in the early Third Reich? Were educators such as former middle school principal Karl P. effectively restored to the positions they had occupied before being purged in 1933? The answers to such questions do more than just illuminate the steps officials took to keep the schools operating; as will be explored here, the specific measures and their effects also raise the possibility that Nazi education authorities were compelled to dismantle elements of the National Socialist school system in order to keep the schools running.

The war's impact on Brandenburg's teachers was not limited to staffing changes at individual schools; Nazi wartime policies also eroded many of the traditional structures and characteristics of the teaching profession. A second interpretative axis of this chapter is the assessment of the ways the wartime ebb and flow of personnel, in addition to related Nazi policies, impacted the workplace experiences of the city's teachers. For them, the demands of the Second World War exceeded simply welcoming new faces to the teachers' lounge; authorities redefined the duties of pedagogues and the conditions under which they were expected to work. Authorities now ordered teachers to lead class field trips to collect materials needed for the war effort and to supplement their required hours of instruction with nightly air raid duty. What did such changes mean for the teachers? Moreover, did the new policies affect only the material conditions under which they lived and worked? Or did their understanding of the professional and social meaning of being a pedagogue change as a result of these wartime education measures? In short, how did notions of professional identity weather the hardships of the Second World War? Furthermore, what was the fate of the NSLB? If all pedagogues—from elementary school teacher to philologist, from zealous Nazi to nonmember of the NSLB—experienced this broad evisceration of the traditional attributes of the teaching profession, is it possible that the social and professional leveling the Nazis long sought came about as a consequence not of their efforts to transform teachers ideologically but of the increasingly desperate measures to win the war?

As will be argued in this chapter, many of the most important changes in the lives of Brandenburg's teachers and in the composition of the city's teaching staff occurred not before but after 1939. To the extent that we can argue that the experience of living in the Third Reich impacted teachers in meaningful ways, much of this impact took place not during the period of the creation and peacetime development of the Nazi dictatorship but during the Second World War. In fact, the city's teachers had been living the war well before Anglo-American bombers and Red Army troops brought their violence and devastation to Brandenburg in the spring of 1945. Moreover, the significance of the wartime changes lasted long after the collapse of the Third Reich, as the collective wartime experiences helped shape the Brandenburg teachers' postwar behavior and attitudes. As the story of these teachers in the period 1939–1945 reveals, the Second World War transformed them in important ways yet also preserved certain continuities. It was this mixture of the new and old, the radical and the traditional, that, as subsequent chapters will illustrate, formed the requisite foundation for the teachers' attitudes and actions under the Soviet occupation and the early GDR. Understanding teachers' eventual role in the creation of the East German Communist state requires that we first investigate their experiences in the Second World War.

The Teaching Staff on the Eve of the Second World War

Five months before the beginning of the Second World War, Brandenburg's teachers and pupils began a new school year. Despite the many changes in German society that followed the Nazi assumption of power in 1933, the city's teaching staff in April 1939 was characterized by, among other things, a high degree of continuity of personnel. Having survived the Third Reich's earlier attempts to purge the city's teaching staff and having weathered the NSLB's failed indoctrination programs, the vast majority—approximately 87 percent—of those teaching in the spring of 1939 had been doing so before January 1933. At the Roland School, for example, only 3 of the 14 instructors had been hired during the previous six years. Almost 90 percent of those at the Hermann Löns and Nicholas schools had entered the profession before the Weimar Republic's dissolution. The 11 men and women working at the Pestalozzi School included only two newcomers from the period 1933–1939.[1] The situation was similar at Brandenburg's middle schools and *Gymnasia*. Although the Augusta Middle School was somewhat smaller than most of the elementary schools, approximately 82 percent of its staff had launched their teaching careers before January 1933.[2] An even greater degree of continuity could be found at the Upper Lyceum; only one of three additions to the teaching staff in the period 1933–1939 was teaching for the first time. Despite a small number of nonpolitically motivated transfers and retirements in the 1930s, the Von Saldern teaching staff remained practically unchanged in this period. As of 1939, 18 of the 22 teachers had also been teaching there prior to January 1933.[3]

Moreover, the addition of the relatively small number of teachers who entered the city's service during the first six years of Hitler's reign does not mean that the newcomers were necessarily young, fervent Nazi teachers like the 24-year-old NSDAP member and Stormtrooper Alfred G., who joined the Rochow School in April 1937. Many of those transferring to Brandenburg's schools had also been teaching well before the Nazi state's creation. Of the seven additions to the Augusta School's teaching staff in the period 1933–1939, four had begun their careers in the Weimar Republic.[4] The Roland School welcomed three new teachers in this period, but none of them began their professional careers after the Nazi "seizure of power." Although the Municipal Intermediate School experienced above average turnover as 10 pedagogues joined its staff in this period, only three of these were new to the profession. A particularly interesting case is that of the men and women teaching at the Hans Schemm School. Created only in 1938 to educate the rapidly increasing number of school-age children, this school had to assemble an entirely new group of pedagogues. Brandenburg officials did not, however, exclusively appoint novice teachers. As of the spring of 1939, the school's 19 pedagogues included 8 who had been teaching in Brandenburg since at least January 1933. Moreover, of the 11 newcomers to the city's teaching staff, 6 had been working in some German school at the time of Hitler's appointment as chancellor. Only 5 of the 19, therefore, began their careers in the Third Reich. Approximately 62 percent of the teachers who began teaching after January 1933 at the nine elementary schools had previously taught elsewhere in Germany.[5] Although novice instructors did begin teaching in Brandenburg in the period 1933–1939, the majority of the teachers who entered the city's service during that period had begun their teaching careers at other German schools, in many cases before the Third Reich.

The high degree of continuity of personnel meant that some of the most important characteristics of the teaching staff remained largely unchanged from 1933 to 1939. Whereas in 1933 more than 66 percent of Brandenburg's teachers were male, that number had crept up to 68 percent by the early summer of 1939. As at the outset of the Third Reich, the gender balance was most pronounced in the secondary schools: 77 percent of the middle and upper school pedagogues were men. The entire teaching staffs of the Municipal Intermediate School and the Von Saldern secondary school were male, for example. Male teachers were even a majority at the girl's secondary school, the Upper Lyceum. The gender imbalance was even more pronounced regarding those who led the schools—the principals and their assistants. In 1939, men were in charge of every elementary, middle, and secondary school, including the city's two schools for girls, the Augusta Intermediate School and the Upper Lyceum. Not only had the gender composition of the city's teaching staff remained essentially the same since 1933 but also they were not, as a group, any younger on the eve of the Second World War. Whereas the average age of the teaching staff was approximately 40 in 1933, six years later it was 45. As at the outset of the Third Reich, there was still no significant age discrepancy between elementary and secondary school teachers, whose average ages were 44 and 46, respectively.[6]

The activities of the local NSLB chapter represented another important element of continuity in the lives of the teachers. The monthly chapter meetings and the more specialized department (Fachschaft) gatherings remained the foundation of the NSLB's program. Consisting of a lecture and a discussion, the meetings explored a single topic, sometimes of an explicitly political nature, though more often of a largely professional or technical nature. In April 1939, for example, local officials organized both a lecture for all members on the history of Brandenburg's garrisons and a daylong workshop for principals and music teachers on the role of music in education. Six weeks later, in May 1939, the vice-principal of the Augusta School lectured the city's pedagogues on the poets and poetry of the Brandenburg region. As part of the larger ideological reeducation effort, local officials also worked with regional and national authorities to coordinate the sending of Brandenburg teachers to the NSLB's training camps in the summer of 1939. In the summer and early fall of 1939 the regional NSLB administered six reeducation camps, in addition to the 28 weekend indoctrination courses held from January to June throughout the province.[7]

Another significant source of continuity, though one that would contribute to the wartime transformation of the teaching staff, was the increasing scarcity of teachers. In the period 1933–1938, Brandenburg's population grew by 33 percent with the influx of workers and their families a result of the city's industrial expansion. The number of school-age children quickly outstripped the number of available teachers. In an effort to alleviate the problem of the crowded classrooms and overwhelmed teachers, city authorities took a series of increasingly drastic measures. In 1936 and 1937, Brandenburg sought to meet its need for pedagogues by creating a small number of new elementary school teaching positions.[8] The situation quickly worsened, however. An entirely new school was built; completed in early 1938 and named the Hans Schemm School, it opened its doors in April 1938.[9] Its teaching staff consisted of men and women recruited from the city and the region. At least seven were ordered to move from less urban locales—where presumably the demand for teachers had not grown as rapidly as in the cities—to Brandenburg. For example, the Potsdam government transferred three teachers to Brandenburg from neighboring Belzig and Falkensee and the more distant Hermsdorf. The rest of the teaching staff had already been working in the city's classrooms and simply changed schools.[10] As of October 1938 the new school employed 19 pedagogues, of whom 12 were men and 4 were receiving their first full teaching appointments. The average age was 38; 12 were NSDAP members, and at least 18 were NSLB members.[11] Though alleviated partially and temporarily by the opening of the Hans Schemm School, Brandenburg's teacher shortage nonetheless remained an acute problem.

The War's Early Effects on the Teaching Staff

The war made itself felt immediately in the city's schools. When the German Wehrmacht invaded Poland on 1 September 1939, a small number of Brandenburg's male teachers were already serving in the military. Six of the thirty male instructors at the Von Saldern secondary school were officially excused from teaching for military service. This small group included four full teachers and two probationary teachers.[12] Some elementary and middle school pedagogues were also conscripted in August 1939. The Fontane School's Walter L. began in 1939 a period of service that would last two years, and Hermann R.'s call-up took him away permanently from both the Rochow School and Brandenburg.[13] Although military conscription posed staffing challenges for the schools' administrators, Brandenburg's school system was initially prepared to deal with the staffing strains, since male teachers' military service had long been a part of school life. City and regional education administration documents indicate that by 1936 men were regularly called up to take part in short-term military training programs and exercises. A teacher at the Jahn School participated in 12 military exercises in the period 1935–1939. Another joined regular military units for three weeks of training in 1937. At least nine teachers underwent significant periods of military training in 1938. One from the Pestalozzi School served for 30 days in 1938, and others were away from the classroom for periods longer than two months.[14]

Education authorities nonetheless quickly realized that previous methods of redressing the shortage would no longer be effective during the war and thus implemented a series of reforms intended to put more teachers in the classroom. Some new measures were intended to alleviate the situation over the long term, and many focused on accelerating the education and certification process for current and future teacher trainees. The Prussian Education Ministry revised the standard training program so that the teachers' academies could certify pedagogues more quickly. Special preparatory courses were created for elementary and middle school graduates who lacked a secondary school diploma, and the required course of study for secondary school graduates was reduced from four to three semesters and soon afterward to two. For students training to become philologists, the number of required semesters of study at the university was reduced from eight to six, the mandatory year of political training at a teachers' college *(Hochschule für Lehrerbildung)* was dropped, the first state exam was simplified, and the probationary training period was reduced to one year. Other measures were intended to have an immediate impact on the shortage. Schools modified curricula and lesson plans so that the teachers could spend more time teaching subjects education authorities deemed important. At the Von Saldern secondary school, for instance, the number of hours dedicated to studying music and art history was reduced in 1940.[15] Such measures, however, either postponed any real improvement to sometime in the future or at best offered immediate but very limited alleviation.

Another method of dealing with the teacher shortage was the rehiring of men and women who had previously taught but had since left the city's service.[16] In the first year of the war, regional and local school authorities appointed a small number of former teachers to provisional positions in various Brandenburg schools. In January 1940, for example, the Potsdam government notified one former teacher, who had resigned in 1929 from the progressive Secular School because of her desire to marry, that she had been assigned to a position as an elementary teacher. At the beginning of the new school year a few months later, education officials informed another former teacher that she would replace a conscripted male middle school teacher.[17] Nor were the secondary schools immune to this larger development. The Von Saldern secondary school put back in the classroom on a part-time basis in the spring of 1940 two retired secondary school teachers, and in the fall of 1939 the Upper Lyceum's principal appointed a retired vocational teacher to take over its home economics classes. By the end of the 1939–1940 school year, four former principals and nine teachers—five women and eight men—had been reinstated.[18]

Despite the increasing need for teachers, the Nazi state initially maintained relatively rigorous replacement standards. In the summer of 1939 the authorities developed guidelines that prohibited local authorities from rehiring civil servants who had been demoted, transferred, retired, or fired for "Marxist" activities or other political reasons, as codified in the Law for the Restoration of the Professional Civil Service. According to an Interior Ministry circular, civil servants punished under the terms of the Restoration Law's political paragraphs could only be reinstated if they met certain requirements such as having clearly and repeatedly demonstrated support for the Nazi state. Exemplary past behavior and current staffing needs, however, could not result in rehirings of purged *Beamte* to positions such as department heads or teachers, since the Nazi state considered these to be "leading or otherwise important positions" that required of the individual "a reliable [*sicher*] ideological attitude."[19] Even shortly after the war had begun, authorities were still largely unwilling to consider individuals who had been purged from the civil service as a consequence of so-called political infractions. Although an Education Ministry circular dated November 1939 no longer categorically excluded all teachers from the pool of former civil servants eligible for reinstatement, the state nonetheless required candidates to have demonstrated their political reliability by extraordinary participation in the activities of the NSDAP or one of its affiliates. Moreover, reinstating such a previously dismissed pedagogue required the approval of the Reich Education Minister and the responsible Nazi Party district leader.[20]

Rehiring former pedagogues was not the only recruitment option available to school administrators. As part of the city's efforts to prevent manpower shortages from disrupting the school system, and demonstrating the state's unwillingness and inability to wait for earlier reforms that expedited teacher training to produce enough pedagogues, Brandenburg's officials began during the war's first year to tap into another important labor source: men and women who wished to teach but lacked the formal certification required to work in the public schools. These individuals, known as lay teachers or school helpers, were a motley collection, consisting of everything from trained gym teachers to private tutors and young female recent secondary school graduates. Although more than a few had received some kind of pedagogical training, or were currently studying to become teachers, almost none had undergone the lengthy and arduous program of study and practical training normally required by the state as preparation for teaching Germany's youth.

Authorization for the school helper program was provided by two Reich Education Ministry measures announced in early 1940. In a decree dated 5 January 1940, the Education Ministry made the official case for loosening the state's traditionally high standards for teacher qualification. Education Minister Rust argued that since more than 32 percent—and sometimes as much as 64 percent—of an area's teaching staff were serving in the Wehrmacht, German communities had to adopt certain emergency measures. Included in the proposals was an authorization for local officials to place in elementary classrooms pedagogues who had received their formal certification in subjects unrelated to what they would soon begin teaching.

Three months later, Rust and others were ready to expand the program dramatically to deal with the worsening situation. An Education Ministry decree of March 1940 set up a completely new teacher training structure. Young men and women who had completed elementary or middle school could now become teachers without finishing secondary school, attending a special preparatory course, or spending years studying at one of the pedagogical academies. Training now consisted of one three-month-long "short course," after which the graduates were to begin teaching under the supervision of an older mentor. At some point in the future—presumably after the end of the war—these school helpers would complete their training with a year of study at a pedagogical academy.[21] What Germany's defeat in 1945 actually brought, as will be discussed in Chapter 4, was not Nazi teacher trainees completing their education but the setting up of a similar program by the Soviets and the East German Communists to create a new cohort of politically reliable pedagogues.

As a result of these directives and the pressing local labor shortage, Brandenburg officials began in 1940 to place school helpers in the classrooms. By the early summer 1940, the student Ilse B. and secondary school graduates Charlotte G., Christel S., and Ursel W. were working as lay teachers in elementary schools. Three more secondary school graduates were working in small schools located in the city's environs.[22] These school helpers were all young women who lived in or around Brandenburg. Although one of them was currently enrolled in a postsecondary school course of study, the others had only recently graduated from secondary school. They represented in the summer of 1940 only a small percentage of Brandenburg's teaching staff, but the number and significance of the relatively untrained school helpers would grow considerably as the war continued.

The War's Radicalization Begins a Transformation

German authorities quickly realized that the limited program of rehirings and the even more limited initiative regarding school helpers were failing to solve the growing problem. The Security Police reported in January 1940 that the German school system was mired in a serious crisis. According to this analysis, the teacher shortage constituted a fundamental element of the current situation:

One of the main causes of the school crisis is identified in all the briefings as the teacher shortage. It has increased during the war to a decisive extent because 15,000 pedagogues are needed at once for the new eastern territory, because a high percentage of teachers continue to be conscripted, and because the communities have commandeered numerous teachers for auxiliary war services [*Kriegshilfsdienste*]. In the opinion of the responsible agencies and of the affected teaching staffs, reforms of the pedagogical courses of study by themselves will in no way alleviate the dearth.[23]

Echoing this alarming description of the national situation, the Brandenburg superintendent informed the Potsdam government at the beginning of the 1940–1941 school year that current practices, especially the prevailing wage system for the school helpers, would ultimately fail to resolve the crisis. Although six secondary school graduates worked in the city and its environs as lay teachers, the superintendent implied that finding more would be difficult, given current wage policies. He concluded: "with this situation it is no wonder if these substitute teachers leave the city's service as fast as possible and those who had wanted to become a teacher turn away from the profession. The currently unbearable shortage of teachers will only thus get worse."[24]

In addition to the current difficulty of attracting young women to work as school helpers, Brandenburg' schools also faced an increased drain both of male teachers to the Wehrmacht and of young men and women to schools in the newly conquered territories to the east. By the middle of 1941, after Germany mobilized more than three million men for the invasion of the Soviet Union, a number of additional Brandenburg teachers were conscripted for military service. Although Brandenburg had constructed the Hans Schemm School in 1938 in order alleviate the city's overcrowded classrooms, in October 1941 approximately 25 percent of the new school's prewar teaching staff was serving in the Wehrmacht. The number of Rochow School pedagogues now at the front had tripled compared to that of two years before. Overall, at least 12 elementary school teachers were in the field in the fall of 1941.[25] Similarly, the number of conscripted secondary school teachers also increased in the period 1939–1941. At least five men from the city's middle schools and more than six secondary school teachers were now in uniform.[26]

Moreover, a small number of Brandenburg's teachers had been transferred to occupied eastern regions, such as the Reich district christened the Wartheland, as part of the Nazi program to "Germanize" these recently conquered areas. As early as May 1940, four elementary school teachers were assigned *(abgeordnet)* to the Katowice District.[27] Two more Brandenburgers, a senior teacher from the Von Saldern secondary school and the Upper Lyceum's director Gustav S., joined them by the end of the summer. Some pedagogues volunteered, presumably out of ideological conviction, to teach in the east. A female secondary school teacher repeatedly applied for and ultimately received permission in late 1940 to move to the Wartheland.[28] The pedagogue Heinrich M., the forty-six-year-old former Social Democrat who in the Third Reich was very active in the Brandenburg NSDAP and NSLB, applied in 1940 to participate in the construction of the new German school system in the Wartheland; Nazi authorities, however, rejected his application because they believed his activism was a consequence of extreme careerism and not genuine National Socialist conviction. Heinrich M.'s efforts to reverse the decision of the *Oberpräsident* and Reich Education Ministry remained unsuccessful. Others—36-year-old Alfred M. and former Secular School teacher and current Nazi Party member Martin L., for example—having been sent to the Wartheland, unsuccessfully lobbied education officials to be allowed to return to Brandenburg. Both spent the rest of the war working outside Brandenburg. Not all transfers were long term. The 39-year-old director of the Upper Lyceum was ordered to the Wartheland in April 1940 by its Reich district governor, but he had returned to Brandenburg by October 1940.[29] Although the short-term transfers often created temporary nuisances for local officials, the long-term displacement of Brandenburg men and women to the eastern territories was part of a larger process that had far-reaching consequences for the composition of the city's teaching staff.

In response to these problems, education officials implemented an array of additional reforms. Hoping to accelerate certification of new pedagogues, the Nazi state continued to dismantle the teacher training system that lay at the heart of German teachers' self-perception as professionals. The Nazi state was not only retreating from the prewar trend of strengthening the academic character of such professional training but also moving quickly to strip it of its academic stature. In early 1941 the Education Ministry abolished the 27 *Hochschulen für Lehrerbildung* and replaced these by the end of 1942 with 160 teacher training institutes *(Lehrerbildunganstalten)*. The great number of institutes and the relative brevity of their courses of study were designed to produce a large number of pedagogues very quickly. Teacher training was thus demoted from a branch of the prestigious higher education system to a more vocationally focused process that represented a return, in many respects, to the teachers' seminars of Wilhelmine Germany. The Nazi state had now erased the gains made as a result of decades of agitation by elementary school teachers and their collective organizations for one of their greatest desires, the "academization" of primary school teacher training.[30] Other reforms were, on the surface, simple administrative measures that facilitated the state's reallocation of teachers between localities and within a particular school system's hierarchy. Important regulations concerning the employment of teachers at secondary schools were relaxed in May 1942. Candidates' files no longer had to be sent to the Education Ministry for review and approval and, most notably, political evaluations from the Nazi Party district leader were no longer required. This seemingly small change represented the erosion—if not the abolition—of a prerogative for which the NSDAP had once fought. Similarly, the Education Ministry issued in July 1943 a decree that permitted state officials to transfer teachers from the numerous municipally administered public schools to the far fewer nationally controlled schools, and vice versa. A largely symbolic measure, this departure from the traditional pre-1933 division of local and federal schools permitted the state to transfer teachers without their or their principals' consent. Finally, education authorities also resorted to forcing pedagogues to teach more for no additional pay. In March 1942 the Brandenburg Province *Oberpräsident* instructed the Education Department of the mayor's office to prohibit local officials from paying a bonus to two teachers at the Von Saldern secondary school in response to an approximately 10 percent increase in their teaching loads.[31]

The heart of the state's response to the worsening labor shortage remained, however, the reemployment of former teachers and the recruitment of school helpers. In the period 1941–1943, Brandenburg's education officials continued to enlist a small number of previously retired men and women. Despite having left the school service in 1938 upon reaching the mandatory retirement age, a 65-year-old former secondary school teacher began instructing in this period at the Municipal Intermediate School. Two former principals joined him at the middle school. Most of these individuals had retired during the previous three or four years as a consequence of reaching the retirement age. At least one replacement, a female secondary school teacher, had previously taught in Stettin and had moved in 1938 to Brandenburg.[32]

In late 1941 Brandenburg's education officials took the noteworthy step of reinstating in their positions two pedagogues who had previously fallen victim to Nazi purges. As a consequence of the Restoration Law's implementation, Potsdam education authorities had demoted in the fall of 1933 the 45-year principal of the Municipal Intermediate School and alleged "Marxist" Karl P. to a less prestigious, less lucrative elementary school position. In August 1934 education authorities had also used section 5 of the Restoration Law to transfer a female teacher from the Upper Lyceum to an elementary school position, although officials claimed at the time that the demotion was a result of staffing needs and not a punitive measure. Thus driven from the school where she had worked for more than 12 years, she retired from teaching less than a year later. As of the fall of 1941, however, both individuals had been reinstated. The woman had been hired out of retirement, and the former principal had been given back his position at the Municipal Intermediate School.[33] The reinstatement of these two represented a significant new departure, a more drastic response to the dramatically worsening situation in the schools. Under the stress of the war, the Third Reich was beginning to abandon the inflexible ideological position that directives issued in the summer and fall of 1939 had clearly expressed regarding the men and women punished by the Restoration Law. By the third year of the war, the Nazi state sought help not only from those pedagogues it had recently deemed too old to teach but also from those men and women it had once concluded were politically unfit to teach Germany's youth.

Despite this initial relaxation of hiring standards and the resultant slight addition of former pedagogues to the teaching staff, Brandenburg's growing staffing crisis forced local officials to expand the school helper program significantly. Whereas in March 1940 the city employed only one school helper, the number had increased 18 months later to at least four.[34] Over the course of the next 14 months, the group of lay teachers grew to at least 14.[35] Such measures, however, did little to alleviate the swelling number of pupils and the worsening shortage of teachers. On more than one occasion, local officials arranged for a teacher to transfer to Brandenburg, only to be told by education officials in the individual's community that the country-wide "serious paucity" of teachers required that Brandenburg provide them with a replacement pedagogue before they could approve the transfer. A clear indication of the explosion in school-age children in the city was the construction at this time of a new elementary school, the Werner Mölders School. It opened in the spring of 1942, but local authorities experienced difficulties in hiring the minimum number of teachers needed.[36] In response, officials recruited even more *Schulhelfer.* By December 1943, a total of more than 45 school helpers had entered the school service since the war began. The vast majority of them were assigned to elementary schools. Whereas single women predominated in the early appointments, by the end of 1943, more and more of the appointees were married. Wartime exigencies were forcing education officials to abandon a number of important Nazi tenets, from ensuring that only politically "reliable" pedagogues taught the future Nazi citizen to removing women, especially married women, from the workplace.[37]

In contrast to these developments, the city's middle and secondary schools made little use of such helpers and instead sought to ensure sufficient personnel by promoting elementary school teachers to secondary school positions. Like the elementary schools, the secondary schools were also suffering by 1943 from the related phenomena of severe overcrowding of the classrooms and a shortage of qualified pedagogues. School officials noted that from 1940 to 1943 the Augusta School's and the Municipal Intermediate School's populations increased 19 and 12 percent, respectively. According to the city's school superintendent, for example, "the conditions at the Municipal Intermediate School are at this time so poor that one can hardly speak of an effective and orderly educational program [*ordnungsgemässen Unterricht*]." Despite the sharp increase in the number of pupils at postelementary institutions and the persistent and worsening shortage of pedagogues in this period, school officials nonetheless officially insisted that middle school and *Gymnasia* replacements possess the basic state certification permitting them to work in the secondary schools.[38] In September 1943 the Brandenburg school superintendent filled some of the vacancies in the city's middle schools by promoting a small group of elementary school teachers who lacked practical experience but had the formal qualifications. Three female teachers were transferred to the Augusta School and three to the Municipal Intermediate School.[39] Since these promotions merely shifted pedagogues from one position to another, the overall teacher shortage remained largely unaffected. Furthermore, promoting elementary teachers only exacerbated the situation in the elementary schools that, in the state's eyes, were already relying too heavily on lay teachers to instruct the pupils. School authorities eventually circumvented official Education Ministry policy and placed seven school helpers in the secondary school classrooms. Although only a university student, a young woman was assigned to the girls' middle school in 1943. She was accompanied by two married women who also had neither experience nor formal qualifications. The suitability of one of these seemed to rest on the fact that she was married to a teacher and that she had spent a year during the late Weimar Republic studying at a teacher training institute.[40] Employment of such lay teachers could and sometimes did represent a significant drop in the quality of the instruction. In September 1942 Brandenburg school officials reported that the school helper assigned to teach English at the Municipal Intermediate School barely knew his subject: "It concerns a 65-year-old man who can also teach English but can under no circumstances do so permanently since he has no pedagogical experience, no pedagogical training, and no certification. All that he can do is simply demonstrate a somewhat sophisticated use of conversational English."[41] Nazi efforts at supplying schools with lay teachers were substantially strengthened by the passage of the Führer Total War decree in January 1943. The German state now required all nonpregnant women between the ages of 17 and 45 to register at local labor offices for possible assignment in a factory, business, or school.[42] Many local women—married and single— were ordered into the schools as a result of this new policy. Between January and December 1943 more than 30 school helpers were assigned to Brandenburg's various schools. They ranged in age from 23 to 56, and the great majority was married. Very few had any sort of formal training recognized by the state, and those who did were usually appointed to one of the secondary schools. Although Brandenburg's superintendent voiced in April 1943 his concerns that one school helper lacked the sufficient basic schooling officially required for the position, city officials nonetheless placed her in a classroom.[43]

As of the end of 1943, Brandenburg school officials had demonstrated flexibility and perseverance in finding men and women to place in the classroom. Male and female retired teachers had been brought out of retirement, even including a small number who had previously been punished under the Restoration Law. Pedagogues from other parts of Germany who found themselves in Brandenburg for various reasons were hired to teach in the city's schools. Local authorities had also increased the number of school helpers between March 1940 and December 1943 from one to more than 45. Despite these efforts, Brandenburg continued to suffer from a severe shortage of teachers.[44]

"Total War" and the Teachers

The authorities' hope that the Führer decree of January 1943 would permanently resolve the teacher shortage soon proved unfounded. As early as the summer of 1943, local officials resumed complaining through official channels about the need for more manpower.[45] These appeals went unanswered, and regional education authorities failed to provide the city with any kind of additional assistance. The school superintendent and municipal education department were thus compelled in the final part of the war, from January 1944 to May 1945, to try to get control over the deteriorating situation by continuing to appoint additional lay teachers. At least 34 school helpers were placed in the Brandenburg schools in the final 17 months of the war. All were female, divided evenly between single and married women.[46] Municipal authorities also hired two women who had been formally trained by the state but had not yet completed probationary periods.[47] In early 1945, in an act that highlighted not only the school system's continuing labor shortage but also Germany's increasingly dire military situation, school authorities placed five refugees from the Russian advance into the city's schools.[48] Although such certified pedagogues brought to the schools a high degree of training and experience, the four women and one man represented an exceptional response to the shortage of teachers. In the final 17 months of the war, school authorities continued a de facto policy—initiated in the spring of 1940 and expanded by early 1943—of relying on inexperienced, poorly trained, and almost exclusively female school helpers to teach the city's pupils.

School authorities recognized that the extensive use of lay teachers posed a serious risk to the traditionally high educational standards that state requirements regarding teacher training and certification had guaranteed for decades. In a speech on "the mission of the German educator" delivered in October 1938, Reich Leader Alfred Rosenberg warned that "a filling-up of the teaching profession with randomly selected auxiliary workers would not result in a healthy youth . . . working together in the service of National Socialism."[49] Prussian secondary school teachers had previously spent many years studying such subjects as literature or history at German universities before undergoing the probationary periods and taking the state exams. Elementary teachers had studied (for a shorter amount of time) a mixture of pedagogy and subject specialties at one of the prewar *Hochschulen für Lehrerbildung*. School helpers without formal qualifications represented a radical departure from this tradition, and authorities worried about the effects that reliance on them would have on the quality of instruction. Objecting in April 1943 to the appointment of a woman he regarded as unqualified for a lay teacher's position in an elementary school, Brandenburg's school superintendent asked the Potsdam *Regierungspräsident* to standardize the hiring procedures for school helpers in the hope that this would ensure a level of quality in the classrooms. Such pleas went unanswered, however, and Brandenburg continued to make widespread use of poorly trained, largely female lay teachers. Only at the very end of the war, as the city's population swelled with refugees, could regional authorities instruct local officials to fill all available teaching vacancies from this newly created pool, which included trained and certified teachers. On at least three occasions, the Potsdam *Regierungspräsident* rejected nominations of lay teachers. In the final six weeks of the war, school authorities welcomed three new teachers, all credentialed and experienced, who had recently arrived in Brandenburg after fleeing from Soviet-occupied areas.[50]

The NSLB during the War

The war's transformative effects impacted not only the composition of the city's teaching staff but also the activities and significance of the NSLB. Originally entrusted with the ideological reeducation of Germany's teaching staff and increasingly plagued during the mid- and late 1930s by financial and institutional troubles, the NSLB was forced during the war to shift its focus and energies from indoctrinating teachers to supporting the war effort. One cannot, of course, claim that the NSLB lost its organizational independence only after and as a consequence of Germany's invasion of Poland. Since its inception in 1927, the NSLB had served the needs of the Nazi movement, most notably in mobilizing support among the teachers. During the war the nature of such instrumentalization changed. Nazi leaders increasingly redirected the NSLB away from transforming teachers into good Nazis and toward rallying pedagogues around Nazi expansion and other war aims. In his remarks on the occasion of the NSLB's release of a new program titled "Week of Martial Education," the Brandenburg chapter leader declared in March 1941 that the teaching staff was happy to provide the city's youth with a martial education *(wehrgeistige Erziehung)*, concluding that instilling such requisite character traits in the pupils "is the pedagogical goal of the school, and accomplishing this goal is the culmination of the work of the National Socialist teacher and educator."[51]

The transformation was evident in Brandenburg in the local NSLB activities, which were, almost without exception, related to the war. In May 1940, for example, NSLB members organized an exhibition of model airplanes built by pupils and teachers. Constructing the planes and gliders was intended to give the pupils practical knowledge of the basic principles of flight as well as raise their interest in the air force. Although pupils had been building model airplanes since the late 1920s, the school program had expanded throughout the 1930s. Recent developments such as an agreement in the spring of 1939 between the NSLB, the city government, and a youth organization not only provided the teachers with more resources for the project but also designated it an increasingly important element of both the schools' curricula and NSLB activities. Slightly less than two years later, state and NSLB officials elevated the construction of model ships to a similar status. In order to ensure that Brandenburg's pedagogues could competently instruct the pupils in this addition to the formal curriculum, in May 1942 NSLB and state officials announced plans for the creation of a special training course for teachers in model ship construction.[52]

Other NSLB activities strove to generate support among teachers for the Nazi war effort by coordinating members' activities with those of other state or party agencies. At a meeting of the local NSLB leadership in November 1940, officials noted that aiding the charity Assistance for the Eastern Territories (Ostlandhilfswerk) constituted one of the three most important current issues facing the chapter. The aim of this project was to support the state in the construction of a Nazi school system in the occupied territories. Members of the NSLB collected money for, among other things, new textbooks, support for German language courses, and repairs to school buildings. Two years later, on the eve of the NSLB's dissolution, its local leaders continued to mobilize the members in auxiliary support activities for other party and state organizations. At a meeting of all local functionaries in September 1942, the leadership stressed the chapter's duty to promote, among other things, the National Labor Service.[53]

The political lectures delivered to the teaching staff—another important and regular element of the local chapter—reflected in the period 1939–1945 the regime's desire to promote war-related issues. The centerpiece of the general chapter meeting in October 1940 was a lecture on constructing a National Socialist school system in the newly annexed Wartheland. "The region needs," the chapter leader argued, "young, industrious, competent teachers possessed of a high sense of idealism so that the entire school system can be synchronized with that of pre-war Germany [Altreich]."[54] Three months later the chapter explored the topic again in a lecture by the chapter leader on the "Struggle of Germanness in the East." Additional speeches and public discussions focused on topics such as the material and spiritual drive of the Japanese and the importance of Germany's navy and naval tradition.[55] As a consequence of this new emphasis on war-related topics, the Brandenburg NSLB spent less time educating its members on prewar National Socialist subjects like the "science" of race and genetics, which were explicitly relevant to teachers and had been a mainstay of chapter activity since at least the early 1930s.

Whereas the NSLB devoted most of its energies to supporting Germany's war effort, the organization increasingly had difficulties fulfilling its primary mission, the ideological transformation of the teaching force. As of 1 September 1939, only 215,000 of the 350,000 teachers in Germany had participated in some kind of formal NSLB reeducation program. Even this statistic, however, may be slightly inflated. According to another NSLB statistical analysis, fewer than 200,000 men and women underwent any ideological training of any sort during this period.[56] The portion of Germany's pedagogues who had participated in NSLB training programs as of September 1939 thus lies between 56 and 61 percent. Exposing more than half of Germany's teachers to some degree of ideological schooling is not an insignificant achievement. Nevertheless, as discussed in Chapter 2, it fell far short of the NSLB's original goal. More significantly, an analysis of NSLB statistics based on the various Gaue illustrates clearly the organization's failure to reach all, or even a significant portion, of the pedagogues in the Brandenburg region. Compared to a national average of approximately 50 percent as of October 1938, only 30 percent of the province's teachers had taken part in an NSLB's reeducation program.[57] Moreover, the 30 percent included not just those who spent time at the NSLB's flagship event, the Schulungslager, but also those who attended other NSLB offerings such as weekend courses and seminars on specific subjects. By the time Germany invaded Poland, only a very small number of teachers living in the Brandenburg region had received ideological training at an NSLB reeducation camp.

The outbreak of the Second World War further curtailed the NSLB's already anemic attempts at proselytizing among Germany's teachers. Although more than 35,000 pedagogues participated in 1939 in some kind of NSLB program, including approximately 12,000 during the period from August to December, in 1940 the NSLB curtailed certain projects like the *Schulungslager* that required large outlays of manpower, time, and money. The training camps for teachers and functionaries, as well as the subject seminars and weekend courses, were closed for the entire year. The NSLB's initial hesitancy gave way by early 1941 to a sense of normality that included the resumption of indoctrination efforts. That year the NSLB coordinated the training of more than 57,000 members, and was even more successful the following year, reaching more than 59,000 members.[58] At first glance these figures illustrate an increase over the annual participation figures for the prewar years, and thus might seem to indicate that the NSLB's political reeducation program had expanded since 1939. The number of participants does not, however, tell the entire story. The wartime figures hide a more significant trend—the NSLB's eschewing of training camps in favor of shorter-term programs that not only minimized costs but also better corresponded to the current restricted availability of teachers and camps.[59] Only 436 of the 801 NSLB-sponsored events for 1941, involving 49 percent of the participants, took place in NSLB training camps. Similarly, a mere half of the activities in 1942, involving only 32 percent of the participants, took place in the *Schulungslager*.[60] Instead of spending seven or ten days experiencing the isolation, martial spirit, and supposed egalitarian camaraderie of the training camp, members were now organized in courses and events that took place in their hometowns and usually lasted only a couple of days. This is not to say that this wartime training was completely ineffective. Doubts about its efficacy can be raised, however, since those very qualities NSLB officials and other Nazis believed to be so central to the indoctrination experience were in fact no longer part of it. Absent the lengthy duration, for example, or the total immersion into a National Socialist community, the experience of being trained by the NSLB less and less represented something special and more and more resembled the kind of technical and pedagogical training sessions to which teachers had long been subjected. If one compares the wartime percentages to those for the 1933–1936 period, the quantitative deemphasis of the *Schulungslager* becomes even more apparent. From 1933 to 1936 the NSLB trained more than 70,000 members in the camps. More important, this represented at least 75—and most likely more than 90—percent of the participants in NSLB reeducation programs in this period.[61] Once the quantitative and theoretical heart of the NSLB's program for the ideological transformation of the teaching staff, the training camps were by 1940 increasingly passed over by the NSLB leadership in favor of measures in better accord with the realities of Germany's manpower and economic situation during the war.

In February 1943 the head of the NSDAP Chancellery, Martin Bormann, decreed the cessation of not only current and future training programs but all NSLB activities. The national treasurer of the party took control of the NSLB's assets and assumed responsibility for its financial commitments to members; all of its administration was dissolved save for a small staff of 22 individuals at the national office. A few small components of this once massive organization—for example, the important periodicals *Der Deutsche Erzieher* and *Hilf mit*—were spun off and administered independently. On the local, regional, and national levels, NSLB activity ceased entirely, and it never again played a significant role in the lives of the teachers.[62]

The shut-down *(Stillegung)* of the NSLB was the culmination of a wartime process of the Nazi Party's encroachment on its prerogatives, fueled by increasing Nazi dissatisfaction with both the organization and its leaders. As early as January 1940, the Nazi Party forced NSLB head Fritz Wächtler to implement a series of rationalization measures designed to improve the NSLB's financial condition. This course of action failed to solve the myriad problems caused by byzantine accounting measures and taxation irregularities, and the Nazi Party imposed an external administration *(Zwangsverwaltung)* on the NSLB in November 1941. At the same time, dissension within its leadership led NSDAP leaders to question the political reliability, efficacy, and significance of both the NSLB and its leaders. These concerns had merged by the beginning of 1943 with the larger, more pressing necessity of eliminating institutions not viewed as essential to the war effort, leading Bormann to end the NSLB's 16-year existence.[63]

A Teaching Staff Transformed

The NSLB's dissolution probably surprised few informed observers. Having long abandoned its primary mission of ideologically transforming the teaching force, it had degenerated over the course of the war into a hollow tool used by state and party for the war effort. Although the NSLB had never been genuinely representative, its dissolution nonetheless removed the last vestige of organizational support at a time when teachers in Brandenburg and elsewhere faced an unprecedented assault on their professional and social identity. The composition of the city's teaching staff was undergoing enormous changes. Once the academic preserve of the teacher, the classroom was now instrumentalized by the state by means of changes to the lesson plans that in effect militarized the curriculum. Moreover, the slide toward total war placed a wide variety of extracurricular demands on pedagogues' time and energies. Some of the clearly nonpedagogical roles assigned to the teachers now included "volunteering for collections of waste materials or healing herbs, taking on nightly air raid or fire brigade duty, signing up for agricultural work or other bureaucratic duty during vacation."[64] In Brandenburg, teachers were dragooned into a wide variety of activities outside of the classroom. Rather than serve as manual laborers themselves, teachers often served as chaperones and on-site tutors for their pupils when they were called up to help the war effort in a wide variety of ways. In the late summer of 1944, almost all of the Von Saldern pupils living in the Ritterakademie's dormitory, along with presumably at least one Brandenburg teacher, participated in an "assignment" in the East (*Osteinsatz*) that lasted eight weeks and most likely was related to helping with the harvest. In a diary entry for May 1944, 65-year-old Von Saldern teacher Otto Söchtig describes spending the school day with a group of pupils in the forest collecting herbs. He also notes in January 1945 that a colleague, Max Georg Hartmann, traveled to the southeastern corner of Brandenburg Province to tutor pupils who were serving as antiaircraft helpers.[65]

Yet such significant intrusions into the regular school routine began much earlier in the war. As early as the spring of 1940, several pedagogues were ordered to the newly created Wartheland, where they were expected to help "Germanize" this recently conquered region of western Poland. Local authorities began to order groups of pupils to serve as antiaircraft helpers beginning in 1942; it can be assumed that city teachers continued to instruct them, though outside the classroom and by less traditional means. In the fall of 1943, for example, the formerly retired and now middle school principal Max K. was ordered to accompany pupils to Berlin, where he was to provide some degree of instruction (*unterrichtliche Betreuung*) to the boys serving as air raid helpers; two months later, he was replaced by the pedagogue Albert H.[66] Personnel records from the Von Saldern secondary school and the Upper Lyceum indicate that 52-year-old Latin teacher Otto B. was instructing antiaircraft helpers as of November 1943, 49-year-old math teacher Heinrich M. did so from February to June 1944, while 46-year-old Johannes D. was tutoring such helpers as of July 1944. The case of 48-year-old secondary school teacher Willi K. illustrates how burdensome and possibly disruptive even a short-term posting close to home could be. Serving as part of an antiaircraft unit stationed outside of Brandenburg in the fall of 1943 meant that he was "on duty" almost around the clock for one week; he taught a full day at the Upper Lyceum and then marched four and a half kilometers to the antiaircraft battery, where he then manned the battery or stood guard for hours before catching a bit of sleep. Following the early morning march back to the city, he reported to the school for another day of teaching.[67] Germany's deteriorating military situation only increased the demand for auxiliary war services, thereby worsening the city's teacher shortage. Having been ordered to release a middle school teacher to tutor boys serving as naval auxiliaries (*Marinehelfer*), Brandenburg's mayor requested that the decision be reversed. Since seven teachers from the Municipal Intermediate School were already serving in the military, only 11 men remained to teach the nearly 600 pupils. Moreover, the school already had to ensure that some boys and their teachers served as antiaircraft helpers. "If we lose another teacher," the mayor argued, "an orderly instruction of pupils [*geordneten Unterricht*] will not be possible at all."[68] Regional authorities ignored the mayor's pleading and removed Kurt P. from the Brandenburg classroom.[69] A particularly regular source of disruption in the lives of Brandenburg pedagogues and their pupils during the war was the Nazi Kinderlandverschickung program of sending schoolchildren and their teachers out of dangerous environments such as industrial cities and into presumably safer rural areas. Records indicate that groups of Brandenburg pedagogues participated in the program from 1941 to at least mid-1944. Five teachers from the Von Saldern secondary school spent several months in Bavarian Engelthal in 1942, for example. At least one of their colleagues participated in the program in the following year. The Upper Lyceum contributed at least three teachers to the program in the period 1941–1944. Five teachers in November 1943, for example, were assigned to chaperone and tutor the more than 250 Brandenburg pupils sent out of the target-rich city and to the relative safety of the Bohemian countryside. This program took experienced teachers Elisabeth G. and Irmgard G. away from Brandenburg for at least eight months.[70] Important in the foregoing discussions of war auxiliary and Kinderlandverschickung programs is both the nature of these "extracurricular" assignments and their frequency. The professional activities of the city's teachers increasingly consisted of duties and obligations that had very little to do with teaching.

Teachers in Brandenburg and elsewhere also suffered from a marked decrease in their material and social standing. The number of hours worked or the number of pupils taught in each class increased at a rate that far outstripped the modest pay raises teachers received in this period, resulting in a real decline in wages. Whereas the average real wage of a secondary school teacher in 1913 had been 533 reichsmarks per month, the real wage in 1941 was only 473 reichsmarks. In contrast, the wages of industrial workers, adjusted for inflation, rose in the same period from 372 to 452 reichsmarks. Unlike engineers, for instance, who could boost their salaries by means of overtime work and special premiums, and thereby compensate for a wartime increase of between 20 and 40 percent in the average cost of living, as compared to that of 1913, teachers were forced to subsist on salaries that still bore the scars of Brüning's austerity measures.[71] In some cases, wage levels were even lowered, and throughout Germany unpaid overtime was demanded of pedagogues. In April 1940, Brandenburg's school superintendent protested against a recent reduction in the wages of a small number of substitute teachers, making it clear that the consequence of such a pay cut was a worsening of the city's teacher shortage because not only would current instructors quit but also those interested in becoming teachers would choose another profession. At Brandenburg's Municipal Intermediate School, to take another example, eight teachers—comprising almost the entire teaching staff—were ordered by education authorities in 1942 to put in overtime in the classroom for no extra pay.[72] The *Oberpräsident* of Brandenburg Province informed all of the region's pedagogues in early 1942 that "now, at a time in which all personnel of every office [*Behörde*] and company is stretched to the limit without special compensation, the teaching staff of the secondary schools must also accept as a temporary war measure an unpaid increase of up to three instructional hours per week on top of their required workload."[73] Finally, pedagogues in Brandenburg and elsewhere also suffered at this time from a marked decline in social prestige, a consequence of their deteriorating economic position as well as other factors. A perceived lack of respect for the profession and its practitioners figured prominently in many individuals' decisions to quit teaching at a time when Germany badly needed educators. As Brandenburg's superintendent noted as early as April 1940, "it is no wonder if . . . those who had wanted to become a teacher turn away from the profession."[74]

These changes were part of a transformative process that some historians have described as a "deprofessionalization" of teachers. According to Charles McClelland, the fundamental characteristics of a "professional" group include a high level of specialized education and training, a system of competency tests, exams, and certifications, high wages and social prestige, and an exclusive right to provide the particular service.[75] During the years 1939–1945 the Nazi state brought about a weakening of each of these aspects of the teaching profession. Education Ministry reforms shortened and diluted the training for all types of pedagogues, affecting the university courses of study traditionally pursued by philologists preparing for secondary school posts, as well as the recently created *Hochschulen für Lehrerbildung* that had finally bestowed academic status on elementary school teachers' training. Rigorous exams and certifications processes were quickly discarded in order to counter the growing teacher shortage by enlisting largely untrained lay teachers. The school helpers also represented a large-scale state-sanctioned assault on the teachers' traditional claim to be the sole group educated and certified by the state to educate Germany's pupils. Moreover, the real value of their wages dropped and the social prestige of teachers and their profession declined precipitously in a wartime Nazi state that valued martial qualities and activism over intellectual accomplishments and development. Konrad Jarausch has concluded:

> the Nazi system impaired professionalism categorically: Training standards declined, certification produced a manpower shortage, economic remuneration fell short of increased work, academic status lines were blurred, practice was hindered, ethics were warped, and free association destroyed. While letting capable experts survive, NS policies stripped the educated occupations of the essence of their "professionalism."[76]

Most important, these transformative processes affected almost every teacher. Philologists and elementary school teachers in Brandenburg and throughout Germany suffered a loss of income and a growing social marginalization. The men and women of the Roland School, for example, were by the end of the war spending more time in the classroom for less money as a consequence of an uncompensated increase in their weekly instructional hours. The growing workload and the worsening workplace conditions meant that fewer and fewer young men and women were interested in replacing the pedagogues who were currently in the military, in the east, performing some other wartime service, ill, or deceased, as Brandenburg's superintendent bemoaned as early as 1940. Similarly, teachers of all kinds— male and female, Catholic and Protestant—were instrumentalized by the state for the war effort. The Wehrmacht's need for able-bodied men did not differentiate between those who had studied at an university and those who had trained at a pedagogical institute. In the fall 1944, for example, large numbers of the prewar male staffs of both the girls' middle school and the Rochow elementary school had been conscripted. And even those teachers who remained in Brandenburg during the war were expected to serve the war both in and out of the classroom. An elite education or high position within the traditional professional hierarchy provided no defense against Nazi state and party demands on teachers' time and activities; both the Von Saldern and the Jahn School teachers chaperoned pupils helping with the harvest, for example, or tutored boys serving in antiaircraft units.

In addition, training and certification standards were not only reissued but also, most important, drastically lowered for those entering the teaching profession. The shuffling of teachers between schools and, more important, between the different school levels lessened the traditionally strong distinctions among pedagogues. In Brandenburg, a small number of elementary school teachers moved up to middle schools and, in a very small number of cases, also taught in the upper schools. Middle school teachers were placed in the upper schools. More significantly, school officials threw open the school doors to, in almost all cases, women with little or no training or experience. Those prewar teachers who made room in the teachers' lounge for an increasing number of *Schulhelfer* were witnessing their de facto collective loss of the exclusive right to teach Germany's pupils. The cumulative effect of these changes was, to a certain extent, the homogenization of the teaching staff. Although differences remained among teachers, the divisions were no longer as clear, prominent, or absolute as before the war. Forces like "deprofessionalization" largely effaced the class, social, and organizational tensions that had fragmented Brandenburg's community of teachers as of January 1933. It was this teaching corps that faced the arrival of the Soviet Red Army and returning German Communists in late April 1945. The ways these war experiences influenced the actions and attitudes of Brandenburg's teachers toward such seminal postwar developments as the Soviet occupation, and, ultimately, the creation of an East German Communist state is the subject of the second half of this book.

CHAPTER 4

Transforming the Teaching Staff under Soviet Occupation

For Johannes S. and his colleagues, as well as for the Brandenburg population in general, the collapse of the Third Reich and the beginning of Soviet occupation in the late spring of 1945 introduced fundamental uncertainties about the future. How long would the occupation last? What kind of political and economic system would succeed that of the Nazis? In what ways would the Allies punish Germany and the Germans for the devastation of the Second World War? On a more personal, though equally relevant, note, the city's teaching staff certainly worried about their jobs and their material circumstances.[1] How were they to provide food and, in the cases of those displaced from their homes, shelter for themselves and their families now that the state and the economy had ceased to function? When, and under what conditions, would the schools be reopened? Would individuals such as Johannes S., who as of the late spring was recovering from wounds sustained as a member of the Volkssturm in "defending" Brandenburg from the Red Army, be permitted to return to the classroom?

Unbeknownst to the men and women of Brandenburg, the Allies, including the Soviets and a small group of German Communists who had spent much of the Third Reich and the Second World War in the Soviet Union, had decided by the spring of 1945 that a central postwar policy concerning Germany would be the eradication of those values, practices, and institutions that, in Allied minds, had led to Hitler and genocidal war. Bent on ensuring that Germany would never plunge Europe into another world war, the Allies planned not only to punish Germany and the Germans but also to reeducate German society. Doing so consisted first and foremost of transforming Germany's "agencies of attitude formation," including its universities, media, and, arguably above all else, schools. Textbooks, maps, and lesson plans were to be immediately purged of their National Socialist, militarist, and authoritarian content, to be replaced, in the eastern occupation zone at least, by school materials that promoted a democratic and "antifascist" agenda. Similarly, the Allies also planned to evaluate Germany's teaching staffs; teachers who had supported the Third Reich—by belonging to the Nazi Party, for example—were to be dismissed and their places at the front of the classroom filled by a new cohort of politically uncompromised pedagogues.[2] The Allies' intention to evaluate Germany's teachers rigorously and thoroughly and to remove those tainted by National Socialism was expressed in this August 1945 statement of the future East German education minister Paul Wandel: "since the education of the youth is of such importance for the German people and so dependent on the personality of the teacher, especially high standards must be applied to the selection of the teachers who will soon work in the schools."[3] What remained to be seen in the summer of 1945 was the degree to which the Allies and their German subordinates would succeed in implementing this controversial and wide-ranging policy.

Since 1945, historians have argued that the Soviet and German Communist officials, in contrast to those who carried out the Allied efforts in western Germany, very successfully implemented their denazification program. Scholars have erroneously concluded—often on the basis of published East German statistics or scholarship—that denazification and demilitarization resulted in the almost complete purge of Germans who had been active politically, socially, culturally, or economically in the Third Reich, including especially civil servants such as teachers and judges. Although a small number of scholars have recently begun to dismantle the decades-old misconceptions surrounding denazification of eastern Germany generally, or in terms of specific areas like higher education and medicine, the traditional fallacy endures regarding a few special spheres of society, for example the schools and the judicial system. Historians have correctly determined that Soviet and German Communist officials were genuinely very interested in denazifying the schools. But such scholars have not (and those writing before 1989 could not have) assessed carefully whether leaders in the Soviet zone of occupation were able to implement all, or even most of what they planned. The collapse of the GDR and the opening of the East German archives has not substantially changed this picture; in many otherwise noteworthy recent works of scholarship, scholars continue to assert the "successful" and "far-reaching" denazification of the teaching staff.[4]

The story of Brandenburg's teachers reveals the conventional narrative to be in need of substantial revision. As this chapter demonstrates, beginning in the summer of 1945 and ceasing in the spring of 1948, Soviet and East German officials implemented a broad range of measures that sought to identify, evaluate, and, if necessary, punish former Nazi teachers. Teachers filled out questionnaires regarding past activities, their personnel files were reviewed, and they were called before special denazification tribunals. Despite its seemingly comprehensive and lengthy nature, however, denazification failed to transform radically the group of men and women teaching in Brandenburg's classrooms. Political considerations, bureaucratic confusions, and, most important, the continued shortage of qualified teachers resulted in an incomplete implementation of the denazification program. Furthermore, mirroring the failure of official efforts to rid the schools of "Nazi teachers" was the less than successful Communist program to create a corps of politically uncompromised and pliant teachers to replace the city's more experienced, though "bourgeois," extant teaching staff. State officials established special training courses that, in an accelerated manner, tried to impart to the generally young trainees basic pedagogical skills as well as so-called "antifascist" ideological lessons. A constellation of factors, including the severe financial, emotional, and material hardships these trainees were forced to endure, prevented authorities from recruiting, training, and maintaining a sufficient number of these *Neulehrer.* The failure of both policies meant that as of the founding of the GDR in October 1949, a majority of the teaching staff consisted of experienced pedagogues who had trained in the Weimar Republic or in the Third Reich and, in some cases, had been Nazi Party members. The story of Brandenburg's teachers from 1945 to 1949 illustrates that in a policy area identified by authorities as absolutely fundamental to the nascent postwar order—the total cleansing of the schools of all remnants of Nazism, especially the National Socialist teachers—the Soviet and German Communist officials failed to accomplish their objectives.

The significance of establishing the remarkable continuity of personnel among the city's teaching staff despite almost three years of denazification efforts exceeds simply correcting the historical record regarding a foundational postwar occupation program. This chapter introduces a theme that will be borne out in the chapters that follow: that the incomplete purge of teachers in Brandenburg and throughout the Soviet zone of occupation had a decisive influence on the later creation of the GDR because so many of the men and women who were expected to play a crucial role in the creation of an "antifascist," socialist state in eastern Germany survived Soviet and German Communist denazification efforts.

Out of the Rubble: Rebuilding Brandenburg's School System

In early May 1945, the Second World War ended for the citizens of Brandenburg.[5] Heralded by the two intensive bombing raids in March and April that destroyed many houses and buildings, seriously damaged much of Brandenburg's industrial plant, and resulted in thousands of casualties, the final battle took place at the end of April. German military, paramilitary, SS, and police forces took the ideologically consistent, though militarily and morally questionable, step of trying to repel the advancing Red Army, given the city's lack of defenses and the large number of refugees and wounded who had flooded into the city over the past months. Upon encountering stiff German resistance that included detonating many of Brandenburg's bridges, Soviet troops bombarded the city for days with artillery, rocket, and tank fire, creating firestorms that swept through neighborhoods. After more than three days of brutal urban fighting, the last of the German troops fled westward, and Soviet troops occupied the city. Governmental authority—including judicial, economic, and police power—was quickly transferred to the local SMA, led by City Commander Colonel P. A. Volkov.[6]

The many Brandenburgers who had sought refuge from the fighting in the surrounding countryside found on their return to the city a landscape of almost unimaginable destruction. The city's industrial plant was heavily damaged, including important manufacturers such as the Opel Works, the Arado airplane factory, the Brothers Wiemann shipyard, and the Brennabor Works. More than 10,000 houses or apartments—almost 50 percent of the available housing—had been destroyed or damaged. The destruction of the city's housing stock was so severe that entire neighborhoods and sections of the city lay in ruins and were no longer habitable. Also obliterated in the fighting were numerous streets and bridges, including, for example, St. Anna Street and the "Millennium Bridge," which formed the city's transportation arteries. Traditional civic and cultural city centers, such as government buildings like the city hall and numerous churches were damaged, as were the municipal hospital, numerous military barracks, all gymnasiums, many department stores and small shops, and much of the rail-yard. Worse yet, the rail lines that connected the city to both Berlin and Magdeburg had been destroyed; Brandenburg was now effectively cut off from the outside world. Rather than a cityscape of medieval spires and modern smokestacks, Brandenburgers in May 1945 saw instead demolished buildings and mountains of debris.[7]

Assaulting the eyes and noses of the survivors were the many corpses littering the streets and courtyards. More than 500 people had died as a result of the March bombing attack, but the April air raids and the battle for the city killed more than 3,000, the great majority of whom were civilians. It took the survivors weeks to bury them all. Thousands more were injured, as a result of either the fighting or the plundering and "other worse excesses," for example rape, that took place during and immediately after the battle.[8]

The city's schools and its teachers suffered greatly as a consequence of the fighting that ended the Third Reich. Every school building, including those turned the previous winter into makeshift hospitals, had been either damaged or fully destroyed. American bombs leveled the Augusta Middle School, for example, and Soviet artillery and rocket fire destroyed the Girls' Upper School. The direct hit on the Von Saldern secondary school in the March bombing also resulted in the deaths of the school principal, who had only been transferred to Brandenburg in 1944, Latin teacher and former Freemason Friedrich K., and a pupil who all had the misfortune of serving that morning as air raid wardens. Secondary school teacher Adalbert O. died while trying to keep the Red Army off the city's Hohenmeyen Bridge. Brought out of retirement in 1940 to replace younger male pedagogues who had been conscripted, 69-year-old former director Max K. was killed by shrapnel early in the fighting at the end of April. Georg M., 57 years old, and Erich F., 55, both longtime teachers in Brandenburg who had been recently conscripted into the Volkssturm like many of their male colleagues, also died in the particularly fierce fighting in and around Brandenburg on 30 April 1945. Nor can the teachers' suffering be measured only by fatality statistics; some pedagogues such as Johannes S. were seriously injured in the fighting, and others like Von Saldern teacher Herbert R. and former Ritterakademie pedagogue Wolfgang L. had their homes destroyed by the bombings.[9]

Such physical damage represented a serious obstacle that would have to be surmounted if the local SMA was to reopen the city's schools, which had been closed in the final stages of the war.[10] The immediate difficulties facing Soviet officials did not end there. In the final months of the war, the German military had impressed many male teachers and pupils into the war effort as tutors to antiaircraft gunners or as members of the Volkssturm.[11] At least 50 male pedagogues, ranging in age from 31 to 59, had fought against the advancing Allies, and a large number of them had thus been killed in the fighting or were as of the summer still in prisoner-of-war camps.[12] Moreover, Brandenburg's pupils were joined by a large number of refugee children, dramatically swelling the school-age population. Whereas approximately 7,600 had attended Brandenburg schools in 1936, successive waves of refugees in 1944 and 1945, combined with the economic migration to the city of 1936–1939, had swelled the number of pupils to 10,000 by the early fall of 1945 and to more than 12,000 by the end of the year.[13] Restarting school life in Brandenburg in May 1945 meant putting a record number of pupils in very few classrooms to be taught by a reduced number of available pedagogues.

Despite these obstacles, German authorities initially planned to reopen the elementary and middle schools on 4 June 1945 and the secondary schools on 11 June 1945. Soviet occupation authorities, however, intervened to block these efforts. Soviet officials instructed their German subordinates to open the schools' doors to the pupils in early June, but the teaching staff were prohibited from conducting any formal and regular instruction of the youth. Instead of studying biology and German literature according to some state-sanctioned curricula, the pupils were to learn about contemporary issues and problems. City authorities advised teachers to structure their lessons around material found in the newspapers authorized by the SMA. It was hoped that this would compel pedagogues to teach only the "most basic and necessary" material.[14]

What this imprecise and subjective term consisted of was soon made clear to the teaching staff. In a letter in early July 1945, Brandenburg's school superintendent informed one principal of the new guidelines for the elementary school classes. In line with the slogan "We're accusing, we're cleaning up, and we're rebuilding," initial daily instruction, the superintendent wrote, would consist of three core elements: a reckoning with Nazi crimes, cleaning up the rubble-filled city, and rebuilding the schools and other fundamental institutions. The study of current events would make clear to the pupils the Nazis' responsibility for the physical, economic, moral, and political destruction of the city and country. Similarly, teachers and pupils were expected to help purge the classrooms of Nazism's physical and intellectual remnants by removing any "fascist or militaristic" images or texts. What this meant for Brandenburg's Ritterakademie—now only a collection of buildings that housed both the Von Saldern secondary school and the Girls' Upper School—was the effacing of all traces of the Prussian aristocratic tradition that had been the defining characteristic of the school: the portraits and coats of arms that adorned the Main Hall (Paradesaal) were removed and painted over, respectively. The circular admonished teachers to avoid mentioning in the classroom anything that might "lead" children back to Nazism's ideological world *(Gedankenwelt)*. Local authorities also ordered teachers and pupils to help restore the physical condition of the surviving schools and their grounds. Many staff members of the Von Saldern secondary school worked to recover its basic administrative and pedagogical resources, a difficult task that included unearthing records from rubble mounds. It took teachers and pupils days to move benches, chairs, bookcases, and other necessary materials from the bombed-out Von Saldern school building into the Ritterakademie. Necessary maintenance also included repairing cobblestone paths and removing the air raid blinds from many school buildings' windows.[15]

The task of clearing, restoring, and rebuilding extended far beyond the schoolyard; pupils and teachers were expected to perform physical labor for the benefit of the city and area. Boys and girls collected medicinal herbs, removed house plaques bearing Nazi symbols, took away air raid signs, and cleaned city parks. Authorities also ordered the teaching staff and its pupils to assist local farmers in agricultural production. The girls at the Oberschule für Mädchen, the former Upper Lyceum, spent a week in July 1945 helping with the harvest in nearby Klein-Kreutz. The children of the Von Saldern secondary school performed a wide variety of services for the city. As of August 1945, 34 pupils had either helped or were continuing to assist farmers with the harvest; ten others had received permission to work in local shops and factories; fifteen had been assigned to help the city provide basic social services. In a campaign called "We're Cleaning Up," Von Saldern teachers and pupils spent 14 days performing various services throughout the city. Some manned collection points in the local museum and in the tax office, where citizens could turn in prohibited Nazi materials. Others gleaned for corn kernels and worked to repair the streets and walkways.[16]

Despite prohibition, some formal instruction remained part of the pupils' daily routine in the summer of 1945. In addition to focusing on current events as a curricular foundation and to devoting significant amounts of time to working in the streets and in the fields, pedagogues also taught important basic skills such as writing and arithmetic, especially to the elementary school pupils. Teachers were admonished to take special care not to use Nazi-era textbooks or lesson plans. School officials also recommended that teachers incorporate songs, drawing, sports, strolls, and, above all else, games into the basic instruction for pupils of all ages. Moreover, such instruction took place under extraordinarily difficult material circumstances. With little to eat and facing great difficulties getting to and from school, high school students in Brandenburg, for example, had to attend school in shifts because the Girls' and Boys' Upper Schools were compelled to share the available classroom space in the Ritterakademie, as its slightly damaged roof and windows made it more acceptable than the more heavily damaged alternatives.[17]

One significant exception to the prohibition against formal specialized instruction was the teaching of the Russian language. Whether out of a desire to improve communication between young Germans and the Russians or out of a belief in the inherent superiority and value of Russian culture, the Soviet military authorities began setting up a system of instruction in Russian as early as June. Although teaching other foreign languages remained prohibited in the summer of 1945, Soviet and German authorities decreed that learning Russian would henceforth be a fundamental element of the curriculum. Permission to teach Russian was initially restricted to a small number of individuals who had been approved by the Soviet authorities, although all teachers were ordered to teach the Russian alphabet. Although it would be too much to see the roots of later East German sovietization efforts in the special place reserved in the summer of 1945 for instruction in Russian, it quickly became an important element of the makeshift curriculum, even taking precedence over mobilizing pupils to clean up the city and leading them on nature hikes. "It must be stressed," noted one teacher at the time, "that Russian instruction . . . may not be interrupted by any distraction."[18]

One of the most pressing and crucial elements of the postwar reconstruction was the reformation of Brandenburg's teachers. As of the late summer of 1945, 221 pedagogues were officially registered as currently teaching in the schools. Sixty-three percent were female, 37 percent male. Although the average age was 47, very few were in their thirties or forties. The staffs of the individual schools were divided between a larger collection of peda-gogues in their fifties or sixties and a smaller cohort in their early twenties.[19] Also significant was the high degree of continuity of personnel. Eleven of the sixteen pedagogues at the Von Saldern secondary school had been teaching since the war began. At one elementary school, this figure was as high as 81 percent. At the Pestalozzi School, the degree of continuity from May 1939 to August 1945 was 100 percent. The figure for the city's entire teaching staff was between 57 and 60 percent.[20] This percentage is in one sense artificially low, since it reflects those who taught only in prewar Bran-denburg and fails to take into account the fact that many newcomers like Elisa Z., who had arrived during the war, were not young lay teachers or school aides but older certified teachers from other parts of Germany. Moreover, at least 75 teachers, or 34 percent, had been members of the Nazi Party, and at least 100 teachers, or 45 percent, had joined the NSLB. Approximately 15 of these PGs—as former *Parteigenossen* came to be known colloquially—had held leadership positions such as cell propagan-dist or cell warden in the Nazi Party, the NSLB or a similar National So-cialist organization. Three of the eighteen current principals and two of the eighteen vice-principals had belonged to the Nazi Party and all but six to the NSLB. The current school leadership was composed of an almost exclusively male group of teachers, ranging in age from 45 to 66, who had almost without exception begun their teaching careers in Brandenburg be-fore January 1933.[21]

Table **4.1** Brandenburg an der Havel teachers as of August 1945

Total number	Male	Female	Average age	NSDAP membership
221	82 (37%)	139 (63%)	47	76 (34%)

Source: Registry of All Teachers at Brandenburg (Havel) Schools, comp. 27 August 1945, Amt für Volksbildung, Abt. Schulamt, StadtA Brandenburg, 2.0.12.30/254, 42–58; city's registry of teachers, StadtA Brandenburg, 2.0.12.25/249; NSLB *Mitgliedskartei* for Gau Kumark, BAB NS12, 2:82–88; School-statistical Lists of the School Supervision District Brandenburg (Havel) for 1939 to 1944, BLHA, Pr. Br. Rep. 2A Regierung Potsdam II Brd., nos. 198–203; NS Lehrerbund Kartei und Akten, Microfilm Publication, A3340, ser. MF, Berlin Document Center, National Archives; and individual personnel files, BLHA, Pr. Br. Rep 34 P.S.K., Personalia, and Domstiftarchiv.

It was these pedagogues whom Soviet and German authorities wished to identify, evaluate, and either dismiss or "reeducate." Paul Wandel, who was a prominent Communist who had returned to Germany with the Red Army and was now running the German Central Administration for Education (Deutsche Zentralverwaltung für Volksbildung, DVfV), wrote in August 1945, before the official reopening of the schools: "since the education of the youth is of such importance for the German people and so dependent on the personality of the teacher, especially high standards must be applied to the selection of the teachers who will soon work in the schools." "That the school system will become a political issue requires teachers who are convinced antifascists," stated a German official speaking before Brandenburg Province's school superintendents in August 1945, "since it was above all teachers who served in the Nazi period as fanatical fascists and amoral opportunists. Even those who simply went along or stood by are dangerous."[22] The publication of the Potsdam Agreement in early August laid out the Allies' broad reform policies for Germany. The Soviet leadership, like its British, American, and French counterparts, believed that no postwar reconstruction could succeed without a thorough removal from public or semipublic positions of former members of the Nazi Party and their affiliated organizations. Teachers were to undergo a program of denazification, demilitarization, and democratization that would be more rigorous and thorough than that to which the Allies intended to subject the entire country. The removal of "more than nominal" PGs from public or semipublic positions, as called for under paragraph 6 of section 3 of the Agreement, placed almost all German teachers into a category that included mayors, ministers, and chiefs of police.[23] Reinforcing the special significance of the schools, and implicitly the teaching staff, paragraph 7 further highlighted the necessity of thoroughly reforming both curricula and pedagogues: "the education system in Germany must be controlled so that the National Socialist and militaristic teachings are removed completely and a successful development of democratic ideas is made possible."[24]

Paragraph 6's explicit focus on those former Nazis who were "more than nominal" revealed a fundamental issue that would bedevil German and Soviet officials up to, and even beyond, the founding of the GDR—the problem of determining individual Germans' implication in Nazism's crimes. If Soviet military commanders and German administrators were to punish every Nazi Party member to the fullest extent, millions could lose their jobs or their property. Such an extreme application of the Potsdam Agreement would most likely alienate a large segment of the population and thereby jeopardize a successful reconstruction of Germany. Similarly, if only certain types of PGs were to be denazified, what criteria should authorities follow in determining their punishments? These issues regarding the postwar transformation of society were raised well before the cessation of hostilities. At the urging of Soviet leaders, leading German Communists living in Moscow drafted in early 1944 an "Action Program" that, as part of its blueprint for the "antifascist-democratic" reconstruction, called for the complete removal of "Hitlerism" from the German state and society and the punishment of its supporters. Emerging from this and additional writings by Walter Ulbricht and Johannes Becher, among other Communists, were two different, and possibly contradictory, positions regarding the nature and function of denazification. German leaders struggled with whether the state's denazification project should concentrate on the reeducation, and thus eventual reintegration, of former Nazis into German society or on their exclusion by means of purges and other punitive measures. Nor were the Soviets able to offer the German Communists much help. To a greater degree than the British, the French, and the Americans, Soviet authorities, motivated by a specific Soviet understanding of fascism, expected the denazification program to result in the total removal from state employment of men and women who had belonged to Nazi organizations; Soviet policies therefore privileged the purge of former Nazis over their possible reeducation and reintegration. Soviet officials, however, quickly found themselves struggling to reconcile their goals with the reality of the situation in eastern Germany. Although they convinced the Germans to adopt the fundamental distinction between nominal and active party members, for example, Soviets' understanding of "active" did not remain constant but was repeatedly modified in 1945 and 1946 as the number and nature of exemptions and qualifications expanded. As a result, Soviet commanders issued or implemented measures in a chaotic and sometimes paradoxical manner that had far-reaching effects on the denazification programs.[25]

The Soviet Zone's denazification policy was therefore not a single, detailed, consistent, and clearly articulated one but was made up of an often contradictory and protean constellation of principles. The large majority of authorities earnestly implemented a broad series of measures and policies intended to punish those who had belonged to the Nazi Party or had "actively" supported National Socialism. Although many pedagogues suffered as a result of punitive measures that included expropriations and the performance of forced labor, two elements of the denazification program were especially relevant for German teachers: the purge from the teaching force of those who had been "actively" involved with National Socialism and their replacement by a corps of young, specially trained and ideologically conformist new teachers.

The Denazification of Brandenburg's Teaching Staff

Measures to identify, evaluate, and, if warranted, punish former Nazi teachers got off to a relatively slow and disorganized start in Brandenburg. As early as 1 May 1945, former members of the Nazi Party, the National Socialist women's organization (NS-Frauenschaft), and the German Women's Enterprise (Deutsches Frauenwerk) were ordered to perform forced labor. Four weeks later, former Nazis, as well as men and boys who had served in military and paramilitary units, were required to register with local officials. In June education authorities began reviewing teachers' curricula vitae for evidence of past political activities and affiliations. Brandenburg's school superintendent approvingly predicted that a number of teachers would be removed from the classrooms as a result of the review. Whereas officials in the Mecklenburg region set up special committees for the examination of individual pedagogues as early as July, the failure to implement similar measures in Brandenburg in June and July belied the superintendent's overly optimistic pronouncement.[26]

On 1 August 1945 at least 83 pedagogues, consisting of 62 men and 21 women and ranging in age from 31 to 59, were formally dismissed from the city's schools.[27] Although seven and ten had been employed in the city's secondary and vocational schools, respectively, more than 45 had taught in the elementary schools. Moreover, a very disproportionate number of middle school pedagogues—17—lost their jobs. More than 40 had belonged to the Nazi Party, some had previously joined the Stormtroopers, and at least one had been a member of the SS. Eleven had held leadership positions ranging from cell leader to block warden in the local party unit or in one of the party's affiliate organizations such as the NSLB and the NSV. More significantly, 52 had recently served in the Wehrmacht or the Volkssturm.[28]

Despite the seemingly impressive scale of this wave of dismissals, closer inspection reveals that it constituted more an administrative accounting of the status quo than a planned purge of former Nazis from the teaching staff. Some of the dismissed individuals had long since moved away from Brandenburg or were temporarily residing elsewhere and currently unable to return and resume teaching. Jahn School elementary teacher Alfred M. was "purged" although records reveal that he had not been in a Brandenburg classroom since 1941, when he was transferred to a school in the "Wartheland." His Jahn School colleague Bernhard S., a former member of the Stormtroopers, was probably equally unconcerned about his dismissal in August 1945; he too had transferred out of the city in 1941.[29] A slightly different case is that of the female vocational school pedagogue Gertrud D., who had fled in April to Hamburg and was officially fired on 1 August. After returning to Brandenburg in September, she registered with local education authorities and resumed teaching when the schools reopened in October. To take another example, Erika G. of the Werner Mölders Girls' School was also dismissed at the beginning of August, only to return to the school's classrooms in July 1946 after presumably finishing some kind of teacher preparation course. Furthermore, many of the female teachers who were fired in August had been teaching only since the spring, and a good number were school helpers who had returned to their normal lives or refugee teachers for whom Brandenburg was only a way station. Young women like Erika D. and Liselotte B., both of whom were in their twenties and had begun teaching in February 1945, did not return to the classroom over the summer and were thus dismissed in August. One of the clearest signs that the terminations were mainly a result of city officials' attempt to update employment records is the fate of Fritz G. A middle school instructor and former NSDAP member who had been teaching since 1934, he was "fired" on 1 August even though he had committed suicide in April.[30]

The fact that 52 of the 83 terminated pedagogues were classified in school records as serving in the military is also very significant. Many of these men most likely either had been only recently released from captivity or were still in prisoner-of-war camps in August 1945. A former member of the SPD and an employee of the Upper Lyceum since 1931, one secondary school teacher returned to Brandenburg after authorities had "fired" him and was soon rehired. Another pedagogue, one who had belonged to the SPD before joining the Nazi Party in the spring of 1933 and who had served during much of the Third Reich as principal of the Pestalozzi School before being sent to the Western Front in November 1944, could not immediately return to Brandenburg after the war's end and was dismissed on 1 August. He eventually was released from captivity and, after securing permission to enter the Soviet Zone and return to the city, reestablished contact with school officials. Records indicate that 46-year-old Erich H. was dismissed in early August while he was still being held in a Russian prisoner-of-war camp. The same was true for former Jahn School director Willi V.; having spent much of the past four years in the military, including most recently in the Volkssturm, he was "fired" from Brandenburg's teaching staff 17 days before he was released from captivity on 18 August 1945. Secondary school teacher and former Nazi Oskar D.'s termination, which occurred three weeks before his official release from the Volkssturm, did not prevent him from returning to the classroom on 1 October. Finally, others, for example—51-year-old elementary school teacher Max J.—simply never returned to the city's schools after being demobilized from the Volkssturm.[31]

The August action nevertheless did remove some Nazis from the teaching staff. In at least three cases, school officials refused to reemploy pedagogues who had belonged to the Nazi Party, had been fired in the summer of 1945, and had sought to regain their positions on returning to Brandenburg. All three men had joined the Nazi Party before June 1937; one had joined in 1931, and one had held an assortment of leadership positions, including district training leader in the German Labor Organization and group leader for vocational schools in the NSLB. Their initial termination thus served as the primary tool for removing them from the classroom. Such cases represented, however, only a fraction of those fired in August.[32]

More important, many known Nazis were not dismissed in August. School officials allowed 75 former Nazi Party members to continue teaching. Furthermore, some men and women who had belonged to the Nazi Party and had been fired in August were rehired in the fall of 1945. One experienced teacher, a former Stormtrooper and NSDAP member previously employed at the Pestalozzi School, was rehired in September. Middle school teacher Friedrich Wilhelm M., a former member of numerous party organizations including the Stormtroopers, was reemployed in a Brandenburg school in early October despite having been officially fired on 1 August 1945. Despite having held a leadership position in the Nazi Party— a criterion that would later categorically prohibit him from teaching—a 47-year-old former Rochow School pedagogue was rehired on 20 August 1945.[33]

The foregoing analysis clearly demonstrates that the August 1945 purge of Brandenburg's teaching staff failed to "completely" remove former "Nazi teachers" from the classroom as Allied officials originally envisioned. Although Soviet and German authorities might have comforted themselves then and later with the knowledge that 83 "unsuitable" or "undesirable" men and women out of a total population of more than 200 pedagogues were prevented from being part of the denazified, demilitarized, and democratized school system, a closer examination of the outcome reveals several important points. The purge was first and foremost an expunging from the employment rolls of those Brandenburgers who were not there in August 1945 to resume teaching, ranging from former Wehrmacht and Volkssturm soldiers now in captivity to underqualified women who, no longer compelled to work as *Schulhelfer,* chose not to return to the schools. Second, a not inconsiderable number of pedagogues who had been members of the Nazi Party or important affiliated organizations such as the Stormtroopers and the NS-Frauenschaft continued to educate the city's youth.

Recognizing the deeply flawed outcome of the initial purge, Soviet and German authorities almost immediately began to agitate for a more effective and thorough reforming of the Soviet Zone's teaching staffs. Following the late August publication of SMA Order No. 40, "Preparing the Schools for Operation," Paul Wandel issued implementation guidelines that signaled an effort both to intensify and to standardize the many denazification efforts taking place throughout the Zone. As part of a wide-ranging series of reforms in preparation for the October reopening of the schools, Wandel ordered regional authorities to employ only men and women who could guarantee that they were "free" of National Socialism and willing to educate the pupils along "democratic" lines. To this end, former members of the Nazi Party or one its affiliate organizations were, except in rare circumstances, to be dismissed or not rehired. Wandel instructed:

> Since the education of the youth is of such importance for the German people and so dependent on the personality of the teacher, especially high standards must be applied to the selection of the teachers who will soon work in the schools. . . . Former members of the NSDAP and its affiliate organizations are as a matter of principle not to be employed. Exceptions can be permitted by provincial administrations for simple, nonactive members only in special cases reported by the responsible school superintendent.[34]

Despite adding greater precision to the SMA order, Wandel failed to clarify a number of unresolved matters, including, most significantly, the issue of which institutions were to be considered Nazi Party "affiliate organizations." Was membership in the NSLB, once the Nazis' primary means of mobilizing pedagogues for National Socialist ends, grounds for exclusion? How exactly would PGs be evaluated and by whom? Moreover, Wandel offered no precise definition of what constituted an "active" or "nominal" former Nazi.[35]

After receiving the DVfV's general instructions, regional administrations quickly drew up detailed programs. In what would become a not uncommon occurrence, policies conceived in Berlin lost some of their original power and direction in the transmission to the local level. The instructions the Potsdam government sent to Brandenburg officials in late August did not require the dismissal of all former Nazis. What had been a relatively small loophole—permitting exceptions only in special cases with the provincial administration's approval—had expanded tremendously. Local school officials were now permitted to employ former Nazis so long as they had not previously held party leadership positions or been "active" in party activities. In order to determine this, regional authorities instructed officials to set up in every district a commission, comprised of the school superintendent and a representative from each of the approved political parties, to review individual cases. The examination would focus on the pedagogue's "entire political attitude" and "instructional usefulness" (*schulische Verwendbarkeit*). It was up to the pedagogues to prove that they had not "actively" served the party and to provide at least two witnesses who would guarantee their future political reliability.[36]

Wasting little time, Brandenburg school officials set up and carried out in September and October the first in a series of centrally coordinated denazification purges. School Superintendent Johannes S., the former deputy principal of the progressive Secular School, closed by Nazi officials in 1933, ordered former Nazis to submit a written statement attesting to their "nominal" status as members of the NSDAP and/or the NS Frauenschaft. He also instructed them to make available at least two "antifascist citizens" to serve as political character witnesses.[37] A commission headed by the superintendent and staffed with other teachers then reviewed the relevant materials and determined whether an individual should suffer consequences.[38]

As a result of the commission's activities, a not insignificant additional number of teachers were dismissed. School officials in October 1945 removed from the classrooms 22 men and women either by refusing to rehire them or by outright termination. Men comprised a slight majority in this group, and many of these pedagogues had been teaching in Brandenburg since the early 1930s. Whereas approximately 48 percent of the teachers dismissed in August had been NSDAP members, 77 percent of those purged in October had belonged to the Nazi Party. Nor was this another episode of city officials updating their employment lists; all of these individuals were present in Brandenburg at the time of their dismissal. This denazification action punished some of the teaching staff's most active and ardent Nazis. Foremost among them was former Ritterakademie principal Professor Ludwig Z., a man who had been one of the first to join the NSDAP, had served in the city's Nazi government, and had returned to the school in June. Another especially active supporter of the Third Reich in Brandenburg and its environs was Albert M.; his 45-year teaching career came to an abrupt end in early October, punishment for his long-standing membership in the NSDAP and the NSLB and his leadership position in the NSV. Still others removed from the classroom at this time were former Nazi Party members who had, however, only been teaching in the city's schools for a short time; Hildegard E. and Hildegard V. were both refugee teachers who joined the teaching staff in 1945. As we will see, this initial vigilance in denazifying the teaching staff proved to be ephemeral; by the time of the founding of the GDR, German authorities were rehabilitating former purged pedagogues, allowing some to resume teaching. Even as notorious a former Nazi as Ludwig Z. was largely "de-denazified" in late 1948![39]

Despite a broad series of punitive measures that included the dismissal of numerous teachers, Soviet authorities quickly concluded that initial efforts in the summer and early fall had largely failed to remove all former Nazis from state and society. In a letter to Wandel in late October, Soviet education authorities accused the DVfV of failing to inform the local commissions of how the program was to be carried out and whom they were to target. Moreover, the Soviets charged Wandel and his associates with failing to supervise the work of the commissions adequately. As a result, the commissions were haphazardly applying the denazification criteria, resulting in too many dismissals in some areas and in others too few. Whereas an overly narrow interpretation of the criterion "active" resulted in the great majority of Erfurt's PGs escaping any punishment, the commission operating in the Brandenburg Province town of Belzig adopted such a broad understanding of "active" membership that it ended up dismissing every teacher. Russian dissatisfaction was expressed pointedly in internal the SMA communications. The head of SMA Education Department, Piotr Solotuchin, informed Major General F. E. Bokov in November that as of 1 October 1945 more than 11,300 former Nazis had been removed from the classrooms of the Soviet Zone, but admitted that the original goal had clearly not been met. Instead of the German school system being free of former Nazis, more than 15,400 continued to teach.[40] That 46 percent of the Zone's teaching staff consisted of PGs was clearly unacceptable to Soviet leaders.

In a lengthy report dated 3 November 1945, the Brandenburg provincial administration energetically countered such criticisms.[41] According to these education officials, German and Soviet authorities had successfully removed all serious Nazis from the classroom. The officials acknowledged, however, that a shortage of replacement instructors, as well as logistical and organizational difficulties, continued to hinder a complete purge of the teachers. Principals and superintendents could not staff their schools solely with pedagogues who had not joined the NSDAP because many of these had not returned from captivity or evacuation centers. Local officials were thus forced to rely on the unskilled school helpers, many of who were considered physically unfit for the reconstruction of the school system. Training courses for the replacement teachers, popularly known as the *Neulehrer,* had not produced enough "qualified" young men and women. Moreover, regional officials raised the politically sensitive issue that the denazification program was inherently flawed: "The treatment of former PGs leads again and again to renewed debates and discussions. The distinction between so-called active and only nominal members is no usable standard. The examinations by commissions—as we have carried out for a long time—is more chance and an emotional grasping than a really perfect solution."[42] Regional officials concluded that the creation of additional commissions would repeat what had already been done and thus accomplish very little.[43]

Such arguments failed to convince Soviet authorities either that previous purges had largely cleared the schools of former Nazis or that the denazification project was intrinsically weak and ineffectual. In January 1946, SMA commander-in-chief Marshal G. K. Zhukov ordered local education departments to create a group of special commissions to review the schools. In addition to determining the conditions of school buildings and the types of materials currently in the classroom, the current and past political affiliation of every teacher was to be investigated and evaluated. The Soviets ordered the commissions to be made up of representatives from local government and the political parties, though this time the membership had been expanded to include representatives of the recently created Free German Trade Union Association (Freie Deutsche Gewerkschaftsbund, FDGB), the Youth Organization (Jugendausschuss), and the Antifascist Women's Organization (Antifaschistische Frauenausschuss).[44] Very likely as a result of such a commission's work in Brandenburg, regional education officials noted in March 1946 that more than 79 percent of the city's 256 teachers did not belong to a political party. Twelve belonged to the SPD, a slightly smaller number than the 14 who had joined the Communist Party, while the CDU and the LDPD had 18 and 7, respectively. Equally if not more disturbing to Soviet and German officials was the continued employment of 81 pedagogues who had belonged to the Nazi Party.[45]

The issuance of Allied Control Council Directive No. 24 in January 1946 represented a milestone in Allied denazification efforts. The measure sought to remove from positions of responsibility—a broad concept that included teachers—all who either had been active Nazis or were currently opposed to the Allies. Unlike previous SMA and Allied decrees, Directive 24 defined in great detail the criteria for denazification. "Active" PGs included those who had held any office—on the local, regional, or national levels—in the NSDAP or one of its organizations, those who had publicly supported either the Nazi regime or its militaristic and racist ideology, and those who had willingly provided substantial moral, material, or political assistance to Nazism. The directive also divided Nazi-era positions and activities into three categories: those requiring immediate removal, those warranting close examination, and those permitting "discretionary removal and exclusion." Teachers who had joined the Nazi Party before 1 May 1937 or had held any office in it or affiliate organizations such as the NSV or the NSLB were to be immediately dismissed. Teachers who embodied the Prussian "Junker tradition" fell into the second category. Finally, pedagogues who had been promoted at an unusually rapid rate during the Third Reich or who had joined the Stormtroopers after 1 April 1933 did not qualify for immediate and automatic termination but could be removed at the authorities' discretion.[46]

Despite the far-reaching and broad powers contained in Directive 24, Soviet and German authorities waited until the end of the year to begin implementing the measure. The Soviets had claimed throughout 1946 that specially appointed denazification commissions—like those operating in Germany's western zones—were not needed in the Soviet Zone because current programs were already removing former Nazis from the state and society. In reality, the Russian and the German Communists were concerned about the effects a new, more extensive denazification initiative would have on German voters, many of whom had been PGs. Although former Nazis had lost their right to run as candidates in an election, they retained the right to elect others to office.[47] In a speech before the SED's executive body in June 1946, Otto Grotewohl expressed the party's fear that the denazification process posed a threat to the SED's success in the upcoming regional and local elections: "The decision must be made very soon because the Nazi fellow travelers [*Mitläufer*] are now, in the face of the approaching elections, searching for an orientation and a political house under whose roof they can crawl, and we must be careful that the CDU has not already snatched away a great portion of these people before we have introduced any measures."[48] It was not until after the conclusion of the district and provincial elections held in September and October of 1946, respectively, that authorities in the Soviet Zone implemented Allied Directive No. 24.[49]

The Brandenburg Commission for the Implementation of Directive 24 finally convened for the first time on 21 December 1946. Consisting of male representatives from the SED, the CDU, the LDPD, the FDGB, and the mayor, the commission focused largely on denazifying a broad group of city employees and small businessmen that included doctors, nurses, musicians from the municipal symphony, gardeners, and white-collar workers. Meeting 12 times between late December 1946 and late March 1947, the commission examined more than 180 cases. Fifteen individuals were dismissed immediately, and 32 lost their licenses to practice a particular occupation. The majority, however, received either light sentences or no punishment at all. Twenty received probation, with the possibility of future dismissal, and 24 were allowed to retain their business licenses. Moreover, the commission ruled that 84 cases did not qualify for denazification according to Directive 24. A large majority of the cases involved women, and a Soviet officer observed at least one of the commission's sessions. The last meeting took place on 26 August 1947. None of the examined cases involved Brandenburg pedagogues.[50]

Only in the fall of 1947 did a denazification commission begin to evaluate the city's teaching staff. Unhappy with both the slow pace of and the growing anger among the German population caused by the current de-nazification program, the SMA had issued in August Order No. 201 as a means of both resolving once and for all the fate of former NSDAP mem-bers and, equally important, bringing the program to a quick conclusion. Significantly, the measure incorporated a number of provisions that facili-tated the full reintegration of nominal PGs into state and society. Now ex-empt from the entire array of postwar orders, decrees, and measures that had circumscribed their political and civil rights, nominal former Nazis could, for instance, run for office. Finally dropping the pretense of not needing formal denazification commissions, Soviet officials ordered their creation; they were to evaluate and, if necessary, remove active Nazis from the government and all other aspects of German life. The commissions had the power to dismiss, ban, decertify, and demote PGs, as well as the option of forwarding individual cases to the judicial authorities for criminal pros-ecution.[51]

On 7 October 1947 the first meeting of the Brandenburg District Denaz-ification Commission took place in the offices of the mayor, Fritz Lange. A former teacher in Berlin, Lange served as the chairman and was assisted by representatives from the CDU, the LDPD, the SED, the FDGB, the Union of People Persecuted by the Nazi Regime (Vereinigung der Ver-folgten des Naziregimes), the Democratic German Women's League (Demokratischer Frauenbund Deutschlands), and the Free German Youth (Freie Deutsche Jugend, FDJ).[52] Seven of the eight were men, and the deputy chairman was a former KPD member and a current SED district ex-ecutive committee member. At least five of the eight had working-class backgrounds, and at least three had suffered imprisonment or forced labor at the hands of the Nazis. As the historian Timothy Vogt has noted, the in-clusion of the so-called antifascist organizations like the FDJ reflected less a genuine attempt to open the process up to a wider array of societal elements than a political maneuver to ensure the SED's dominance in the commis-sion, since the representatives of the FDGB, FDJ, Union of People Perse-cuted by the Nazi Regime, and Democratic German Women's League were usually SED members. This was certainly the case in Brandenburg, where all four, as well as the mayor and the deputy chairman, belonged to the SED.[53] That the endeavor was not free from Soviet oversight was made clear in this first meeting; the CDU representative, who had been nomi-nated by his party only after a rancorous controversy had effectively nulli-fied the original candidate, had not yet been approved by the SMA.[54]

Meeting a week later, the Commission examined the first eight individuals, three of whom were teachers.[55] Established at this time was the basic procedure the Commission would follow over the course of the next 19 weeks: following a reading of the charges, the chairman questioned the accused about his or her past political memberships and activities, especially public appearances or writings interpreted as having lent support to the National Socialist state. Incriminating evidence—usually consisting of state and party documents such as questionnaires, professional resumés, and NSDAP membership cards, as well as of newspaper reports, announcements, and photographs—was introduced in order to refute the defendant's testimony or to substantiate the Commission's claims. Witnesses then testified either on behalf of or against the accused. The Commission closed the proceedings by voting on the applicability of Directives 24 or 38 to the accused's case and, if necessary, also determined the appropriate punishment. The entire process usually lasted a little longer than one hour.[56]

Over the course of four months, the Commission reviewed more than 60 cases, including those of 15 teachers. The two charges most frequently leveled against the pedagogues were falsification of official questionnaires and propagandizing on behalf of the Nazi state. Most defendants brought with them witnesses—usually fellow teachers or school principals—whose testimony, they hoped, would exonerate them. On more than one occasion, incriminating evidence was presented by witnesses, often former or current pupils, who had been summoned by the Commission. One vocational school teacher was called before the Commission twice.

The SMA's Order No. 35, issued on 26 February 1948, officially and permanently ended the formal denazification campaign throughout the Soviet Zone, including in Brandenburg.[57] On completion of its activities, the Commission had decided that six pedagogues should be allowed to teach despite their previous affiliations with the NSDAP or, in one case, the SS. One teacher was found guilty of propagandizing in informal settings on behalf of the Nazi Party and of actively supporting the NSV but was nonetheless permitted to continue teaching. Convinced by multiple accounts of one defendant's "antifascist" behavior, the Commission concluded that he had been used by the Nazi Party, formally exonerated him, and instructed school officials to reinstate him immediately. Unlike these lucky few, the majority of the teachers examined by the Commission received punitive sentences. Eight were immediately dismissed from their current positions and prohibited from teaching in the future. Having previously lost his position and seeking to return to the classroom, the former Von Saldern director Walter H., who had worked so hard in the Third Reich to transform his school and its teaching staff along National Socialist lines, was banned from ever teaching again. When sentencing one former Pestalozzi School instructor, the Commission made it clear that his former membership in the SPD was crucial in establishing his complicity and determining his punishment; possibly motivated by traditional Communist hostility toward Social Democrats, SED member Lange sharply denounced the "defector" (*Überläufer*) for his "treason." Lange and his fellow committee members judged the activities of former Ritterakademie principal Professor Ludwig Z. serious enough to justify banning him from all "antifascist organizations," dismissing him from any leadership positions in "public or semipublic jobs," prohibiting him from all types of teaching and public speaking, continuing his imprisonment, and transferring his case to the criminal courts.[58]

The straightforward description of the Commission's modus operandi and analysis of its verdicts, however, fail to illuminate the protean nature of the process. With most, if not all, of the terms and conditions of the denazification process open to some kind of interpretation, the Commission exhibited significant flexibility in its examination of the 15 cases involving teachers. One defendant was found guilty of having propagandized on behalf of the NSDAP and actively supported Nazism to such a degree that he had been awarded a NSV service medal, yet this 49-year-old elementary school teacher was allowed to keep his job. Another pedagogue—a 63-year-old who had been teaching at the Saldria since 1914—was held to much higher standards and was terminated and banned as a consequence of his Nazi Party membership and one pupil's allegations of mild anti-Czech discrimination. Commission members ruled that Von Saldern pedagogue Karl G., a German nationalist and supporter of the "Confessing Church" whose run-ins with Nazi officials is described in Chapter 2, could continue working in the city's schools but could no longer teach history or current events as punishment for what can only be described as a minor omission on his questionnaire. To take another example, the Commission established that a 67-year-old vocational school teacher lied on his questionnaire regarding his "supporting" membership (*fördernde Mitgliedschaft*) in the SS but refused to assign a punishment, passing his case off to local school authorities. A denunciatory letter to the provisional government, combined with the unearthing of more incriminating documents, led to the teacher's second appearance before the Commission and his subsequent termination and ban. In two of the cases heard in the first meeting, the Commission singled out speeches given by the teachers as proof of propagandizing on behalf of the Third Reich. Yet the Commission ultimately reached two very different verdicts, concluding that one pedagogue had been used by the Nazis, despite a history of affiliation with rightist parties, and the other had actively supported the Nazi state. Moreover, factors such as membership in the rightist German National People's Party or the NSV were accorded varying degrees of importance in different hearings. Nor were the decisions always reached unanimously. In at least three cases, Commission members disagreed over both determinations of complicity and the assigning of appropriate punishments, with a dissenter on at least one occasion basing his objections on concerns about the shortage of teachers.[59]

Similarly, the efficacy of Brandenburg's denazification of its teaching staff was closely linked to the city's enduring shortage of teachers. On more than one occasion local officials resisted fully implementing a purge that would only exacerbate the problem. In an effort to balance two contradictory SMA imperatives, the necessity of both purging PG teachers and employing enough teachers to instruct the pupils, city authorities in the period up to the spring of 1946 allowed some "active" former Nazis to remain in the classroom. The SMA recognized at this time the deleterious effect the purges were having on staffing, even going so far as to permit German officials to exempt PG teachers from a harsher, broader denazification order issued in November 1945, if their removal would completely close a school.[60] Brandenburg officials' willingness to weigh their relatively new imperative of denazifying the teaching staff against the traditional mission of teaching the city's children became an issue again during the activities of the Commission between late 1947 and early 1948. Denazification transcripts reveal that concerns about replacing needed teachers who might be dismissed because of past affiliations with the Nazi Party and other National Socialist organizations were considered when deciding the individuals' fate. Testifying in November 1947 before the city's denazification commission on behalf of a former Nazi and Stormtrooper, the principal of the Fontane School pleaded for clemency for 51-year-old Otto B. partially on the grounds that there were too few teachers in Brandenburg. To take another example, the CDU representative on the Commission agreed to purge one former secondary school teacher but requested that the dismissal be postponed until after a replacement had been found.[61]

Training a New Generation of Teachers? Brandenburg's *Neulehrer*

Intimately related to the denazification purges were state efforts to recruit and train a new generation of teachers. Initially planning on dismissing tens of thousands of German teachers because of their Nazi pasts, Soviet and German Communist officials implemented a series of measures in the period 1945–1949 in the hopes of creating a new, substitute body of instructors. The massive influx of pupils from former eastern German regions like East Prussia and the Sudetenland added even greater pressure to the imperative of finding new teachers. Finally, and most important, fundamental political and ideological motivations lay behind the search for new teachers. Soviet and German Communist authorities planned to train pedagogically inexperienced and politically uncompromised young Germans in order to create important allies in the construction of a new, "antifascist-democratic" German state and society. In August 1945 Paul Wandel had demanded: "Only those teachers can be employed who can guarantee that they will educate the youth according to true democratic principles, free of Nazi and militaristic beliefs [*Gedankengänge*]. . . . The goal is . . . to empower teachers to become, in this decisive epoch of our history, convinced pioneers [*bewusste Vorkämpfer*] for a political, spiritual, and moral democratic rejuvenation of our national life."[62] In a public appeal for the reform of the school system, the leadership of both the KPD and SPD echoed Wandel's words in October, calling for a "new type of democratic, responsible and capable teacher" who alone would be able to transform the pupils into "agents" of a peaceful, "antifascist" and democratic reconstruction.[63]

The earliest measures to create *Neulehrer* were not dictated by the SMA in Karlshorst or the nascent DVfV in Berlin but were conceived and administered locally. In Brandenburg, the first program for the training of a new group of teachers began in June 1945. Under the direction of 57-year-old Johanna M.—a "known personality in nationalist circles" who had, among other things, once served as the local chairwoman of both the Women's Committee of the rightist German National People's Party and the nationalist and conservative Queen Louise League and was now the deputy principal of the Görden School—a three-month-long training program began for 35 Brandenburgers. She was responsible for instructing the participants in basic pedagogy; joining her were three colleagues—including a 39-year-old former Nazi Party and NS-Frauenschaft member and an experienced instructor formerly associated with the regional teachers' academy—who endeavored to convey how one teaches subjects such as music and singing, Russian, and most important, contemporary political issues.[64] The 35 *Neulehrer* finished their three-month training in September and joined the more experienced and formally trained pedagogues in the classrooms as the 1945–1946 school year commenced in October.[65]

By the late summer, Soviet and leading German education authorities were establishing stricter control over local measures to train the *Neulehrer.* The implementation directive for SMA Order No. 40 set out basic guidelines regarding critical topics like the selection of participants and the nature of the training program. According to Wandel, *Neulehrer* should be young, should be preferably female, and, most importantly, should have proven "democratic convictions" (*eine schon bewährte demokratische Gesinnung*). Of secondary importance were pedagogical ability and educational qualifications.[66] Additional guidelines lent even greater specificity to the DVfV's recommendations. Brandenburg authorities were informed that the most appropriate age for participants was between 20 and 30 and that an "antifascist" attitude was a necessary precondition. Trainees whose formal education ended at graduation from elementary school were still eligible so long as they met the other criteria.[67] The students were to spend their mornings learning about pedagogical and methodological issues as well as listening to lectures on political topics; afternoons were to consist of supervised teaching exercises and drills.[68] In response, Brandenburg education officials set up in the fall of 1945 a second course for *Neulehrer* scheduled to last for eight months. Forty men and women enrolled in the course in October. One such individual was 23-year-old Eva-Maria B. Having interrupted her schooling in the late 1930s to work for the Ernst Paul Lehmann toy company, she returned to high school during the war, ultimately earning her graduation certificate. The call for candidates to enroll in the city's first *Neulehrer* course found a volunteer eager not to become a teacher but to learn a profession that would enable her to survive in postwar Brandenburg and, more immediately, relieve her of having to clear rubble.[69]

The men and women who graduated in the spring of 1946 were, in the words of one former Brandenburg *Neulehrer,* "thrown into the schools."[70] Due to the extreme shortage of qualified teachers, *Neulehrer* were expected to perform the work of a full teacher, including at least 30 hours of instruction per week. Moreover, they were expected to teach under incredibly challenging circumstances. Eva-Maria B., for example, was assigned to teach a second grade class of 60 children, ranging from 7 to 14 years old. In addition to having to find a way to instruct so many pupils and of such varying ages, she had very little room—her pupils sat "three to a seat"—and lacked almost entirely any supplies and materials: no workbooks, for example, and no textbooks or teaching aides. As beginning pedagogues, they were assigned a mentor, usually an experienced *Altlehrer* (an established, credentialed teacher), who occasionally sat in on their classes and whose classes the *Neulehrer* observed; both individuals met for two hours a week to discuss pedagogical matters and specific problems.[71] The shortage of teachers also meant that *Neulehrer* were not assigned solely to the elementary schools but also taught in the middle and secondary schools. At least one *Neulehrer* began working in the spring of 1946 at the Upper Lyceum, the Von Saldern secondary school, and the Boys' Intermediate School. These were most likely individuals who had the secondary school graduate certificate, and some had possibly undergone a slightly more specialized training in the *Neulehrer* course.[72]

Despite initiatives like Brandenburg's second training course, the Soviets increasingly voiced criticism of the nature and the efficacy of the German efforts. Solotuchin demanded that Paul Wandel and the DVfV reform the current programs so that central or regional education authorities exercised greater control, thereby ensuring that the *Neulehrer* would be trained more quickly—a pressing need given the dramatic shortage of teachers in the Soviet Zone—and that more suitable candidates would be selected.[73] Less than a month later, Solotuchin broadened both his criticisms and his reform proposals. Concluding that the various courses were not producing sufficient numbers of new pedagogues and estimating that 29,000 *Neulehrer* needed to be trained by the beginning of the 1946–1947 school year in order to meet the Zone's manpower needs, Solotuchin called for the expansion of the system of training courses. Provincial administrations were to set up by 1 January 1946 a Zone-wide network consisting of courses that lasted either three to four months or six to eight months, depending on the participants' educational backgrounds. Authorities were to provide the trainees with, if necessary, small stipends and ration cards equal to those of an industrial worker. Solotuchin's proposals were codified in SMA Order No. 162, issued on 6 December 1945.[74]

As a result of the changes, Brandenburg received more than 80 *Neu-lehrer.* Having graduated from the course begun in October 1945, 34 newly trained pedagogues began working in June 1946. An additional 50 men and women joined the teaching staff in September 1946 after having recently completed an eight-month program held as a result of Order No. 162.[75] Although the extra manpower helped relieve the shortage, school officials had expected to receive far more *Neulehrer.* Fifteen percent of those who began studying in October 1945 failed to become teachers in Brandenburg. Similarly, of the 170 who entered the January 1946 training course, only 50 ended up in the city's classrooms.[76] The sizeable attrition that took place throughout 1946 perpetuated a shortage of teachers that had plagued Brandenburg as early as October 1945 and continued to affect the city's schools up to and beyond the founding of the GDR in the fall of 1949.[77] Brandenburg was not getting enough *Neulehrer* to resolve staffing difficulties caused either by the war or by postwar developments like the flood of refugee pupils. That the placement of the 50 men and women represented the last wave of large-scale *Neulehrer* appointments to the city's schools was an especially ominous portent.

The situation in Brandenburg exemplified the failure of Solotuchin's changes to alter significantly the dismal situation that confronted school administrators and teachers alike. Principals still faced a dramatic shortage of teachers. In August 1945 Brandenburg Provincial Administration vice-president Fritz Rücker called the attention of the region's school superintendents to the "most urgent problem"; localities lacked sufficient teachers to teach the children.[78] By the year's end, the situation had not changed. Regional education officials complained to their Berlin superiors that the shortage threatened not only the instruction of the children but also the effective training of the *Neulehrer.* Instead of the prescribed relationship of one politically uncompromised and experienced teacher supervising the practical training of one *Neulehrer,* the Provincial Education Department reported in November:

> We are quickly approaching the situation in which one uncompromised pedagogue serves as mentor to 10 *Neulehrer.* We are forced under these circumstances to place *Neulehrer* in positions for which they are not pedagogically suited, namely instructing first-year pupils and working in single-classroom schools. . . . [Despite our efforts], it will nevertheless be a long

time before all positions are filled such that pedagogues can teach without requiring supervision and assistance.[79]

The prediction proved correct as the situation not only failed to improve significantly over the next couple of years but in fact worsened. One DVfV official reported in December 1946 that the "catastrophic" shortage of teachers in the region necessitated an intentional lowering of pedagogical standards within the schools. Although the official considered it "extremely dangerous," he nevertheless authorized certain districts, including Brandenburg, to employ *Schulhelfer*, individuals who lacked even the rudimentary training of the *Neulehrer*.[80]

Such efforts did little to improve the situation. At the Second Pedagogical Congress of Brandenburg Province, held in July 1947, the persistent shortage of trained pedagogues was an important part of Minister Fritz Rücker's speech to the assembled administrators. He admitted that officials had failed up to this point to create a qualitatively and quantitatively sufficient teaching staff for the region. As a result, important state initiatives such as the expansion of so-called unitary schools *(Einheitsschulen)* in the countryside had been retarded.[81] Finally, even as late as July 1948, communities like Brandenburg continued to struggle to find enough reasonably qualified teachers to instruct the ever increasing number of pupils. Despite three years of local and regional efforts to train *Neulehrer*, the city still lacked approximately 47 teachers, or roughly 15 percent of the total teaching staff.[82]

A primary reason for the persistence of the teacher shortage was the profound difficulties in recruiting and, equally important, retaining *Neulehrer*. As early as February 1946, regional officials voiced concerns that the trainees were overwhelmed with the rigors of the brief but intensive course of study.[83] Local administrations like Brandenburg were often unable to provide students with basic material necessities such as adequate housing, clothing, or stipends. The *Neulehrer* Herbert S. later recalled that the months he spent preparing to teach were "difficult": the housing shortage compelled him to travel 22 kilometers to and from Brandenburg every day by bicycle, and food was always scarce. The participants of the *Neulehrer* course held in Potsdam beginning in January 1946 were forced to spend their first couple of nights sleeping in such undesirable environments as the city jail.[84] Moreover, some trainees enrolled in the courses simply as a means of ensuring their survival, and their commitment to becoming *Neulehrer* lasted only as long as local authorities provided for them or nothing more attractive became available. Not only did Eva-Maria B. originally not want to become a teacher, but one of her two *Neulehrer* colleagues at her first job was a former housewife who took the training course so that she could make ends meet following the death of her husband, a former pedagogue. Herbert S. became a *Neulehrer* only after his Wehrmacht past precluded him from pursuing his dream of working as a forester. None of these had become *Neulehrer* for ideological reasons. To take another example, Karl-Heinz R. worked various odd jobs in the initial postwar months before signing up for a course "since many teachers were needed."[85] As a result, many young men and women quit the training. Twenty-three percent of the participants of the January–August 1946 courses held in the Soviet Zone withdrew from the program. Fifteen percent of the Brandenburg candidates failed to complete the eight-month course begun in October 1945.[86]

These difficulties continued to stymie Soviet and German efforts throughout the period 1945–1949. The SMA's plans for 11- and 12-month courses to begin in May 1946 and August 1946, respectively, met with very little interest. Approximately 10,000 fewer *Neulehrer* than expected reported for work in September 1946.[87] As fewer people signed up for training, as more teachers left the profession, and as the number of pupils continued to increase, *Neulehrer* courses continued to be held, largely as a result of education officials struggling to preserve personnel levels attained in 1945 and 1946; earlier hopes of replacing the entire teaching staff with a new cohort of young pedagogues became increasingly unrealistic. Much smaller than for the period 1945–1946, the number of *Neulehrer* trained between 1947 and 1949 only increased modestly the total number of teachers in the Soviet Zone. As late as 1949, German officials called for an additional 10,000 to 15,000 men and women to register to become *Neulehrer*.[88]

Nor did completing the training guarantee that the Neulehrer would remain in the classrooms. In fact, many of the same factors that convinced some to drop out of the training programs hampered the efforts of school officials to retain others. Perceived as either professionally unqualified or as lackeys of the Soviet occupation government, many of the newly credentialed young men and women encountered significant distrust and opposition from both the general populace and their fellow teachers.[89] In addition to admonishing the teaching staff at an assembly in June 1948 to stop using the terms *Neulehrer* and its opposite, *Altlehrer,* Brandenburg's school superintendent conceded that 25 or 30 percent of the novice pedagogues would not be up the task before them, noting that some would change jobs as soon as the economic situation improved.[90] The *Neulehrer* also suffered from low wages and were often compelled to perform additional odd jobs in order to secure basic supplies such as food and wood. According to one *Neulehrer* from Brandenburg Province, the typical regular salary disbursements did not enable one "to buy even two loaves of bread on the black market." Recalling the low wages of the early postwar years, a former Brandenburg *Neulehrer* claimed in an interview in 2000 that teaching had been "a bit of a side job [*Nebenberuf*]"; securing the basic necessities such as food had taken precedence over his school obligations.[91] In July 1946 the SMA issued Order No. 220 in an effort to improve the situation. *Neulehrer* wages were raised but remained well below those of formally trained pedagogues. Whereas *Neulehrer* earned 3,800 reichsmarks a year, elementary school and middle school pedagogues earned 4,100 and 4,800 reichsmarks, respectively. *Neulehrer* did not receive the full wage increase until after their fifth year of employment and were excluded from receiving performance bonuses. Despite Order No. 220, the situation did not improve significantly because regional and local authorities rarely implemented the changes fully, ultimately provoking the German and Soviet administrations of Brandenburg Province in both early and late 1947 to issue sharply worded statements reminding rural authorities and mayors of their financial and material obligations to the *Neulehrer.* The SED School Commission for Brandenburg Province noted in May 1949 that the implementation of Order No. 220 continued to encounter "serious difficulties" on the local level.[92]

As a result of these financial, emotional, and material hardships, many novice and experienced teachers fled the profession. More than 12 percent of Brandenburg's *Neulehrer* had quit as of December 1947. Education authorities noted that more than half of these had either moved to another occupation zone or quit for political reasons. Less than four months later, another analysis of the teaching staff revealed that still more Brandenburger *Neulehrer* had quit.[93] Local education officials reported in September 1948 that an additional group—comprising more than 13 percent of the city's instructional staff—had ceased to teach in Brandenburg in the period October 1947 to September 1948. Of the 20 teachers who left the city's service from March to October 1948, at least two fled the Soviet Zone, and both were *Neulehrer*.[94] The situation in Brandenburg exemplified a Zone-wide problem that increasingly worried Soviet and German authorities. The fluctuation within the teaching staff was particularly strong in the first three postwar years and remained a serious problem up to and beyond the founding of the GDR.[95] Recognizing the disruptive effects the substantial turnover was having on state and party efforts to transform the school system, education authorities noted in August 1949 that approximately 100 teachers per region per month were leaving the profession. Inquiries revealed that the primary issues causing *Neulehrer* to quit included the disdainful attitude of the general population, the lack of available housing, the often substandard quality of the meals provided, the "extremely inadequate" provisioning (*äusserst mangelhafte Versorgung*) of clothing, and a lack of support from school administrators. In 1949 East Berlin authorities strove to staunch the flow of teachers out of the schools with a series of reforms that included improving the provisioning of teachers with shoes and clothes.[96] The pedagogues who fled to the western zones did so for a variety of reasons. Many left the Soviet Zone as a consequence of a Communist repression that included the persecution of the churches and the suppression of free and independent political activities. Others were motivated by economic concerns, hoping that in the West there would be better access to goods or greater opportunities for themselves or their families.[97]

Conclusion

That both denazification and the *Neulehrer* program had largely failed became clear to most observers by 1948. Soviet officials and leading German Communists had originally sought the total removal of those pedagogues who had—as "fanatical fascists and amoral opportunists"—supported the Third Reich. As the chairman of the Brandenburg District Denazification Commission stated in November 1947, he and his colleagues were to apply "especially high standards" when evaluating the National Socialist pasts of teachers, judges, and policemen.[98] Although many former Nazi Party members were dismissed from Brandenburg's schools in the period 1945–1948, a significant number of PGs continued to teach. The case of a Von Saldern secondary school teacher who had belonged, at different times, to the German National People's Party and the NSDAP and had once lectured on the importance of militarily "riding" against the East yet was rehabilitated by the Brandenburg Denazification Commission in early 1948 was not exceptional. First appearing in the summer of 1945, various commissions examined the city's teaching staff over the course of almost three years but ultimately dismissed relatively few people. Directly related to this imperfect implementation of Soviet and German denazification measures was the failure to recruit, train, and retain a new generation of young, politically uncompromised *Neulehrer.* These teachers comprised as of March 1948 less than 50 percent of the Brandenburg teaching staff.[99] Although many *Neulehrer* were trained and placed in the schools, a majority of the teaching staff consisted of experienced pedagogues who had trained in the Weimar Republic or in the Third Reich and, in some cases, had been Nazi Party members. As the school superintendent remarked in September 1948, "a large part of the teaching staff went through that system of schools and education, grew up used to thinking in a way that we want to overcome." "The teachers at the high school are almost exclusively old, academically trained secondary school pedagogues," Brandenburg's school superintendent lamented in an official evaluation of a Brandenburg high school less than two years later, "who in the best of cases venture all the way to liberal democracy but cannot find their way to Marxism."[100] At the same time that German Communists were foundng a new, allegedly democratic and antifascist state, local and regional education officials were only too aware of the largely unsuccessful efforts of the previous four years to replace the older, ideologically "tainted" teachers with a new generation of politically uncompromised pedagogues.

The primary obstacle to Soviet and German plans for the transformation of the teaching staff was the extensive and enduring shortage of qualified teachers. The paucity of pedagogues was a constant concern of local, regional, and central authorities from the end of the war up to, and even beyond, the founding of the GDR. Brandenburg schools lacked enough men and women to teach a pupil population that had been growing steadily since the war's end and had swelled by December 1949 to more than 14,500.[101] In addition to failing to implement the denazification measures fully, German and Soviet authorities sought to solve the problem by carrying out a widespread program of rehiring purged pedagogues in 1946–1949. There were indications that such a policy was in the works as early as the summer of 1946. In June, just months after the publication of Directive 24, Brandenburg Province authorities issued detailed secret instructions to school superintendents setting out what kind of former Nazis were eligible for reemployment and how many.[102] Shortly thereafter, the DVfV distributed guidelines to local and regional authorities regarding the rehiring of teachers who had once belonged to the NSDAP. German officials admitted that former Nazis were fundamentally "not suited" to be a "moving force [*Träger*] of the new school" but nonetheless authorized their reemployment, though at this time only on a small scale and after careful scrutiny by local and regional authorities.[103] By the late fall of 1946 and early winter of 1947, even as the local Commissions for the Implementation of Directive 24 were busy carrying out the second wave of purges in Brandenburg and elsewhere, Soviet and German authorities were forced to make modifications to the denazification program in order to maintain sufficient manpower in the schools. "It is to be pointed out that the question of the past is not even the most important thing," Brandenburg Province's official hiring guidelines stated. Instead, "the democratic school requires that the teacher be a political pioneer of especially great activity."[104] Current behavior, and not past political actions and affiliations, was the more important criterion. According to former *Neulehrer* Eva Maria B., local education officials rehired in 1947 at least one teacher who had been politically purged in 1945.[105]

By the late 1940s, Soviet and German authorities had significantly expanded the scope and nature of the means through which local education authorities could rehire former Nazis. The SMA's Order No. 35, dated 25 February 1948, broadened the group of PGs who were eligible for reemployment.[106] The number and size of legal "loopholes" that enabled former Nazis to return to the classrooms continued to grow in 1948.[107] Records indicate that at least one other pedagogue, who had worked in Brandenburg after the war and had been eventually dismissed because of his Nazi Party affiliations, was rehired as late as 1949. Former *Neulehrer* Karl-Heinz R. recalled in an interview conducted in 2000 the reinstatement in the early 1950s of two former Nazi teachers, including one who had been an active Stormtrooper. Such efforts to rehabilitate fully former Nazis culminated in the October 1952 decree "Reinstatement of former NSDAP Members in the Schools."[108]

No case illustrates the increasing willingness of authorities over the course of the 1940s to amnesty local individuals who played a crucial role in setting up and running the Third Reich than that of Professor Dr. Ludwig Z.

Active in rightist political circles in the German Empire and Weimar Republic, Ludwig Z. joined the NSDAP in 1932 and, after Hitler's appointment to the chancellorship, left the Ritterakademie for a series of high positions in Brandenburg's municipal government. He was imprisoned after the war, prohibited by the local denazification commission in October 1947 from holding any type of leadership position in the workplace or in society, and sentenced in January 1948 to five years' imprisonment and the confiscation of his property. Ten months later, however, his sentence was revised; instead of five years, he received nine months, which he had already served. Moreover, as he described in a letter to former pupils, the "main point" of the reduced punishment was that "all other 'expiatory measures' [*Sühnemassnahmen*] were rescinded." It is very possible, had he not been almost 80 years old, that in addition to getting back his books and furniture he would have also been permitted to teach again. Age, and not Soviet and German Communist notions of justice, prevented this notorious Nazi pedagogue from returning to the classroom.[109]

Additional factors hindered the denazification project and thereby hobbled efforts to transform the teaching staff. Some German, and to a lesser extent even some Soviet, officials were unwilling to participate in or oversee an accurate and thorough accounting of teachers' role under the Nazis. As former SMA Education Department functionary Piotr Nikitin has stated, education issues—including the transformation of the teaching staffs—were for years not a high priority for Soviet officials. This institutional negligence was exemplified in the lack of plans or firm guidelines within the SMA that plagued early efforts to reform the schools.[110] To take another example, Provincial Administration vice-president Fritz Rücker—the man in charge of all aspects of public education in the Soviet zone—delivered a speech in 1945 that illustrated the tendencies of some administrators to absolve teachers fully or partially of responsibility for Nazism's crimes. Rücker stated:

> Sadly, the teachers had idly observed how young people were filled with the poison of Hitler's propaganda—racial theories, militarism and a pernicious ideology. . . . Under these circumstances, under the always increasing teaching loads, with more crowded classrooms, with commemorative ceremonies and extracurricular obligations, etc. the teachers were overburdened and made incapable of any resistance. . . . Finally, the majority of

teachers became apathetic and resigned. Seduced by the idea of the Great German Reich and in the hope of leadership in it, they followed National Socialism.[111]

In this version of the recent past, teachers had impassively watched while others had indoctrinated the girls and boys. The logical conclusion was that these allegedly disempowered and disengaged pedagogues bore little responsibility for Nazism's crimes.[112] Nor were such attitudes and actions confined to senior administrators. Local "antifascist" committees not infrequently obstructed the early purges carried out in the summer of 1945, often protecting men and women with clearly active Nazi pasts.[113]

Moreover, such individuals were aided in their efforts by a protean and evolving distinction between "active" and "nominal" that created ample space in which, if they wished, they could slightly impede or obstruct the full implementation of the denazification measures. Initial Soviet policies and actions in the summer and early fall of 1945, though imperfect themselves, soon gave way to an approach characterized by inconsistencies about exactly who should be purged, resulting in an significant broadening of the loopholes.[114] Subsequent directives and orders codified the increasingly finely drawn distinctions, in effect increasing the numbers of former Nazis who no longer qualified as "active" and thus could escape punishment. German authorities on more than one occasion contributed to this confusion and its resultant weakening of the denazification program. In the winter of 1945–1946, for example, regional officials issued contradictory denazification standards. Whereas the first vice-president, Bernhard Bechler, instructed local authorities to dismiss all former PGs, others in the Brandenburg Province administration issued guidelines stipulating that replacement teachers need to be "qualified," a vague concept that was often used to prevent experienced and needed PGs from being dismissed.[115] Confusion gave cover to local officials predisposed to protecting former Nazis or more concerned with keeping state services like the schools and the administration running than with fully purging teachers. The situation was confusing enough that the Brandenburg Commission for the Implementation of Directive 24 unanimously complained on the record that contradictory government orders were hindering its efforts to determine which small businessmen should lose their licenses to practice business.[116]

Finally, the efforts of German Communists to reconcile a desire to purge former Nazis from state and society on the one hand with a growing recognition of the importance of influencing the voting behavior of former Nazis in the postwar democratic order on the other significantly affected the pace and scale of denazification efforts. Not only did Soviet and German authorities refrain from implementing Directive 24 until after the regional and communal elections were held in the fall of 1946, most denazification measures, including the forced labor conscriptions and the prohibition on owning televisions or radios, were suspended in mid-1946.[117] Nor were the fears of the SED and the SMA without merit. As early as February 1946, education officials noted with alarm that many teachers were joining the CDU.[118] More than two years later, the situation had improved only marginally. The CDU and LDPD together had more members among the teachers than the SED as of March 1948; more than 49 percent of all teachers had not joined any political party.[119] More ominous and worrisome for the authorities was the political behavior of the *Neulehrer*. Many chose to remain at arm's length from the established parties and the political and social reconstruction of Germany.[120] If they did become politically engaged, many *Neulehrer*—like their more experienced colleagues— joined the CDU and LDPD instead of the SED.[121]

Although Soviet and German Communist officials in the initial postwar years sought to implement the broader denazification program with special rigor in the schools, the results of their efforts were not exceptional in comparison to the program's impact in other areas of eastern German society. Historian Ralph Jessen's exemplary analysis of the incomplete transformation of eastern German university faculty, for example, illustrated a roughly similar process with a comparable outcome: what was called the "storming of the ivory tower" took longer than scholars had previously assumed and unfolded in a more contradictory fashion than had long been believed. More important, the first 10 years witnessed important historical continuities in professors' professional lives, and material shortages played an important role in obstructing SED reforms.[122] Future studies of other communities' experiences with the postwar transformation of their school systems will most likely bear out the experiences of teachers like Johannes S., Johanna M., and Eva-Maria B., since the crucial elements of their story—for example, the shortage of qualified teachers that plagued Brandenburg, the sometimes contradictory and poorly executed official policies, and the difficulty of attracting and retaining new teachers—could almost certainly be found, though admittedly to varying degrees, throughout the Soviet Zone. With the failure of Soviet and German administrations to transform Brandenburg's teaching staff by dismissing experienced but politically compromised pedagogues and replacing them with a new cohort of young, "democratic" teachers, the task of convincing Brandenburg's teachers to work with the postwar East German order—an important development that nevertheless fell short of the original goal of creating a pliant, ideologically trustworthy and activist teaching staff—would be accomplished by the postwar teachers' union.

CHAPTER 5

The Creation of a Genuine
Teachers' Union

With the denazification campaign under way, Brandenburg's school superintendent ordered the city's teachers in December 1947 to submit an additional, more detailed questionnaire that provided information regarding,
among other things, their previous political memberships and activities. As
head of the local chapter of the GLE, Willi S., a 59-year-old SED member
who had once also belonged to the SPD and the NSLB, first sought to persuade the school superintendent to refrain from enforcing the December
order, since he feared it would create unrest among the pedagogues. When
the superintendent refused to do so, Willi S. took the drastic step of instructing GLE members to ignore the superintendent's measure. This
brief but significant episode ended with local education authorities denouncing such "obstructionist action" to regional officials in Potsdam.[1]

At first glance, the actions of Willi S. seem quite surprising. According to
traditional notions of the nature and activities of trade unions in the Soviet
Zone and GDR, especially as they underwent the process of sovietization,
such independence was next to impossible. For decades, scholars have depicted trade unions as "handmaidens" of the SED, "transmission belts"
that helped the ruling Communist party implement its wishes in the workplace.[2] Yet Willi S. and the GLE refused to follow state and party officials
blindly, and did so at a time when the GLE was supposedly losing its remaining autonomy. The actions of the Brandenburg chapter, however,
most likely did not surprise the superintendent, for they were but the latest example of the GLE actively campaigning on behalf of its members.

From its inception, the GLE had served as the pedagogues' advocate vis-à-vis the state; it had, for example, worked first with Soviet and then with German Communist officials to ensure that its members had enough to eat, sufficient clothing, and adequate housing. It also worked to secure the teachers' interests in larger political and social processes such as the denazification campaign, as Willy S.'s story illustrates. In the period 1945–1949, the relationship between the GLE and the state was marked at times by harmonious cooperation and at times by irreconcilable adversity.

This chapter tells for the first time the story of the origins and early actions of the postwar GLE, illuminating the special role it played in striving to improve the conditions under which pedagogues worked and lived, and especially its efforts to seek better wages, housing, food, and clothing from Soviet and German authorities. That the GLE intervened with education officials to facilitate the reinstatement of purged teachers, for example, or pressured local authorities to pay pedagogues' salaries certainly contributes to our understanding of the challenges pedagogues faced in the workplace and at home. More important, determining the nature and degree of the GLE's activism on behalf of teachers also helps answer several fundamental questions regarding teachers' attitudes toward the emerging postwar state and society. First, did Brandenburg's teachers support their local union? What do the membership data, for example, reveal about teachers' attitudes toward this new, unitary professional organization that so differed from the Weimar-era organizations familiar to these pedagogues? Similarly, how did their previous experiences with the NSLB affect their relationship with the GLE? Did the legacy of the NSLB's 12-year existence influence their perceptions of and attitudes toward the postwar union? Second, what was the relationship between Brandenburg's teaching staff, its union, and the nascent postwar political system? Did support for the GLE translate into teachers joining political parties like the SED? Or was it possible for teachers to embrace one but not the other? Teachers' actions in these areas shed light on their attitudes toward the nascent "democratic" and "antifascist" state and society. Faced with the apparent hostility of the state, expressed most powerfully in the lengthy denazification process, and the indifference of the ruling SED, was the GLE the primary means through which pedagogues interacted with the emerging East German Communist state and society?

The Resurrection of Trade Unions in Eastern Germany

Absent for more than a decade as a consequence of National Socialist policies enacted in the early years of the Third Reich, independent trade unions reappeared in Brandenburg in the summer of 1945. The SMA had authorized the creation of trade unions in its Order No. 2, issued on 10 June 1945. According to this decree, "the working population in the Soviet Zone of Occupation in Germany is to have the right to unite in free trade unions and organizations to protect the interests and rights of all working people."[3] The unions were empowered to make collective agreements with employers, to set up welfare and insurance funds, and to promote educational and cultural development through union institutions. Despite the formal existence of a plurality of organizations, the Soviets rejected the idea of resurrecting Germany's traditional union movement—one characterized by deep organizational, political, and ideological divisions among the various unions—and therefore insisted from the beginning on a single organizational structure to replace the previous unions. Moreover, the Soviet military authorities closely supervised the unions, requiring them, for example, to register with the SMA, to submit their membership lists, and to follow SMA instructions. Finally, Order No. 2 repealed all National Socialist laws and decrees regarding unions and other professional associations.[4]

The establishment of trade union chapters on the local and regional level quickly followed the creation of nascent central institutions in June. The Preparatory Union Committee for Greater Berlin, consisting of Communists, Social Democrats, and future leaders of the CDU, issued on 15 June a call for the founding of unions throughout the Soviet Zone. The unions' primary activities were to consist of combating the remnants of National Socialism, aiding in Germany's reconstruction, engaging in instructional activities and, most important, representing all types of workers. Mirroring developments in traditionally unionized industries such as mining and manufacturing, a teachers' union began to take shape in the summer of 1945. In late June, an Organizational Committee of Teachers made up of Berlin pedagogues established contact with the Preparatory Union Committee, and the founding of the GLE followed on 16 July 1945. Consisting largely of Social Democrats with prior experience in school administration or teachers' associations during the Weimar Republic, the union leadership soon made clear to the Berlin education officials their intentions to develop the GLE in a manner consistent with the Preparatory Union Committee's June declaration and with traditional, pre-1933 union activities. Whereas Paul Wandel, head of the German Central Administration for Education, hoped to use the nascent organization primarily as a tool to aid the administration in the control and transformation of the teaching staff, the GLE instead intended to represent the social, economic, and legal interests of teachers.[5]

Within weeks, the initial call for unions and the concomitant developments in Berlin were already showing preliminary results in Brandenburg. In July 1945, the leadership of the local committee of the FDGB announced to city officials and workers both the existence of the nascent unions and the procedures for obtaining membership. The process for recruiting state employees—a category that included school teachers—involved a slightly different path than in the factories, whose officials convened workers' assemblies to discuss the issue of unions and to distribute materials such as a questionnaire required of every potential member. Instead the local union officials asked municipal departments to coordinate the distribution and collection of the membership questionnaires. Finally, officials made it known that the unions would not inherit the financial resources of their pre-1933 predecessors; potential members were thus encouraged to donate money.[6]

At the regional conference of school superintendents held less than a month later, Dr. Johann Dembowski introduced the GLE's basic organizational structure and its intended role in German society. Rejecting the highly heterogeneous constellation of teachers' organizations that had characterized Germany before 1933, Dembowski announced the planned creation of a single teachers' union, one that would encompass all the pedagogues of Brandenburg Province. Dembowski's position was consistent with the general postwar Communist approach to organizing the unions, one that originated in the belief that the extreme disunity of the working classes had facilitated Hitler's rise to power. Moreover, Brandenburg's teachers and their professional organizations were to give up their supposed traditional position of disengagement from political and public affairs. Pedagogues in postwar Germany were "to join with and march along the general stream" as one component of the larger FDGB. Similarly, GLE officials also expected the union and its members to participate in the political and ideological reconstruction of Germany—to be, as Dembowski's described it, "political." He refrained, however, from explaining what this important, though vague and potentially ominous, characterization might mean.[7]

Much of the very early history of the GLE in Brandenburg Province and its communities remains shrouded in mystery. Although the regional organization's founding congress took place in June 1946, state and party records indicate that some form of teachers' union was operating well before that. At assemblies held in the districts of Potsdam and Teltow, pedagogues agreed in October 1945 to situate a future professional organization institutionally within the FDGB. Similarly, Potsdam education officials at this time discussed the possibility of seeking the assistance of the region's GLE organization in carrying out the state's program of teacher retraining. Unionization efforts soon spread to other cities and communities, and by December 1945 a provisional regional executive—consisting of the retired school superintendent Adolf Buchholz and four other men from the areas *(Gebiete)* of Potsdam, Teltow, and Templin—had been formed.[8] More important, membership records for late 1945 and early 1946 confirm the existence of a teachers' union. More than 260 Brandenburg pedagogues had joined the national GLE organization as of the winter of 1945–1946. Despite revealing a not insignificant degree of fluctuation, subsequent monthly membership statistics demonstrate that considerable numbers of teachers were joining the union. As of March 1946, more than 200 of the city's pedagogues and "educators"—a term that included the kindergarten and nursery school teachers—had joined the GLE. Shortly thereafter, an additional 32 individuals joined, bringing the union's total membership for April and May to 244.[9]

In the late spring these men and women selected three delegates to attend the founding congress of the GLE's regional chapter, held in Potsdam in early June 1946. Of the three delegates, two had belonged to the SPD and were currently school principals and SED members, one had served as the superintendent of schools and was currently an LDPD member, and all were older than 57 and had been teaching in Brandenburg since well before 1933. The delegates selected a Regional Executive Committee—consisting of Brandenburg's three delegates and 22 additional teachers—and elected a few individuals to attend a future Zone-wide conference.[10] With the administrative matters finished, state and union functionaries gave speeches that delineated the form and purpose of the GLE. According to the chairman of the Regional Executive Committee, Adolf Buchholz, the union's foundation *(Kernstück)* was "the creation of a united teaching staff, consisting of all who teach, from kindergarten to the university."[11] The GLE's organizational hierarchy consisted of zonal, regional, and, on the lowest level, district chapters; the GLE initially refrained from establishing individual school organizations, analogous to the factory union organizations that formed the foundation of the more traditional unions in the FDGB, as a consequence of the wide dispersion of individual teachers throughout the zone. Together with the district executive committee, a future district teachers' council was to serve as "the representative of the interests of the teaching staff" *(Vertreter der Belange der Lehrerschaft)*.[12] Firmly anchored within the organization of the FDGB, the GLE pledged to treat all pedagogues—members and nonmembers—in a fair and "democratic" fashion and to right a historical wrong by actively supporting female teachers, including promoting them to positions of responsibility outside the classroom. Also established at the conference was a statement of the GLE's political function in postwar society:

> We trade unionists [*Gewerkschaftler*] must structure the union in such a way that it carries out the political tasks of the new democratic Germany, according to the principles and duties of the FDGB, which were approved by the Zonal Conference in February, because the union has duties different from those of any union organization in the past. It is to concern itself not only with questions regarding vacations, wages, pensions, etc., but is also responsible for all that happens in our state, from our smallest domain to the entire state [*Reich*]. You as teachers have the highest responsibility for this.[13]

The GLE's primary political role would be to assist in the creation of a peaceful and democratic Germany by liberating the youth from harmful influences such as militarism and racial mania *(Rassenwahn)*.[14]

Promoting the Material Interests of the Teaching Staff

Although the GLE in the period 1945–1949 did not ignore its political mission, its officials at this time nevertheless concentrated on working for the material well-being of its members. Most pedagogues were struggling to survive in a postwar order in which their traditional employer—the government—was not in a position to provide the full array of customary benefits and services. In response, the union became the sole organizational advocate working to secure for teachers the necessities they needed to live.

Its program at first consisted of securing basic necessities like housing, clothing, firewood, and food, often obtaining for its members what German and Soviet authorities had promised but failed to deliver. Its scope of action quickly grew to include lobbying authorities to improve teachers' salaries, housing opportunities, and work conditions.

According to the FDGB constitution adopted at the founding congress in February 1946, the union's primary tasks included working to improve the conditions of labor, a broad concept that included but was not limited to wages and benefits, and securing the workers' right to participate in the larger decision-making processes, known as codetermination, regarding the reconstruction of German industry and economic life.[15] One general strategy unions used to fulfill these tasks at this time was direct agitation vis-à-vis the German and Soviet authorities. After the teachers of the Brandenburg Province had gone more than eight weeks in the fall of 1945 without having been paid their wages, the nascent teachers' union began to lobby the regional administration. The Provisional Executive Committee of the regional union organization reported in December 1945 that negotiations with the Potsdam government had resulted in a pledge by the administration to pay the back wages quickly. Union officials at this time also raised a controversial issue that remained at the heart of union-state struggles for the next couple of years: the right of the union to have a voice in personnel matters such as hiring and promotions within the regional administration.[16]

The GLE continued to pressure the administration to pay teachers' wages regularly and promptly. The failure of the regional government to compensate teachers in the first half of 1946 for their work in the fall of 1945 resulted in a sustained volley of complaints and criticism from the union and individual teachers. Such efforts eventually bore fruit. In mid-June the SMA reprimanded the provincial administration's director of personnel and finance for his "bureaucratic and heartless attitude regarding the payment of the teachers' wages."[17] A few weeks later, regional officials in Potsdam paid the pedagogues and thereby finally made good on their December 1945 promise regarding these outstanding wages.[18]

In addition to ensuring the regular payment of salaries, the GLE sought to increase the amount teachers were paid. The SMA issued a decree in October 1945 ordering employers—including local and regional governments—to compensate white-collar employees according to precapitulation levels. Order No. 100's provisions regarding the salaries and additional financial supplements such as housing bonuses due to school administrators and teachers represented a significant improvement over the provincial administration's current compensation program. The region's pedagogues, however, did not see an immediate improvement in their pay because in late 1945 and early 1946 Potsdam officials resisted adopting the Soviet program. The regional GLE responded by lobbying various regional authorities. Such efforts contributed to Potsdam's eventual implementation of Order No. 100 in July 1946.[19] Similarly, union officials at this time unsuccessfully tried to convince the regional authorities that teachers deserved to have their salaries based on age and not on tenure within a particular school system. Given that numerous pedagogues had changed schools or school districts or had returned to the classroom from retirement as a consequence of the war, the GLE's success in its insistence on age-based wage categories would have benefited the many older men and women teaching in municipalities like Brandenburg.[20]

Although substantially improving the "material and legal situation" *(materielle und rechtliche Lage)* of teachers throughout the zone, SMA Order No. 220, issued in July 1946, failed to resolve the problem completely. The measure's most significant reform was its reclassification of wage categories such that elementary school teachers were henceforth to be paid between 4,100 and 7,100 reichsmarks per year, an increase of more than 20 percent. The order also recalibrated the housing supplements pedagogues were to receive, stipulated the preferential distribution of coupons for shoes, clothing, and other goods, and guaranteed small plots of land for teachers who lacked their own gardens.[21] The GLE soon discovered that education and finance authorities were not fully implementing Order No. 220 and in some cases were actively obstructing it. Teachers continued to be paid according to the old, less remunerative wage levels, and education officials still refused to give teachers a degree of codetermination in deciding salary questions. Noting that Order No. 220 reflected a Soviet commitment to improving pedagogues' wages and living conditions, Brandenburg's GLE leadership in October 1946 unanimously voted to seek SMA assistance in this matter if the German regional administration continued to resist the reforms.[22] The union also had to pressure city agencies to comply fully with the other provisions of Order 220. The GLE chapter worked together with the city's teachers' council to convince the city housing agency to agree to give preference to homeless teachers in its allocation of available housing, compelled the Trade and Welfare Department to increase the amount of

clothes, shoes, and shoe soles allotted to teachers, and forced shoe repair-
men to keep a list of all resolings performed so that the union could verify
that teachers had received their share.[23]

Another union strategy for improving pedagogues' lives was the campaign for the creation of teachers' councils. Allied authorities established
with Control Council Decree No. 22, issued in April 1946, the right of all
workers to create workplace councils. Officially classified a type of public
employee *(öffentliche Angestellten),* teachers thus had the right to form
councils that would "represent [their] professional, economic and social
interests."[24] To be set up at district, regional, and zonal levels, teachers'
councils were to work with and influence administrations whose policies
"decisively" impacted, for example, teachers' employment status and wage
and food ration levels. Despite the strong similarities in purpose and the
potential for conflict between the union and the proposed councils, the
GLE welcomed their creation. According to union officials, the teachers'
councils were to supplement or aid the work of the GLE since they would
also represent those pedagogues who had not joined the union. Moreover,
these councils represented a potential magnification of the union's bargain-
ing power with the state, especially since Decree No. 22 explicitly granted
workplace councils the right of codetermination. Although education officials de facto refused to recognize the GLE's demand for the right of codetermination in matters such as personnel issues, union officials planned
to take unofficial control of the teachers' councils and thereby use them to
preserve and, when possible, improve the material, social, and legal situation of the teaching force:

> After detailed consideration of the given preconditions and of acquired ex-
> perience, the Union of Teachers and Educators has reached the conclusion
> that teachers' councils are to be created to work with the proper adminis-
> trative agencies. The union is of the opinion that in the preparations and ex-
> ecution of the elections, as well as in the activities of the teachers' councils,
> the union will have in its capacity as representative the decisive influence
> over more than 80 percent of the teachers. Only in this way will the realiza-
> tion of the provisions contained in article 7 of Law No. 22 be guaranteed.
> The best trade unionists must become members of the teachers' councils.[25]

This attitude toward the teachers' councils was significantly different from
the other unions' characteristic relationships with their workers' councils.
Helke Stadtland notes that Communist and union officials in the period

1945–1948 pursued various strategies to neutralize the councils as a representative organ of the workers. The GLE, however, was the driving force behind the creation of the teachers' councils; the councils were not part of the immediate postwar education system landscape, as was the case with the thousands of workers' councils that sprang up in the late spring and summer of 1945, and therefore were not independent competitors for the workers' allegiance. The GLE from the very beginning crafted the councils to serve as an "executing organ" *(ausführende Organ)*.[26] Rather than eclipsing or replacing the union's role vis-à-vis the state, the councils were to serve as another vehicle for union agitation.

Brandenburg's teachers' council began operating in March 1947 under the leadership of a 59-year-old school principal who had been teaching in the city since 1930 and had once belonged to the SPD and the NSLB. This council's creation marked the end of a long struggle between the GLE and education authorities. Although the union began calling for the creation of councils as early as late 1945, nothing was accomplished that winter or the next spring. In June 1946 the regional chapter took up the issue again, declaring at the founding congress its intention to implement teachers' councils on the zonal, regional, and district levels. Negotiations continued for more than half a year, and only in the winter of 1946–1947, after the resolution of disagreements between the Education Ministry and the union, was an accord reached regarding the councils' official rights and function. They were to play both a "consultative" and a "participatory" role in the German education system. Local and regional authorities, for example, were to consult them on individual cases involving the hiring, promoting, transferring, disciplining, and even dismissing of pedagogues. More direct participation consisted of the councils having "a seat and a vote" (*Sitz und Stimme*) on issues relating, among other things, to teachers' continued training, the regulation of holidays, the allotment of government apartments, and the creation and administration of social service facilities for teachers and pupils.[27]

The composition of the Brandenburg teachers' council operating in the second half of 1947 sheds light on the kind of pedagogue the local teaching staff elected to represent its interests. Elected in the late spring of 1947, the council consisted of five men and two women, all but one of whom had been teaching in Brandenburg since the 1930s. Although one young woman was a *Neulehrer* who had been trained in the first three-month-long course held in the fall of 1945, the other six pedagogues had been NSLB members and currently held high positions such as school superintendent and school principal. Their average age was 50. Elected as the council's chairman was the 62-year-old GLE Regional Executive Committee and LDPD member Johannes S.[28]

Performing a variety of relevant functions that included operating as a clearinghouse for teachers' concerns and issues, Brandenburg's council quickly established itself as an important ally and advocate of the city's teachers. At the meeting held on 26 June 1947, it reviewed on a case-by-case basis various appeals, grievances, and claims submitted by individual pedagogues. It voted, for instance, to permit one previously dismissed Nazi teacher to tutor pupils. Successfully thwarting the efforts of the mayor to fire a teacher because of the content of a talk he had delivered before the war, the council refused to issue a statement denouncing the pedagogue. The requests of four purged Nazi teachers for reinstatement were reviewed, and the council gave its support to three of them. Ultimately deciding to postpone the matter for further review, the council even went so far as to consider endorsing the application of one of the city's most notorious Nazi pedagogues, a former driving force behind the NSLB district chapter, for the right to give extracurricular academic instruction to pupils. At a meeting held on 30 August 1948, the council objected to the authorities' decision to transfer to outside the district a secondary school teacher who had been working in Brandenburg since 1931, citing Brandenburg's need for such highly trained and experienced pedagogues.[29]

The council also assisted the union in protecting currently employed teachers. In one episode in the early fall of 1947, the union, in concert with at least some political parties, protested regional education officials' recent efforts to punish and even fire teachers for alleged "political inadequacy" (*politische Unzulänglichkeit*). The Education Ministry responded by distributing revised guidelines to principals and school superintendents that prohibited summary dismissals of pedagogues. Teachers suspected of not supporting the "antifascist" postwar order were instead to be investigated, a process that included interviewing both the accused and witnesses, with the council participating in the process. The results of the investigation, as well as the council's opinion in the matter, were then to be forwarded to the regional Education Ministry's personnel department.[30] Although neither GLE chapters nor teachers' councils could completely protect teachers from dismissals or demotions, their inclusion in disciplinary proceedings unrelated to denazification enabled them to work to blunt the state's efforts to target individual teachers for political reasons.

The Teachers' Union and Denazification

One of the most effective means by which the GLE won the support of most teachers was its intervention on their behalf in the denazification process that lasted from 1945 to 1948. The union formally and informally served as an advocate of both individual teachers and eastern Germany's teaching staff generally in negotiations with Soviet and German authorities. Usually falling short of outright opposition, GLE lobbying of local and regional authorities focused from the outset on securing lenient treatment by Brandenburg's denazification commissions and eventually expanded to include supporting reinstatement appeals of purged pedagogues. A letter written by a high-ranking union functionary to German officials illuminates both the GLE's theoretical position and tactical course of action regarding denazification. While acknowledging the importance of transforming the teaching staff and even recognizing the complicity of many teachers in the Third Reich's crimes, the union nonetheless argued against a thorough purge of pedagogues. According to the GLE, postwar Germany's current needs argued against broad punitive measures:

> We must stress even more emphatically that among the many teachers who were only nominal members of the Nazi Party there are individuals who are not only useful but wanted, yes, who are necessary in a democratic Germany for service in the education of our youth and whose assistance we cannot do without. It would not only be a wrong committed against these teachers but would in addition seriously endanger the entire education project if, from the beginning, one were to equate them with those Nazis described above [in the letter] and without exception remove them immediately from the schools.[31]

Moreover, the union argued that most party members had been coerced to join the NSDAP and, in fact, millions had inwardly "hated the system." Threats and extortion, often at the hands of ambitious NSDAP local group leaders, had driven many teachers and other civil servants into the Nazi Party. Teachers, the union argued, were no more susceptible to Nazism than other professional groups, although the "monstrous pressure" pedagogues had been subjected to was unique. Finally, it was erroneous to assume a correlation between simple membership in the NSDAP and pro-Nazi attitudes and actions; many nonmembers in fact had supported Hitler and his policies. The letter concluded:

> We see not only a great injustice but also a danger for the democratic Germany that is developing if these workers, who are absolutely willing to rebuild and who according to their disposition are antifascists like us, are forced into the camp of reaction and negation, of resistance and rejection. Do we want to repeat the mistake of the Weimar Republic, which failed at the outset to win over to its side the proletarianized bourgeois circles?[32]

There is no record of union officials involving themselves in the first stage of denazification, the series of summary dismissals conducted by local German and Soviet officials in the summer and early fall of 1945. Explanations for the union's noninvolvement include both the nature of the early purges—the August dismissals, for example, as noted, largely represented an administrative accounting of the teaching staff in Brandenburg—and the fact that, since the FDGB and the GLE's founding congresses did not take place until the spring and summer of 1946, respectively, the city's teachers still lacked formal institutions through which they could express their collective voice vis-à-vis the authorities.

The publication of Allied Control Council Directive No. 24 in January 1946 represented a significant broadening and intensification of denazification efforts. In an effort to remove from positions of responsibility—a concept that included teachers—all who either had been an active Nazi or were currently opposed to the Allies, the measure detailed not only the criteria for denazification but also set out state actions regarding a lengthy catalog of Nazi-era positions and activities. Almost immediately union officials made their reservations known. In a letter to Paul Wandel, head of the DVfV, GLE Executive Committee member Köhn argued that civil servants and other white-collar workers were again being unfairly singled out for scrutiny and possibly punishment. Köhn admonished Wandel to ensure that current denazification measures applied to all German economic groups, including tradesmen and businessmen. Should the state continue to dismiss politically reliable, professionally capable, and irreplaceable pedagogues, he warned, "it will mean an evisceration of the activists for a democratic Germany and a strengthening of the forces of reaction."[33]

Beginning in the second half of 1946, the GLE stepped up its advocacy as a consequence of state agencies starting to direct their denazification efforts at teachers. The regional chapter began to complain as early as October 1946 about the many cases in which the Brandenburg Province administration had summarily dismissed or transferred pedagogues.[34] Moreover, the union's influence moved beyond mere criticism, once trade unions began to participate directly in the local and regional denazification commissions. As the FDGB representatives to Brandenburg's Commission for the Implementation of Directive 24, two trade unionists in late 1946 and early 1947 had a voice in evaluating former Nazis, helping to determine their complicity and possibly assigning punishment. An FDGB official joined representatives from each political party and from "democratic" organizations such as the FDJ and the Democratic German Women's League in staffing the Brandenburg Denazification Commission that in late 1947 and early 1948 investigated the city's teachers, among other social and professional categories. The FDGB's participation, however, did not guarantee that a teacher or a GLE functionary served on the Commission. The three FDGB men involved in city denazification efforts from 1946 to 1948 were neither teachers nor members of the teachers' union. The voting record of one of the men, a 50-year-old electrician who had belonged to the SPD before and after the Third Reich, nonetheless illustrates the not insignificant advocacy role unions could play on the Denazification Commission. On more than one occasion, he opposed some of his fellow committee members, including Brandenburg's Communist mayor, and voted to allow former Nazis to continue working in the schools.[35]

Rather than leaving teachers' fates in the hands of a couple of FDGB officials, the teachers' union also pursued alternative strategies in its efforts to defend members' interests. One tactic was explicit noncompliance with administrative measures. A contest of wills took place in December 1947 between the Brandenburg union chapter and local authorities regarding teachers' compliance with a recent order issued by the school superintendent requiring them to submit an additional, more detailed questionnaire covering, among other things, their previous political memberships and activities. Objecting to this document, the chairman of the union chapter, an SED member, enlisted the teachers' council's assistance in an attempt to persuade the school superintendent not to implement the measure on the grounds that it would spark new unrest among the pedagogues. Faced with the school superintendent's obstinacy, however, the union appealed to its members to ignore the measure. The episode ended with the super-intendent filing a protest with Potsdam regarding this "obstruction-ist action."[36]

In addition to working to blunt the effects of the denazification mea-sures, the union also campaigned to reinstate some teachers who had been dismissed as a consequence of their Nazi activities and affiliations. Follow-ing the recent publication of an administration measure that formally per-mitted the rehiring of Nazis under certain conditions, the regional GLE chapter in November 1947 boldly decided to cease its usual practice of consulting with Soviet authorities before taking action regarding the rein-statement of individual teachers. Issued in March 1948, SMA Order No. 35 represented the formal end of denazification. In addition to shutting down the commissions, the decree broadened the kind and number of cat-egories of former Nazi teachers who could be reemployed by the schools. Teachers who wished to be considered for reinstatement had to apply to an Evaluating Commission comprised of the school superintendent and union representatives. The GLE of Brandenburg Province even went so far as to compel the Education Ministry in August 1948 to agree, when filling posi-tions with former Nazis, to give preference to men and women currently living in Brandenburg Province before hiring former Nazis transferring into the region.[37]

Around the same time, Brandenburg's GLE chapter and teachers' coun-cil were closely examining individual pedagogues' cases in order to deter-mine who qualified for reemployment. Having reviewed 16 cases, the GLE in February 1948 rejected outright a small number of them. Of the rest, half were set aside for further review and half received the union's endorse-ment for reinstatement. Picking up where the union had left off, the teach-ers' council five months later formally asked the school superintendent to intervene with education officials in Potsdam so that a number of former Nazis—including some whose reinstatement had been considered in the February meeting—could be rehired. Those who were approved to return to the classrooms included an equal mixture of men and women, some of whom had held leadership positions in the NSV, the League of German Girls, or even the NSDAP. Almost half had begun teaching in Branden-burg before Hitler's assumption of power.[38] Moreover, records indicate that such efforts could be successful. To take one example, a former party member and Nazi welfare organization block leader who received the local union leadership's endorsement was returned to the classroom, where he remained well into the 1950s. Other individuals continued for years to seek reinstatement. Finally, even high-ranking GLE officials pursued quasi-independent policies of seeking to place individual Nazis back into the classroom. As part of a general denunciation of the political climate within the city's schools and teaching staff, Brandenburg's Communist school superintendent accused GLE chapter chairman and regional Executive Committee member Johannes S. of working to rehabilitate and reinstate two former Nazis, one of whom ultimately was rehired.[39] Although there was never a simple or automatic mechanism of reentry for dismissed Nazis, the union and the affiliated teachers' council sought successfully to return some to the schools.

Membership among Brandenburg's Teachers in the GLE and the SED

As a result of an enduring and multifaceted advocacy campaign—one that lasted from the union's inception up to and through the GDR's creation—the GLE became an important institution to which pedagogues collectively and individually turned for assistance. One important manifestation of this was the union's exceptional success in convincing pedagogues to join it. Recruitment efforts for the FDGB among Brandenburg teachers yielded impressive results long before the formal establishment of a local chapter. Membership levels for Brandenburg's GLE in the spring of 1946 hovered between 200 and 250. Following the formal creation of both a regional and a local chapter at the founding congress held in June 1946, membership levels increased significantly, reaching close to 350 by October and remaining at that level for the rest of the year. This upward surge was maintained throughout 1947, and by the spring of 1948 Brandenburg's GLE had more than 400 members.[40] A closer examination of membership levels at individual Brandenburg schools at this time illustrates more clearly the extremely high degree of support among teachers for the union. At 12 of the 14 elementary or secondary schools in April 1948 every pedagogue had joined the GLE. There was no noteworthy difference in membership percentages between the elementary and secondary institutions; teachers at both were equally supportive of their professional organization, a situation that was significantly different from that of the NSLB in the early Third Reich. There were also no significant differences in the membership patterns between men and women and between older teachers and younger pedagogues.[41] These membership data powerfully illustrate the degree to which the teaching staff had been transformed since 1933. The tradition of an organizationally fragmented teaching staff that had persisted well into the Third Reich—exemplified by secondary school teachers' reluctance to join the NSLB and by its structure in departments that corresponded to customary divisions, and that had only been erased by the deprofessionalization process that accompanied the Second World War—did not reemerge in the postwar era. Membership rose to just under 500 by the end of 1948 and remained there up to the founding of the GDR in October 1949.[42]

Whereas their trade union colleagues in the GLE successfully recruited teachers with consistent and serious efforts, German Communists began to try to win over the city's teaching staff only slowly and with some confusion. That the Brandenburg KPD began as early as September 1945 to concern itself with the teaching staff's composition, its activities, and, most significantly, the right of the KPD to influence the hiring and placement of pedagogues seemed to signal its interest in local school issues. But Brandenburg's Communists failed to follow through on this initiative, choosing instead to conform to a de facto overall KPD political and ideological strategy that focused party energies and efforts in this immediate postwar period on more traditional Communist sources of support such as industrial laborers.[43] Accordingly, the largely nonexistent efforts of local party functionaries failed to increase the very small number of teachers who had joined the KPD. By the winter of 1945–1946, there were only three KPD members among a teaching staff of 268 men and women. Twelve had joined the SPD. Even more ominous, the great majority—172, or 64 percent—had decided against joining any political party, a significant phenomenon that would continue through the GDR's early years. Nor did the situation improve in the spring and summer of 1946. A small increase in memberships as of March 1946 was as much a result of officials simply merging the memberships of the SPD and KPD—despite the still incomplete merger of the two parties—as of party efforts to win over sympathetic pedagogues. This increase was more than matched by a spike in the number of teachers who still refused to join any party. Following the forced merger of the SPD and the KPD, the SED could claim to speak in June 1946 for only 9 percent of the city's teachers; 79 percent of them were "without any formal political affiliation" (parteilos).[44]

Despite being aware of the teachers' clear lack of interest in joining the SED, and increasingly fearful that politically active pedagogues were flocking to the CDU and the LDPD, Brandenburg's Communists nonetheless failed throughout 1946 to do much, if anything, to improve the situation.

Plans to participate in teachers' assemblies in order to evaluate later what was said and done at them were followed by frank admissions of the party's inability to accomplish even these very limited goals. Such inconsistent and halfhearted efforts yielded lackluster results. After more than 18 months of Communists playing a predominant role in the postwar reconstruction of the state, society, and economy, a process that included putting not inconsequential numbers of *Neulehrer* in the classroom, the SED could count only 57 pedagogues—17 percent of the city's total—among its members in December 1946. Although the percentage of politically unaffiliated pedagogues had decreased to 61 percent, the number of combined CDU and LDPD members now exceeded that of the SED for the first time.[45]

The creation in December 1946 of a special group of pro-SED teachers could be interpreted as an example of a new commitment by the party to mobilize, control, and even expand more effectively its current membership base within the schools. The centerpiece of the first meeting—and a significant step in institutionalizing greater party control over this group of pedagogues—was the election of a three-person executive committee that consisted solely of individuals who had begun teaching in Brandenburg in the fall of 1945. Regular meetings of this "SED Teachers' Group" would enable the party to inform members of SED developments and decisions and to indoctrinate individuals by means of directed political discussions, all in a manner that theoretically improved on traditional means of and structures for mobilization. The report of the initial meeting, however, clearly reveals the continued general apathy among teachers—in this case even among the pro-Communist teachers—that had posed an obstacle from the beginning. Although more than 60 of the city's 375 teachers had joined the SED by the fall of 1947, less than half were present for the group's inaugural meeting. Nor did things improve for the SED Teachers' Group. Party officials in October 1947 were forced to convene another constitutive meeting to select a new executive, since the previous leaders had all recently left Brandenburg. Even fewer pro-Communist teachers bothered to attend this time; only 16 of the 63 pedagogues turned up.[46]

These SED efforts proved largely ineffectual, and the number and percentage of pedagogues who had joined the party did not increase significantly. For example, only 3 of the 16 teachers at one Brandenburg secondary school were party members in March 1947. Dwarfing this pro-Communist faction in the school were both the six teachers who belonged to either the CDU or LDPD and the seven who were *parteilos*. By the time the school year ended four months later, one of the SED members had switched to the LDPD, further reducing the numerical and symbolic strength of the SED in this particular school. Membership in the GLE during the same period remained at 100 percent.[47]

Subsequent developments such as increased SED efforts in August 1947 to recruit *Neulehrer* did little to change the teaching staff's overall party affiliations. As of October 1947, 22 percent of Brandenburg's teaching staff had joined the SED. An additional 16 and 12 percent were members of the LDPD and CDU, respectively. The remaining 50 percent of the city's pedagogues had no formal affiliations to a political party. Nor did the situation change significantly in the following year. Of the almost 300 teachers in the elementary and secondary schools in late 1948, only 73 (25 percent) belonged to the SED, a slight increase from the 57 pedagogues in October 1947. Of the 300, 149 were classified as *parteilos* (50 percent) and 287 had joined the FDGB (97 percent).[48]

A comparison of the SED membership data of Brandenburg's teachers with that of the entire teaching staff of the region underscores the relatively lukewarm support for the party among Brandenburg teachers, as seen in the table below.

The low membership statistics were only one manifestation of a much larger problem facing the SED. Local party dissatisfaction with the attitudes of the city's teachers was also an expression of a more general fear that German Communists were failing to create a teaching staff that would assist in the transformation of German society. "The Party is dissatisfied with the political views and orientation of the younger and older teachers

Table 5.1 Percentage of teachers who were KPD/SED members

	Winter 1945/1946	Winter 1946/1947	October 1947	May 1948
Brandenburg an der Havel	10%	17%	22%	25%
Brandenburg Province	18%	35%	38%	35%

Source: Untitled statistical analyses, BLHA, Rep 205A Ministerium für Volksbildung, no. 217: 7 and 14, and "Stand der Schulen," no. 216: 4; "Volksbildung 1947 in Brandenburg," StadtA Brandenburg, 2.0.12/1/225, 5; "Bericht über das Brandenburger Schulleben vom Mai 1945 zum Mai 1948," StadtA Brandenburg, 2.0.12/17/241, 166; "Stand der Organisation" for 28 February 1947, 31 October 1947, and 13 May 1948, BLHA, Ld. Br. Rep 333 SED-Landesvorstand Brandenburg, no. 223: 11, 24, and 76.

[*Neu- und Altlehrer*]," one regional SED functionary claimed at a March 1948 meeting of party and state education officials, unknowingly echoing similar complaints made years earlier by Nazi state and party officials. Necessary reforms, he argued, included improving the ideological training of pro-Communist teachers as well as according them greater institutional influence in the education system.[49] Admitting that the large majority of the city's teachers were not affiliated with political parties and decrying the lack of teacher participation in "democratic" organizations such as the FDJ, Brandenburg's school superintendent in June 1948 identified the political education of the city's teachers as an "absolute necessity" of future state and party work.[50]

On the eve of the founding of the GDR in 1949, Brandenburg SED officials continued to complain vociferously about the city's teaching staff. At a Secretariat Meeting of the Brandenburg SED held in May 1949, deputy school superintendent and SED member Fritz S. reported "that of the 450 teachers, 80 belong to the SED, though one can describe only a few of these as activists. There exists here a firmly built bourgeois teachers' organization. Of the 24 principals only 6 are SED members and of these only 3 are dependable. The LDP[D] and the CDU predominate at various schools; not a single secondary school teacher is associated with the SED."[51] To rectify the situation in places like Brandenburg, one regional SED official in June 1949 advocated dealing with the matter forcefully "in order to eliminate all unsuitable forces."[52]

As the SED quickly discovered, "unsuitable forces" among Brandenburg's teachers included much more than just the *parteilos* and other non-Communists. The SED was dissatisfied with the attitudes and actions of those teachers who, in the eyes of the German Communists, should have been actively working to build a "democratic" education system: men and women who had either joined the party and/or who were responsible for training the next generation of pedagogues. Regional SED officials in December 1947 rebuked the Brandenburg chapter of the party for the poor performance of its Teachers' Group. A month earlier, regional SED officials had complained to the Education Ministry about the staff at Brandenburg's teacher training institute for the Russian language. Examples of the instructors' alleged "political indifference" included critical statements they had made on a number of topics. In a discussion that was supposed to commemorate the Russian Revolution, the instructor had advised the students to form their own opinions regarding the event. To take another example, a teacher in a class discussion had clearly expressed his dislike of the "democratic" cooperatives the state and party were introducing to the Zone.[53]

Conclusion

The failure of the SED to mobilize the great majority of the city's teachers in the period 1945–1949 does not indicate a general and widespread rejection of the postwar order. Although the majority of Brandenburg's pedagogues remained *parteilos* in this period, almost all of them joined one new organization, the GLE. They joined the teachers' union for many reasons, but the most important was not state or party compulsion but the union's clear record of effective advocacy on behalf of the teachers. Complaining about the widespread political apathy among pedagogues in Brandenburg and Magdeburg, education officials noted in the spring of 1947 that "the teachers yearn for clarification of their economic and legal situation and for a final resolution to the incriminating questionnaires."[54] The GLE worked to address these concerns. From pressuring authorities in 1945 to pay teachers' salaries to endorsing some former Nazis' reinstatement applications, the union's activities responded to some, even though not all, of the pedagogues' fears, concerns, and desires. Reviewing the union activities of the past year, GLE Central Committee chairman Richard Schallock stated in December 1946: "we have in our common struggle accomplished for our colleagues a lot in terms of economic support and some in terms of legal protection. 1947 will confront us with great tasks . . . Particularly our social and legal safeguarding will be extraordinary work for our organization."[55]

Fundamental to the GLE's willingness and ability to "safeguard" teachers' interests were the committed, politically nonradical men and women who ran the Brandenburg chapter. The school superintendent in early 1950 described the nature of the local union and its leadership:

> The conference [to elect a new Executive Committee] displayed the usual picture, the complete predominance of the petit bourgeois [*kleinbürgerlich*] teaching staff of Brandenburg, under the strict intellectual leadership of the former school superintendent Senkpiel, who has been working in Brandenburg for 40 years. Except for the group of socialist teachers and the representatives of the Russian Seminar, a sense of self-awareness or even

class-consciousness was not noticeable. Instead, there was an almost slavish [*helotenhaft*] dependence on those running the union conference.[56]

This "usual picture" had been sustained by a 15-person local Executive Committee that consisted of six Liberal Democrats, two Christian Democrats, one National Democrat, five Communists, and one *parteilos*. Efforts by the school superintendent in the spring of 1949 to add young Communists to the committee were rebuffed by Johannes S., who eventually convinced the teaching staff to appoint instead three young LDPD pedagogues. Left with no more than a third of the union leadership, the SED had been prevented from taking control of Brandenburg's GLE. Seven of the pedagogues elected in 1949 had been teaching since at least before the war. Moreover, more than one-third of the leadership had been hired since August 1945 and had joined either the LDPD or CDU.[57] With such men and women running the chapter, the local union did not have a difficult job of projecting a serious, politically moderate image to the city's teachers.

In a number of ways, from the leadership's composition to its activities, the teachers' union clearly demonstrated to the city's teachers the significant difference between itself and the NSLB. Whereas the GLE saw itself as the teachers' representative, the NSLB had refused to consider itself a traditional trade union and instead had focused its efforts on disseminating National Socialist propaganda and ideologically transforming Germany's teaching force. As one NSLB functionary stated in the 1930s, "the NSLB never focuses its struggle on professional, bureaucratic, pay or hiring questions. Its will has always centered on the ideological penetration of German education, the fight for political power in the state and the cleansing of our cultural life from all Marxist destructive tendencies."[58] Similarly, the GLE's abstinence from direct or substantial participation in the political and ideological indoctrination of teachers both distinguished it from its predecessor and illuminates another reason why so many Brandenburg teachers supported it. Although it did assist state authorities in limited forms of political and pedagogical retraining in the summer and fall of 1945, the state quickly assumed primary responsibility for all forms of continued education and training. Unlike the NSLB, the GLE did not set up and administer training camps in the city or region.[59] In the eyes of the pedagogues who began teaching before the war and continued to do so after 1945, the many examples of the GLE's advocacy of their interests contrasted sharply with the actions and attitude of the NSLB.

The GLE also distinguished itself from the NSLB by striving to maintain its relative political autonomy, even to the extent of sometimes disagreeing or clashing with the SED. Struggling to fulfill its potentially contradictory obligations to both the "democratic" postwar order and to East Germany's pedagogues, the GLE charted a precarious course in its policies. The regional GLE chapter in December 1946 reiterated its fundamental prohibition on privileging one party over another. More important, such statements were backed up by union actions. SED officials were angry, for instance, that GLE preparations for union elections in early 1947 did not involve the SED. Almost two years later, the GLE again felt the need to demonstrate its institutional autonomy. Following a wave of severe criticism of the regional union by the SED and the FDJ, GLE officials strongly defended their actions, calling on the union to continue to act independently of the SED and the administration.[60]

On the eve of the founding of the GDR, the GLE fulfilled an important function in its members' lives, and by doing so helped to integrate them into the postwar "democratic" order. The union's ability to sustain itself in the face of the coming sovietization of the state and society would have enormous significance for the teachers, especially regarding their response to the social, political, and economic discontent that sparked the first popular revolt against the East German government, the Uprising of 17 June.

CHAPTER 6

The Sovietization of Teachers and Their Union

The founding of the GDR in October 1949 changed very little for Brandenburg's GLE. The District Executive Committee remained in the hands of non-Communist pedagogues who were committed to fighting for the teaching staff's material, legal, and social improvement. In his report on the union's district delegate conference that took place in early 1950, one local Communist official described the Brandenburg chapter:

> The conference showed clearly from the very beginning that the forces of the bourgeois parties were beyond a doubt stronger and were aware of their strength . . . there were several serious clashes between the colleagues from the bourgeois parties and the colleagues from the SED, though it was very clear that the bourgeois parties, as a result of the fairly united manner of the SED teachers, formed an equally united front. Thus Colleague [Johannes] S. appeared to be the most powerful figure within the Brandenburg teaching staff as well as the leader of the bourgeois group. Election results for the position of Chairman revealed 64 votes for S. (LDP[D]), 37 for K. (SED), one invalid return. . . . For the position of Deputy Chairman 62 votes were again given to the representative of the bourgeois parties (CDU). . . . One reason [for these results] lies in the poor political composition of the entire teaching staff. If one considers [party] membership alone, there are as many SED teachers as there are pedagogues who support the two bourgeois parties (LDP[D] and CDU) combined. Moreover, the SED has met with absolutely no response from the teaching staff because the school superintendent has

up to now not understood [the need] to work together with the progressive and useful parts of the bourgeois teaching staff.[1]

Divided almost equally between men and women, the citywide union leadership (now officially referred to as the *Betriebsgewerkschaftsleitung,* BGL) elected in March 1950 consisted of seven Liberal Democrats, seven Christian Democrats, one National Democrat, two SED members, and five individuals without any formal political affiliation. Older pedagogues who had been teaching in Brandenburg since the late 1930s continued to make up a sizeable portion—just under a third—of the 20 teachers elected to the BGL. A slightly larger number of committee members were *Neulehrer* who supported non-Communist parties such as the CDU, the LDPD, and the National Democratic Party. Although an additional seven BGL members had begun teaching in Brandenburg after 1945 under less discernible circumstances that could include having been transferred to the city or having arrived as refugees from the East, none had joined the SED. The conference delegates' refusal to support a SED list of candidates consisting largely of Communists represented a direct repudiation of the party's conception of who should run the union.[2]

Local and regional union officials continued to defend the interests of the teaching staff despite the significant political changes that had taken place in the Soviet Zone between 1945 and 1949. In late 1950 when Potsdam failed to provide the required amount of coal to the region's teachers, regional union officials telegraphed a threat to notify the press; the day after the union sent the telegram, the coal was delivered. Moreover, the union continued to pressure the regional government to supply teachers with, for example, special clothes suitable for working with pupils in laboratories or machine shops. Similarly, efforts continued to return to the classroom pedagogues who had been dismissed in connection with the denazification process. The union also tried to shield its members from government interference. In late 1949 when the school superintendent began a campaign to replace many of the older, *Altlehrer* principals with younger, presumably more politically acceptable teachers, onetime postwar school superintendent Johannes S., a Liberal Democrat and former deputy principal of the Weimar-era Secular School, led the union in a lengthy "tough struggle" with the administration—a largely successful effort to retain the experienced pedagogues.[3]

These continuities of personnel, attitude, and activities were soon seriously challenged by the Communist state and party. This chapter investigates the sovietization of the teaching staff and its union that began in the late 1940s and accelerated in the early 1950s. Unlike existing accounts of the sovietization of the East German state and society, however, the story of Brandenburg's teachers illustrates the significant difficulties the SED state faced in implementing its policies. This chapter examines the process by which the teachers' union was transformed by East German Communists into a genuine "transmission belt" designed to support SED activities and policies, seeking to determine whether, for example, the changes occurred much later than has been traditionally understood and were actively contested by the teaching staff. To what extent can one speak of an incomplete victory for the SED state as of the mid-1950s? Had the union by 1953 completely redirected its efforts away from securing the material needs of the teaching staff and toward the political mobilization of the teachers? Or do the actions of Brandenburg's GLE into the 1950s illustrate the continuity of certain practices and attitudes from the presovietized period? Finally, did the experience of East German Communists in retooling the GLE to serve as a political and ideological instrument mirror the serious difficulties the Nazis encountered in their efforts to mobilize Germany's teachers politically by means of the NSLB?

In addition to analyzing GLE practices in the period 1949–1953, this chapter also seeks to determine the extent of the political and ideological co-optation of Brandenburg's teachers by means of a detailed study of their behavior during the greatest challenge to the nascent East German dictatorship, the Uprising of 17 June 1953. Three important questions are raised here: first, did the city's teachers join the more than 15,000 Brandenburgers who assaulted manifestations of the SED state, including representatives of the state and the party, or did they refrain from any participation in the violent expression of popular dissatisfaction? As enormous mobs sacked the local SED headquarters, for example, stormed the city's jail, and nearly hanged a judge in a central square, did the pedagogues stay in their classrooms or take to the streets? Second, if the pedagogues failed to revolt, how do we explain their absence? The answer is not that the uprising was exclusively an eruption of working-class discontent with factory or workplace conditions, for neither the causes of the uprising nor the composition of the participants were limited to one class. Rather, two interrelated factors require further analysis: Brandenburg teachers' deep-seated and long-developed ability to adapt with a minimum of friction to radically changing political, social, and economic circumstances and the GLE's continued functioning as an integrative link between its members and the state. Might the teachers' actions during the uprising mark a culmination of more than 20 years of limited participation in the major events and processes in Germany? Finally, what impact did such behavior—not only during the uprising but also inside the classroom in the early 1950s— have on the East German dictatorship? Did the enduring continuities—of personnel, attitude, and activities—ultimately stabilize or undermine the Communist regime? The story of Brandenburg's teachers in the early GDR, culminating in the Uprising of 17 June, raises the possibility that Germany's teachers stabilized the East German dictatorship in much the same way they had Hitler's state in the Third Reich.

The Incomplete Sovietization of the GLE

Despite the efforts of men like Johannes S., in the course of the late 1940s the teachers' union underwent a process of sovietization that transformed its mission, structure, and functionary corps. Officials of the SED and the central GLE made significant personnel changes within the regional and local union leadership. By the spring of 1949, the central union and party authorities had orchestrated the replacement of some older members of the Brandenburg Province Executive Committee with younger functionaries who were both "unburdened" by pre-1933 union traditions and likely to have been deeply influenced by the SED; Alfred Wilke had taken over the chairmanship of the regional executive committee from Adolf Buchholz, a founding father and longtime head of the regional chapter. As one of its first acts, the new leadership formally adopted as guiding principles (*Leitgedanken*) the so-called Bitterfeld Resolutions, a set of directives that, among other things, emphasized the union's role in politically mobilizing its members. Whereas the union had been originally created for the defense of teachers' economic and social interests, it was now more concerned with helping the state meet its education goals by means of the "tighter organization of education [and] the fulfillment of the lesson plans." In order to accomplish these goals, the regional leadership more than doubled the union's budget for the political training of teachers so that they could learn to "feel and act in a democratic sense." As part of this, the GLE launched a campaign to eradicate the allegedly reactionary "objectivist" worldview held by most East German teachers. Similarly, the regional organization worked with the state and party to disseminate Communist propaganda. In the fall and winter of 1950, for example, officials designated as a "special task" of the union the propagation of the content of the recent Prague Decrees, a tendentious call by the Soviet Union and other Eastern Bloc states for the demilitarization and reunification of the two German states.[4]

In June 1949 the union's structure was transformed. The central leadership stripped the previously democratically elected regional executive committee of its powers, thereby reducing it simply to rubber-stamping decisions and plans made by a nonelected executive, a "Sekretariat" consisting of the committee's chairman, deputy chairman, and head of the union bureaucracy. Similarly, the local committees or citywide leaderships lost their executive powers and were now authorized only to implement instructions received from the district and central leaderships. Finally, the union added to its organizational hierarchy a new level: union officials were to organize a school union group (*Schulgewerkschaftsgruppe*) in every school. These groups, lead by an executive (*Schulgewerkschaftsleitung*), would constitute the lowest level of the union structure. Since they extended the direct reach of the central union organization beyond the local level, as had previously been the case, the school union groups offered state, party, and union leaders potentially better means for mobilizing East Germany's teachers. In April 1950 union officials reported that as a consequence of both the proliferation of *Schulgewerkschaftsgruppen* and the appointment of pro-Communist union members as the groups' executives, the union's ability to carry out its programs had improved significantly.[5] The reorganization represented, in theory at least, the adoption of a Soviet organizational model—characterized by a politically conformist group of leaders and functionaries bound to one another in a highly centralized and hierarchical relationship by the bonds of what was called democratic centralism—for purposes other than representing workers' material and legal interests.[6]

These changes were not limited to the regional GLE but were part of a gradual and multifaceted process that was transforming all of the Soviet Zone's unions as well as their umbrella organization, the FDGB. Beginning in the late 1940s, this organization reconsidered its central role in East German society; instead of primarily representing its members' "material and legal situation," it increasingly saw its mission as the political and ideological mobilization of workers on behalf of the Communist Party and the state. The FDGB conference held in November 1948 in Bitterfeld, for instance, unleashed a campaign against *Nurgewerkschaftlertum* or "pure trade unionism," based on the Communist rejection of trade unions that emphasized representing workers instead of ideologically educating and mobilizing the masses. Recognizing the resistance of traditional and largely independent factory councils to the union's and the party's plans for the creation of a more politically and economically pliant workplace in which socialist norms regarding industrial discipline could be achieved, FDGB officials at the Bitterfeld conference announced the replacement of factory councils with a form of workers' representation that was formally subsumed in the trade union association. These local union leaderships would represent the lowest level of the trade union organization, but they would be, unlike the factory councils, directly accountable to the regional and central trade union organizations. Before officials could either start using the union for political purposes or set up a statewide system of local union leaderships, a more politically loyal, ideologically conformist group of union leaders and functionaries had to be created. Purges in 1948 and 1949 increased the number and influence of hard-line SED members in the FDGB by removing many former SPD members and some less radical Communists from its leadership and administration. Taken as a whole, the reforms represented a significant loss of independence both for the union vis-à-vis the SED and the state and for the local and regional union organizations vis-à-vis central leadership.[7]

After the creation of the GDR, the intensity and pace of the union's sovietization increased. The clearest expression of this process was its new constitution, adopted at its third congress in the late summer of 1950 and ratified at a zonal congress in February 1951. The changes embodied in the new constitution also effected the FDGB's subordinate organizations, including the GLE. Its Communist leaders adopted the principles of democratic centralism and reordered the GLE's set of operational priorities such that working to secure better wages and housing for teachers now ranked behind cajoling them to work harder. Members' duties now included respecting, increasing, and protecting collectivized property (*Volkseigentum*) and "using all of one's strength for the fulfillment und even early completion of the Five-Year Plan."[8] A policy paper neatly summarized the role of the transformed teachers' union:

The Union . . . works constantly toward raising the political consciousness of its members. The union educates its members in the spirit of proletarian internationalism. . . . The union supports state planning and steering of the economy. It mobilizes its members for the fulfillment of the Five-Year Plan. . . . It stands firmly behind the class struggle. Its goal is a socialist ordering of society. It is a school of democracy and socialism. The Union . . . leads a decisive struggle against all manifestations of opportunism, against *Nurgewerkschaftlertum* and bureaucratic tendencies because only in this way can the fighting power and unity of the union be strengthened and the great social tasks carried out. It can only successfully lead this struggle if criticism and self-criticism become a component of all union activities. . . . All the union's work has the goal of enlightening the workers in the German democratic schools about the tasks that arise from their societal mission and providing them with all the necessary ideological, professional, and material help necessary to carry out these tasks.[9]

Brandenburg's GLE chapter did not escape the sovietization process, even though it started relatively late and proceeded gradually and somewhat fitfully. State and party officials recognized that the precondition for any substantive transformation of the local chapter was a purge of its leadership. Previous attempts at creating a more conformist leadership, one in which more Communist teachers served, had failed. School Superintendent M. in the spring of 1949 proposed adding two younger, SED teachers to the allegedly gerontocratic union leadership. He encountered serious opposition from chapter officials, however, who ultimately thwarted his plans by orchestrating instead the appointment of three Liberal Democrats.[10]

Communist agitation against Brandenburg's BGL—especially its composition and general attitude—became more substantial immediately after the SED defeat in the chapter elections held in the spring of 1950 and increased over the next 12 months. In the spring of 1951, on the eve of elections for a new, sovietized BGL, Brandenburg party leaders wrote that "the composition of the leadership does not correspond in any way to the makeup of our city. The work of the teachers' union was also not satisfactory. The BGL saw its entire mission as worrying about material things (coffee, apples, and shoes, etc.)."[11] Beginning in the winter of 1950–1951 and accelerating in the spring, local SED officials and education authorities, in conjunction with the regional GLE, began a campaign to overthrow

Brandenburg's BGL. The first move was a wave of complaints and "requests" sent to the regional GLE leadership, first by Communist teachers' groups and then, days later, by school union groups. The letter from the SED Teachers' Group for the Goethe School, Girls Division, for example, demanded a reorganization of the BGL because of its allegedly poor ideological and technical training activities.[12] "The BGL demonstrated in its activities of the past year that it in no way is equal to its tasks," another SED teachers' group claimed. "Its work is only stuck in a *Nurgewerkschaftlertum* that fails to extend to the local groups [*Grundeinheiten*]."[13] Despite the vitriol of some of these letters, almost half of Brandenburg's union school groups submitted nothing. Moreover, officials conceded that no more than "approximately" 40 percent of the pedagogues who had attended the teachers' assemblies convened in some schools at the request of the regional union had voted for the BGL's recall.[14]

The letter campaign gave the regional union leadership a pretext to intervene. At an emergency union meeting held in mid-February 1951, after denouncing Brandenburg's BGL, the regional leadership dissolved it and assumed its rights and responsibilities. Claiming that the BGL had "done all it could to improve the teachers' economic situation," Johannes S. publicly defended it and its actions, but to little effect. Elections for a new BGL were scheduled for mid-April.[15] Although the FDGB and Communist mass organizations such as the FDJ and the Democratic German Women's League were supposed to nominate the candidates, the SED quickly drew up a list of acceptable candidates and then, in March, met with the FDGB and the other Communist mass organizations to discuss the SED's "suggestions." Of the 17 men and women the SED then proposed, 9 were SED members. Neither the Liberal Democrats, the Christian Democrats, nor the National Democrats were to command a large, potentially oppositional block of representatives; the SED intended to limit these non-SED parties' potential influence by dividing the remaining eight positions somewhat equally among them. Finally, the fact that none of the candidates were *parteilos* meant that all of them were by virtue of their party affiliations formally part of the established political structure and thus not beyond the SED's reach.[16]

On 14 April 1951 delegate teachers selected by the teaching staffs of the individual schools assembled at a district delegate conference in order to review and then vote on the proposed candidates. In pathos-laden opening remarks, a regional teachers' union official stated that the aim was to "elect

colleagues who will guarantee an improvement in the political and pedagogical work [of the union] and thus guarantee peace. Today the best and
most progressive forces must be elected to the BGL so that a mother will
never again weep over her son."[17] In order to ensure this, state, party, and
union officials had mobilized and most likely pressured the individual
school union groups to select proregime delegates. Although the teaching
staff was divided at this time, with roughly half of its members having no
formal affiliation with any party and only a third belonging to the SED, 31
(53 percent) and 19 (33 percent) of the 58 delegates were SED and *parteilos*, respectively. Similarly, the percentage of delegates representing the
CDU or LDPD was smaller than the teachers' traditional level of support
for these two parties—approximately 20 percent since the late fall of 1946.
The SED had successfully created an unrepresentative and presumably
more pliant group of delegates.[18]

A closer examination of the candidates reveals, however, both the strength
and limitations of the SED's power. In March, after the SED had put forward its 17 suggested candidates, the FDGB and the SED-dominated Communist mass organizations, had not nominated them all but had considered
only 13 of them. Moreover, these 13 had been forced to compete against an
additional 17 candidates that these organizations had added.[19]

The SED's screening of the candidates at the conference, nonetheless,
enabled it to direct the proceedings and ultimately to shape the composition of the new local leadership. Faced with a number of candidates who
had not been nominated by the SED, state and party officials used these
candidates' nonmembership in various "democratic" organizations as an
ideological and political bludgeon to weed them out on the grounds that
they could not be considered committed activists. Candidates who had not
joined the Society for German-Soviet Friendship (Gesellschaft für Deutsch-
sowjetische Freundschaft, DSF)—a creation of the Communist Party—
were grilled, even verbally attacked, so severely that some chose to
withdraw from the election. In more than one instance, the delegates dis-
qualified a teacher who refused to join the DSF. The case of one female
teacher employed in Brandenburg schools since before the war illustrates
particularly well the degree of control the SED exercised in the overtly political proceedings. As part of their public evaluation of her suitability, officials and other members demanded to know why she had not joined the
DSF and the Democratic German Women's League. Her claim that her
teaching itself demonstrated a commitment to East Germany and its values

failed to satisfy her inquisitors; they put a number of questions to her regarding Russian history and pedagogy. The candidate defended her actions by stating that "it is important to be a freedom fighter [*Friedenskämpfer*], and that does not depend on memberships," quoting a well-known statement by GDR minister-president Otto Grotewohl. Unconvinced, her opponents moved to strike her from the candidates' list. The objection of one delegate that she deserved to serve on the BGL in order to represent the interests of the many older Brandenburg pedagogues was met with the response that younger, presumably pro-SED teachers could also serve the needs of their older colleagues. Her name was removed from the list following a very close vote.[20]

The composition of the new BGL represented a clear victory for the SED. Only two men and one woman were reelected. More than half of the BGL's members now belonged to the ruling party, and all but one had started teaching in Brandenburg's schools after the war. Occupying only 5 of the 17 seats, women continued to constitute a minority, a decrease of 50 percent from the previous year. Moreover, the average age of the 11 for whom biographical data could be found was 30; since state records indicate that none of the other six had been teaching before 1945, their ages were very possibly not significantly different from those of their BGL colleagues.[21] Representing the culmination of party and FDGB political machinations, the new elections marked the formal end of the traditional union leadership of Brandenburg's teachers.

The purge of the BGL did not result in the complete sovietization of the GLE of Brandenburg. Just as recent scholarship has shed light on the difficulties encountered by the state and party in ensuring that their directives, orders, and policies were implemented on the regional and local levels, the history of Brandenburg's GLE in the early 1950s illustrates a fundamental duality of purpose and action, of intention and realization.[22] Serving two masters in an imperfect and occasionally contradictory manner, the union functioned as both a traditional union and a sovietized mass organization.

The local GLE pursued a strategy of political and ideological engagement that included mobilizing teachers' support for SED activities and policies. In June 1951 the GLE held a conference in order to inform Brandenburg's teachers and educators of recent FDJ, FDGB, and Education Ministry decisions, orders, and guidelines, as well as to promote government projects such as the role of the coming International Youth Games in

East Germany's peace campaign. In September 1951, Brandenburg's teachers' union (now renamed the Union of Teaching and Education: Gewerkschaft Unterricht und Erziehung, GUE) organized a rally to support purported efforts by the government to effect German unity and world peace. Holding signs that read "Carry Out the Government Decree" and "Unification with Our West German Brothers" and accompanied by music from FDJ bands, three large groups of teachers and pupils marched through the city to an assembly point, where they then heard speeches from local union officials explaining the recent East German unification initiatives and the GUE's plans to support them.[23] To take another example, union officials in October 1951 resolved to drum up support among its members for the DSF. "Since various [DSF] groups are still very weak, it is our special task to recruit new members. We want to intervene by visiting meetings, those meetings that fit into our general mission to be precise. Only 60 percent of Brandenburg's teachers are members of [the DSF]. This percentage must change considerably."[24] Dutifully fulfilling its function as a "transmission belt" for the state and the party, the supposedly sovietized union also set aside one afternoon each month for the purpose of training its members in Soviet pedagogy and regularly disseminated SED propaganda by means of "wall newspapers" (*Wandzeitungen*) and other public displays.[25]

In the period 1951–1953, however, the GUE also continued to advocate on behalf of its members' interests and still struggled, though in diminished fashion and under more difficult circumstances, to improve the conditions under which teachers' lived and worked. One important area of operational continuity for the local leadership was its continuing effort to reemploy teachers who had been dismissed because of their Nazi-era activities. Only a couple of months after the spring 1951 election, the leadership considered and more than once decided to support individual cases for reinstatement. The BGL, curiously, endorsed one female former Nazi's application even though the school superintendent had complained a year earlier that Johannes S.'s efforts to rehire her demonstrated the unprogressive nature of a local leadership led by him.[26] The case of a former elementary school principal who wished to return to the classroom illustrates the curious mixture of ideology, party politics, and staffing demands that often informed the BGL's decisions regarding the treatment of former Nazis. Appearing before the Brandenburg leadership, this principal admitted to having joined the Nazi Party in 1933 "out of conviction" and even having briefly held a leadership position in it. His postwar employment as a "coach-driver and rag-and-bone man [*Kutscher und Lumpensammler*]" proved to some local union leadership members that he had been transformed by the postwar "democratic" reforms. One, a National Democrat, supported the applicant, stating that "we take the view that every person has the right to work, and, to be precise, at that which corresponds to his abilities."[27] Other union leaders realized the applicant's usefulness to a school system still struggling to fill classrooms with pedagogues. The BGL voted to support his application following the declaration of one young Communist teacher that "we at the Goethe School (Boys) urgently need a specialized pedagogue [*Fachlehrer*] for physics and chemistry. He would certainly be the right man."[28] In another case considered in the fall of 1951, the union leadership endorsed the application of a man who had joined the Nazi Party and served in the *Waffen SS*.[29] Of the seven petitions considered in the period June 1951–May 1952, five were endorsed and two were rejected. Even these rejections were somewhat conditional: in one case the BGL did not rule out the possibility of reconsidering its decision at a future date, and in the other case the BGL forwarded the teacher's appeal for reinstatement to regional authorities despite the absence of an endorsement.[30]

Brandenburg's BGL also continued to work to improve the material conditions of teaching. The leadership in October 1951 discussed the dearth of shoes and bicycles that continued to plague pedagogues. The GUE resolved to remind Brandenburg authorities of government decrees that instructed local administrations to treat teachers and children preferentially when distributing coupons for shoes. Since the official and unofficial requirements of teaching continued to overwhelm teachers in Brandenburg and throughout the GDR and since many pedagogues responded by fleeing either the classroom or the country, the GUE increasingly concerned itself with the general health of its members. Following an examination of the high rates of illness among teachers conducted by the regional chapter, Brandenburg's chapter investigated the situation at two representative schools and concluded: "the teachers are often strained to their utmost limits. The majority suffer from an overtaxing of their nerves [*nervliche Überreizung*]." Illness had forced more than a third of the city's teaching staff to miss work at some point in the previous four months, and approximately 10 percent were out sick as of 11 January 1952. Union officials eventually decided to campaign to create what would be the region's second school infirmary, to be staffed by a medical officer, a doctor and a nurse.[31]

In the early 1950s the GUE continued to serve as a central clearing-house for the Brandenburg teaching staff's diverse needs and desires. Officials performed an array of services on behalf of the teaching staff, including lending money to those in need and helping to resolve bureaucratic matters involving pedagogues. At the request of a teacher seeking to spend more time preparing for the second round of state certification exams, local union officials lobbied the local CDU leadership to release him temporarily from his duties as a city councilor on the party's district executive committee.[32] In another case, the union negotiated a solution to a dispute between a pupil's father and a teacher. Having established the veracity of the father's accusation that the pedagogue broke the law by severely beating his son in class, the union went to extraordinary lengths to satisfy the concerns of both the father and the teacher and to keep the matter from escalating into a much larger and less tractable problem. The union's original hope of fashioning a compromise that would allow the pedagogue to remain in the classroom—and thereby prevent a worsening of Brandenburg's persistent teachers' shortage—proved illusory. Realizing that this elementary school teacher had struck students on more than one occasion and that he in fact wished to quit the profession as a consequence of the mental and emotional stress of teaching, the teachers' union decided to send him off to recuperate and then to help him find a job in another line of work.[33]

The Uprising of 17 June 1953 in Brandenburg

The ability of the city's pedagogues to insulate themselves from intimate involvement in the major political developments of the time—a defining characteristic of the teaching staff since at least the Third Reich—was put to the test in the Uprising of 17 June. Motivating more than 15,000 Brandenburgers to take to the streets were a rise in political oppression and a decline in living standards that occurred in the early 1950s as a consequence of an array of government measures seeking to transform the East German state and society. Following a meeting with Stalin in Moscow in early April 1952, SED leaders returned to East Germany intent on implementing a series of radical reforms that included building up military forces, collectivizing agriculture, and eliminating private enterprise. At the SED's Second Party Conference, held in June 1952, Communist leaders announced this new program of "building socialism," and state and party officials immediately set about realizing it. A new system of 15 administrative districts replaced the traditional federalist structure with one that was highly centralized and therefore more easily controlled by Berlin. An agricultural collectivization program launched in the summer of 1952 a series of brutally repressive measures targeting farmers that turned the stream of refugees to West Germany into a flood that included more than 2,000 farmers per month in the period January–April 1953. The decision in January 1953 to "neutralize" the Christian youth association Junge Gemeinde because of its alleged role as a front organization for the West represented an important skirmish in the intensifying "church struggle" (*Kirchenkampf*) between the SED and the Protestant church. Education authorities expelled students and fired teachers as part of the state's harassment of individuals affiliated with the Junge Gemeinde. At least one Brandenburg pedagogue and 74 secondary school pupils were forced to leave school.[34]

The expulsions represented only one of a number of radical changes that had been sweeping through the schools since the late 1940s. Although it was not until the 1950s that authorities were able to produce a sufficient supply of teaching materials and schoolbooks, education officials beginning in 1946 drew up and distributed hastily produced but ideologically correct pamphlets as a temporary solution.[35] History pedagogues began using in the classroom works with titles like *The German Peasants' War*, *The History of Russia*, and *Japanese Imperialism*. Allegedly free of the militarism and "reaction" thought to be characteristic of previous textbooks, the new geography pamphlets were intended to "awake in the pupils an understanding for lands and peoples . . . especially for the Soviet Union."[36] Since schools had been compelled as part of the denazification campaign to collect and dispose of all Nazi-era textbooks, the demand for materials far exceeded the supply of new textbooks and even of the pamphlets. As a result, many pedagogues taught from Weimar-era textbooks that had been "revised": pages containing politically unsuitable material had been ripped out or particular passages crossed out. Even in a subject as important to the authorities as Russian instruction, teachers lacked sufficient teaching materials. Almost a year after the pupils of Brandenburg Province began learning Russian in the summer of 1945, the schools had not received any of the 45,000 schoolbooks regional education officials ordered. As of early 1947, the situation had improved only slightly. Although education authorities had published some new pamphlets for use in history and Russian classes, most pupils studying biology, geography, mathematics, physics, and chemistry still used Weimar-era materials. In preparation for the 1947–1948 school year, education officials were only able to publish enough school texts for every other pupil. The government's capacity to publish and distribute teaching materials improved in the period 1947–1949; by the time the GDR was founded, many pupils were learning from new schoolbooks.[37]

Material shortages did not prevent education authorities from overhauling the curricula. German officials had as early as 1946 issued amended syllabi that reflected the postwar political and ideological situation. All pupils in grade 5 and above were required to learn a foreign language, which for most was Russian. In the second year of Russian instruction, pupils were to learn about "life and the characteristic conditions in the Soviet Union" and "the historical, political, and social development of Russia and the Soviet Union." To facilitate the implementation of the new history syllabus, pedagogical specialists and university professors in the fall of 1946 lectured to those responsible for training history teachers on topics such as "the history of the workers' movement for the elementary and secondary schools" and "teaching the Age of Imperialism." In 1947 education authorities introduced the very politicized subject of civics (*Gegenwartskunde*) into the vocational schools' curriculum. Conceived of as a continuation of elementary school history classes, *Gegenwartskunde* was to "'promote the realistic political education of the youth.' The young people are to become ready for a democratic way of life and for participation in a future democratic state."[38]

Beginning in the late 1940s, the sovietization of the ruling party and state intensified the politicization of the curricula. Officials lengthened the school day at vocational schools in an effort to "fight Americanism" (*Amerikanismus*) by increasing pupils' knowledge and honing their skills. New guidelines issued in February 1950 for the secondary schools' certification exams attest to the curricula's ideological nature. Successful oral interview answers in the subject of German were to demonstrate "above all knowledge of the most recent literature and of seminal social science works, as well as demonstrating knowledge of progressive literature, especially Soviet literature." Beginning in mid-1950, education authorities required all pupils in the four upper years of elementary school to study *Gegenwartskunde*. The topics to be covered in the mandatory class included "American Aggression in Korea," "The Five-Year Plan as the Path to Prosperity and Peace," and "Stalin—The Leader of the World Peace Movement." Officials offered teachers suggestions on incorporating the subject into the curricula. One recommended essay topic was "Fighters for Peace." A correct answer consisted of a discussion of a "freedom fighter" who "bravely stood up against the war mongers and the Anglo-American imperialists and their lackeys." Suitable examples of such peace activists included "exceptional" individuals like Stalin and West German KPD Bundestag deputy Max Reimann. Officials expected teachers to incorporate *Gegenwartskunde* into seemingly apolitical subjects like mathematics. For pupils in the seventh grade, education authorities deemed the following math problem appropriate: "Of the 6,681 workers in the Solingen cutlery industry, only 3.9 percent are 27 years old or younger. How many workers . . . are 27 years old or younger?" Officials suggested that teachers complete the exercise by noting that the large West German "concerns" were failing to train apprentices, thereby causing a "crisis" of too few skilled workers. Similarly, secondary school teachers were expected at this time to incorporate contemporary political issues into all elements of the curricula. Possible essay topics for pupils studying German included "Why the Path to Peace Lies through a Unified Germany" and "The Five-Year Plan Is a Plan for Peace."[39] By means of such methods, officials hoped to achieve their goal—"to anchor firmly in the youth a love for the German Democratic Republic and its President, Wilhelm Pieck. The youth—who once again have a fatherland in the German Democratic Republic—should be raised to be active peace activists struggling for the unification of Germany and for a friendship with the Soviet Union, the Peoples' Democracies, and everyone who loves peace."[40] Although these changes represented a significant departure from the pre-1945 curricula, teachers in Brandenburg implemented the Education Ministry's directives without noticeable resistance. Some did so out of conviction and others simply because it was their job. Not a few—those who had joined the SED, for example, or were active in the DSF—likely thought the reforms would help transform the schools into genuine "antifascist" institutions of learning. These teachers, the majority of whom began teaching after the war, surely satisfied the demand of one Brandenburg school principal that Germany's teachers be "politically trained and conscious pedagogues" so that they could "stand behind the social issues of the day." For the far greater number of those who were *parteilos* or like Johannes S. had joined a non-SED party, the question is not whether they taught the new curriculum—they surely did—but why they did so—extolling Stalin in class or assigning essays on American aggression. For the teachers who had worked in the schools in the Third Reich and in whom pre-SED notions of the teacher's role and duties could still be found, as well as for the many *Neulehrer* who refused to join the SED or work outside of the classroom to build a new socialist utopia, they taught the sovietized curriculum because the state ordered them to. According to one *Neulehrer*, being a teacher meant "doing what was required" of you and "obeying" certain things [*gewisse Dinge einhalten*], regardless of one's personal beliefs.[41] As previous chapters have shown, a similar dynamic existed during the Third Reich; teachers' actions in the early 1950s, including during the Uprising of 17 June, demonstrate its continuation into the postwar era.

As part of the SED's "building socialism" program, the sovietization of the schools accelerated. The party decreed that the purpose of education had changed, that teachers and schools were now to transform pupils into "socialist patriots" capable of defending East Germany and its alleged accomplishments against the allegedly many external and internal enemies. To this end, classrooms and hallways were to be adorned with images of the "leaders of the working class and other progressive personalities," for example, and teachers were to commit themselves to work with the SED youth organizations. According to an SED Politbüro decision of 29 July 1952, teachers were to have "an attitude consciously full of fighting spirit [*bewusst kämpferische Einstellung*] toward the construction of socialism."[42] Officials were well aware that many German pedagogues, as shown in earlier chapters, lacked the "fighting spirit" now demanded of them. One solution to the problem lay in ensuring that future teachers were up to the task. Authorities therefore reformed the system of teacher training and the state-sanctioned curricula. Another solution was increasing state scrutiny of and pressure on the teachers currently in the classroom. To this end, officials carried out an examination of secondary school pupils and teachers in order to determine their suitability for the new educational mission; special district commissions reviewed the pedagogues' records, ultimately dismissing slightly under 10 percent of the teaching staff. Similarly, the SED instituted a reorganization of the Education Ministry, significantly centralizing the hierarchy and placing greater numbers of party members in all levels of school administration. At the same time, the state and party issued a flood of propaganda regarding the importance of the

Soviet model in pedagogy and other educational areas, culminating in a decision in May 1953 by the Council of Ministers to adopt completely the Soviet model for East Germany's entire school system.[43]

Financing the new programs, especially those related to East Germany's militarization and the shift toward investing in heavy industry, placed an extraordinary burden on the GDR's economy and society. In early 1953, officials made deep cuts in the budgets for various social services in an effort to alleviate the increasing pressure on public finances that had arisen as a consequence of expenditures on rearmament and disruptions caused by collectivization. Unable to obtain aid from the Soviet Union, authorities also raised property and income taxes and turned to the idea that productivity increases could be a way of simultaneously reducing real wages and boosting output. Aware that previous attempts at raising the traditionally low work norms by means of collective work agreements had failed, East German officials unleashed a massive campaign to introduce what they called "technically determined work norms," culminating in May 1953 with the state decreeing a 10 percent increase in the workers' quotas. Since many workers relied on the bonuses that came with the regular overfulfillment of artificially low work norms, the announced increase represented a potential 25 to 30 percent cut in real wages.[44]

Whereas the intended implementation of the raised quotas represented a soon-to-be-realized hardship for workers, many East Germans by the spring of 1953 had already been suffering as a consequence of the SED's drive to "build socialism." The flight of thousands of farmers to West Germany as well as the disruptions caused by both the collectivization campaign and the industrialization drive resulted in a food shortage that began in the fall of 1952 and continued well into 1953. The situation was even direr for the approximately two million people who faced a radical reduction in their regular food supply following an April 1953 decree that took ration cards away from all self-employed people such as craftsmen and shopkeepers. Similarly, the state's marshalling of economic resources for heavy industry, in addition to the general supply problems and bottlenecks characteristic of a planned economy, resulted in a dramatic decline in the production of consumer goods. Government officials recorded in the first half of 1953 a shortage of goods such as shoes, paper, textiles, clothes, and foodstuffs like fruit, vegetables, potatoes, and butter. One former *Neulehrer* later recalled the widespread discontent in Brandenburg at this time over the "constant" shortages of goods such as toilet paper, cheese, and meat. Finally, a wave of arrests and imprisonments had accompanied the regime's efforts to intensify the struggle against so-called class enemies. Farmers who failed to meet their requisitioning targets were fined, and many were jailed. Some small business owners were punished for allegedly having committed "economic" crimes like corruption or sabotage. Similarly, many politically active clergy members and church employees were arrested. The number of prison inmates jumped from approximately 30,000 in the summer of 1952 to more than 61,300 in the late spring of 1953.[45]

As a result of the generally worsening situation, East Germans in the months leading up to June 1953 were expressing in small, usually anonymous or private ways their growing dissatisfaction. Party and secret police informants noted at this time a widespread unhappiness with the current policies among the people and even among SED functionaries. Aware of the situation, Soviet leaders in early June ordered East German leaders to rescind the policies that were clearly alienating the population and worsening the economy. On 9 June, the East German government repealed most of the repressive and onerous measures: the production of consumer goods was to be increased, for example, and oppressive taxes that had been levied on a wide range of groups that included farmers, tradesmen, and retailers were abolished. The government publicly acknowledged that policies such as the *Kirchenkampf* and the harsh delivery quotas required of individual farmers had been mistakes.[46]

On 12 June, the SED organ *Neues Deutschland* published a speech by minister-president Otto Grotewohl in which he promised the revocation of the education reforms initiated since January, including the requirement that teachers "accept" *(anerkennen)* Marxism-Leninism as a condition of their employment and the state's assumption that the level of instruction in the schools could be raised by dismissing hundreds of allegedly ideologically unsuitable pedagogues. Grotewohl announced the complete repeal of the dismissals, demotions, and forced retirements of secondary school teachers that had been decreed by the Education Ministry in its campaign to transform East Germany's teaching staff. On 15 June 1953, education minister Else Zaisser formally ordered school administrators to implement these reforms.[47]

For many Germans, the reforms were too little and too late. In Brandenburg, the popular discontent did not dissipate but instead erupted on 12 June, five days before the Uprising of 17 June. Having learned that the owner of a taxi service was not going to be released from jail as part of the liberal "New Course" the SED government had announced for the GDR, a small group of the owner's employees appeared at Brandenburg's district courthouse, demanded his release, and even went so far as to threaten the state prosecutor. Following the authorities' refusal, the men soon returned, accompanied by additional employees and a growing number of by-standers. The small group of protestors metamorphosed over the course of the day into a disorganized and increasingly violent crowd of more than 2,000 people. Efforts to force their way into the courthouse's jail in order to secure the prisoner's release failed, and the protestors then turned their wrath on another organ of state power, the FDJ. Having spotted the first secretary of the district FDJ on the street, the crowd attacked and severely beat him. After a number of small brawls broke out involving some protestors, the crowd eventually dispersed in the late evening.[48]

The real manifestation of this popular anger and dissatisfaction was the extraordinary series of antistate, antiparty disturbances that took place on 17 June. Although the New Course represented a broad series of concessions by the East German state, officials had not repealed the 10 percent norm increase for industrial workers, and this failure, compounded by an article defending the norms that appeared in the 16 June edition of the FDGB's newspaper, set into motion the Uprising of 17 June. On 16 June, East Berlin construction workers spontaneously went on strike and marched through parts of East Berlin before ultimately assembling in front of the House of the Ministries and demanding that the government abolish the new quotas. After failing to force SED head Walter Ulbricht or minister-president Otto Grotewohl to appear and hear their demands, the large demonstration ended with workers calling for a general strike to be held the next day.[49]

As a result of the previous day's events in Berlin, police and authorities throughout East Germany were already officially in a heightened state of alert on the morning of 17 June. Having heard about what had transpired in Berlin, workers from Brandenburg's construction firms, the Branden-burg Steel and Rolling Mill, the Tractor Factory, and other state-run People's Own Enterprises (Volkseigener Betrieb) walked off the job on the morning of 17 June 1953 and made their way to the city center. Within less than an hour, more than 15,000 people had gathered throughout the city. Loosely divided into four or five groups, the demonstrators proceeded to destroy symbols of state and party power. More than a thousand stormed the district headquarters of the SED, having first overwhelmed the 10 policemen who had been sent to guard it. Ignoring the party officials' pleas to cease and disperse, the crowd proceeded to destroy the building and its contents. For more than an hour, protestors—including women and children—plundered the furnishings and fittings and threw documents out of the windows into a canal.[50]

At the same time or shortly thereafter, a very large group of demonstrators assembled before the city's district courthouse. Part of the crowd forced its way through the windows and quickly reached the courtyard of Brandenburg's jail. From there, the demonstrators bombarded the jail's guardrooms and offices with stones and shots fired from firearms stripped from policemen. Although the crowd failed to break into the cell-block, the warden and other officials chose to negotiate. A delegation of five demonstrators entered the jail and demanded that the guards be disarmed and the "political prisoners" released. Following a brief negotiation, the officials agreed. With the assistance of Brandenburg's former criminal judge Harry Benkendorf, the delegation reviewed the files of the imprisoned men and women and questioned individual prisoners about their alleged crimes. From the outset, the delegation distinguished between "criminals" who had been arrested for offenses such as theft—and thus did not deserve to be released—and "political prisoners" who had been convicted of crimes such as "resistance against the state." Forty-two identified as political prisoners were ultimately released from jail.[51] Realizing that Benkendorf, who had the extreme misfortune of having returned to Brandenburg that day in order to inform the city's courts of recent Ministry of Justice directives in connection with the New Course, was in the building, the crowd demanded that he appear before it. "Immediately a massive howling set in," he stated in a later report about the day's events. "There were many shouts like 'we want to have the dog that sentenced so many, he should now get what he deserves.'" Brought outside in handcuffs that he himself had to locate, he was attacked by the crowd and severely beaten. His ordeal ended after he was marched to the town square and there, in front of the crowd, admitted his "guilt" for his "sins." Only with great effort was the crowd persuaded not to hang him right there but to allow him to go to a hospital.[52]

While protestors stormed and demolished the FDGB headquarters, the DSF's House of Friendship, the district administration building, and the FDJ's youth clubhouse, a crowd of more than 6,000 was demonstrating in front of the district headquarters of the police. Inside were Brandenburg's mayor and SED district chairman, as well as other high-ranking officials and policemen. Throwing stones and firing pistols, groups of protesters successfully forced their way into the building's courtyard and into the headquarters itself. Between 20 and 30 demonstrators fought their way to the building's second floor, where they were forcefully halted by Soviet army troops and local policemen.[53]

At this point, the tide began to turn for the demonstrators. Soviet troops from the motorbike and howitzer battalions of the Tenth Tank Division moved into the city. In the early afternoon, Brandenburg's Soviet military commander proclaimed a state of emergency. Germans were forbidden to be on the streets between 8 p.m. and 6 a.m.; those who disobeyed would be tried before a military tribunal.[54] On 18 June, some Brandenburg citizens nonetheless tried to continue the demonstrations. Many of those from the Steel and Rolling Mills and the Ernst Thälmann Shipyards refused to resume working, demanding instead that the government implement free elections and other reforms. By the end of the day, however, strikers from these and other workplaces had failed to rally their fellow workers, and almost all reported for the evening shift. The Uprising of 17 June was over. East German and Soviet authorities immediately set about arresting hundreds of people believed to be the uprising's "ringleaders" and recapturing the great majority of the "liberated" prisoners.[55]

While thousands were laying siege to government buildings and physically assaulting officials, Brandenburg's teachers and pupils remained in the classroom and almost without exception continued their normal routine. There were minor disturbances, to be sure. At the Theodor-Neubauer School, political banners and portraits were ripped down, and the school closed its doors early. Some parents pulled their children out of class. At another school, teaching was suspended at 10:30 a.m., and the teachers removed banners, posters, and portraits from the school walls. A couple of other schools halted classes and sent their pupils home. The vast majority of the schools—including the many located in the city center—were unaffected by the day's events. At Eva-Maria B.'s school, for instance, the teachers were aware of the various developments on the streets but nevertheless spent the day proctoring exams. This experience was shared by Karl-Heinz R. and his colleagues; they ended their workday only after the pupils had finished taking their exams. Most significantly, none of Brandenburg's teachers took part in the protests, and not a single teacher was arrested that day or in the following weeks and months. Reaching its own conclusions about the noninvolvement of East Germany's pedagogues—including Brandenburg's—in the uprising, the GUE Central Committee noted the "energetically correct, loyal attitude of the teachers."[56]

After German and Soviet authorities had restored order fully in Brandenburg, they took stock of the uprising, endeavoring to prevent a recurrence by investigating the uprising's causes, development, and effects. Noting that protesters had demanded free and secret elections, the revocation of the new work norms, and a lowering of prices in state-run shops and called for a change in government (Sturz der Regierung), the abolition of German-German borders, and the removal of Allied troops from Berlin, authorities hurriedly implemented many elements of the New Course: local manufacturers agreed to produce more consumer goods, the social welfare system was expanded, the state allocated greater resources to housing construction, the government relaxed requirements for receiving credit, many confiscated businesses were returned to their owners, property was returned to individuals who had fled the GDR and since returned to Brandenburg, and more than 50 Brandenburg individuals associated with the Junge Gemeinde—including one teacher—were returned to the classroom.[57] The state, however, also punished those who had allegedly played leading roles in the uprising. According to police statistics, more than 90,000 people in the Potsdam District had taken part. Slightly fewer than 600 people were arrested in the region in the nine days following the uprising. Of these, more than 350 were soon released; 162 were transferred to the Ministry of State Security and 32 to the Soviet military authorities.[58]

Conclusion

One cannot claim that Brandenburg's teachers failed to participate on 17 June because the uprising was exclusively an eruption of working-class discontent with factory or workplace conditions. In Brandenburg and elsewhere in the region, diverse elements of East German society joined these protests, which often violently attacked symbolic and literal representatives of the state and party. In the city of Rathenow, white-collar employees of the state-run retail stores and consumers' collective took part in the uprising; 600 "mostly bourgeois individuals" (vorwiegend bürgerliche Kräfte)—in the words of Communist officials—from the Freisack community administration protested by "rampaging" through the town, destroying state propaganda, and trying to force their way into city hall.[59] A small number of pedagogues in other areas of the region and the Soviet Zone did take part. Authorities arrested five pedagogues in the Magdeburg District for their activities but failed to arrest two additional teachers who had participated and then fled. One teacher in the Halle District led a group of recently released prisoners in destroying the district's schools. One East Berlin pedagogue wrote: "we do not want to be slaves. We want to declare our solidarity with the construction workers." Other pedagogues protested in alternative ways. Some teachers quit the party or the FDJ. The majority of teachers at one school refused to sign a declaration of support to be sent to the government. The state ultimately tried and convicted four teachers for their roles as "provocateurs" during the uprising.[60] Although many of the repressive educational reforms had been repealed on the eve of the uprising, these people were nonetheless motivated by the deteriorating general situation in East Germany, characterized by a growing scarcity of consumer goods, an increase in taxes, and a campaign of repression targeting the regime's so-called economic, political, and intellectual enemies.

The great majority of pedagogues—and all of those in Brandenburg—refrained from joining the demonstrations and protests due to a constellation of factors. Although at least one well-known historian has argued that "intellectuals" did not participate because the uprising, first, reminded them of Nazi mass violence, and second represented an attack by the Western consumerist social model on the socialist state and society, the case of Brandenburg does not bear this out. Extant records do not indicate that men like Johannes S. interpreted the decentralized and populist destruction of the 17 June uprising as a throwback to the state- and party-directed violence of the Third Reich, nor do the many posthumous accounts justify seeing teachers' reticence as a rejection of an "Americanized western culture and society." Unlike intellectuals such as Johannes R. Becher, Brandenburg's pedagogues were not ardent supporters of the regime who felt threatened by the events.[61] Instead, the failure to mobilize against the East German state in 1953 represented the latest manifestation of Brandenburg's teaching staff's ability to adapt to radically changing political, social, and economic circumstances. From at least as early as January 1933, the teaching staff demonstrated a remarkable mutability, successfully weathering—without ever fully supporting—first the Nationalist Socialist order and now the Communist regime. Cloaked in their highly developed professional identity as civil servants, Brandenburg's pedagogues neither resisted the sovietization process begun in the late 1940s nor actively supported it.

Their behavior on 17 June exemplified, in the words of one local SED teacher and functionary, this "Don't disturb me" attitude *(Rühr-mich-nicht-an Einstellung)*. Except for a few isolated episodes, the schools remained open, and teachers continued to teach. Men and women who were teaching at the time were aware, in most cases, of the extraordinary events taking place in the city, yet they stayed on the job. Subsequent party and state investigations did not uncover any significant degree of participation. Similarly, Brandenburg's teachers did almost nothing to stop or contain the demonstrations. In fact, the Brandenburg SED punished some teachers who belonged to the party for their "capitulatory" behavior *(wegen kapitulantenhaften Verhaltens)* and criticized others for their inactivity. The SED punished these pedagogues not for anything they did but rather for what they did not do; instead of sitting out the uprising, the party had expected them to defend the state and party actively, even if that entailed mobilizing against the demonstrators in the streets. The SED Central Committee concluded that East Germany's pedagogues had failed both to show a "just and aggressive attitude" and to come to the party's aid.[62]

A second important factor in explaining the teachers' political reticence in June 1953 was their residual faith in a union that, though constrained, continued to work to improve their working and living situations. The union had been able to help Brandenburg's pedagogues maintain their position of political inactivity because the union in the period 1949–1953 had continued to serve two masters, the SED and East Germany's teachers. By 1953, the GUE had become a curious mixture of a sovietized mass organization and a professional representative *(Interessenvertreter)*.[63] This dualistic nature had become apparent to union officials by 1952. A discussion within Brandenburg's local union leadership in March 1952 revealed the union's different roles in East German society:

> The first question is—what do you expect of your union?
>
> . . .
>
> Colleague W., Rochow School, commented: one requires the representation of the interests of the individual vis-à-vis the employer.
>
> . . .
>
> Colleague P., Goethe School (Boys): . . . Its concerns are to direct labor [*die Arbeitskräfte anzuleiten*] and to accomplish productive work. Worrying

about the individual is still not a central consideration for the regional or local union chapters. Union functionaries have not correctly understood their mission of caring for the individual. . . .

. . .

Colleague S., Betriebsberufsschule Bau-Union: The most important task is to improve the ideological work. . . ."

. . .

Colleague S., Rochow School: . . . The main point [of union activity] is to fight for a united fatherland and long-desired peace treaty.[64]

More than a year later, on the eve of the uprising, the union was still wrestling with its dualistic nature.[65]

In its capacity as a "handmaiden" to the SED, the union campaigned to mobilize its members to support the party's program of "building socialism" and regularly informed the party of teachers' attitudes. The effects of sovietization had even begun to undermine union efforts to secure material goods for its members. Rather than pressuring state agencies to raise wages, union officials now received allotments of goods such as radios and distributed them as rewards for particularly "loyal" or "active" members.[66] The GUE in the early 1950s remained an institution that pedagogues nonetheless turned to for assistance. By serving as a central, quasi-governmental clearinghouse for teachers' concerns and issues, the union performed an important integrative function in nascent GDR society. Although the SED would increasingly eviscerate the GUE union in the 1950s, it was still sufficiently strong enough in 1953 to continue to provide an institutional haven where Brandenburg's teachers could weather major developments such as the sovietization of the schools and East Germany's first popular uprising.

Conclusion

Almost a year after the failed uprising of June 1953, Brandenburg's political authorities continued to complain about the allegedly "nonprogressive" behavior of the city's teaching staff. Officials decried its "purely technical" *(rein fachlich)* attitude toward the ruling party's program of treating the children of workers and farmers preferentially in the schools. Communist officials were also unhappy that pedagogues were only "formally" following Education Ministry directives regarding the compulsory participation of teachers in the FDJ. Also of concern were the continued difficulties of the SED in recruiting pedagogues; as of 15 March 1954, only 27 percent of the teaching staff belonged to the party, and a majority refused to join any party.[1]

The roots of the complaints in 1954 were the same as those of the authorities' satisfaction in 1953, when the city's teachers had refrained from participating in the June uprising. In both cases, state and party officials were reacting to a mentality and set of established practices among teachers that constituted core elements of the teachers' collective biography that had not ended in 1933 but had continued through the Third Reich and into the GDR. This continuity of professional attitudes and customs was a fundamental feature of pedagogues' experiences under both dictatorships and manifested itself in two principal and related forms: a marked disengagement from and a high degree of adaptability to the major ideological developments of the period. First, although the National Socialists successfully demanded a high degree of compliance with their education reforms, a large majority of the teachers refrained from supporting the new regime beyond teaching the revised lesson plans or participating in the Nazi school festivals. The number of pedagogues who had joined the Nazi Party by the spring of 1933 was minuscule. Six years later, on the eve of Germany's invasion of Poland, the situation had changed, but not to the degree desired by the state and party; a majority of the teachers at the elementary schools, for instance, had not joined the NSDAP. Illustrative is the experience of Von Saldern director and ardent Nazi Walter H. Hired in large part to win over to National Socialism a teaching staff that had since 1933 largely stood apart from the "national revolution" and its various new demands of Germans, Walter H. failed to do so. Instead, as he complained to his superiors over the years, the "convinced reactionaries," the "opposition group," and the "subterranean currents" were fundamentally undermining, by means of "passive resistance," his efforts—were, in fact, "agitating against the National Socialist movement." Walter H. and other Nazi officials, having failed to win the hearts and minds of most pedagogues, effectively settled instead for teachers' compliance, for example, in teaching the revised curriculum.

The unwillingness of Brandenburg's teaching staff to support the ruling party beyond the legal or administrative requirements of their jobs continued in the postwar era. Although the teachers taught the new lesson plans and used the revised textbooks, most chose not to join a party, and only a minority—approximately 10 percent in 1946 and 27 percent in 1954—became Communists. "Only about 160 of our teachers are politically organized, and more than half are *parteilos*," Brandenburg's Communist school superintendent noted in September 1948; "but even the politically organized teachers are politically inactive."[2] Walter H.'s postwar successors criticized repeatedly and sincerely the "old" teachers who "cannot find their way to Marxism" and who instead allegedly impeded the construction of a "democratic" and "antifascist" Germany with their "bourgeois" attitudes and behavior. We need to appreciate the sincerity of such expressions of dissatisfaction and disappointment. Both National Socialists and Communists sought to save a Germany each believed was gravely injured—a victim, according to the former, of the ills of modern society and, according to the latter, of genocidal war and dictatorship. Neither in words nor in deeds did either believe time was on its side when it came to fundamental reforms such as the "restoration of the professional civil service" or denazification. The "coolness" displayed by Brandenburg's teachers toward National Socialism or Communism was therefore a genuine concern.

Moreover, we can and should interpret membership data as indicators of degrees of support because both the Nazis and the East German Communists did. Whether one joined a political party is admittedly an imperfect gauge of one's commitment to that party or even its regime; individuals joined the Nazi or Socialist Unity parties for a variety of reasons, motivated by personal conviction, for example, or by external pressure from state and party officials. Moreover, not every party member was an activist, as the cases of some Brandenburg teachers show, nor was every supporter formally affiliated with the party. Nonetheless, whether one joined the NSDAP mattered both to the Nazis in the Third Reich and to the Soviet and East German Communists in the postwar era. An individual's affiliation with certain organizations was a central element of both the Nazi and Communist purges, for example. Even though the SED largely failed to convince most teachers to join, it nevertheless closely monitored teachers' membership rates.

The corollary of teachers providing both dictatorships with only a modicum of support for their revolutionary projects was the teacher's remarkable ability to adapt to each regime. Pedagogues like Johannes S. or Johanna M. stood at the front of classrooms in the Weimar Republic, the Third Reich, and the GDR. They taught first from nazified and then from sovietized textbooks. For some, the wartime effort of tutoring antiaircraft helpers turned into the postwar effort of rebuilding individual schools. They joined first the NSLB and then the GLE. Having once attended lectures on Nazi racial science, they now marched with their students for world peace.

Contributing to the teaching staff's ability to preserve a degree of collective professional detachment and showcasing its adaptability was a second fundamental continuity: the continuity of personnel in the period 1933–1953. The great majority of men and women teaching in 1939 had been doing so since before Hitler was appointed chancellor. Measures such as the Restoration Law and the anti-Masonic decrees did not result in a significant purge of the city's teaching staff. The professional biography of Johannes S. illustrates this point particularly well. Affiliated early in his career with Brandenburg's Secular School, an institution particularly despised by the Nazis for its progressive pedagogy and its alleged leftist political leaning, and a member of the Freemasons until 1935, he was not dismissed from the city's service.[3] The Second World War diminished somewhat this remarkably high degree of continuity. Large numbers of conscripted male pedagogues were eventually replaced by additional sources of labor, consisting of mostly female school helpers but also including a not insignificant number of older teachers who had left the city's service since 1933. Despite these changes, which were the unplanned consequences of the war, the majority of Brandenburg's teachers reporting to the schools in the fall of 1945 were experienced ones.

Some of the teachers, however, had belonged to the Nazi Party or to one of its affiliate organizations such as the Stormtroopers. Beginning in the summer of 1945, Soviet and German Communist officials implemented a massive denazification program in an effort to purge Germans who had actively supported National Socialism. Eastern German teachers were required to fill out special questionnaires and submit to questioning by denazification committees. Education authorities made teachers' records available to state and party officials. Ultimately, the denazification committees passed judgment on the political suitability of individual pedagogues. Despite such seemingly extensive efforts to rid the schools of Nazis, "militarists," and "reactionaries," Brandenburg's teaching staff weathered the denazification process largely unaffected. As of the official cessation of denazification in early 1948, a small number of former Nazis had been investigated and punished, but many who had belonged to the Nazi Party or had been active in a National Socialist organization continued to teach. Moreover, authorities in the late 1940s and early 1950s quietly rehired some of those former Nazis who had been purged. In December 1949 the local SED leadership decided it would not object to the rehiring of a former secondary school teacher who had once belonged to the Nazi Party and who had served as a leader *(Rottenführer)* in the Stormtroopers.[4] The history of the local leadership of the GLE also illustrates the degree and significance of the continuity of personnel. Year after year, Brandenburg's teachers elected men and women who were older, professionally trained and credentialed, and non-Communists. In 1950, two years after the state and party initiated the sovietization of the schools, a majority of the local leadership had been teaching since before the war, and almost none of them were affiliated with the SED. Although such experienced pedagogues were removed from positions of power in the union and the schools by 1952, many of them continued to teach East Germany's pupils.

That so many of Brandenburg's teachers found themselves in the classroom both before 1939 and after 1945 enables us to analyze the impact the Third Reich had on those tasked with building an East German society and state. The relationship between Brandenburg's teaching staff and the SED demonstrates clearly that 12 years of Nazism and six years of war did not predispose Brandenburg's teachers toward a "democratic" postwar society and polity as defined by the Communists. The political bankruptcy of Nazism, evident to even the most hardened Brandenburg National Socialist by the time the Red Army brutally conquered the city in April 1945, did not translate into unconditional or wholehearted support for Communism. Extant records do not reveal a willingness on the part of most pedagogues to make a complete break with the Nazi past by throwing themselves into the restructuring of eastern Germany. Whether having recently been demobilized from the Wehrmacht or the Volkssturm or having tried to keep instructing the pupils under the sharply deteriorating wartime conditions, teachers such as Johannes S. focused in the postwar era on rebuilding their personal and professional lives. For this, GLE advocacy was much more important than the SED programs. If the GLE served to channel teachers' interests and energies away from SED mobilization projects, it also kept the teaching staff connected to the developing East German order, making clear its relevance to pedagogues in an immediate and material sense. The result of such activities was not just deliveries of shoes and the payment of back wages; as has been argued here, the nonparticipation in the June uprising can be explained in part by the continued relevance of the teachers' union as well as by the teachers' enduring traditional professional self-conception. Like East Germany's population in general, the men and women of Brandenburg's teaching staff were suffering as a result of political, social, economic, and cultural developments associated with the sovietization of the GDR. During the uprising, however, they stood at the front of the classroom, teaching a politicized curriculum with sovietized course materials, while more than 15,000 of their neighbors expressed their discontent. And by doing so, they helped to stabilize Germany's second dictatorship, as they had done in a similar way and to a similar degree in its first dictatorship.

This is not to say that the experiences of the city's pedagogues during the Third Reich did not have an effect on the teaching staff. As of 1933 it was fractured along social, political, and professional lines and was a largely male professional group led almost exclusively by men. The wartime influx of mostly untrained or poorly prepared female school helpers, combined with a widespread deprofessionalization of teaching that occurred at the same time, substantially diminished some of the traditional social, gender, and professional distinctions among pedagogues. In the exceptional war-time situation, teachers were promoted to positions for which they were unqualified, and the state failed to distinguish among types of teachers when ordering them to perform clerical tasks in the city's administration. Similarly, the experience of having been strong-armed into the Nazi NSLB helped facilitate the inclusion of the teaching staff, from philologists to elementary school teachers, into a single, postwar teachers' union. Extant records do not indicate that Brandenburg's teachers sought to resurrect the old unions or to structure the emerging postwar professional organization along the traditionally fractured lines. Although there were tensions between the *Neulehrer* and their more experienced colleagues, among the many *Altlehrer*—men and women who comprised a majority of the teaching staff at this time—the traditional lines of conflict failed to reappear after the war.

That a large number of Brandenburg's teachers experienced both German dictatorships enables us to compare and contrast the two in novel and important ways. One of their most important similarities was the intent and means with which they sought to transform the teaching staff. The National Socialists and Communists both saw teachers as a professional group that was to play a crucial role in the transformation of German society, creating via education Nazis in the Third Reich and "antifascists" in the postwar era. Officials as different as Hans Schemm and Paul Wandel shared a belief in the absolute necessity of overhauling the teaching staff as an early and crucial step in the larger remaking of Germany. Moreover, both the National Socialists and the Communists not only believed the teaching staff needed itself to be transformed before it could play its part in the creation of a new Germany but also sought to bring this about primarily by eliminating "unsuitable" pedagogues. The unsuccessful purges of both regimes were carried out by remarkably similar processes: soon after acquiring power, the authorities collected completed questionnaires, testimonials, and personnel files and then forwarded the materials to tribunals specially appointed to evaluate the candidates' political suitability. The process was lengthy, and neither the Nazi nor the Communist regime was able to bring the matter to a close according to its original timetable. More significant, both purges achieved similar results: the far from complete removal of those teachers whose previous political actions or affiliations violated the standards of the new state and party. This underimplementation was the consequence of a number of factors, the most important of which was a constellation of formidable structural obstacles. In the Third Reich, the shortage of certified teachers played an important role in limiting the political purges. Faced with too few pedagogues for a population of pupils that was expanding rapidly and unable at this time to abandon the traditionally high standards regarding teachers' qualifications, local and regional education officials in Brandenburg took advantage of the decentralized and confused nature of the Nazi purges to hold on to their valuable manpower, regardless of individuals' former political and organizational affiliations. Nor could education officials hope for a substantially greater supply of trained pedagogues in the near future. The Nazi failure to raise teachers' wages or promote their social standing meant that many bright secondary school graduates chose other professions. These factors enabled Brandenburg's school superintendent and some principals to retain teachers who previously had been affiliated with the SPD or the Freemasons and even during the war to rehire pedagogues who had been purged in the first years of the Third Reich.

The Soviets and East German Communists inherited a similar situation. Of the many intractable problems facing the postwar administration, the dearth of trained teachers ranked high. Given that some pedagogues were in prisoner-of-war camps or were otherwise missing, local education officials needed every available teacher in order to keep the pupils—many of whom were refugees—in the classroom. This imperative, however, quickly clashed with that of denazifying the schools. The original scale for the removal of politically "unsuitable" teachers, as envisioned by Soviet and East German Communists in the summer and fall of 1945, necessarily entailed a significant loss of manpower. Terminating every teacher who had been a member of the NSDAP or one of its affiliate organizations like the NSLB or the NSV threatened to derail the authorities' plans for resuming the full-scale schooling of the Zone's pupils. Although Soviet and German authorities had hoped to ensure a sufficient number of teachers by hurriedly training tens of thousands of inexperienced and underqualified men and women, too few *Neulehrer* were created. To the great surprise of education officials, not enough people signed up for the expedited courses, and a significant number either failed to complete the training or soon quit the profession. Continuing low wages and lack of respect accorded by society to the profession contributed further to the scarcity of pedagogues; bright secondary school graduates instead sought careers in more prestigious or remunerative fields. In response, local and regional officials modified, often covertly, the denazification program. The provisions of measures such as SMA Order No. 24 were watered down in subsequent implementation decrees. To take another example, local denazification commissions like Brandenburg's took the manpower shortage into account when evaluating former Nazis, and authorities were willing to rehire former Nazis in order to meet manpower needs. For one Communist member of the local teachers' union leadership in 1951, a secondary school's need for a qualified science teacher outweighed a particular candidate's National Socialist past.[5] The professional history of Johannes S. and his colleagues reveals that fundamental impediments prevented the Nazi and Communist dictatorships from fully realizing their revolutionary plans.

Whereas the attempts of the Nazi and Communist states to transform the teaching staff bore resemblances in their origins, development, and efficacy, the role and significance of the NSLB and the GLE differed from each other significantly. The NSLB was created for the ideological indoctrination and political mobilization of Germany's teaching staff. The NSLB's indoctrination efforts consisted of a panoply of measures, from the dissemination of propaganda to public lectures to its most important tool, the training camp. Factors like bureaucratic infighting and a lack of regular and sufficient funding prevented the NSLB from fully implementing its reeducation program. In one sense, the history of the NSLB's indoctrination efforts is one of postponements, conceptual and practical downsizings, and a premature end. As a result, the NSLB's efforts to transform the teaching staff impacted far fewer teachers and to a much lesser extent than was originally planned. Moreover, the NSLB did not address issues such as wages and working conditions, which had been the traditional focus of the pre-Nazi teachers' associations. Accordingly, the NSLB ensured superficial compliance, such that the teachers obediently attended required assemblies and outings—but they grumbled about the burden or the cost while they did so. That Brandenburg authorities appointed a so-called Nazi Old Fighter to the directorship of the Von Saldern secondary school in 1937 in order to mobilize an indifferent teaching staff exemplifies the failure of the city's pedagogues to participate in NSLB activities to a degree satisfactory to the Nazi state. As the director of the Ritterakademie noted in 1935, membership in a Nazi organization alone was no guarantee of true belief in or support for National Socialism.[6]

Unlike the NSLB, the postwar teachers' union quickly established itself as a legal and professional advocate under whose banner the city's teachers rallied. From its inception, the GLE focused on fighting for the economic, social, and professional advancement of its members. In addition to campaigning for higher wages, it lobbied officials in the postwar period for an improvement in the provisioning of teachers with food, clothing, teaching supplies, and housing. Similarly, the GLE interceded with denazification commissions on behalf of individual pedagogues. Such actions proved immensely popular, and the GLE quickly established itself as a central clearinghouse that teachers turned to for many needs. Important elements of the GLE's advocative role were challenged by but ultimately survived the sovietization program. Although the sovietization of the GLE—and especially the replacement of the traditional non-Communist local leadership with one dominated by SED loyalists—seriously eroded the union's de facto autonomy and thereby affected the relationship between the union and its members, the teachers' union in the early 1950s nevertheless continued to promote and defend the teachers' material, social, and professional interests.

The story of Brandenburg's teaching staff in the period 1933–1953 illuminates some important points regarding the functioning of Germany's two dictatorships and the experiences of millions of Germans under the Communist and Nazi regimes. Committed to transforming society, the Nazis and Communists were forced to adjust their revolutionary plans in accordance with the materials with which they had to work, not least of which was the attitude and behavior of a German populace that could not simply be exchanged for another. Similarly, the professional and personal lives of Germany's teachers underwent extraordinary changes as both regimes sought to transform the individuals responsible for educating those regimes' future citizens. In a response that most likely was not limited to the men and women standing in the front of Germany's classrooms, the teaching staff exhibited a remarkable ability to adapt to the political, social, and economic changes they endured. With a biography more significant for its general applicability that for its exceptionalism, Johannes S. lived under four political regimes, endured economic collapse on more than one occasion, and experienced two world wars. Neither an ardent supporter nor a principled resistor, he—like his fellow teachers, other civil servants, and millions of his compatriots—served Germany's two dictatorships in a complex and varied fashion.

Notes

Introduction

1. "Bericht über die Kreisdelegiertenkonferenz in Brandenburg am 7.3.50," 27 March 1950, BLHA, Rep 347 FDGB Landesvorstand GUE, no. 990, 13–14; "Bericht über den Ortsvorstande und die BGL der Lehrergewerkschaft in Brandenburg," 29 June 1949, BLHA, Rep 347 FDGB Landesvorstand GUE, no. 1031; and the city's registry of teachers, StadtA Brandenburg, 2.0.12.25/249. In accordance with German federal and Brandenburg state law, I have anonymized the names of Brandenburg's teachers.

2. "Nachweisung über die Zugehörigkeit von Beamten zu Freimaurerlogen, anderen Logen oder logenähnlichen Organisationen und deren Ersatzorganisationen," draft report from Regierungspräsident Potsdam to the Education Ministry, 30 September 1935, BLHA, Pr. Br. Rep 2A Regierung Potsdam II Gen., no. 733. Teachers' biographical information was compiled from a diverse group of sources. Most important was the city's registry of teachers, StadtA Brandenburg, 2.0.12.25/249. The registry provides such crucial background information as the dates on which individual teachers entered and left the city's service, and lists individual teachers' political and organizational affiliations. Another significant source is the NSLB's membership card catalogue *(Mitgliedskartei)* for Gau Kurmark, BAB, NS 12, 2:82–88. Individual files from the BLHA's Provinzialschulkollegium record group and from the DStA helped fill in some of the gaps. Regarding his supervision of early denazification efforts, see Circular from School Superintendent S., 5 September 1945, StadtA Brandenburg, 2.0.12.116/958, 79. Statistical information regarding teachers' membership

in the NSDAP can be found in Konrad Jarausch and Gerhard Arminger, "The German Teaching Profession and Nazi Party Membership: A Demographic Logit Model," *Journal of Interdisciplinary History* 20:2 (1989), 201–202.

3. City's registry of teachers, StadtA Brandenburg, 2.0.12.25/249; Report, 10 April 1946, StadtA Brandenburg, 2.0.12.115/957, 36; School-statistical List of the School Supervision District Brandenburg (Havel) for 1939, BLHA, Pr. Br. Rep 2A Regierung Potsdam II Brd., no. 198; Brandenburg an der Havel Magistrat to Potsdam Regierungspräsident, 25 January 1929, BLHA, Pr. Br. Rep 2A Regierung Potsdam II Brd., no. 169.

4. Benita Blessing, *The Antifascist Classroom: Denazification in Soviet-occupied Germany, 1945–1949* (New York: Palgrave, 2006), 13–36 and 159–186; John Rodden, *Repainting the Little Red Schoolhouse: A History of Eastern German Education, 1945–1995* (New York: Oxford University Press, 2002), 54–59, 393; Gert Geissler, *Geschichte des Schulwesens in der Sowjetischen Besatzungszone und in der Deutschen Demokratischen Republik 1945 bis 1962* (Frankfurt am Main: Peter Lang, 2000), 187; Sonja Häder, "Von der 'demokratischen Schulreform' zur Stalinisierung des Bildungswesens—Der 17. Juni 1953 in Schulen und Schulverwaltung Ost-Berlins," in Jürgen Kocka, ed., *Historische DDR-Forschung: Aufsätze und Studien* (Berlin: Akademie Verlag, 1993), 196.

5. "Beschluss des Politbüros zur Verbesserung des Schulwesens," BLHA, Rep 333 SED Landesvorstand Brandenburg, no. 1205, 34.

6. Geissler, *Geschichte des Schulwesens*, 191–192 and 204–205.

7. Confidential letter from District Secretary of Brandenburg GLE chapter Günther S. to Province Brandenburg GLE, 21 August 1950, and "Bericht über den Ortsvorstande und die BGL der Lehrergewerkschaft in Brandenburg," 29 June 1949, BLHA, Rep 347 FDGB Landesvorstand GUE, no. 1031.

8. *Brandenburger Anzeiger,* 25 February 1933, "Für Brandenburg" section.

9. *Brandenburger Anzeiger,* 30 January, 25 February, and 11 March 1933, "Für Brandenburg" section; School-statistical List of the School Supervision District Brandenburg (Havel) for 1939, BLHA, Pr. Br. Rep 2A Regierung Potsdam II Brd., no. 198; city's registry of teachers, StadtA Brandenburg, 2.0.12.25/249; StadtA Brandenburg, 2.0.12.117/959; Otto Söchtig, "Tagebuchaufzeichnungen eines Lehrers von 1944 bis 1946," in Arbeitskreis Stadtgeschichte im Brandenburgischen Kulturbund e.V., ed., *Das Jahr 1945 in der Stadt Brandenburg: Eine Anthologie mit Darstellungen, Tagebuchaufzeichnungen und Lebenserinnerungen an das Ende des Zweiten Weltkrieges in der Stadt Brandenburg*, 3rd ed. (Brandenburg an der Havel: Werbe-Profi, 2001), 80–89.

10. Although scholars have studied Nazi and Communist education policies, the bulk of the research has focused on pedagogical and ideological developments and has largely overlooked teachers' and teacher organizations' roles in and experiences under each dictatorship; see, for example, Manfred Heinemann, ed., *Erziehung und Schulung im Dritten Reich* (Stuttgart: Klett-Cotta, 1980), Hans-Jochen Gamm, *Führung und Verführung: Pädagogik des Nationalsozialismus*, 2nd ed. (Frankfurt am Main: Campus Verlag, 1984), Arthur Hearnden, *Education in the Two Germanies* (Oxford: Blackwell, 1974), and Margrete Siebert Klein, *The Challenge of Communist Education: A Look at the German Democratic Republic* (New York: East European Monographs, 1980). Nor has the opening of various East German archives substantially altered our understanding of the issues; much of the writing on postwar education has continued to focus on subjects such as curricular changes or eastern German universities or has examined the experiences of teachers and their professional organizations in an incomplete or unsatisfactory manner, often as a result of either an overly broad perspective that obscures and distorts what really took place in communities like Brandenburg or reliance on a source base that makes extensive use of suspect East German scholarship. See for example Rodden, *Repainting the Little Red Schoolhouse*, 30–31, 43–45. Other more noteworthy works of recent scholarship on East Germany's education system include John Connelly, *Captive University: The Sovietization of East German, Czech, and Polish Higher Education, 1945–1956* (Chapel Hill: University of North Carolina Press, 2000), David Pike, *The Politics of Culture in Soviet-occupied Germany, 1945–1949* (Stanford: Stanford University Press, 1992), Norman Naimark, *The Russians in Germany* (Cambridge, Mass.: Harvard University Press, 1995), Blessing, *Antifascist Classroom*, and Geissler, *Geschichte des Schulwesens*.

11. Quoted in Kurt Schwedtke, *Adolf Hitler's Gedanken zur Erziehung und zum Unterricht: Eine Schulpolitische Studie*, 3rd ed., (Frankfurt am Main: Verlag Moritz Diesterweg, 1934), 36.

12. Brigitte Hohlfeld, *Die Neulehrer in der SBZ/DDR 1945–1953: Ihre Rolle bei der Umgestaltung von Gesellschaft und Staat* (Weinheim: Deutscher Studien Verlag, 1992), 11 and 85.

13. "Sorge um die Lehrerschaft," *Märkische Volksstimme*, 29 July 1946, 2.

14. Ritterakademie director to Oberpräsident Kube, 27 September 1935, BLHA, Pr. Br. Rep 34 P.S.K., no. 5303.

15. Walter Holöhr, "Jugend muss von Jugend geführt werden," in *Festschrift zur 350 Jahr Feier der v. Saldern*, BLHA, Pr. Br. Rep 34 P.S.K., no. 5364, 153.

16. Report on the Sekretariat meeting of 3 May 1949, BLHA, Rep 334 SED Kreisleitung Brandenburg, no. 8, 125.

17. Brandenburg an der Havel School Superintendent, "Nachtrag—Mein Urteil über die Goetheschule für Mädchen (Oberschule) Brandenburg (Havel)," 20 May 1950, BAB DR 2/5720, 230.

18. The promise of such an approach has been recognized by scholars such as Konrad Jarausch, Günther Heydemann, Michael Schwartz, and Hermann Wentker; see Konrad Jarausch, "Jenseits von Verdammung und Verklärung: Plädoyer für eine differenzierte DDR-Geschichte," in John A. McCarthy, Walter Grünzweig, and Thomas Koebner, eds., *The Many Faces of Germany: Transformations in the Study of German Culture and History* (New York: Berghahn Books, 2004), 195; Günther Heydemann, "Die DDR-Vergangenheit im Spiegel des NS-Regimes," *Internationale Schulbuchforschung* 22 (2000), 407–416; Henrik Bispinck, et al., "Die Zukunft der DDR-Geschichte," *Vierteljahrsheft für Zeitgeschichte* 53:4 (2005), 554–556.

19. Ralph Jessen, *Akademische Elite und kommunistischer Diktatur: Die ostdeutsche Hochschullehrerschaft in der Ulbricht-Ära* (Göttingen: Vandenhoeck und Ruprecht, 1999), especially 35–48; Achim Leschinsky, "Schule in der Diktatur: Die Umformung der Schule im Sowjetkommunismus und im Nationalsozialismus," in Dietrich Benner and Heinz-Elmar Tenorth, eds., *Bildungsprozesse und Erziehungsverhältnisse im 20. Jahrhundert: Zeitschrift für Pädagogik, supp. 42,* (Weinheim: Beltz Verlag, 2000), 116–138; Achim Leschinsky and Gerhard Kluchert, *Zwischen Zwei Diktaturen: Gespräche über die Schulzeit im Nationalsozialismus und in der SBZ/DDR* (Weinheim: Deutscher Studien Verlag, 1997); Elizabeth H. Tobin and Jennifer Gibson, "The Meanings of Labor: East German Women's Work in the Transition from Nazism to Communism," *Central European History* 28:3 (1995), 301–342; Lutz Niethammer, Alexander von Plato, and Dorothee Wierling, *Die Volkseigene Erfahrung: Eine Archäologie des Lebens in der Industrieprovinz der DDR: 30 biografische Eröffnungen* (Berlin: Rowohlt, 1991); Peter Hübner, ed., *Niederlausitzer Industriearbeiter 1935 bis 1970: Studien zur Sozialgeschichte* (Berlin: Akademie Verlag, 1995); Hermann Wentker, *Justiz in der SBZ/DDR 1945–1953: Transformation und Rolle ihrer zentralen Institutionen* (Munich: R. Oldenbourg Verlag, 2001), 584–605. Not all explorations of the issue of continuity are successful, however; Rodden, *Repainting the Little Red Schoolhouse*, 51–53, and Hermann Ottensmeier, *Faschistisches Bildungssystem in Deutschland zwischen 1933 und 1989: Kontinuität zwischen Drittem Reich und DDR* (Hamburg: Verlag Dr. Kovac, 1992), address the issue of continuity in the GDR but in a superficial, simplistic, and unenlightening manner.

20. Otto Tschirch, *Geschichte der Chur- und Hauptstadt Brandenburg an der Havel* (Brandenburg [Havel]: J. Wiesike, 1936), 1–3 and 9–13; Klaus Hess, *Brandenburg so wie es war* (Düsseldorf: Droste Verlag, 1992), 7–10, 27–28 and 31, and Winfried Schich, ed., *Beiträge zur Entstehung und Entwicklung der Stadt Brandenburg im Mittelalter* (Berlin: de Gruyter, 1993), v; Georg Holmsten, *Brandenburg: Geschichte des Landes, seiner Städte und Regenten* (Berlin: edition arani, 1991), 46; Udo Geiseler and Klaus Hess, ed., *Brandenburg an der Havel: Lexikon zur Stadtgeschichte* (Berlin: Lukas Verlag, 2008), 27, 75–81, 200–201, 255–257, 294–295. Although the Dominsel was only formally incorporated into the city in 1928–1929, it had been a de facto part of Brandenburg an der Havel since the nineteenth century.

21. Eberhard Schmieder, "Wirtschaft und Bevölkerung," in Hans Herzfeld, ed., *Berlin und die Provinz im 19. und 20. Jahrhundert* (Berlin: de Gruyter, 1968), 354–355; B. Graeser, ed., *Monatsschrift für Preussisches Städtewesen*, vol. 1, *Jahrgang 1855* (Frankfurt an der Oder: Verlag der Hofbuchdruckerei von Trowitzsch und Sohn, 1955), 162; Schich, *Beiträge*, x; Hess, *Brandenburg*, 57–59, and Tschirch, *Geschichte*, 211–212.

22. Hess, *Brandenburg*, 59–61 and 71; Tschirch, *Geschichte*, 220–223 and 247; and Schmieder, "Wirtschaft und Bevölkerung," 365. See also Roger Daniel, *Brennabor: "Die Fabrik." Die Industriegeschichte der Brennabor-Werke* (Lappersdorf: Kerschensteiner Verlag, 2005).

23. Tschirch, *Geschichte*, 228, Hess, *Brandenburg*, 81–82, and *Brandenburger Warte*, 11 March 1933, "Brandenburgische Schöppenstuhl" section.

24. Tschirch, *Geschichte*, 248–249.

25. Ibid., 251; Gordon Craig, *Germany 1866–1945* (New York: Oxford University Press, 1978), 509–510; Hess, *Brandenburg*, 82–83; *Brandenburger Anzeiger*, 11 March 1933, "Für Brandenburg" section. Brandenburg's other political parties as of 1919 were the German Democratic Party, the German National Peoples' Party, the Christian Peoples' Party, the Independent Social Democratic Party, and the Trade Middle Class (Gewerbliche Mittelstand). In the 1927 elections, the Bourgeois Working Group won 14 seats, the Communist Party's influence was reduced from 6 to 5 seats, and the new List of the Middle received 3 seats. See also Gerd Rühle, *Kurmark: Die Geschichte eines Gaues* (Berlin: Verlag Alfred Lindemann, 1934).

26. Hess, *Brandenburg*, 71; Tschirch, *Geschichte*, 255; *Brandenburger Anzeiger*, 18 January 1933, "Für Brandenburg" section.

27. See, for example, "Rote Pädagogen," *Brandenburger Warte*, 11 March 1933, and "Abwehrfront gegen die Schulreaktion," *Brandenburger Zeitung*, 26 January 1933; Frank Brekow, "Die Schule als

gesamtgesellschaftliche Aufgabe," in Gerd Heinrich, Klauss Hess, Winfried Schich, and Wolfgang Schössler, eds., *Stahl und Brennabor: Die Stadt Brandenburg im 19. und 20. Jahrhundert* (Potsdam: Verlag für Berlin-Brandenburg, 1998), 322.

28. *Brandenburger Anzeiger,* 11 March 1933, "Für Brandenburg" section.

29. Ibid.

30. "Abwehrfront gegen die Schulreaktion," *Brandenburger Zeitung,* 26 January 1933.

31. Representative of the many examples are "Säuberung des Schulwesens" and "Das Schulwesen wird weiter gesäubert: Der Eiserne Besen bleibt in Aktion!" *Brandenburger Warte,* 13 May 1933 and 3 June 1933. The paper also gleefully published a series of lists of Social Democrats, including teachers, who had recently left the SPD or who currently belonged to a Marxist "kitchen" *(Garküche)* like the Republican Club.

32. Tschirch, *Geschichte,* 250 and 255; Wolfgang Kusior, *Die Stadt Brandenburg im Jahrhundertrückblick: Streiflichter durch eine bewegte Zeit* (Berlin: Verlag Bernd Neddermeyer, 2000), 35; Karl-Heinz Röhring, "Parteien und Wahlen," in Heinrich et al., *Stahl und Brennabor,* 202; Hess, *Brandenburg,* 83; *Brandenburger Anzeiger,* 6 March 1933, "Für Brandenburg" section. According to the local newspaper, the city's population as of 31 December 1932 was 64,357; *Brandenburger Anzeiger,* 5 January 1933, "Für Brandenburg" section. See also Rühle, *Kurmark.*

33. Winfried Schich, "Die Kulturlandschaft im 19. und 20. Jahrhundert—Von der vorindustriellen Stadt zum Standort der Grossindustrie," and Detlef Kotsch, "Bürgerquartier und Kasernen—Brandenburg als Garnisonstadt (1815–1945)," in Heinrich et al., *Stahl und Brennabor,* 30 and 125–140, respectively; Kusior, *Die Stadt Brandenburg,* 48 and 50; Klaus Hess, "Rückblende 1945—Die Stadt Brandenburg vor über 50 Jahren," in Arbeitskreis Stadtgeschichte in Brandenburgischen Kulturbund e.V., *Das Jahr 1945,* 10–11, 15. See also Gudrun Bauer, Wolfgang Fritze, Doreen Geschke, Heiko Hesse, and Edith Sitz, eds., *Unfreiwillig in Brandenburg: Kriegsgefangene und Zwangsarbeiter in der Stadt Brandenburg in zwei Weltkriegen* (Berlin: Verlag Bernd Neddermeyer, 2004).

34. Schich, "Die Kulturlandschaft," 35; Hess, "Rückblende 1945," 18–19; Klaus Hess, "Republik und NS-Diktatur: Die Stadtverwaltung und der Stadtkreis in der Phase des Ausbaus der Stadt zum zweitgrössten Industrieort der Provinz Mark Brandenburg (1918–1945)," in Heinrich et al., *Stahl und Brennabor,* 72 and 76; Kusior, *Die Stadt Brandenburg,* 41–42 and 47.

35. Kusior, *Die Stadt Brandenburg,* 42–45, 51–52; *Brandenburger Zeitung,* 1 March 1933; *Brandenburger Anzeiger,* 5 April and 4 August 1933, "Für Brandenburg" section.

36. Klaus Hess, "Besatzungszeit und SED-Herrschaft (1945–1989)," in Heinrich et al., *Stahl und Brennabor*, 149–164; Kusior, *Die Stadt Brandenburg*, 72–94; Geiseler and Hess, *Brandenburg an der Havel*, 155 and 367–368; *Der Kurier*, no. 3, 24 November 1946, DStA; School Superintendent Willi L. to Deputy Principal Otto S., 11 July 1945, StadtA Brandenburg, 2.0.12.116/958, 28.

37. Hess, "Besatzungszeit," 149–164; Kusior, *Die Stadt Brandenburg*, 95–104; Burghard Ciesla, ed., *"Freiheit wollen wir": Der 17. Juni 1953 in Brandenburg* (Berlin: Ch. Links Verlag, 2003), 16–32; Arnulf Baring, *Uprising in East Germany: June 17, 1953* (Ithaca, N.Y.: Cornell University Press, 1972), 1–51; Mike Dennis, *The Rise and Fall of the German Democratic Republic, 1945–1990* (New York: Longman, 2000), 57–63; Mary Fulbrook, *Anatomy of a Dictatorship: Inside the GDR* (New York: Oxford, 1995), 179–183; Andrew I. Port, *Conflict and Stability in the German Democratic Republic* (New York: Cambridge University Press, 2007), 70–72.

38. Kusior, *Die Stadt Brandenburg*, 46–47, 60; Deborah Dwork and Robert Jan van Pelt, *Holocaust: A History* (New York: Norton, 2002), 262–263; Robert S. Wistrich, *Hitler and the Holocaust* (New York: Modern Library, 2003), 226–227.

1. National Socialism's Assault on German Teachers

1. Regarding the purge of senior civic leaders, see *Brandenburger Anzeiger*, 20 March 1933, special ed.; *Brandenburger Anzeiger*, 2 March 1933, "Für Brandenburg" section; see also the numerous, usually gleeful, reports of dismissals and punishments in the *Brandenburger Warte*, March to July 1933.

2. *Brandenburger Anzeiger*, 27 February 1933, "Für Brandenburg" section. For biographical information on Neef, see Erich Stockhorst, *Fünftausend Köpfe: Wer war was im Dritten Reich* (Bruchsal/Baden: blick + bild Verlag, 1967), 305.

3. "Lebt wohl, ihr roten genossen," "Rote Pädagogen," and "Säuberung des Schulwesen," *Brandenburger Warte*, 4 and 11 March and 13 May 1933; "Wühlereien gegen die vaterländische Schule: Schuldige ertappt," *Brandenburger Warte*, 4 February 1933.

4. Confidential circular, Education Ministry, 25 October 1938, BLHA, Pr. Br. Rep 2a Regierung Potsdam II Gen. no. 733.

5. See for example Michel Kater, *Hitler Youth* (Cambridge, Mass.: Harvard University Press, 2004), 40–42. Although not focusing on pedagogues, Dan Silverman makes clear the shortcomings of the Nazi purges in "Nazifica-

tion of the German Bureaucracy Reconsidered: A Case Study," *Journal of Modern History* 60 (1988), 496–539.

6. Included in the 18 schools are all of Brandenburg's primary, middle, and secondary schools. The few kindergartens, as well as the very small military school *(Heeresfachschule)* and the educational arm of the municipal jail, have been excluded from my analysis because they employed in total only a handful of teachers and because so few records exist regarding them and their activities. For a historical overview of the city's schools, see Frank Brekow, "Die Schule als gesamtgesellschaftliche Aufgabe," in Gerd Heinrich, Klaus Hess, Winfried Schich, and Wolfgang Schössler, eds., *Stahl und Brennabor: Die Stadt Brandenburg im 19. und 20. Jahrhundert* (Potsdam: Verlag für Berlin-Brandenburg, 1998), 315–329.

7. Albrecht von dem Bussche, *Die Ritterakademie zu Brandenburg* (Frankfurt am Main: Peter Lang, 1989), 43–50 and 91–96; regarding the pupils' elite status, see Oberpräsident Mark Brandenburg to Reich Education Minister, 3 March 1942, BAB, R4901/5144, as well as biographical entries of Ritterakademie cadets, undated, in R4901/5144; H.-J. Hahn, *Education and Society in Germany* (Berg: New York, 1998), 35 and 62; International Institute of Teachers College, Columbia University, *Guidebook to Some European School Systems* (New York: Bureau of Publications, Teachers College, Columbia University, 1927), 20–21; I. L. Kandel, *The Reorganization of Education in Prussia: Based on Official Documents and Publications*, trans. I. L. Kandel and Thomas Alexander (New York: Bureau of Publications, Teachers College, Columbia University, 1927), 72, 94–95, 98; A. E. Meyer, *Public Education in Modern Europe: A Review of Pre- and Post-war Education* (New York: Avon Press, 1928), 93; Rainer Bölling, *Sozialgeschichte der deutschen Lehrer: Ein Überblick von 1800 bis zur Gegenwart* (Göttingen: Vandenhoeck und Ruprecht, 1983), 16; according to the 1928 directory of teachers, approximately 1,043 pupils out of Brandenburg's 5,657 total pupils studied at the academic secondary schools, Lehrer-Verband der Provinz Brandenburg, ed., *Lehrer-Verzeichnis für die Provinz Brandenburg* (13. Jahrgang, Liegnitz: Carl Seyffarth, 1928), 29–33.

8. On *Mittleschulen* and the *Mittlere Reife*, see Hahn, *Education and Society in Germany*, 57; International Institute, *Guidebook*, 19–20; Bernd Zymek, "Schulen, Hochschulen, Lehrer," in Dieter Langewiesche and Heinz-Elmar Tenorth, eds., *Handbuch der deutschen Bildungsgeschichte: Die Weimarer Republik und die nationalsozialistische Diktatur, vol. 5, 1918–1945* (Munich: C. H. Beck, 1989), 156–175; and Bölling, *Sozialgeschichte*, 18–19.

9. International Institute, *Guidebook*, 18; Zymek, "Schulen," 166; for a general discussion of the Secular School, see Meyer, *Public Education*, 114–115; see Lehrer-Verband der Provinz Brandenburg, *Lehrer-Verzeichnis für die Provinz Brandenburg*, 29, and *Die Erzieher der Kurmark 1936: Verzeichnis der Parteidienststellen, Schulbehörden, Lehranstalten und Lehrkräfte* (Berlin: Verlag "Nationalsozialistische Erziehung," 1936), 107. Although the 1928 directory of teachers lists only 5,657 pupils in Brandenburg, this tally appears not to include pupils from all 18 schools. The more inclusive 1936 directory lists 7,645. Franz Breskow writes that there were 6,685 pupils in the city as of 1930, Franz Breskow, *Brandenburger Schulen von 1300–1990*, unpublished manuscript, StadtA Brandenburg, 115.

10. See Lehrer-Verband der Provinz Brandenburg, *Lehrer-Verzeichnis für die Provinz Brandenburg*, 29–35, *Die Erzieher der Kurmark 1936*, 107–112, and Breskow, *Brandenburger Schulen*, 115. Since the formal and informal pedagogical interaction between vocational school teachers and elementary and secondary school teachers was quite minimal, the very small number of teachers of the Städtische Handelsanstalt and the Gewerbliche Berufsschule are excluded from my analysis.

11. Statistical information regarding the teaching staff's characteristics was compiled from the diverse group of sources listed in the introduction, note 2.

12. As of 1931 only 24.4 percent of German secondary school teachers and 26.1 percent of Prussian elementary school teachers were women; however, women comprised 46.2 percent of all German middle school teachers, Konrad Jarausch, *The Unfree Professions. German Lawyers, Teachers, and Engineers, 1900–1950* (New York: Oxford University Press, 1990), 240, and Bölling, *Sozialgeschichte*, 10 and 14.

13. This statistic was drawn from a comparison of tables of "instruction hours" (*Unterrichtsstunden*) for the Ritterakademie for the period 1931–1934, DStA, BR 328/488, as well as from information found in Lehrer-Verband der Provinz Brandenburg, *Lehrer-Verzeichnis für die Provinz Brandenburg*, 33, *Die Erzieher der Kurmark 1936*, 107, and the registry of teachers, StadtA Brandenburg, 2.0.12.25/249. In contrast, only 48 percent of the city's population in June 1933 were male; *Statistisches Jahrbuch für Preussen*, ed., Preussischen Statistischen Landesamt, (Berlin: Verlag der Preussischen Statistischen Landesamt, 1934), 30: 258–259.

14. Registry of teachers, StadtA Brandenburg, 2.0.12.25/249; Lehrer-Verband der Province Brandenburg, *Lehrer-Verzeichnis für die Provinz Brandenburg*, 29–35, and *Die Erzieher der Kurmark 1936*, 107–112. In this respect, Brandenburg represents an anomaly since, according to Bölling,

female teachers were more concentrated at this time in the German middle and secondary schools, *Sozialgeschichte*, 11.

15. Ibid., and Konrad Jarausch and Gerhard Arminger, "The German Teaching Profession and Nazi Party Membership: A Demographic Logit Model," *Journal of Interdisciplinary History* 20:2 (1989), 202. For general information on the political topography of Brandenburg, see Laurenz Demps, "Die Provinz Brandenburg in der NS-Zeit (1933–1945)," in Ingo Materna and Wolfgang Ribbe, eds., *Brandenburgische Geschichte* (Berlin: Akademie Verlag, 1995), 620; a *Brandenburger Anzeiger* article notes that the KPD received the third greatest number of votes from city voters in both the November 1932 and March 1933 parliamentary elections, *Brandenburger Anzeiger*, 6 March 1933, "Für Brandenburg" section. The extant information, while sufficient to enable historians to establish a broad overview of city's pedagogues' political affiliation with non-Nazi parties, does not permit accurate determinations of the teacher type–political party correlations discussed in Bölling, *Sozialgeschichte*, 131–132, Jarausch, *Unfree Professions*, 70–71, and Jarausch and Arminger, "German Teaching Profession," 197–225.

16. *Brandenburger Anzeiger*, 13 January 1933 and 10 March 1933, "Für Brandenburg" section.

17. See "Wühlereien gegen die vaterländische Schule: Schuldige ertappt," *Brandenburger Warte: Kampfblatt der nationalen Bewegung und der vaterländischen Organisationen und Verbände, Der Deutsche Vorwärts*, Brandenburg ed., 4 February 1933, articles in the "Chronik der Heimat" section of the local Social Democratic newspaper *Brandenburger Zeitung*, 9 and 17 January 1933, and various teachers' biographies compiled as part of the postwar denazification trials, in minutes of meeting nos. 2 to 10 of Brandenburg (Havel) Denazification Commission, BLHA, Rep 203 Ministerium des Innern Entnazifizierung, no. 791.

18. See note 13 and extant personnel files for the city's secondary school teachers, BLHA, Pr. Br. Rep 34, Personalia; for a description of the various teachers' professional organizations, see the collection of essays in Manfred Heinemann, ed., *Der Lehrer und seine Organisation* (Stuttgart: Ernst Klett Verlag, 1977); Sebastian Müller-Rolli, "Lehrer," in Langewiesche and Tenorth, *Handbuch der deutschen Bildungsgeschichte*, 240–256; Johannes Erger, "Lehrer und Nationalsozialismus: Von den traditionellen Lehrerverbänden zum Nationalsozialistischen Lehrerbund (NSLB)," in Manfred Heinemann, ed., *Erziehung und Schulung im Dritten Reich, pt. 2, Hochschule, Erwachsenenbildung* (Stuttgart: Klett Cotta, 1980), 206–228; Bölling, *Sozialgeschichte*, 98–101; and Jarausch, *Unfree Professions*, 31–66.

19. "Wühlereien gegen die vaterländische Schule: Schuldige ertappt," *Brandenburger Warte*, 4 February 1933. For mention of the corporal punishment decree, see "Erweiterung des Züchtigungsrechts," *Brandenburger Zeitung*, 14 February 1933.

20. "Quer Durch Brandenburg," series of articles in *Brandenburger Warte*, 25 February 1933, 4 March 1933, 11 March 1933, and 18 March 1933, and Erich B.'s defense of his actions, BLHA, Pr. Br. Rep 34 P.S.K., no. 5315.

21. "Das Grosse Aufräumen: Die rotten Ketten sind gesprengt: Die Genossen fliegen," *Brandenburger Warte*, 25 March 1933, and *Brandenburger Anzeiger*, 20 March 1933, "Für Brandenburg" section.

22. "Der Mann, der immer auf die Füsse gefallen ist . . . Strauch rausgeflogen!" *Brandenburger Warte*, 8 April 1933.

23. Hans Mommsen, *Beamtentum im Dritten Reich* (Stuttgart: Deutsche Verlags-Anstalt, 1966), 39–46.

24. Ibid., 31 and 39; J. Noakes, and G. Pridham, eds., *Nazism 1919–1945, vol. 2, State, Economy and Society 1933–1939: A Documentary Reader* (Exeter, England: University of Exeter Press, 2000), 29; Jane Caplan, "The Politics of Administration: The Reich Interior Ministry and the German Civil Service, 1933–1943," *Historical Journal* 20:3 (1977): 720. Caplan notes that the Restoration Law was the Nazis' first "universally applicable statute," superseding individual states' laws and applying to all civil servants throughout Germany, 721.

25. Third Implementation Decree of 6 May 1933, RGBl I, 175, reprinted in G. A. Grotesend and Dr. C. Cretschmar, *Das gesamte deutsche und preussische Gesetzgebungsmaterial: Die Gesetze und Verordnungen sowie die Ausführnings-Anweiswage, Erlasse, Verfügungen usw. der preussischen und deutschen Zentralbehörden* (Düsseldorf: L. Schwann Verlag, 1933): Jahrgang 1933, 1:326–27, and 432. In the Third Implementation Decree issued by the Prussian State Ministry on 15 June 1933, the Restoration Law is defined for the first time as applying to teachers of public elementary and middle schools as well as of private secondary schools and vocational schools, 658–659.

26. Ibid., 326–327, 344, 432–433. The distinction between "political" and "nonpolitical" *Beamte* centered on how long individuals had occupied their civil service positions. Whereas "political" *Beamte* were expected to demonstrate their suitability on the basis of their proven civil service careers, a "nonpolitical" civil servant was to demonstrate his or her suitability for a recently occupied or soon to be occupied position "on the basis of his earlier theoretical or practical activities as well as on the basis of the honorableness of his attitudes and deeds", 433.

27. The Restoration Law provided for two additional categories of exemptions: for those who lost a father or son(s) in the First World War and for those who were currently working abroad; Noakes and Pridham, *Nazism*, 30. The exemptions were included at the insistence of Reich president Paul von Hindenburg; Mommsen, *Beamtentum*, 48. However, the Implementation Decree of 6 May 1933 closed some of the original law's loopholes. Having fought in the First World War no longer sufficed; now one had to have seen combat and also remained a civil servant with a distinguished record without interruption since the war's end; Grotesend and Cretschmar, *Gesetzgebungsmaterial*, 435.

28. Grotesend and Cretschmar, *Gesetzgebungsmaterial*, 344 and 435. Despite article 3's increasingly stringent anti-Semitic nature, the state nonetheless expanded in the third implementation decree the exemption for "non-Aryan" veterans if they fought against the "enemies of the national revolution" in the Baltics, Upper Silesia, and elsewhere, 435.

29. Noakes and Pridham, *Nazism*, 30.

30. Grotesend and Cretschmar, *Gesetzgebungsmaterial*, 344 and 435–436.

31. According to Mommsen, article 4 constituted the Restoration Law's "politically decisive core" that provided the state with its full power of attorney (*Generalvollmacht*), *Beamtentum*, 49.

32. Grotesend and Cretschmar, *Gesetzgebungsmaterial*, 327 and 436; Jane Caplan notes that these two provisions formed the heart of Frick's administrative reconstruction of the German civil service, "Politics of Administration," 720–721.

33. Mommsen argues that the state officially wished to effect the changes quickly in order to minimize the anticipated sense of unease and disquiet among the civil servants, *Beamtentum*, 44; Noakes and Pridham, *Nazism*, 31.

34. Included in the Decree of the Prussian Education Ministry, 14 June 1933, BLHA, Pr. Br. Rep 2a Regierung Potsdam II Gen., no. 733.

35. Directive of the Prussian Education Ministry, 11 July 1933, ibid. The committees were also referred to in the official correspondence as Liaison Commissions (*Vertrauenskomissionen*).

36. Report of the Personnel Committee for the Cleansing of the Civil Service of the Potsdam Government, 24 May 1933, ibid.

37. Ibid. According to the activity report, the Committee planned to require teachers who were suspected of being "unsuitable" to swear an oath of support. This oath would then be put into the teacher's official personnel file and could be the basis of any future disciplinary action if the teacher should in some way disregard the oath.

38. Report from Regierungspräsident Potsdam to Prussian Ministry of Education, 7 October 1933, ibid.

39. Directive from Prussian Education Ministry, 14 June 1933, 22 June 1933, and 28 July 1933, ibid; also Ferdinand G. to Brandenburg Province Oberpräsident, 4 August 1933, BLHA, Pr. Br. Rep 34 P.S.K., no. 5261.
40. Circular from the Prussian Education Ministry, 6 October 1933, BLHA, Pr. Br. Rep 2a Regierung Potsdam II Gen., no. 733.
41. Circular from the Prussian Ministry of the Interior, 9 August 1933, and Express Letter, Prussian Ministry of Education to Oberpräsidenten and Regierungspräsidenten, 12 August 1933, ibid.
42. Circular of the Prussian Ministry of Education, 28 November 1933, ibid. For individual teachers' materials provided in connection with the Restoration Law, see their personnel files, BLHA, Pr. Br. Rep 34 P.S.K., Personalia.
43. Circular of the Prussian Ministry of Education, 27 December 1933, BLHA, Pr. Br. Rep 2a Regierung Potsdam II Gen., no 733.
44. "Nachweisung über beurlaubte Lehrer," undated report from Potsdam Regierungspräsident, and Report of the Personnel Committee for the Cleansing of the Civil Service of the Potsdam Government, 24 May 1933, BLHA, Pr. Br. Rep 2A Regierung Potsdam II Gen, no. 733; see the relevant articles in *Brandenburger Warte*, 25 February, 1 April, 22 April, and 8 July 1933; Brandenburg Magistrat to Potsdam Regierung, Education Department, 12 April 1933, BLHA, Pr. Br. Rep 2A Regierung Potsdam II Brd., no. 124.
45. "Nachweisung über beurlaubte Lehrer," undated report from Potsdam Regierungspräsident, and Report of Personnel Committee for the Cleansing of the Civil Service of the Potsdam Government, 24 May 1933, BLHA, Pr. Br. Rep 2A Regierung Potsdam II Gen, no. 733. For information on their postpurge fates, see transfer notices in BLHA, Pr. Br. Rep 2A Regierung Potsdam II Brd., no. 124, the directory of teachers, in *Die Erzieher der Kurmark 1936*, 107–112, and School-statistical List BLHA, Pr. Br. Rep 2A Regierung Potsdam II Brd., no. 199.
46. For the fates of individual teachers, see transfer information BLHA, Pr. Br. Rep 2A Regierung Potsdam II Brd., no. 124, and the periodical by the regional education agency, *Amtliches Schulblatt für den Regierungs-Bezirk Potsdam*, nos. 8–28, 1933; *Brandenburger Anzeiger*, 8 March 1933, "Für Brandenburg" section; Protocol no. 7 of the meeting of the Brandenburg (Havel) Denazification Commission, 2 December 1947, BLHA, Rep 203 Ministerium des Innern Entnazifizierung, no. 791; *Die Erzieher der Kurmark 1936*, 107–112, and correspondence between Brandenburg Magistrat and Regierungspräsident Potsdam regarding the hiring of Erich F., Ursula M., and Johannes F., BLHA, Pr. Br. Rep 2A Regierung Potsdam Brd., no. 169. The continued employment of many Secular School teachers was confirmed by Karl-Heinz R., interview by author, August 2000. See also

Kusior, *Die Stadt Brandenburg im Jahrhundertrückblick*, 44; Ute Frevert, *Women in German History: From Bourgeois Emancipation to Sexual Liberation* (New York: Berg, 1988), 219.

47. "Aus der Mitgliederliste des 'Republikanischen Clubs' Brandenburg," *Der Warthe*, 4 June 1933, and "Die bonsokratischen Verhältnisse an der Handelslehranstalt Brandenburg-Ha.," report, both atttached to correspondence, Potsdam Regierungspräsident to Education Minister, 31 August 1933, BAB R4901/7849.

48. "Die bonsokratischen Verhältnisse an der Handelslehranstalt Brandenburg-Ha," BAB R4901/7849.

49. Report from Regierungspräsident Potsdam to Prussian Economics and Labor Minister, 31 August 1933, BAB R4901/7849.

50. Regierungspräsident Potsdam to Prussian Economics and Labor Minister, 31 August 1933, and draft letter, Prussian Economics and Labor Minister to Karl L., 18 January 1934, BAB R4901/7849.

51. Regierungspräsident Potsdam to Prussian Economics and Labor Minister, 31 August 1933, and draft transfer notice, Prussian Economics and Labor Minister to Alfred H., 4 February 1934, ibid.

52. Registry of teachers, StadtA Brandenburg, 2.0.12.25/249; Lehrer-Verband der Province Brandenburg, *Lehrer-Verzeichnis für die Provinz Brandenburg*, 29–35, and *Die Erzieher der Kurmark 1936*, 107–112; table of personnel data, DStA, BR106/272; "Quer Durch Brandenburg," 4 March, 25 March, 13 May 1933, "Rote Pädagogen," 11 March 1933, and "In den Ferien: Zeit der Reinigung der Schulen!" 10 June 1933, *Brandenburger Warte*; Director Ferdinand G. to Provinzialschulkollegium, BLHA, Pr. Br. Rep 34 P.S.K., no. 5261. The director also publicly defended both Julius S. and Heinrich M. in a letter to the *Brandenburger Warte*, 25 March 1933.

53. See correspondence, summer and early fall, personnel files, Heinrich M. and Paul G., BLHA, Pr. Br. Rep 34 P.S.K., Personalia, nos. M 288 and 41/1, respectively; "Lebt wohl, ihr roten genossen," *Brandenburger Warte*, 4 March 1933.

54. Report, BLHA, Pr. Br. Rep 34 P.S.K., no. 5313; registry of teachers, StadtA Brandenburg, 2.0.12.25/249. Regarding the tragic fate of Erich B., see the correspondence and reports in his personnel file, including Upper Lyceum principal Gustav S. to Brandenburg Province Oberpräsident, 3 July 1933, BLHA, Pr. Br. Rep 34 P.S.K., Personalia, no. B 234.

55. Quoted in Jarausch, *Unfree Professions*, 130.

56. Helmut Neuberger, *Freimaurerei und Nationalsozialismus: Die Verfolgung der deutschen Freimaurerei durch völkische Bewegung und Nationalsozialismus* (Hamburg: Bauhütten Verlag, 1980), 1:158–160, 2:118–119. Neuberger notes that during the Weimar Republic the liberal-bourgeois

"humanist" branch of German Freemasonry, as opposed to the Prussian lodges collectively and colloquially known as the Old Prussians, had openly embraced Social Democracy, the democratic parties, and the labor movements, and thereby helped convince Nazis and rightists of Freemasonry's "anti-German" character, 1:168–169.

57. Quoted in Ralf Melzer, *Konflikt und Anpassung: Freimaurerei in der Weimarer Republik und im "Dritten Reich"* (Vienna: Braumueller, 1999), 186.

58. Ibid., 27, 123–153. Examples of continued state and party actions against Freemasons in this period include the prohibition from joining the paramilitary *Stahlhelm* in December 1933, Hermann Göring's decree of January 1934 regarding lodges' voluntary dissolution, and the NSDAP Supreme Party Court's decision in early 1934 banning most Freemasons from joining the Nazi Party, ibid.

59. Ibid., 133, 136–139, and 150; Neuberger, *Freimaurerei*, 2:104–106.

60. Decree from Brandenburg Province Oberpräsident, 13 August 1935, and internal letter, Brandenburg Province Oberpräsident to Head of the Secondary Schools Department, 10 July 1935, BLHA, Pr. Br. Rep 34 P.S.K., no. 3786, 28 and 32–34; Neuberger, *Freimaurerei*, 2:124.

61. Report from Oberpräsident, 27 August 1935, BLHA, Pr. Br. Rep 34 P.S.K., no. 3786, 39–55, and Report from Regierungspräsident to Education Ministry, 30 September 1935, BLHA, Pr. Br. Rep 2a Regierung Potsdam II Gen., no. 733.

62. Letter from Education Ministry, 3 October 1936 and 18 February 1937, BLHA, Pr. Br. Rep 34 P.S.K., no. 3786, 76 and 86.

63. Olaf Thiede and Jörg Wacher, eds., *Chronologie Potsdam und Umgebung: Die Kulturlandschaft von 800 bis 1918: Brandenburg, Potsdam, Berlin*, vol. 3, *Ereignisse und Bauwerke* (Potsdam: Druckerei und Buchbinderei Christian und Cornelius Rüss, 2007), 1042–1045; personnel files, Brandenburg's secondary school teachers, BLHA, Pr. Br. Rep 34, Personalia; Report from Brandenburg Province Oberpräsident, 27 August 1935, BLHA, Pr. Br. Rep 34 P.S.K., no. 3786, 45–46.

64. "Nachweisung über die Zugehörigkeit von Beamten zu Freimaurerlogen, anderen Logen oder logenähnlichen Organisationen und deren Ersatzorganisationen," draft report from Regierungspräsident Potsdam to Education Ministry, 30 September 1935, BLHA, Pr. Br. Rep 2A Regierung Potsdam II Gen., no. 733.

65. Letter from Education Ministry, 18 February 1937, BLHA, Pr. Br. Rep 34 P.S.K., no. 3786, 86.

66. Memorundum of Potsdam Regierungspräsident, 24 June 1937, and attached draft letter, Regierungspräsident to Ministry of Education, BLHA, Pr. Br. Rep 2a Regierung Potsdam II Gen., no. 733.

67. Neuberger, *Freimaurerei*, 2:118 and 144.

68. Saul Friedlander, *Nazi Germany and the Jews*, vol. 1, *The Years of Persecution, 1933–1939* (New York: HarperCollins, 1997), 26. Although it is difficult to speak of a detailed program regarding Jews, points 4, 5, 6, 8, and 23 of the NSDAP Twenty-Five-Point Program address various aspects of the so-called Jewish Question, ibid.

69. Noakes and Pridham, *Nazism*, 2:530–535; Friedlander, *Nazi Germany and the Jews*, 137–143, 145–151. In his remarks before the Reichstag, Hitler stated that "the first and the second laws repay a debt of gratitude to the Movement, under whose symbol Germany regained its freedom, in that they fulfill a significant item on the program of the National Socialist Party," 142.

70. Friedlander, *Nazi Germany and the Jews*, 149. The Reich Citizenship Law of 15 September 1935 and the First Supplementary Decree of the Reich Citizenship Law of 14 November 1935 are reprinted in Noakes and Pridham, *Nazism*, 2:536–538.

71. Express letter from Reich Education Ministry, 30 September 1935, BLHA, Pr. Br. Rep 2a Regierung Potsdam II Gen., no. 733.

72. Decree of Prussian Education Ministry, 14 June 1933, BLHA, Pr. Br. Rep 2a Regierung Potsdam II. Gen., no. 733.

73. Ibid., Circular from Reich Ministry of Education, 12 December 1935.

74. Ibid., Circular from Reich Ministry of Education, 7 September 1936.

75. Ibid., Decree from Regierungspräsident Potsdam, 4 January 1937. The pledge consisted of the statements "I am not aware [*mir ist nicht bekannt*] that my wife is descended from Jewish parents or grandparents" and "I am not aware that I am descended from Jewish parents or grandparents."

76. Ibid., Draft letter from Regierungspräsident Potsdam, 4 March 1937.

77. Ibid., Decree of Education Ministry, 18 November 1937, with attached Interior Ministry Circular, ibid.; Jarausch, *Unfree Professions*, 145–146; Noakes and Pridham, *Nazism*, 539.

78. Delia and Gerd Nixdorf, "Politisierung und Neutralisierung der Schule in der NS-Zeit," in Hans Mommsen and Susanne Willems, eds., *Herrschaftsalltag im Dritten Reich: Studien und Texte*, (Düsseldorf: Schwann im Patmos Verlag, 1988), 256.

79. Jarausch, *Unfree Professions*, 145–146.

80. Report, BLHA, Pr. Br. Rep 2A Regierung Potsdam II Spezifica, no. 152.

81. Handwritten report "Über jüdisch versippte Lehrpersonen, die gemäss no. 6 BBG in den Ruhestand versetzt worden," draft letter from Regierungspräsident Potsdam to Minister of Education, 23 August 1937, and circular from Education Ministry, 13 August 1937, BLHA, Pr. Br. Rep 2a Regierung Potsdam II Gen., no. 733.

82. Prussian Minister for Economics and Labor to Frans S., 29 June 1937, copy, Regierungspräsident Potsdam to Reich Education Ministry, 31 March 1941, and Reich Education Ministry to Regierungspräsident Potsdam, 23 April 1941, BAB, R4901/7849.

83. Demps, "Die Provinz Brandenburg in der NS-Zeit," 625.

84. Confidential circular of Education Ministry, 25 October 1938, BLHA, Pr. Br. Rep 2a Regierung Potsdam II Gen., no. 733.

85. Quoted in I. L. Kandel, *The Making of Nazis* (1935; reprint, Westport, Conn.: Greenwood Press, 1970), 42.

86. Ibid.

87. Registry of teachers, StadtA Brandenburg, 2.0.12.25/249; Lehrer-Verband der Province Brandenburg, *Lehrer-Verzeichnis für die Provinz Brandenburg*, 29–35, and *Die Erzieher der Kurmark 1936*, 107–112; *Brandenburger Anzeiger*, 31 March 1933 and 28 March 1934, "Für Brandenburg" section; report, BLHA, Pr. Br. Rep 2A Regierung Potsdam I, no. 5260.

88. Ibid. For information about Dr. Ludwig Z.'s diverse political involvements starting in the spring of 1933, see the transcript of his denazification hearing, BLHA, Rep 203 Ministerium des Innern Entnazifizierung, no. 791.

89. Dr. Ludwig Z. to Provinzialschulkollegium, 8 July 1933, BLHA, Pr. Br. Rep 34 P.S.K., no. 5294.

90. Gustav S. to Brandenburg Province Oberpräsident, to Provinzialschulkollegium, and to *Brandenburger Warte*, BLHA, Pr. Br. Rep 34 Provinzialschulkollegium, no. 5315; correspondence between Ferdinand G. and Provinzialschulkollegium, March 1933, BLHA, Pr. Br. Rep 34 Provinzialschulkollegium, no. 5261; Neuberger, *Freimaurerei und Nationalsozialismus*, 2:134; Nixdorf, "Politisierung und Neutralisierung," 228.

91. The closings did not affect the training of Prussia's secondary school teachers, who pursued a four-year course of study at one of the traditional universities. Beginning in the early 1930s, however, education officials did implement measures such as a *Numerus clausus* in order to reduce the number of students preparing to become secondary school pedagogues; Bölling, *Sozialgeschichte*, 113–116 and 152–153.

92. Harald Scholtz and Elmar Stranz, "Nationalsozialistische Einflussnahmen auf die Lehrerbildung," in Heinemann, *Erziehung und Schulung im Dritten Reich* 2:110–111 and 116–117; Bölling, *Sozialgeschichte*, 148. In an effort to expand and accelerate the production of new teachers, Nazi officials in 1939 introduced special teacher training courses *(Aufbaulehrgänge)* for young men and women with only elementary or middle school qualifications, 116.

93. Rolf Eilers, *Die nationalsozialistische Schulpolitik: Eine Studie zur Funktion der Erziehung im totalitären Staat* (Köln: Westdeutscher Verlag, 1963), 74.

94. Kusior, *Stadt Brandenburg,* 50–51; Tschirch, *Geschichte,* 254; see correspondence between Brandenburg School Superintendent Schmidt and Potsdam Regierungspräsident 1934–1937, BLHA, Pr. Br. Rep 2A Regierung Potsdam II Brd. no. 124; Notes of Oberregierungsrat Heckel, 14 November 1938, BAB R4901/5144; draft letter, Potsdam Regierungspräsident to Reich Education Ministry, 10 January 1939, BLHA, Pr. Br. Rep 2A Regierung Potsdam II Brd., no. 152; Brekow, "Die Schule," 323.

95. Bölling notes that although the cost of living sank by 20 percent in the period 1930–1932, the loss of up to 40 percent of their wages nevertheless represented a painful devaluation of their income, a situation that continued into the Third Reich. According to Jarausch, real wages for secondary school teachers decreased from 454.2 to 420.5 Marks per month in the period 1928–1936; in 1913 the real wage had been 533 Marks per month. Bölling, *Sozialgeschichte,* 122, and Jarausch, *Unfree Professions,* 249.

96. Secondary school teachers experienced some economic relief as early as 1936 when their income rose as a consequence of the transfer of their pay scale from the Prussian wage system to that of the Reich; Bölling, *Sozialgeschichte,* 150 and 154–155, and Jarausch, *Unfree Professions,* 205.

97. Michael H. Kater, "Hitlerjugend und Schule im Dritten Reich," *Historische Zeitschrift* 228 (1979), 596–597; Jarausch, *Unfree Professions,* 132–133, 156–162; Bölling, *Sozialgeschichte,* 116–125, 153–155; Scholtz and Stranz, "Nationalsozialistische," 116.

98. Memorandum of Potsdam Regierungspräsident, 24 June 1937, and attached draft letter, Regierungspräsident Bismarck-Schönhausen to Education Ministry, BLHA, Pr. Br. Rep 2a Regierung Potsdam II Gen., no. 733.

99. Jarausch, *Unfree Professions,* 158–161.

100. Kater, "Hitlerjugend," 579, 581 and 593; Zymek, "Schulen, Hochschulen, Lehrer," in Langewiesche and Tenorth, *Handbuch der deutschen Bildungsgeschichte,* 190–193; Langeweische and Tenorth, "Bildung, Formierung, Destruktion," in ibid., 20, and Tenorth, "Pädagogisches Denken," in ibid., 139; Jarausch, *Unfree Professions,* 120; and Bölling, *Sozialgeschichte,* 136–142; Nixdorf, "Politisierung und Neutralisierung," 229. For a useful survey of the regime's polycratic nature, see Ian Kershaw, *The Nazi Dictatorship: Problems and Perspectives of Interpretation,* 3rd ed. (London: Arnold, 1993), 59–79.

2. The Incomplete Revolution of the NSLB

1. *Brandenburger Anzeiger,* 12 and 13 June 1933, 15 and 26 February 1933, and 13 May 1933, "Für Brandenburg" section. In contrast to the dearth of publicity surrounding the NSLB, the *Brandenburger Anzeiger* reported

extensively at this time on the various activities of local chapters of other National Socialist organizations such as the Nationalsozialistisches Kraftfahrkorps, the Hitler Jugend, the Nationalsozialistische Betriebszellenorganisation, and the NSDAP.

2. Gertrud Kahl-Futhman, *Hans Schemm Spricht: Seine Reden und sein Werk* (Bayreuth: Gauverlag Bayerische Ostmark, 1936), 162. Although Schemm and other Nazis regularly spoke of a "teachers' community" *(Lehrerschaft)*, Brandenburg's teachers did not constitute a single, city-wide, clearly defined community. Nor did they collectively take part in the city's civil society, although individual teachers certainly participated by means of various clubs and other associations; see Jürgen Kocka's useful essay "Civil Society in Historical Perspective," in John Keane, ed., *Civil Society: Berlin Perspectives* (New York: Berghahn Books, 2007), 37–50.

3. Kahl-Futhman, *Hans Schemm Spricht*, 162.

4. See for example Götz Aly, *Hitler's Beneficiaries: Plunder, Racial War, and the Nazi Welfare State* (New York: Metropolitan, 2007), 30, Peter Fritzsche, *Life and Death in the Third Reich* (Cambridge, Mass.: Belknap Press, 2008), Robert Gellately, *Backing Hitler: Consent and Coercion in Nazi Germany* (New York: Oxford University Press, 2001), and the essays in David Bankier, ed., *Probing the Depths of German Antisemitism: German Society and the Persecution of the Jews, 1933–1941* (New York: Berghahn Books, 2000).

5. The NSLB *Mitgliedskartei* for Gau Kurmark, BAB NS12, 2:82–88; registry of teachers, StadtA Brandenburg, 2.0.12.25/249; individual files, BLHA, Provinzialschulkollegium record group and DStA; *Die Erzieher der Kurmark 1936*, and NS Lehrerbund Kartei und Akten, Microfilm Publication A3340, Series MF, Berlin Document Center, National Archives, Washington, D.C.; *Verzeichnis der Parteidienststellen, Schulbehörden, Lehranstalten und Lehrkräfte* (Berlin: Verlag "Nationalsozialistische Erziehung," 1936), 107–112; *Brandenburger Anzeiger*, 30 September 1937, "Für Brandenburg" section.

6. Marjorie Lamberti, "German Schoolteachers, National Socialism, and the Politics of Culture at the End of the Weimar Republic," *Central European History* 34:1 (2001), 74.

7. *Brandenburger Anzeiger*, 2 March and 12 June 1933, "Für Brandenburg" section.

8. Willi Feiten, *Der Nationalsozialistische Lehrerbund—Entwicklung und Organisation: Ein Beitrag zum Aufbau und zur Organisationsstruktur des nationalsozialistischen Herrschaftssystems* (Weinheim: Beltz Verlag, 1981), 40–42. Schemm first made contact with the Nazi Party in 1923 and soon afterward became very active in the local Bayreuth chapter,

rising by 1928 to the position of district governor of Upper Fra-
conia.

9. Ibid., 44–45.

10. Ibid., 46.

11. Ibid., 44–45.

12. Ibid., 47.

13. Lamberti, "German Schoolteachers," 74, and Feiten, *Nationalsozialistische Lehrerbund*, 48–49. According to Michael Kater, beginning in mid-1932 "the various restrictions imposed on the openly activist Nazi public servants by the states of Prussia and Baden, and sporadically by other state governments, were either revoked or could be openly ignored," *The Nazi Party: A Social Profile of Members and Leaders 1919–1945* (Cambridge, Mass.: Harvard University Press, 1983), 61.

14. According to Lamberti, 12,000 of Germany's approximately 300,000 teachers in March 1933 were NSLB members, "German Schoolteachers," 81. Konrad Jarausch notes that there were 11,000 members "by early 1933," *The Unfree Professions: German Lawyers, Teachers, and Engineers, 1900–1950* (New York: Oxford University Press, 1990), 99.

15. Feiten, *Nationalsozialistische Lehrerbund*, 50.

16. As quoted in ibid., 53.

17. Compiled from *Mitgliedskartei* for Gau Kurmark, BAB NS12, 2:82–88, registry of teachers, StadtA Brandenburg, 2.0.12.25/249, and individual files, BLHA Provinzialschulkollegium record group and DStA. For a comparative analysis of the NSLB admission rates in 1933 for eight *Gaue*, see Heinrich Küppers, *Der katholische Lehrerverband in der Übergangszeit von der Weimarer Republik zur Hitler-Diktatur* (Mainz: Matthias-Grünewald Verlag, 1975), 123.

18. *Brandenburger Anzeiger*, 17 August 1933, "Für Brandenburg" section.

19. Friedericke Matthias, Leader of NSLB Reich Section II, to Regional Association of the Prussian Senior Civil Servants, 5 November 1933, copy, BAB NS12/869; membership information compiled from *Mitgliedskartei* for Gau Kurmark, BAB NS12, 2:82–88, registry of teachers, StadtA Brandenburg, 2.0.12.25/249, and individual files, BLHA Provinzialschulkollegium record group and DStA.

20. *Brandenburger Anzeiger*, 21 November 1933, "Für Brandenburg" section.

21. Following the so-called Potsdam of the Teaching Staff at Magdeburg, the NSLB targeted the teachers' associations on the regional and local levels. League officials hoped to "hollow out" and thus destroy the associations by co-opting their members into the NSLB, Rolf Eilers, *Die nationalsozialis-*

tische Schulpolitik: Eine Studie zur Funktion der Erziehung im totalitären Staat (Köln: Westdeutscher Verlag, 1963), 79.

22. Karl Dietrich Bracher, *The German Dictatorship* (New York: Praeger, 1970), 214–227; *Brandenburger Anzeiger,* 26 August 1933, "Für Brandenburg" section.

23. See the personnel records for the men of the Von Saldern and Ritterakademie schools, BLHA, Pr. Br. Rep 34 P.S.K., Personalia. The problem of "double membership" plagued the NSLB throughout its struggle to dissolve the non-Nazi teachers' professional associations, Eilers, *Die nationalsozialistische Schulpolitik,* 83.

24. Rainer Bölling, *Sozialgeschichte der deutschen Lehrer: Ein Überblick von 1800 bis zur Gegenwart* (Göttingen: Vandenhoeck und Ruprecht, 1983), 129; Sebastian Müller-Rolli, "Lehrer," in Dieter Langewiesche and Heinz-Elmar Tenorth, eds., *Handbuch der deutschen Bildungsgeschichte: Die Weimarer Republik und die nationalsozialistische Diktatur, vol. 5, 1918–1945* (Munich: C. H. Beck, 1989), 250–252; Rainer Bölling, "Zur Entwicklung und Typologie der Lehrerorganisation in Deutschland," in Manfred Heinemann, ed., *Der Lehrer und seine Organisation* (Stuttgart: Ernst Klett Verlag, 1977), 2:23–24, and Eilers, *Die nationalsozialistische Schulpolitik,* 76.

25. Feiten, *Nationalsozialistische Lehrerbund,* 55, and Eilers, *Die nationalsozialistische Schulpolitik,* 76 and 132. For a discussion of the function of and services provided by, for example, the German Teachers' Association, see Rainer Bölling, *Volksschullehrer und Politik: Der Deutsche Lehrerverein 1918–1933* (Göttingen: Vandenhoeck und Ruprecht, 1978), 55–104.

26. Feiten, *Nationalsozialistische Lehrerbund,* 56–57. Eilers writes that on 31 March 1933 Schemm had called on the teachers' organizations to turn over to the National Socialists their associations' leadership positions, on both the national and local levels, and the control of their press departments, *Die nationalsozialistische Schulpolitik,* 76–77.

27. Feiten, *Nationalsozialistische Lehrerbund,* 57.

28. Eilers, *Die nationalsozialistische Schulpolitik,* 77; Feiten, *Nationalsozialistische Lehrerbund,* 58; Bölling, *Volksschullehrer und Politik,* 221–223. The author recounts a weekend meeting, held 20–21 May 1933, between NSLB *Gauobmänner* and association leaders in which the Philologist Association voiced its serious opposition to the DEG, claiming that the philologists would be outvoted by the more numerous elementary school teachers, ibid. Konrad Jarausch writes that the Philologist Association issued in late May a warning as to the "grave danger that valuable organizations will be destroyed or atomized without being replaced by an organic

whole that is not only externally but internally united and really alive," reprinted in *Unfree Professions,* 119.

29. Feiten, *Nationalsozialistische Lehrerbund,* 60–61, and Eilers, *Die national-sozialistische Schulpolitik,* 78.

30. Eilers, *Die nationalsozialistische Schulpolitik,* 82–83, and Feiten, *National-sozialistische Lehrerbund,* 67. Remaining tasks included the compulsory dissolution of a number of small confessional teachers' associations, the legal proscription of teachers' membership in non-NSLB professional organizations, and the legal transfer of associations' assets to the NSLB, all of which were accomplished under Wächtler's supervision, Eilers, *Die nationalsozialistische Schulpolitik,* 83.

31. *Brandenburger Anzeiger,* 7, 9, and 21 August 1933, 29 November 1933, 11 December 1933, and 15 June 1934, "Für Brandenburg" section.

32. *Brandenburger Anzeiger,* 26 October 1933, "Für Brandenburg" section.

33. See Kurmark District Treasurer Heinrich Wallrabenstein to League Reich Leadership, 16 December 1933, BAB NS12/1018; *Brandenburger Anzeiger,* 29 September and 21 November 1933, "Für Brandenburg" section; Kurmark District Leader Martin Müller to NSLB Reich Leadership, 8 November 1933, BAB NS12/1018.

34. Officials of the NSLB were still discussing a year later the relationship between financial burdens and members' discontent, including the lingering anger over the House of German Education; see "Bericht über die Stimmung in der kurmärkischen Erzieherschaft," attached to letter, NSDAP Kurmark District Leadership to NSLB Reich leadership, 8 November 1934, BAB NS12/1018.

35. Reprinted in Eilers, *Die nationalsozialistische Schulpolitik,* 3.

36. NSLB Kurmark District Treasurer Wallrabenstein to NSLB Reich Leadership, 4 August 1936, and NSLB Kurmark District Leadership to Reich Manager Kolb, NSLB Reich Leadership, 8 May 1936, BAB NS12/864; NSLB Kreis Züllichau-Schwiebus to NSLB Reich Leadership, 17 March 1936, BAB NS12/1018.

37. *Brandenburger Anzeiger,* 23 September 1933, 20 March 1934, 14 and 30 April 1934, and 26 August 1937, "Für Brandenburg" section.

38. Feiten, *Nationalsozialistische Lehrerbund,* 114–120; Fritz Wächtler, "Volksgemeinschaft-Schicksalgemeinschaft," *Der Deutsche Erzieher: Reichszeitung des NSLB,* Gau Kurmark ed., vol. 3, 1 February 1939, 50–51. Wächtler's article also indicates that in addition to publishing the student magazine *Hilf mit,* the NSLB organized essay contests for pupils, helped build schools, and financed a barge that was intended to expose small groups of German pupils to German culture and geography by traveling along Germany's rivers.

39. Hauptstelle Schrifttum, Jugendschriftstelle to Principal Fritz Günther, 28 July 1936, BAB NS12/999; Feiten, *Nationalsozialistische Lehrerbund,* 123; for examples of NSLB publications and their diverse readership, see NSLB correspondence, BAB NS12/997.

40. Kahl-Futhman, *Hans Schemm Spricht,* 162.

41. Feiten, *Nationalsozialistische Lehrerbund,* 176.

42. Ibid., 176–177.

43. *Brandenburger Anzeiger,* 4 September 1934 and 17 August 1933, "Für Brandenburg" section.

44. *Brandenburger Anzeiger,* 4 February 1937, "Für Brandenburg" section.

45. *Brandenburger Anzeiger,* 23 November 1933, 18 and 26 January 1934, 23 April 1934, 3 May 1934, 8 and 18 June 1934, 7 and 22 September 1934, 23 and 24 October 1934, and 13 November 1934, "Für Brandenburg" section.

46. Quoted in Adolf Mertens, *Schulungslager und Lagererziehung* (Dortmund: Druck und Verlag von W. Crüwell, 1937), 4.

47. Arbeitsgruppe Pädagogische Museum, ed., *Heil Hitler, Herr Lehrer: Volksschule 1933–1945 Das Beispiel Berlin* (Reinbek bei Hamburg: Rowohlt, 1983), 126–127, and Feiten, *Nationalsozialistische Lehrerbund,* 177 and 182. The camp system consisted of three tiers: the A-Training was the basic indoctrination program intended for every German teacher: the B-Training, representing a lengthier and more intensive indoctrination in National Socialism, was for the top 10 percent of the basic program's graduates, and the C-Training was a three-week program for the "creation of the educators' leadership corps," see "Schulungsaufbau," diagram, BAB NS12/1455. For the centrality of the *Schulungslager* in the Nazi teacher training system, see also Werner Sacher, "Lehrerfortbildung im Spannungsfeld zwischen Staat und Lehrerorganisation," in Heinemann, *Der Lehrer und seine Organisation,* 114.

48. Arbeitsgruppe Pädagogische Museum, *Heil Hitler, Herr Lehrer,* 128.

49. Ibid., 127.

50. Mertens, *Schulungslager,* 37 and 73; Feiten, *Nationalsozialistische Lehrerbund,* 178; Arbeitsgruppe Pädagogische Museum, *Heil Hitler, Herr Lehrer,* 128; "Schulungsaufbau und Lehrpläne des NS-Lehrerbundes," Carl Wolf, BAB NS12/1455. For detailed analysis of the divisions within Brandenburg's teaching staff, see Chapter 1.

51. Wilfried Breyvogel, "Volksschullehrer und Faschismus—Skizze zu einer sozialgeschichtlichen Erforschung ihrer sozialen Lager," in Heinemann, *Der Lehrer und seine Organisation,* 338, and Arbeitsgruppe Pädagogische Museum, *Heil Hitler, Herr Lehrer,* 127–128. This desire to erase differences among teachers did not extend to unifying men and women; the NSLB camps were segregated along gender lines, see, for example, "Die

Schulungsarbeit der Gauwaltung," *Nationalsozialistische Erziehung* 8:17, 1. September 1939, 375–376.

52. Arbeitsgruppe Pädagogische Museum, *Heil Hitler, Herr Lehrer,* 126.

53. *Brandenburger Anzeiger,* 6 August 1937, "Für Brandenburg" section.

54. See personnel files, secondary school teachers, BLHA, Pr. Br. Rep 34, Personalia; quotation from Walter H.'s report to *Oberpräsident,* 29 February 1940, BLHA, Pr. Br. Rep 34, M 288. Against the possible charge that the files might not be complete, it should be noted that they show that teachers often went to great lengths to make sure their files were complete and up to date, especially regarding items on which they believed the regime would look favorably.

55. "Prozentsatz der Geschulten," statistical analysis, 1 January 1935, BAB NS12/1455. See also "Prozentsatz der lagermässig Geschulten," statistical analysis, NSLB Training Department, 2 January 1936, BAB NS12/1455.

56. NSLB Reich Leadership to NSLB Kurmark District, 22 February 1935, and NSLB Kurmark District to NSLB Reich Leadership, 19 March 1935, BAB NS12/1018; undated activity report from Training Department, NSLB Kurmark District, BAB NS12/913; and NSLB Kurmark District Dr. Gerhard Hoppe to Reich Schulung Leader Carl Wolf, NSLB Main Office for Educators, 10 May 1935, BAB NS12/1018.

57. NSLB Reich Schulung Leader Carl Wolf to District Schulung Leader Hoppe, 13 May 1935, NSLB Kurmark District Leadership, Martin Müller, to Education Ministry, 7 June 1935, NSLB Kurmark District Leadership, Gerhard Hoppe, to NSLB Reich Leadership, Carl Wolf, 17 August 1935, NS12/1018, and "Sommerschulung des NSLB 1935," statistical analysis, BAB NS12/1455.

58. "Lagerschulung 1933–1.5.1936," 15 May 1936, BAB NS12/1455; NSLB Kurmark District Leadership, Gerhard Hoppe, to NSLB Reich Leadership, Carl Wolf, 17 August 1935, BAB NS12/1018. The NSLB records reveal a slight discrepancy regarding the total number of pedagogues trained that summer. Hoppe's letter claims 1,980, while a later NSLB letter states the total at 2,200, in addition to making clear that the participants had volunteered, see NSLB Kurmark District, Finance Department, to Reich Leadership, Finance Department, 25 February 1936, BAB NS12/1018.

59. Kurmark District Schulung Leader Hoppe to Reich Schulung Leader Wolf, 13 December 1935, Müller to Oberregierungsrat Kolb, 31 January 1936, Kurmark District Leadership to Reichs Leadership, 24 March 1936 and 8 April 1936, circular from Kurmark District NSLB Schulung Department to all NSLB Kurmark District Kreisamtsleiter, 21 April 1936, and

NSLB Reich Leadership to Kurmark District Leadership, 30 April 1936, BAB NS12/1018; Feiten, *Nationalsozialistische Lehrerbund*, 181.

60. Feiten, *Nationalsozialistische Lehrerbund*, 181. Citing similar statistics for total numbers of educators trained in the camps, Konrad Jarausch nonetheless claims that the number of teachers in 1937 represented two-fifths of Germany's teaching staff, *Unfree Professions*, 153.

61. See the completed questionnaire regarding costs of membership in the regional NSLB from Kurmark District Treasurer Wallrabenstein to Reich Leadership, Treasury Department, 21 June 1937, BAB NS12/864.

62. "Tätigkeitsbericht Gau Kurmark, Abteilung Schulung, no. 3, Zeit 1.10.–31.12.37," BAB NS12/927; "Schulungsstatistik bis Oktober 1938," BAB NS12/1455.

63. "Die Schulungsarbeit der Gauwaltung," *Nationalsozialistische Erziehung*, 8:17, 1 September 1939, 375–376.

64. Jarausch, *Unfree Professions*, 153. Participation statistics vary widely from *Gau* to *Gau* and from *Kreis* to *Kreis*; whereas some subdistricts succeeded in placing 95 percent of their members in camps, only 35 percent of the Kassel Subdistrict's NSLB members attended a camp, Breyvogel, "Volksschullehrer und Faschismus," 339.

65. NSLB Gauamtsleitung Gau Kurmark to NSLB Reichsleitung, 11 July 1934, BAB NS12/1018.

66. Feiten, *Nationalsozialistische Lehrerbund*, 153 and 170–174, and Eilers, *Die nationalsozialistische Schulpolitik*, 78–84. See also draft circular from NSLB Reich Leadership official Carl Wolf, 3 March 1936, to all NSLB Gauamtsleiter and Gauschulungswalter, BA R4901/4607.

67. Jarausch, *Unfree Professions*, 153.

68. Feiten, *Nationalsozialistische Lehrerbund*, 182; Wilhelm Deist, *The Wehrmacht and German Rearmament* (Toronto: University of Toronto, 1981), 36–44, and Rudolf Absolon, *Die Wehrmacht im Dritten Reich*, vol. 3, *3. August 1934 bis 4. Februar 1938* (Boppard am Rhein: Harald Boldt Verlag, 1975), 23–24, 82–85, and 111.

69. School-statistical List of School Supervision District Brandenburg (Havel) as of 1 May 1939, BLHA, Pr. Br. Rep 2A Regierung Potsdam II Brd., no. 198; Barton Whaley, *Covert German Rearmament, 1919–1939: Deception and Misperception* (Frederick, Md.: University Publications of America, 1984), 69.

70. Michael H. Kater, "Hitlerjugend und Schule im Dritten Reich," *Historische Zeitschrift* 228 (1979): 596–597; Jarausch, *Unfree Professions*, 132–133, 156–162; Bölling, *Sozialgeschichte*, 116–125, 153–155.

71. Wolfgang Kusior, *Die Stadt Brandenburg im Jahrhundertrückblick: Streiflichter durch eine bewegte Zeit* (Berlin: Verlag Bernd Neddermeyer,

2000), 50–51; Otto Tschirch, *Geschichte der Chur- und Hauptstadt Brandenburg an der Havel* (Brandenburg (Havel): J. Wiesike, 1936), 254; see correspondence between Brandenburg School Superintendent Schmidt and Potsdam Regierungspräsident 1934–1937, BLHA, Pr. Br. Rep 2A Regierung Potsdam II Brd., no. 124; Notes of Oberregierungsrat Heckel, 14 November 1938, BAB R4901/5144; draft letter, Potsdam Regierungspräsident to Reich Education Ministry, 10 January 1939, BLHA, Pr. Br. Rep 2A Regierung Potsdam II Brd., no. 152; Frank Brekow, "Die Schule als gesamtgesellschaftliche Aufgabe," in Gerd Heinrich, Klaus Hess, Winfried Schich, and Wolfgang Schössler, eds., *Stahl und Brennabor: Die Stadt Brandenburg im 19. und 20. Jahrhundert* (Potsdam: Verlag für Berlin-Brandenburg, 1998), 323.

72. Jarausch, *Unfree Professions*, 153.

73. Kahl-Furthmann, *Hans Schemm Spricht*, 164.

74. School-statistical List of the School Supervision District Brandenburg (Havel) for 1939, BLHA, Pr. Br. Rep 2A Regierung Potsdam II Brd., no. 198, *Mitgliedskartei* for Gau Kurmark, BAB NS12, 2:82–88, registry of teachers, StadtA Brandenburg, 2.0.12.25/249, individual files, BLHA Provinzialschulkollegium record group, BLHA, Pr. Br. Rep 34 P.S.K., Personalia, from DStA, and from NS Lehrerbund Kartei und Akten, Microfilm Publication A3340, ser. MF, Berlin Document Center, National Archives; Wolfgang F., interview by author, summer 2005.

75. Personnel file, Rudolf R., BLHA, Pr. Br. Rep 34, Personalia, no. R 267.

76. Ibid., especially Brandenburg NSDAP Kreisleiter Schöttler, report to Kurmark NSDAP leadership, 21 November 1938, and police report, 15 December 1938. Rudolf R. was not punished for his actions, as the regional NSDAP leadership informed Brandenburg's *Kreisleiter* and school superintendent, "in view of the general opinion of the Reich and Gau leaderships regarding the action of 9. and 10. November," NSDAP, Gauleitung Mark Brandenburg to Brandenburg School Superintendent, draft letter, 7 February 1939, BLHA, Pr. Br. Rep 34, Personalia, no. R 267. For background on the *Reichspogrom* in Brandenburg, see *Brandenburger Anzeiger*, 11 November 1938, "Antijüdische Demonstrationen in Berlin und in der Kurmark," and Irene Diekmann, "Zur Geschichte der jüdischen Gemeinde," in Heinrich et al., *Stahl und Brennabor*, 306–309.

77. Personnel records, BLHA, Pr. Br. Rep 34 P.S.K., Personalia, nos. 86 and N 113/a.

78. Ibid., no. G 119.

79. School-statistical List of School Supervision District Brandenburg (Havel) for 1939, BLHA, Pr. Br. Rep 2A Regierung Potsdam II Brd., no. 198, *Mitgliedskartei* for Gau Kurmark, BAB NS12, 2:82–88, registry of teach-

ers, StadtA Brandenburg, 2.0.12.25/249, individual files, BLHA
Provinzialschulkollegium record group, BLHA, Pr. Br. Rep 34 P.S.K.,
Personalia, and from DStA, and NS Lehrerbund Kartei und Akten, Micro-
film Publication A3340, ser. MF, Berlin Document Center, National
Archives.

80. See, for example, NSDAP Gauleitung Mark Brandenburg to Oberpräsident, 26 June 1942, BLHA, Pr. Br. Rep 34 P.S.K., Personalia, no. R 267,
and see for instance the announcements and brief reports of NSLB meetings published throughout 1934 in *Brandenburger Anzeiger*, "Für Brandenburg" section.

81. Report attached to letter, Von Saldern secondary school Schulobmann
to Oberpräsident Kube, 28 April 1937, BLHA, Pr. Br. Rep 34 P.S.K.,
no. 5261.

82. See correspondence and press clippings, including principal of Von
Saldern Secondary School to Provinzialschulkollegium, 15 March 1933,
BLHA, Pr. Br. Rep. 34 P.S.K. no. 5261; *Mitgliedskartei* for Gau Kurmark, BAB NS12, 2:82–88, registry of teachers, StadtA Brandenburg,
2.0.12.25/249, and individual files, BLHA Provinzialschulkollegium record
group, BLHA, Pr. Br. Rep 34 P.S.K., Personalia, no. K 361, and from
DStA.

83. Personnel file, BLHA, Pr. Br. Rep 34 P.S.K., Personalia, no. G 281.

84. Brandenburg Province Oberpräsident to Reich Education Minister,
31 October 1936, BAB R4901/5138.

85. Brandenburg Province Oberpräsident to Reich Education Minister,
18 March 1938, BAB R4901/5138; for membership information, see annual "Bericht über das Schuljahr" for 1933–1939, BLHA, Pr. Br. Rep 34
P.S.K., no. 5264; *Mitgliedskartei* for Gau Kurmark, BAB NS12, 2:82–88,
registry of teachers, StadtA Brandenburg, 2.0.12.25/249, and individual
files, BLHA Provinzialschulkollegium record group.

86. Personnel files, BLHA, Pr. Br. Rep 34 P.S.K., Personalia, nos. R 267,
G 119, and H 334.

87. Ritterakademie director to Oberpräsident Kube, 27 September 1935,
BLHA, Pr. Br. Rep 34 P.S.K., no. 5303.

88. Draft letter, Reich Minister for Religious Affairs to Brandenburg Province
Oberpräsident, 19 November 1936, DstA, BR 4696/1324.

89. See for example Fritzsche, *Life and Death*, Aly, *Hitler's Beneficiaries*, Gellately, *Backing Hitler*, David Bankier, *The Germans and the Final Solution*
(Oxford: Blackwell, 1992), Bankier, *Probing the Depths*.

90. *Brandenburger Anzeiger*, 16 February 1937 and 4 September 1934, "Für
Brandenburg" section; in periodical, "Schulchronik," *Schulspiegel: Blätter
des Oberlyzeums-Brandenburg/Havel* 23:7, December 1935.

91. See for example essays in Robert Schandley, ed., *Unwilling Germans? The Goldhagen Debate* (Minneapolis: University of Minnesota Press, 1998), and Bankier, *Probing the Depths.*

92. See Ritterakademie principal Georg Neuendorf to Brandenburg Province Oberpräsident, 2 June 1935, BLHA, Pr. Br. Rep 34 P.S.K., no. 5303, and draft letter, Reich Education Minister to Brandenburg Province Oberpräsident, Secondary School Department, 17 October 1936, BAB R4901/5144.

93. For a more detailed account of the nazification of everyday life in the schools, see Wolfgang Keim, *Erziehung unter der Nazi-Diktatur, vol. 2, Kriegsvorbereitung, Krieg und Holocaust* (Darmstadt: Wissenschaftliche Buchgesellschaft, 1997), 48–56.

94. *Schulspiegel: Blätter des Oberlyzeums-Brandenburg/Havel,* 6th–9th eds., June 1933 to December 1937; Oberstudiendirektor Ferdinand Grussendorf, Reports on the School Year, 1932/33 to 1939/40, BLHA, Pr. Br. Rep 34 P.S.K., no. 5264; *Die Ritterakademie: Mitteilungsblatt des Vereins ehemaliger Zöglinge der Ritterakademie zu Brandenburg an der Havel,* no. 1, July 1938, DstA, BR 664/330, 1–2, and Reports on the School Year, 1931/32 to 1936/37, BLHA, Pr. Br. Rep 34 P.S.K., no. 5295.

95. Wolfgang Keim, *Erziehung unter der Nazi-Diktatur, vol. 1, Antidemokratische Potentiale, Machtantritt und Machtdurchsetzung* (Darmstadt: Wissenschaftliche Buchgesellschaft, 1995), 91, and "Erlass des preussischen Kultusministers . . . zur Vererbungslehre und Rassenkunde," reprinted in Heinrich Kanz, ed., *Der Nationalsozialismus als pädagogisches Problem: Deutsche Erziehungsgeschichte 1933–1945* (New York: Peter Lang, 1984), 83. Quotation from Albert Ständer's essay "Nationalsozialistischer Geschichtsunterricht" in *Festschrift zur 350 Jahr Feier der v. Saldern,* BLHA, Pr. Br. Rep 34, no. 6264. As a result of the new curricular guidelines issued in the period 1937–1939, teachers devoted five classroom hours per week to "physical education" *(Leibeserziehung),* a sign of its importance that was matched by only one other subject, German; Keim, *Erziehung unter der Nazi-Diktatur,* 2:43.

96. Kurt-Ingo Flessau, *Schule der Diktatur: Lehrpläne und Schulbücher des Nationalsozialismus* (Munich: Ehrenwirth Verlag, 1977), 19–20, 53–58.

97. Quoted in ibid., 74.

98. Ibid., 58–61.

99. Ibid., 82–83 and 87.

100. Quoted in ibid., 64.

101. Ibid., 91–92, and Ute Frevert, *Women in German History: From Bourgeois Emancipation to Sexual Liberation* (New York: Berg, 1988), 221.

102. Oberstudiendirektor Ferdinand Grussendorf, Report on School Year 1932/33, published as *Die Saldria: Von Saldernsches Reformrealgymna-*

sium und Oberrealschule zu Brandenburg Havel, May 1933, and Report
on School Year 1938/39, sent by Oberstudiendirektor Walter Holöhr to
Brandenburg Province Oberpräsident, 9 June 1939, BLHA, Pr. Br. Rep 34
P.S.K., no. 5264. For the Ritterakademie, see Reports on School Year,
1931/32 to 1936/37, BLHA, Pr. Br. Rep 34 P.S.K., no. 5295.

103. Keim, *Erziehung unter der Nazi-Diktatur,* 2:47–48. For more information
on the nature, history, and extent of the "reform" of the schoolbooks,
see Flessau, *Schule der Diktatur,* 108–169, 144, and 152, Horst Gies,
Geschichtsunterricht unter der Diktatur Hitlers (Köln: Böhlau Verlag,
1992), 25–75, Benjamin Ortmeyer, *Schulzeit unterm Hitlerbild: Analysen,
Berichte, Dokumente* (Frankfurt am Main: Fischer Taschenbuch Verlag,
1996), 49–54, and individual essays in Franziska Conrad, Martin Götting,
and Inge Naumann, eds., *Erziehung im Nationalsozialismus: Gutenberg-
schule und Diltheyschule 1933–1945* (Geisenheim: Druckerei Nagel,
1992), 57–121.

104. Kahl-Futhman, *Hans Schemm Spricht,* 166.

105. Feiten, *Nationalsozialistische Lehrerbund,* 197.

3. Keeping the Schools Running during the War

1. Compiled from School-statistical List of the School Supervision District
Brandenburg (Havel) as of 1 May 1939, BLHA, Pr. Br. Rep 2A Regierung
Potsdam II Brd., no. 198, as well as city's registry of teachers, StadtA Brandenburg, 2.0.12.25/249, NSLB *Mitgliedskartei* for Gau Kurmark, BAB
NS12, 2:82–88, and NS Lehrerbund Kartei und Akten, Microfilm Publica-
toin A3340, ser. MF, Berlin document Center, National Archives, Washington, D.C.

2. Ibid.

3. Compiled from the Upper Lyceum's "Stellenplan für die vollbeschäftigten
Lehrkräfte an den nichtstaatlichen öffentlichen höheren Lehranstalten für
die weibliche Jugend," as of 1 May 1940 and of 1943/1944, BLHA, Pr. Br.
Rep 34, P.S.K., no. 5313, Von Saldern's annual "Bericht über das Schuljahr" for period 1932/1933 to 1938/39, in BLHA, Pr. Br. Rep 34, P.S.K.,
no. 5264, and ibid.

4. School-statistical List of the School Supervision District Brandenburg
(Havel) as of 1 May 1939, BLHA, Pr. Br. Rep 2A Regierung Potsdam II
Brd., no. 198 and city's registry of teachers, StadtA Brandenburg,
2.0.12.25/249, NSLB *Mitgliedskartei* for Gau Kurmark, BAB NS12,
2:82–88, and NS Lehrerbund Kartei und Akten, Microfilm Publication A3340, ser. MF, Berlin Document Center, National Archives.

5. Ibid., and miscellaneous transfer notices from Potsdam Regierungspräsident, BLHA, Pr. Br. Rep 2A Regierung Potsdam II Brd., nos. 124, 125,
   126, and 127.

6. Ibid., and the Upper Lyceum's "Stellenplan für die vollbeschäftigten
   Lehrkräfte an den nichtstaatlichen öffentlichen höheren Lehranstalten für
   die weibliche Jugend," as of 1 May 1940 and of 1943/1944, BLHA, Pr. Br.
   Rep 34, P.S.K., no. 5313, Von Saldern's annual "Bericht über das Schuljahr" for period 1932/1933 to 1938/39, in BLHA, Pr. Br. Rep 34, P.S.K.,
   nos. 5264.

7. Gauwaltung Kurmark des Nationalsozialistischen Lehrerbundes, ed.,
   *Nationalsozialistische Erziehung: Kampf- und Mitteilungsblatt des Nation-
   alsozialistischen Lehrerbunds für den Gau Kurmark*, 8:7, 1 April 1939,
   169; 8:10, 18 May 1939, 237; and 8:17, 1 September 1939, 375–376.

8. Correspondence, Oberbürgermeister Brandenburg an der Havel, Kultur-
   und Schulamt to Potsdam Regierungspräsident, via Superintendent
   Schmidt, 3 April 1936, and to Potsdam Regierungspräsident, via Superintendent Max Wolff, 17 April 1937, BLHA, Pr. Br. Rep 2A Regierung Potsdam II Brd., no. 125.

9. Correspondence, Oberbürgermeister Brandenburg an der Havel, Kultur-
   und Schulamt to Potsdam Regierungspräsident, via School Superintendent
   Max Wolff, 14 April 1938, BLHA, Pr. Br. Rep 2A Regierung. Potsdam II
   Brd., no. 125. In fact, Brandenburg's Oberbürgermeister believed that the
   number of pupils so overwhelmed the current school system that the city
   should build both a new elementary and high school, Heckel, note to file,
   14 November 1938, BAB R4901/5144. Moreover, this lack of teachers
   existed not only in Brandenburg but also throughout Germany. Articles in
   the NSLB publication *Der Deutsche Erzieher* occasionally spoke of the
   "catastrophic scarcity of teachers"; see for example "Der Lehrer als Kamil-
   lenblütensammler," *Der Deutsche Erzieher: Reichszeitung des NSLB*,
   Gau Kurmark ed., 6 and 18 March 1939, 188.

10. Correspondence, Oberbürgermeister Brandenburg an der Havel, Kirchen-
    und Schulamt to Potsdam Regierungspräsident, via School Superintendent
    Max Wolff, 14 April 1938, BLHA, Pr. Br. Rep 2A Regierung Potsdam II
    Brd., no. 125.

11. Statistical information compiled from School-statistical List of the School
    Supervision District Brandenburg (Havel) as of 1 May 1939, BLHA, Pr. Br.
    Rep 2A Regierung Potsdam II Brd., no. 198, and miscellaneous transfer
    notices from Potsdam Regierungspräsident, BLHA, Pr. Br. Rep 2A
    Regierung Potsdam II Brd., no. 125.

12. "Bericht über das Schuljahr 1939/40," 5 June 1940, sent by Oberstudien-
    direktor Walter H. to Brandenburg Province Oberpräsident, Education

Department, BLHA, Pr. Br. Rep 34, P.S.K., no. 5264. At least one secondary school instructor, Ritterakademie's Kurt B., transferred permanently in late 1937 to the military; correspondence, Generalkommando III Armeekorps to Ritterakademie, 31 January 1938, DStA, BR92u/271.

13. School-statistical List of the School Supervision District Brandenburg (Havel) as of 1 May 1940, BLHA, Pr. Br. Rep 2A Regierung Potsdam II Brd., no. 199, and city's registry of teachers, StadtA Brandenburg, 2.0.12.25/249.

14. School-statistical List of School Supervision District Brandenburg (Havel) as of 1 May 1939, BLHA, Pr. Br. Rep 2A Regierung Potsdam II Brd., no. 198.

15. Harald Scholtz and Elmar Stranz, "Nationalsozialistische Einflussnahmen auf die Lehrerbildung," in Manfred Heinemann, ed., *Erziehung und Schulung im Dritten Reich, pt. 2, Hochschule, Erwachsenbildung* (Stuttgart: Klett Cotta, 1980), 116–117; Konrad Jarausch, *The Unfree Professions: German Lawyers, Teachers, and Engineers, 1900–1950* (New York: Oxford University Press, 1990), 185; "Bericht über das Schuljahr 1940/41," 10 October 1941, sent by Oberstudiendirektor Walter H. to Brandenburg Province Oberpräsident, Education Department, BLHA, Pr. Br. Rep 34, P.S.K., no. 5264.

16. See Education Ministry directives dated 1 September 1939 and 20 January 1940, discussed in "Amtliche Erlasse," *Deutsche Wissenschaft Erziehung und Volksbildung: Amtsblatt des Reichsministeriums für Wissenschaft, Erziehung und Volksbildung und der Unterrichts-Verwaltungen der Länder* 2:6, 20 January 1940, 36–37.

17. See correspondence and transfer notices between Potsdam Regierungspräsident and individual teachers, BLHA, Pr. Br. Rep 2A Regierung Potsdam II Brd., no. 125. Although sources do not explicitly indicate whether the female teachers applied for the positions, the general failure of Nazi officials in the period before 1943 to enforce nascent legal measures requiring women to work suggests that the teachers chose to reenter the classroom, Ute Frevert, *Women in German History: From Bourgeois Emancipation to Sexual Liberation* (New York: Berg, 1988), 222–224.

18. "Bericht über das Schuljahr 1940/41," BLHA, Pr. Br. Rep 34, P.S.K., no. 5264, and Abschrift correspondence between Brandenburg Province Oberpräsident, Education Department, and Upper Lyceum Director Gustav S., 19 October 1939, BLHA, Pr. Br. Rep 34, P.S.K., no. 5313; Oberbürgermeister Brandenburg an der Havel, Education Office, to Potsdam Regierungspräsident, 15 March 1940, BLHA, Pr. Br. Rep 2A Regierung Potsdam II Brd., no. 161.

19. Circular from Reich Minister of the Interior to Government Division Heads and Personnel Departments, 20 June 1939, BLHA, Pr. Br. Rep 2a Regierung Potsdam II Gen., no. 733.

20. Circular from Reich Education Minister, 30 November 1939, BLHA, Pr. Br. Rep 2a Regierung Potsdam II Gen., no. 733.

21. *Deutsche Wissenschaft, Erziehung und Volksbildung* 6:4, 20 February 1940, 123, and Scholtz and Stranz, "Nationalsozialistische Einflussnahmen auf die Lehrerbildung," 117.

22. Correspondence, Oberbürgermeister Brandenburg an der Havel, Kirche und Schulamt to Potsdam Regierungspräsident, 10 June 1940, and District Superintendent Max W. to Potsdam Regierungspräsident, 24 April 1940, BLHA, Pr. Br. Rep 2A Regierung Potsdam II Brd., no. 125.

23. Secret Security Police Report, 19 January 1940, BAB R4901/alt 21/724, 30–31.

24. Correspondence, District Superintendent Max W. to Potsdam Regierungspräsident, 24 April 1940, BLHA, Pr. Br. Rep 2A Regierung Potsdam II Brd., no. 125.

25. Gerhard L. Weinberg, *A World at Arms: A Global History of World War II* (Cambridge: Cambridge University Press, 1994), 264, and School-statistical List of the School Supervision District Brandenburg (Havel) as of October 1941, BLHA, Pr. Br. Rep 2A Regierung Potsdam II Brd., no. 200.

26. Correspondence, Oberbürgermeister Brandenburg an der Havel, Kirche und Schulamt to Potsdam Regierungspräsident, 4 June 1941, BLHA, Pr. Br. Rep 2A Regierung Potsdam II Brd., no. 152, "Bericht über das Schuljahr 1940/41," 10 October 1941, sent by Oberstudiendirektor Walter H. to Brandenburg Province Oberpräsident, Education Department, BLHA, Pr. Br. Rep 34, P.S.K., no. 5264, Sonderführer (and Upper Lyceum Director) Gustav S., Feldpostnumner 22053, to Potsdam Regierungspräsident, Education Department, 2 November 1941, BLHA, Pr. Br. Rep 2A Regierung Potsdam II Brd., no. 125, and *Die Ritterakademie. Mitteilungsblatt des Vereins ehemaliger Zöglinge der Ritterakademie zu Brandenburg an der Havel* 1:17, March 1941, DStA, BR 664/330.

27. *Amtliches Schulblatt für den Regierungs-Bezirk Potsdam,* 16 May 1940, 42–44; see also draft delegation letters, Potsdam Regierung to Martin L. and Max N., 22 April 1940, and to Alfred M., 3 May 1940, BLHA, Pr. Br. Rep 2A Regierung Potsdam II Brd., no. 125.

28. Von Saldern Secondary School "Bericht über das Schuljahr 1940/41," 10 October 1941, BLHA, Pr. Br. Rep 34 P.S.K., no. 5264, and Upper Lyceum Director Gustav S. to Brandenburg Province Oberpräsident, 11 April 1940, and Oberbürgermeister Brandenburg an der Havel, Kirche und Schulamt to Brandenburg Province Oberpräsident, 1 February 1941, BLHA, Pr. Br. Rep 34 P.S.K., no. 5313, and Reichstatthalter Posen to Brandenburg Province Oberpräsident, Education Department, 21 October 1940, Pr. Br. Rep 34 P.S.K., no. 5315.

29. Personnel file, Heinrich M., BLHA, Pr. Br. Rep 34, Personalia, no. M 288; correspondence, Director Gustav S. to Brandenburg Province Oberpräsident, Education Department, 11 April 1940 and 15 October 1940, BLHA, Pr. Br. Rep 34, P.S.K., no. 5313.

30 Arbeitsgruppe Pädagogische Museum, ed., *Heil Hitler, Herr Lehrer: Volksschule 1933–1945 Das Beispiel Berlin* (Reinbek bei Hamburg: Rowohlt, 1983), 221; Charles McClelland, *The German Experience of Professionalization: Modern Learned Professions and Their Organizations from the Early Nineteenth Century to the Hitler Era* (New York: Cambridge University Press, 1991), 221.

31. Education Ministry decree, 1 May 1942, BAB R4901/alt R21/84, 195; Education Ministry circular, 5 July 1943, reproduced in circular from Brandenburg Province Oberpräsident, Secondary School Education Department, 17 July 1943, BLHA, Pr. Br. Rep 34, P.S.K., no. 3884; and draft letter, Brandenburg Province Oberpräsident, Education Department, to Oberbürgermeister Brandenburg an der Havel, Kirchen- und Schulamt, 16 March 1942, BLHA, Pr. Br. Rep 34, P.S.K., no. 5259.

32. See, for example, School-statistical List of the School Supervision District Brandenburg (Havel) as of 1 May 1940, BLHA, Pr. Br. Rep 2A Regierung Potsdam II Brd., no. 199, and School-statistical List of the School Supervision District Brandenburg (Havel) as of October 1941, BLHA, Pr. Br. Rep 2A Regierung Potsdam II Brd., no. 200; also BLHA, Pr. Br. Rep 2A Regierung Potsdam II Brd., nos. 125 and 126; Director Gustav S. to Brandenburg Province Oberpräsident, Education Department, 29 August 1941, BLHA, Pr. Br. Rep 34, P.S.K., no. 5313, and Brandenburg's registry of teachers, StadtA Brandenburg, 2.0.12.25/249.

33. Handwritten draft letter, Postdam Regierung to Brandenburg Magistrat and Potsdam School Superintendent, 4 October 1933, and Regierungpräsident, note to file, 18 March 1935, BLHA, Pr. Br. Rep 2A Regierung Potsdam II Brd., no. 124; copy of Education Ministry certificate, dated 11 August 1934, and Director Gustav S. to Brandenburg Province Oberpräsident, Education Department, 29 August 1941, BLHA, Pr. Br. Rep 34, P.S.K., no. 5313; and School-statistical List of the School Supervision District Brandenburg (Havel) as of October 1941, BLHA, Pr. Br. Rep 2A Regierung Potsdam II Brd., no. 200.

34. Data compiled from School-statistical List of the School Supervision District Brandenburg (Havel) as of October 1941, BLHA, Pr. Br. Rep 2A Regierung Potsdam II Brd., no. 200, and transfer notices, BLHA, Pr. Br. Rep 2A Regierung Potsdam II Brd., no. 125.

35. Data compiled from correspondence and transfer notices in BLHA, Pr. Br.

Rep 34, P.S.K., nos. 5313 and 5264, and BLHA, Pr. Br. Rep 2A Regierung Potsdam II Brd., no. 126.

36. See correspondence between Brandenburg and Einbeck, November 1940, and between Brandenburg and Osnabruck, June and July 1941, BLHA, Pr. Br. Rep 2A Regierung Potsdam II Brd., no. 125. For difficulties in staffing the Werner Mölders School, see Oberbürgermeister Brandenburg an der Havel, Kirchen- und Schulamt to Potsdam Regierungspräsident, 8 July 1941, BLHA, Pr. Br. Rep 2A Regierung Potsdam II Brd., no. 125.

37. Data compiled from correspondence and transfer notices, BLHA, Pr. Br. Rep 34, P.S.K., nos. 5313 and 5264, and in BLHA, Pr. Br. Rep 2A Regierung Potsdam II Brd., no. 126. See also Frevert, *Women in German History*, 207–208 and 217–219.

38. Oberbürgermeister Brandenburg an der Havel, Kultur- und Schulamt to Potsdam Government, 1 September 1943, and City School Superintendent to Potsdam Government, 25 October 1943, BLHA, Pr. Br. Rep 2A Regierung Potsdam II Brd., no. 153.

39. Oberbürgermeister Brandenburg an der Havel, Kultur- und Schulamt, to Superintendent Speer and to Potsdam Government, 1 September 1943, Theodor Körner School (Middle School for Boys) Directory as of 1 October 1943, dated 14 October 1943, and Augusta School Directory as of 1 October 1943, dated 12 October 1943, BLHA, Pr. Br. Rep 2A Regierung Potsdam II Brd., no. 153.

40. School Superintendent to Potsdam Government, Education Department, 25 October 1943, BLHA, Pr. Br. Rep 2A Regierung Potsdam II Brd., no. 153. For the appointments to the Upper Lyceum see the school's "Stellenplan für die vollbeschäftigten Lehrkräfte an den nichtstaatlichen öffentlichen höheren Lehranstalten für die weibliche Jugend, Stand. 1. Mai 1942," and correspondence between Principal Gustav S. and Potsdam Government regarding Hildegard K., Elly-Lotte M., and Rosemarie K., BLHA, Pr. Br. Rep 34, P.S.K., no. 5313. For the appointments to the middle schools, see Pr. Br. Rep 2A Regierung Potsdam II Brd., nos. 152 and 153, and Upper Lyceum Principal Gustav S. to Brandenburg Province Oberpräsident, Education Department, 1 September 1943 and 20 April 1943, BLHA, Pr. Br. Rep 34, P.S.K., no. 5313.

41. Oberbürgermeister Brandenburg an der Havel, Kultur- und Schulamt to Potsdam Government, 8 September 1942, BLHA, Pr. Br. Rep 2A Regierung Potsdam II Brd., no. 153.

42. Frevert, *Women in Germany History*, 223, and Elizabeth H. Tobin and Jennifer Gibson, "The Meanings of Labor: East German Women's Work in the Transition from Nazism to Communism," *Central European History* 28:3 (1995), 307–308.

43. School Superintendent Speer to Potsdam Regierungspräsident, Education Department, 2 April 1943, BLHA, Pr. Br. Rep 2A Regierung Potsdam II Brd., no. 126.

44. Regarding the shortage in the middle schools, see Oberbürgermeister Brandenburg an der Havel, Kultur- und Schulamt to Brandenburg Province Oberpräsident, Education Department, 27 August 1943, BLHA, Pr. Br. Rep 34, P.S.K., no. 5313, and to Postdam Regierungpräsident and to School Superintendent Speer, 1 September 1943, BLHA, Pr. Br. Rep 2A Regierung Potsdam II Brd., no. 153. For the cooptation of Berlin teachers in Brandenburg schools, see Oberbürgermeister Brandenburg to Potsdam Regierungspräsident, 17 September 1943, BLHA, Pr. Br. Rep 2A Regierung Potsdam II Brd., no. 126.

45. Oberbürgermeister Brandenburg an der Havel, Kirchen- und Schulamt to Brandenburg Province Oberpräsident, Education Department, 27 August 1943, BLHA, Pr. Br. Rep 34, P.S.K., no. 5313.

46. Statistical information gathered from the collection of transfer notices, Potsdam Regierungspräsident to Oberbürgermeister Brandenburg an der Havel and Brandenburg School Superintendent for the period January 1944 to April 1945, in BLHA, Pr. Br. Rep 2A Regierung Potsdam II Brd., nos. 126 and 127, and Pr. Br. Rep 34, P.S.K., no. 5313.

47. Copy of transfer notice, Potsdam Regierungspräsident to Trainee Teacher (*Lehramtsanwärterin*) Emma R. and to Brandenburg School Superintendent, 19 September 1944, and copy of transfer notice, Potsdam Regierungspräsident to Trainee Teacher Margot M. and to Brandenburg School Superintendent, 23 January 1945, BLHA, Pr. Br. Rep 2A Regierung Potsdam II Brd., no. 127.

48. See correspondence between Potsdam Regierungspräsident and Oberbürgermeister Brandenburg an der Havel regarding Charlotte N., Hanna B., Otto Z., and Helga H., BLHA, Pr. Br. Rep 2A Regierung Potsdam II Brd., no. 127, and Oberbürgermeister Brandenburg an der Havel, Kultur- und Schulamt to Potsdam Regierungspräsident via School Superintendent Speer, 20 March 1945, BLHA, Pr. Br. Rep 2A Regierung Potsdam II Brd., no. 153.

49. Reprinted in Heinrich Kanz, ed., *Der Nationalsozialismus als pädagogisches Problem: Deutsche Erziehungsgeschichte 1933–1945* (New York: Peter Lang, 1984), 240.

50. School Superintendent Speer to Potsdam Regierungspräsident, Education Department, 2 April 1943, BLHA, Pr. Br. Rep 2A Regierung Potsdam II Brd., no. 126; Potsdam Regierungspräsident to Oberbürgermeister Brandenburg an der Havel, 22 February 1945, and draft letters, Potsdam Regierungspräsident to Oberbürgermeister Brandenburg an der Havel, 22 February 1945 and 23 February 1945, BLHA, Pr. Br. Rep 2A Regierung Potsdam II

Brd., no. 127; see notices of appointment for Charlotte N., Hanna B., and Otto Z., BLHA, Pr. Br. Rep 2A Regierung Potsdam II Brd., no. 127.

51. "Eindrucksvolle Kundgebungen in den Kreisen . . . Kreis Brandenburg-Zauch-Belzig. Die Wehrmacht braucht Leistungsmenschen," *Mitteilungsblatt des NSLB Gauwaltung Mark Brandenburg* 4, April 1941, 30–31. Beginning in 1939, the NSLB published the *Mitteilungsblatt* as the regional supplement to the now national ed. of *Der Deutsche Erzieher.*

52. "Soldatischer Geist im Unterricht," *Der Deutscher Erzieher. Reichszeitung des NSLB* 7 (1940), 237, and Jarausch, *Unfree Professions,* 178; "Die Entwicklung des Flugmodellbaues in Brandenburg (Havel)," *Mitteilungsblatt* 7, July 1940, 50–51; "Aus der Arbeit der Kreise . . . Kreis Brandenburg-Zauch-Belzig," *Mitteilungsblatt* 5, May 1942, 20.

53. "Aus der Arbeit der Kreise . . . Kreis Brandenburg-Zauch-Belzig: Arbeitstagung des Kreisstabes," *Mitteilungsblatt* 11, November 1940, 86; "Ostlandhilfswerk des NSLB," *Der Deutscher Erzieher: Reichszeitung des NSLB* 7, 1940, 214; "Aus den Kreisen . . . Kreis Brandenburg-Zauch-Belzig: Tagung der Kreisabschnittswalter," *Mitteilungsblatt* 9, September 1942, 36.

54. "Aus der Arbeit der Kreise . . . Kreis Brandenburg-Zauch-Belzig: Schulaufbau im Wartheland," *Mitteilungsblatt* 10, October 1940, 79.

55. Ibid., and "Schülerwettbewerb 'Seefahrt ist not!' . . . Kreis Brandenburg-Zauch-Belzig," *Mitteilungsblatt* 5, May 1942, 20, and 6, June 1941, 42–43.

56. "Anzahl der im NSLB geschulten Erzieher (Stand 1.9.1939)," table, BAB NS12/1455. The exact figure was 197,745; see "Zusammenstellung Übersicht: Die Schulung der Erzieher durch den NSLB," table, 8 April 1940, BAB NS12/1455.

57. Ibid., and "Schulungsstatistik bis Oktober 1938," BAB NS12/1455.

58. "Zusammenstellung Übersicht: Die Schulung der Erzieher durch den NSLB," table, 8 April 1940, and "Zusammenstellung Übersicht: Die Schulung der Erzieher durch den NSLB," table, undated, BAB NS12/1455.

59. Willi Feiten, *Der Nationalsozialistische Lehrerbund: Entwicklung und Organisation* (Weinhem: Beltz Verlag, 1981), 185–186.

60 Compilations *(Zusammentstellungen)* for 1941 and 1942, Schulung Department, NSLB, BAB NS12/1455.

61. "Lagerschulung 1933–1.5.1936," 15 May 1936, BAB NS12/1455. Since the file does not include participation statistics on a month-by-month basis, one can only very roughly approximate the percentage of camp attenders to general NSLB participants on the basis of two separate sets of data, that for the period 1933 to May 1936 and that for the period 1933 to December 1936; "Zusammenstellung Übersicht: Die Schulung der Erzieher durch den NSLB," table, 8 April 1940, BAB NS12/1455.

62. Feiten, *Der Nationalsozialistische Lehrerbund*, 185, 192, 197, and 199, and Jarausch, *Unfree Professions*, 195.
63. Feiten, *Der Nationalsozialistische Lehrerbund*, 192–193 and 197–199.
64. Jarausch, *Unfree Professions*, 179.
65. *Der Kurier*, inaugural issue, DstA BRV 132/128, 2–3, and Otto Söchtig, "Tagebuchaufzeichnungen eines Lehrers von 1944 bis 1946," in Arbeitskreis Stadtgeschichte im Brandenburgischen Kulturbund e.V., ed., *Das Jahr 1945 in der Stadt Brandenburg: Eine Anthologie mit Darstellungen, Tagebuchaufzeichnungen und Lebenserinnerungen an das Ende des Zweiten Weltkrieges in der Stadt Brandenburg*, 3rd ed. (Brandenburg an der Havel: Werbe-Profi, 2001), 80.
66. See note 30; also Brekow, "Die Schule als gesamt gesellschaftliche Aufgabe," in Gerd Heinrich, Klaus Hesse, Winfried Schich, and Wolfgang Schössler, eds., *Stahl und Brennabor: Die Stadt Brandenburg im 19. und 20. Jahrhundert* (Potsdam: Verlag für Berlin-Brandenburg, 1998), 316, and Brandenburg School Superintendent to Potsdam Regierungspräsident, 10 September 1943 and 4 November 1943, BLHA, Pr. Br. Rep 2A Regierung Potsdam Abt II, no. 1311.
67. Personnel files, BLHA, Pr. Br. Rep 34 P.S.K., Personalia, no. B 371, M 288, and K 77/1.
68. Brandenburg Mayor to Potsdam Regierungspräsident, 20 July 1944, BLHA, Pr. Br. Rep 2A Regierung Potsdam Abt II, no. 1311.
69. Notice from Sonderbeauftragte des Reichserziehungsministerium für den Einsatz von Marinehelfern (HJ) im Marineoberkommando to Potsdam Regierungspräsident, 3 March 1945, ibid.
70. See personnel records, BLHA, Pr. Br. Rep 34, Personalia, nos. 113/a, K 327, D 89, ST-20, K 77/1, and B 452/1, as well as various transfer notices and correspondence, BLHA, Pr. Br. Rep 2A Regierung Potsdam II Brd., nos. 126, 127, and 153.
71. Jarausch, *Unfree Professions*, 186 and 249; Dietmar Petzina, Werner Abelshauser, and Anselm Faust, *Sozialgeschichtliches Arbeitsbuch, vol. 3, Materialien zur Statistik des Deutschen Reiches 1914–1945* (Munich: C. H. Beck Verlag, 1978), 98, and Gerhard Bry, *Wages in Germany 1871–1945* (Princeton: Princeton University Press, 1960), 361–362 and 422–429. The last of the austerity measures was rescinded in 1950, Jarausch, *Unfree Professions*, 205.
72. Correspondence, District Superintendent Max W. to Potsdam Regierungspräsident, 24 April 1940, BLHA, Pr. Br. Rep 2A Regierung Potsdam II Brd., no. 125; Oberbürgermeister Brandenburg an der Havel, Kirche und Schulamt to Potsdam Regierungspräsident, 14 April 1942, and Potsdam

Regierungspräsident draft response, 2 July 1942, BLHA, Pr. Br. Rep 2A Regierung Potsdam II Brd., no. 126.

73. Brandenburg Province Oberpräsident, memo, 16 March 1942, copy, BLHA, Pr. Br. Rep 2A Regierung Potsdam II Brd., no. 126. On this being carried out in Brandenburg, see BLHA, Pr. Br. Rep 34, Personalia, no. R 267.

74. Jarausch, *Unfree Professions*, 178 and 186; Renate Morell, "Organisierte Volksschullehrerbewegung vom Ende des Zweiten Weltkrieges bis zur Konstituierung der 'Gewerkschaft Erziehung und Wissenschaft': Ein sozialgeschichtlicher Beitrag zu Geschichte und Ideologie der Volksschullehrerschaft in Deutschland" (Ph.D. diss., Philipps-Universität Marburg, 1977), 51–53; correspondence, District Superintendent Max W. to Potsdam Regierungspräsident, 24 April 1940, BLHA, Pr. Br. Rep 2A Regierung Potsdam II Brd., no. 125.

75. McClelland, *German Experience*, 14. Elements of the "deprofessionalization" process also include the transformation of the teachers' working conditions, the "militarization of the content of professional practice," and the widespread and multifaceted co-optation of pedagogues for the war effort, Jarausch, *Unfree Professions*, 172–200.

76. Jarausch, *Unfree Professions*, 200.

4. Transforming the Teaching Staff under Soviet Occupation

1. See Otto Söchtig, "Tagebuchaufzeichnungen eines Lehrers von 1944 bis 1946," excerpted diary, in Arbeitskreis Stadtgeschichte im Brandenburgischen Kulturbund e.V., ed., *Das Jahr 1945 in der Stadt Brandenburg: Eine Anthologie mit Darstellungen, Tagebuchaufzeichnungen und Lebenserinnerungen an das Ende des Zweiten Weltkrieges in der Stadt Brandenburg*, 3rd ed. (Brandenburg an der Havel: Werbe-Profi, 2001), 84–87.

2. See for example Lothar Kettenacker, "The Planning of 'Re-education' during the Second World War," in Nicholas Pronay and Keith Wilson, eds., *The Political Re-education of Germany and Her Allies after World War II* (London: Croom Helm, 1985), 59–82; Timothy Vogt, *Denazification in Soviet-occupied Germany: Brandenburg, 1945–1948* (Cambridge, Mass.: Harvard University Press, 2000), 2–28; Steven P. Remy, *The Heidelberg Myth: The Nazification and Denazification of a German University* (Cambridge, Mass.: Harvard University Press, 2002), 124–130.

3. "Ausführungsbestimmungen zum Befehl des Obersten Chefs der sowjetischen Militärverwaltung über die Wiedereröffnung der Schulen vom 25.8.1945," sent by Paul Wandel to regional administrations, BAB DR2/4717, 74.

4. For a detailed discussion of the historiography regarding denazification, see Vogt, *Denazification*, 10–16. Regarding recent challenges to the traditional narrative, see Ralph Jessen's remarkable *Akademische Elite und kommunistische Diktatur: Die ostdeutsche Hochschullehrerschaft in der Ulbricht Ära* (Göttingen : Vandenhoeck und Ruprecht, 1999), and Anna-Sabine Ernst, *"Die beste Prophylaxe ist der Sozialismus": Ärtze und medizinische Hochschullehrer in der SBZ/DDR 1945–1961* (New York: Waxmann Münster, 1997). A particularly good example of the persistence of misconceptions regarding the denazification of eastern German schools is John Rodden's history of East German education, in which an uncritical reliance on East German statistics and an undifferentiated, statewide perspective prevents him from accurately analyzing such important early developments as the denazification of eastern Germany's teaching staff and the implementation of the "Law on the Democratization of the Schools," *Repainting the Little Red Schoolhouse: A History of Eastern German Education, 1945–1995* (New York: Oxford University Press, 2002), 30–31, 43–45. See also for example Konrad Jarausch, *After Hitler: Recivilizing Germans, 1945–1995* (New York: Oxford University Press, 2006), 53, Benita Blessing, *The Antifascist Classroom: Denazification in Soviet-occupied Germany, 1945–1949* (New York: Palgrave, 2006), 48–49, and Mary Fulbrook, *The People's State: East German Society from Hitler to Honecker* (New Haven: Yale University Press, 2005), 199–200.

5. Klaus Hess and Anke Richter, "Die Stadt Brandenburg im Jahre 1945," in Werner Stang, ed., *Brandenburg im Jahr 1945: Studien* (Potsdam: Brandenburgische Landeszentrale für politische Bildung, 1995), 199.

6. Ibid., 199–201. For a basic overview of the complex organization of the SMA in Germany, see Stefan Cruezberger, *Die sowjetische Besatzungsmacht und das politische System der SBZ* (Weimar: Böhlau Verlag, 1996), 28–39, Norman Naimark, *The Russians in Germany* (Cambridge, Mass.: Belknap Press, 1995), 9–36, and Jan Foitzik, *Sowjetische Militäradministration in Deutschland (SMAD) 1945–1949* (Berlin: Akademie Verlag, 1999). For an excellent and detailed description of the SMA's Education Department, see Piotr I. Nikitin, *Zwischen Dogma und gesunden Menschenverstand: Wie ich die Universitäten der deutschen Besatzungszone "sowjetisierte": Erinnerungen des Sektorleiters Hochschulen und Wissenschaft der Sowjetischen Militäradministration in Deutschland* (Berlin: Akademie Verlag, 1997), 29–32.

7. Frank Brekow, "Die Havelstadt im Zweiten Weltkrieg—Verschliess und Zerstörung," in Gerd Heinrich, Klaus Hess, Winfried Schich, and Wolfgang Schössler, eds., *Stahl und Brennabor: Die Stadt Brandenburg im 19. und 20. Jahrhundert* (Potsdam: Verlag für Berlin-Brandenburg, 1998),

142–147; Olaf Groehler, "Der Luftkrieg gegen Brandenburg in den letzten Kriegsmonaten," in Stang, *Brandenburg im Jahr 1945,* 22–23, and Hess and Richter, "Die Stadt Brandenburg," 197, Otto Söchtig, "Tagebuchaufzeichnungen," 82–83; *Der Kurier,* no. 3, 24 November 1946, DStA, 1.

8. Olaf Groehler, "Der Luftkrieg gegen Brandenburg in den letzten Kriegsmonaten," 22–23, and Hess and Richter, "Die Stadt Brandenburg," 197, Söchtig, "Tagebuchaufzeichnungen," 82–83; Brandenburg an der Havel Registry Office to Socialist Unity Party District Leader Sage, 2 November 1952, StadtA Brandenburg, 2.0.2.110/583, 24–25; Ludwig Ziehen, "Die letzten Kampftage in Brandenburg," *Der Kurier,* no. 41, 1 June 1953, DStA, 3.

9. Brekow, "Die Havelstadt," 142–147; Söchtig, "Tagebuchaufzeichnungen," 82–83; StadtA Brandenburg, 2.0.12.25/249; Wolfgang Kusior, *Die Stadt Brandenburg im Jahrhundertrückblick: Streiflichter durch eine bewegte Zeit* (Berlin: Verlag Bernd Neddermeyer, 2000), 63–69; Ludwig Ziehen, "Die letzten Kampftage in Brandenburg," *Der Kurier,* no. 41, 1 June 1953, DStA, 3; Report, 10 April 1946, StadtA Brandenburg, 2.0.12.115/957, 40–42.

10. Officials first closed the city's secondary schools, including the vocational institutions, as early as October 1944. The elementary schools continued to function until the spring of 1945. See correspondence, Oberbürgermeister Brandenburg an der Havel, Kultur- und Schulamt to Potsdam Regierungspräsident, 19 October 1944, and series of appointment requests, March 1945, Brandenburg Kultur- und Schulamt to Potsdam Regierungspräsident, BLHA, Pr. Br. Rep 2A Regierung Potsdam II Brd., no. 127.

11. Notifications regarding the confiscation of Brandenburg school buildings can be found in BLHA, Pr. Br. Rep 2A Regierung Potsdam II Brd., no. 127.

12. Teachers' service in the Volkssturm compiled from registry of teachers, StadtA Brandenburg, 2.0.12.25/249. Johannes S., who as of August 1945 was both the Rochow School's principal and the city's school superintendent, served from October 1944 to late April 1945 and, having been injured, spent much of the summer in a field hospital.

13. *Die Erzieher der Kurmark 1936, Verzeichnis der Parteidienststellen, Schulbehörden, Lehranstalten und Lehrkräfte* (Berlin: Verlag "Nationalsozialistische Erziehung," 1936), 107; Hess and Richter, "Die Stadt Brandenburg," 215; "Bericht über das Brandenburger Schulleben von Mai 1945 zum Mai 1948," StadtA Brandenburg, 2.0.12.17/241, 164. The number of pupils in the Brandenburg region increased more than 30 percent in the period 1939–1945; Lothar Mertens, "Die Neulehrer: Die 'grundlegende Demokratisierung der deutschen Schule' in der SBZ und die Veränderung in der Lehrerschaft," *Deutsche Studien* 102:26 (June 1988), 196.

14. Brandenburg School Superintendent Willi L. to Mayor Max Herm, 29 May 1945, StadtA Brandenburg, 2.0.12.24/248, 1; circular, School Superintendent Willi L. to all schools, 4 July 1945, StadtA Brandenburg, 2.0.12.116/958, 23–24.

15. School Superintendent Willi L. to Deputy Principal Otto S., 7 July 1945, StadtA Brandenburg, 2.0.12.116/958, 26; *Der Kurier*, no. 3, 24 November 1946 and no. 13, 1 August 1948, DStA, 1 and 1–2; circular from President of Provincial Administration Mark Brandenburg to all school superintendents, copy, 24 October 1945, StadtA Brandenburg, 2.0.12.116/958, 120; correspondence, 24 August 1945, and reports, Principal Otto S. to Education Department, StadtA Brandenburg, 2.0.12.116/958, 68–72; Söchtig, "Tagebuchaufzeichnungen," 84–87; circular from School Superintendent Willi L., 4 July 1945, StadtA Brandenburg, 2.0.12.116/958, 23–24.

16. Circular from School Superintendent Willi L., 12 July 1945, StadtA Brandenburg, 2.0.12.116/958, 30, and Zylka, Head of the Brandenburg an der Havel Education Office, to Saldria Secondary School, 25 July 1945, StadtA Brandenburg, 2.0.12.116/958, 38; circulars from School Superintendent Willi L., 4 July 1945 and 12 July 1945, StadtA Brandenburg, 2.0.12.116/958, 23–24 and 30; Report, Saldria Secondary School to Brandenburg's Education Office, 24 August 1945, StadtA Brandenburg, 2.0.12.116/958, 68, and Von Saldern Principal Otto S. to School Superintendent Johannes S., 27 August 1945, StadtA Brandenburg, 2.0.12.116/958, 68–72; see also Söchtig, "Tagebuchaufzeichnungen," 86.

17. Directive from School Superintendent Willi L., 21 July 1945, StadtA Brandenburg, 2.0.12.116/958, 35; Söchtig, "Tagebuchaufzeichnungen," 85–86. Nor was the Ritterakademie the perfect solution; the two schools had to share the available space not only with each other but also with government agencies and other institutions, including the municipal retirement home, which had appropriated parts of the Ritterakademie; *Der Kurier*, no. 2, 15 April 1946, and no. 13, 1 August 1948, DStA, 2 and 1–2, respectively.

18. Georg-Max H., Von Saldern Secondary School, note, 24 August 1945, StadtA Brandenburg, 2.0.12.116/958, 65; minutes of School Principal Conference, 13 August 1945, StadtA Brandenburg, 2.0.12.26/250, 119–120; Directive from School Superintendent Willi L., 21 July, 1945, StadtA Brandenburg, 2.0.12.116/958, 35; Norman Naimark notes that much of Soviet cultural policy can be explained by the Soviets' sense of cultural superiority, *Russians in Germany*, 440.

19. Registry of All Teachers at Brandenburg (Havel) Schools, compiled 27 August 1945, Amt für Volksbildung, Abt. Schulamt, StadtA Brandenburg, 2.0.12.30/254, 42–58.

20. Statistics compiled from August 1945 Registry of All Teachers at Brandenburg (Havel) Schools, StadtA Brandenburg, 2.0.12.30/254, and the city's registry of teachers, StadtA Brandenburg, 2.0.12.25/249.

21. Membership information compiled from August 1945 Registry of All Teachers at Brandenburg (Havel) Schools, StadtA Brandenburg, 2.0.12.30/254, and the city's registry of teachers, StadtA Brandenburg, 2.0.12.25/249, and NSLB *Mitgliedskartei* for Gau Kurmark, BAB NS12, 2:82–88; School-statistical Lists of the School Supervision District Brandenburg (Havel) for years 1939 to 1944, BLHA, Pr. Br. Rep 2A Regierung Potsdam II Brd., nos. 198–203. The data for NSLB membership is less complete due to the organization's failure to maintain updated membership records in the final months of the war.

22. "Ausführungsbestimmungen zum Befehl des Obersten Chefs der sowjetischen Militärverwaltung über die Wiedereröffnung der Schulen vom 25.8.1945," sent by Paul Wandel to regional administrations, BAB DR2/4717, 74, and "Bericht über die pädagogische Tagung in Potsdam vom 29.–31. August 45," BAB DR2/488, 4–5.

23. Vogt, *Denazification*, 2–3, and Historische Gedenkstätte des Potsdamer Abkommens, ed., *The Potsdam Agreement: Selected Documents Concerning the German Question 1943–1949* (Berlin: Staatsverlag der Deutschen Demokratischen Republik, 1967), 56–58.

24. Brigitte Hohlfeld, *Die Neulehrer in der SBZ/DDR 1945–1953: Ihre Rolle bei der Umgestaltung von Gesellschaft und Staat* (Weinheim: Deutscher Studien Verlag, 1992), 20.

25. Vogt, *Denazification*, 2, 8, 23–28, 35, and 56; Hohlfeld, *Die Neulehrer*, 27.

26. Hess and Richter, "Die Stadt Brandenburg," 202; Report from Superintendent Willi L. to Mayor Max Herm, 27 June 1945, StadtA Brandenburg, 2.0.2.16/16, 2; for Mecklenburg's early denazification activities, see Office of the Department of Culture and Education, President of the Land Mecklenburg-Vorpommern, to Director of the German Central Administration for Education, 31 October 1945, BAB DR2/421, 72.

27. City's registry of teachers, StadtA Brandenburg, 2.0.12.25/249. Much of the information regarding membership in the NSDAP and related organizations, however, was drawn from the School-statistical Lists of the School Supervision District Brandenburg (Havel) for 1939 to 1944, BLHA, Pr. Br. Rep 2A Regierung Potsdam II Brd., nos. 198–203, and from the Registry of All Teachers at Brandenburg (Havel) Schools, compiled 27 August 1945, StadtA Brandenburg, 2.0.12.30/254, 42–58.

28. Ibid.

29. Ibid.

30. Ibid.

31. Ibid.
32. Ibid., and *Mitgliedskartei* for Gau Kurmark, BAB NS12, 2:82–88.
33. Ibid.
34. "Ausführungsbestimmungen zum Befehl des Obersten Chefs der sowjetischen Militärverwaltung über die Wiedereröffnung der Schulen vom 25.8.1945," sent by Paul Wandel to regional administrations, BAB DR2/4717, 74.
35. Ibid.
36. Correspondence from Education Department, Provincial Administration, Mark Brandenburg, 23 August 1945, StadtA Brandenburg, 2.0.12.26/250, 20. Moreover, former Nazi Party members were not to work in small schools, especially in the often rural, one-room elementary schools.
37. Circular from School Superintendent Johannes S., 5 September 1945, StadtA Brandenburg, 2.0.12.116/958, 79.
38. Report, 10 April 1946, StadtA Brandenburg, 2.0.12.115/957, 36.
39. City's registry of teachers, StadtA Brandenburg, 2.0.12.25/249, and "Protokoll no. 3 Sitzung der Entnazifizierungskommission der Stadtkreis Brandenburg/Havel vom 23.10.1947," BLHA, Rep 203 Ministerium des Innern Entnazifizierung, no. 791. According to regional authorities, a total of more than 14,000 former Nazis were purged from the late spring of 1945 to the year's end. With more than 2,800 dismissed, teachers were the group that lost the second greatest number of individuals, behind the more than 3,700 purged from the local and regional administrations; see Report, Ministry of the Interior, Brandenburg Provincial Administration, BLHA, Rep 203 Ministerium des Innern Entnazifizierung, no. 8, 207. Regarding Ludwig Z.'s rehabilitation, see *Der Kurier,* no. 10, 1 February 1948, and no. 16, 1 February 1949, DStA, BRV 132/128, 1 and 2–3, respectively.
40. Education Department, SMA of Germany, to Paul Wandel, 23 October 1945, BAB DR2/421, 46–47; Report from Piotr Solotuchin to Major General F. E. Bokov, Member of Military Council of SMA, November 1945, BAB DR2/959, 1–2. Russian archival restrictions reintroduced as of summer 2000 prevented me from examining Soviet attitudes and actions regarding the evaluation and purge of teachers in Brandenburg; for SMA reports on the denazification program for the entire Soviet Zone, see GARF, f. 7317, op. 54, d. 7–8, 10, 15, and op. 55, d. 1–2.
41. "Bericht zum Punkt 1 der Halleschen Tagesordnung über die Durchführung des Befehls des Marschalls Schukow über die Wiedereröffnung der Schulen," 3 November 1945, BAB DR2/280, 275–279.
42. Ibid., 278–279.
43. Ibid., 279.

44. Mayor Lange to School Superintendent Johannes S., 24 January 1946, StadtA Brandenburg, 2.0.2.16/16, 3.

45. Statistics for Brandenburg (Havel), as of 1 March 1946, BAB DR2/280, 229, and statistics for Brandenburg (Havel), as of 1 March 1946, BLHA, Rep 205A Ministerium für Volksbildung, no. 215, 7.

46. Directive No. 24, "Entfernung von Nationalsozialisten und Personen, die den Bestrebungen der Alliierten feindlich gegenüberstehen, aus Ämtern und verantwortlichen Stellungen," reprinted in Ruth-Kristin Rössler, ed., *Die Entnazifizierungspolitik der KPD/SED 1945–1948: Dokumente und Materialien* (Goldbach: Keip Verlag, 1994), 64–80; Vogt, *Denazification*, 83.

47. Vogt, *Denazification*, 72, 77–78, and 81–82.

48. Otto Grotewohl's speech before meeting of SED Executive Body, 18–20 June 1946, reprinted in Rössler, *Die Entnazifizierungspolitik*, 92.

49. Ibid., 33–35. According to Rössler, such political calculations continued to worry high-ranking SED leaders like Ulbricht as late as December 1947, 47.

50. Minutes of meeting nos. 1–12 of Commission for the Implementation of Directive No. 24, 26 December 1946 to 26 March 1947, BLHA, Rep 203 Ministerium des Innern Entnazifizierung, no. 63, 1–235; "Personen die bei der Durchführung der Direktive 24 mit Zwangsmassnahmen belegt wurden," table, BLHA, Rep 203 Ministerium des Innern Entnazifizierung, no. 663; "Statistischer Bericht über die Ergebnisse der Durchführung der Direktive 24 des Allierten Kontrollrates vom 1. Januar 1947 bis 17. August 1947," Land Brandenburg, BLHA, Rep. 203 Ministerium des Innern Entnazifizierung, no. 8, 28.

51. Rössler, *Die Entnazifizierungspolitik*, 147–148; correspondence from chairman of Commission for the Implementation of Directive 24, Brandenburg Province, to Deputy Chief of SMA, Abteilung Inneres, 4 September 1947, BLHA, Rep. 203 Ministerium des Innern Entnazifizierung, no. 8, 107–108.

52. Minutes of constituent meeting of Brandenburg (Havel) Denazification Commission, 7 October 1947, BLHA, Rep 203 Ministerium des Innern Entnazifizierung, no. 791.

53. Vogt, *Denazification*, 98. See personnel questionnaires and curricula vitae for individual commission members, BLHA, Rep 203 Ministerium des Innern Entnazifizierung, no. 790.

54. Minutes of constituent meeting of Brandenburg (Havel) Denazification Commission, 7 October 1947, BLHA, Rep 203 Ministerium des Innern Entnazifizierung, no. 791.

55. Minutes of meeting no. 2 of Brandenburg (Havel) Denazification Commis-

sion, 14 October 1947, BLHA, Rep 203 Ministerium des Innern Entnazifizierung, no. 791.

56. See minutes of meeting nos. 2–10 of Brandenburg (Havel) Denazification Commission, BLHA, Rep 203 Ministerium des Innern Entnazifizierung, no. 791.

57. Ibid; Rössler, *Die Entnazifizierungspolitik*, 29.

58. See minutes of meetings nos. 2–10 of Brandenburg (Havel) Denazification Commission, BLHA, Rep 203 Ministerium des Innern Entnazifizierung, no. 791. The Commission also passed on to the criminal courts the case of the secondary school pedagogue and city archivist who had helped Brandenburg's mayor Dr. Wilhelm Sievers prepare his regular reports to the Nazi secret police. Although the denazification commission failed to call before it everyone who had belonged to or even actively participated in the NSDAP or one of its affiliated organizations, the percentage of teachers purged (53 percent) was significantly higher than in, for example, the "skilled trades" (31 percent) or "health care" (9 percent) professions. Vogt, *Denazification*, 158–169.

59. Minutes of meetings nos. 2–10 of Brandenburg (Havel) Denazification Commission, BLHA, Rep 203 Ministerium des Innern Entnazifizierung, no. 791.

60. Report dated 10 April 1946, StadtA Brandenburg, 2.0.12.115/957, 36; Hohlfeld, *Die Neulehrer*, 49.

61. See minutes for meeting no. 6 as well as for meeting nos. 2–10 of Brandenburg (Havel) Denazification Commission, BLHA, Rep 203 Ministerium des Innern Entnazifizierung, no. 791.

62. "Ausführungsbestimmungen zum Befehl des Obersten Chefs der sowjetischen Militärverwaltung über die Wiedereröffnung der Schulen vom 25.8.1945," distributed as an attachment from Paul Wandel, DVfV, to provincial administrations, BAB DR2/4717, 74–75.

63. Hohlfeld, *Die Neulehrer*, 11 and 85.

64. *Brandenburger Anzeiger*, 30 January, 25 February, and 11 March 1933, "Für Brandenburg" section; Report, 10 April 1946, StadtA Brandenburg, 2.0.12.115/957, 37; Report from School Superintendent Willi L. to Mayor Herm, 27 June 1945, StadtA Brandenburg, 2.0.2.16/16, 2; biographical data found in city's registry of teachers, StadtA Brandenburg, 2.0.12.25/249, and School-statistical Lists of the School Supervision District Brandenburg (Havel) for years 1939 to 1944, BLHA, Pr. Br. Rep. 2A Regierung Potsdam II Brd., no. 198–203.

65. "Bericht über das Brandenburger Schulleben von Mai 1945 zum Mai 1948," StadtA Brandenburg, 2.0.12.17/241, 164.

66. "Ausführungsbestimmungen zum Befehl des Obersten Chefs der sowjeti-

schen Militärverwaltung über die Wiedereröffnung der Schulen vom 25.8.1945," distributed as an attachment from Paul Wandel, DVfV, to provincial administrations, BAB DR2/4717, 76–77.

67. "Richtlinien für die Schulräte zur Durchführung der Ausbildung von Schulhelfern," StadtA Brandenburg, 2.0.12.26/250, 24.

68. "Bericht über die pädagogische Tagung in Potsdam, vom 29.–31. August 45," BAB DR2/488, 5.

69. Report by School Superintendent Johannes S., 2 July 1946, StadtA Brandenburg, 2.0.12.17/241, 175; and Eva-Maria B., interview by author, 3 August 2000.

70. Eva-Maria B., interview by author, 3 August 2000.

71. Ibid.

72. City's registry of teachers, StadtA Brandenburg, 2.0.12.25/249; according to Geissler, as early as 1946 the *Neulehrer* courses were training specialists (*Fachlehrer*), *Geschichte des Schulwesens*, 183–184.

73. Piotr Solotuchin, Education Department SMA, to Paul Wandel, 23 October 1945, BAB DR2/421, 46. For more on Russian attitudes and actions on the zonal level regarding the *Neulehrer* program, see GARF f. 7317, op. 54, d. 7–8, and 10.

74. Memorandum, Solotuchin to Major General F. E. Bokov, Military Council, SMA, November 1945, BAB DR2/959, 1–3; SMA Order no. 162, 6 December 1945, copy, BAB DR2/910, 8. See also Information Report from Solotuchin to Major General M. I. Dratvin, Command Headquarters, SMA, 25 March 1946, GARF, f. 7317, op. 54, d. 7, l. 5.

75. "Bericht über das Brandenburger Schulleben von Mai 1945 zum Mai 1948," StadtA Brandenburg, 2.0.12.17/241, 164.

76. Report by School Superintendent Johannes S., 2 July 1946, StadtA Brandenburg, 2.0.12.17/241, 175.

77. Correspondence, District School Superintendent to Brandenburg School Superintendent, 28 December 1945, StadtA Brandenburg, 2.0.12.117/959, 157, and Report of School Superintendent Johannes S., 19 October 1945, StadtA Brandenburg, 2.0.12.26/250, 129.

78. "Bericht über die pädagogische Tagung in Potsdam, vom 29.–31. August 45," BAB DR2/488, 2.

79. "Bericht zum Punkt 1 der Halleschen Tagesordnung über die Durchführung des Befehls des Marschalls Schukow über die Wiedereröffnung der Schulen," 3 November 1945, BAB DR2/280, 277.

80. Dr. Gertrud Rasenow, "Stand der Neulehrerausbildung in der Provinz Brandenburg," 18 December 1946, BAB DR2/201, 16.

81. Fritz Rücker, speech at Second Pedagogical Congress of Province Brandenburg, 22 July 1947, copy, BAB DR2/269, 41. The *Einheitsschulen* re-

placed the traditional system, in which pupils were selected at the age of 10 for their postprimary schooling, with a new school structure in which all pupils remained together in the elementary school for a total of eight years before attending either an academic secondary school or a vocational school; see H.-J. Hahn, *Education and Society in Germany* (New York: Berg, 1998), 97.

82. Minutes of meeting of principals, 14 July 1948, StadtA Brandenburg, 2.0.12.26/250, 169–171.

83. "Bericht über die 2. Tagung der Schulräte der Provinz Brandenburg vom 27. Februar bis 2. März 1946," 4 March 1946, BAB DR2/488, 18.

84. "Bericht über die Überprüfung der Volksbildungsabteilung bei der Provinzialverwaltung in Potsdam and beim Oberlandrat in Brandenburg," 24 September 1946, BAB DR2/823, 98; and Herbert S., interview by author, 2005. See also Gert Geissler, *Geschichte des Schulwesens in der Sowjetischen Besatzungszone und in der Deutschen Demokratischen Republik 1945 bis 1962* (Frankfurt am Main: Peter Lang, 2000), 120.

85. Geissler, *Geschichte des Schulwesens*, 122; Karl-Heinz R. and Eva-Maria B., and Herbert S., interviews by author, August 2000 and Summer 2005, respectively.

86. Hohlfeld, *Die Neulehrer*, 117–118; Report from School Superintendent Johannes S., 2 July 1946, StadtA Brandenburg, 2.0.12.17/241, 175. Hohlfeld notes that only 88 percent of all participants in the region completed their training, *Die Neulehrer*, 120.

87. Hohlfeld, *Die Neulehrer*, 148; Geissler, *Geschichte des Schulwesens*, 122–123.

88. Hohlfeld, *Die Neulehrer*, 148, 152–153, and 194; Geissler, *Geschichte des Schulwesens*, 124.

89. Hohlfeld, *Die Neulehrer*, 60, 80, 161–162.

90. Minutes of district teachers' meeting, 11 June 1948, StadtA Brandenburg, 2.0.12.26/250, 161–162.

91. Quoted in Hohlfeld, *Die Neulehrer*, 82; Herbert S., interview by author, 2005.

92. Hohlfeld, *Die Neulehrer*, 154–156. Fleeing to the western zones was the single most popular cause for what was called the *Lehrerflucht* in this period; of the 20 Brandenburg *Neulehrer* who quit the elementary or academic secondary schools, two gave no reason for leaving the profession, five chose to change jobs, six were dismissed for political reasons, and seven fled the Soviet Zone, "Neulehrer-Statistisk: Bestand, Ohne Berufsschulen, Stichtag 20.12.47," sent from School Superintendent M. to Education Ministry, Statistics Department, BLHA, Rep 205A Ministerium für Volksbildung, no. 362, and "Bericht über die Sitzung der Landesschulkom-

mission vom 23. Mai 1949," SAPMO-BArch DY 30/IV 2/9.05/38, 32. See also report from I. D. Artiukhin to Major General Lukyancheko, Command Headquarters of SMA, 19 January 1948, GARF, f. 7317, op. 54, d. 10, l. 8.

93. Neulehrer statistics as of 20 December 1947 and 1 March 1948, BAB DR 2/196, 83 and 85.

94. Due to the relative imprecision with which education officials categorized teachers' reasons for leaving, it is possible that some of six who left for "other reasons," for instance, did in fact flee the Zone, "Statistik über das Ausscheiden von Lehrkräften," for Brandenburg/Havel, Education Ministry, Land Brandenburg, 23, and minutes of district teachers' conference, 20 September 1948, StadtA Brandenburg, 2.0.12.26/50, 181.

95. "Bericht über das Schulwesen des Landes Brandenburgs," 20 May 1949, BAB DR2/280, 266–267, and letter to editorial board of *Berliner Zeitung*, 28 June 1949, copy, SAPMO-BArch DY30/IV 2/9.05/38, 62.

96. "Fluktuation der Lehrer," 9 August 1949, BAB DR2/911, 77–78. Specific material improvements were also included in the "Kulturplan" issued by the German Economic Commission and the DVfV in March 1946; Hohlfeld, *Die Neulehrer*, 194.

97. Volker Ackermann, *Der "echte" Flüchtling: Deutsche Vertriebene und Flüchtlinge aus der DDR 1945–1961* (Osnabrück: Universitätsverlag Rasch, 1995), 126–195, Helge Heidemeyer, *Flucht und Zuwanderung aus der SBZ/DDR 1945/1949–1961: Die Flüchtlingspolitik der Bundesrepublik Deutschland bis zum Bau der Berliner Mauer* (Düsseldorf: Droste Verlag, 1994), 53–62, Joachim S. Hohmann, ed., *Lehrerflucht aus SBZ und DDR 1945–1961: Dokumente zur Geschichte und Soziologie sozialistischer Bildung und Erziehung* (Frankfurt am Main: Peter Lang, 2000), 13–19.

98. Minutes of meeting no. 6 of Brandenburg (Havel) Denazification Commission, BLHA, Rep 203 Ministerium des Innern Entnazifizierung, no. 791.

99. Neulehrer statistics as of 1 March 1948, BAB DR2/196, 85.

100. Report, 30 September 1948, StadtA Brandenburg, 2.0.12.17/241, 197; and Brandenburg an der Havel School Superintendent's "Nachtrag—Mein Urteil über die Goetheschule für Mädchen (Oberschule) Brandenburg (Havel)," 20 May 1950, BAB DR2/5720, 230.

101. "Tätigkeitsbericht über das gesamte Aufgabengebiet des Dezernates für Volksbildung für die Zeit vom 1. Juli 1949 bis 30. November 1949," Education Department, Brandenburg an der Havel, 1 December 1949, StadtA Brandenburg, 2.0.12.17/241, 33, and "Bericht über das Schulwesen des Landes Brandenburgs," 20 May 1949, BAB DR2/280, 266–73, and "Fluktuation der Lehrer," 9 August 1949, BAB DR2/911, 77–78.

102. Circular from Province Brandenburg Administration, Education Department, to Oberschulräte and School Superintendents, 29 June 1946, BAB DR2/947, 37. Although Ralph Jessen argues that reinstated "brown" professors often proved to be more obedient and adaptable than their non-Nazi colleagues who were still teaching after 1945, there is no reason to believe that East German officials expected this to be the case at the time of the reinstatements. As he notes, purged professors were rehired partly due to Soviet pressure on German authorities. Regarding school teachers, extant records give no indication that local or regional education officials anticipated that rehired PG teachers would be especially loyal or obedient. If such a dynamic turned out eventually to be true, it was not something they expected while making the early reinstatements. More plausible is the argument that authorities rehired Nazi teachers because of the dramatic teacher shortage; Jessen, *Akademische Elite*, 297–302.

103. Correspondence, Paul Wandel, DVfV, to provincial administrations, 15 July 1946, BAB DR2/421, 2.

104. Guidelines for personnel departments of Oberschulräte, BAB DR2/947, 55.

105. Eva-Maria B., interview by author, 3 August 2000.

106. Draft circular, 5 March 1948, BAB DR2/421, 130.

107. "Protokoll der Sitzung der Leiter der Personalabteilungen in den Volbildungsministerien, 31.3–1.4.1948," copy, BAB DR2/947, 74–75.

108. Note from Hermann Gerigk to Mr. Kauter, Brandenburg Province Ministry of Education, 24 September 1949, BLHA, Rep 205A Ministerium für Volksbildung no. 104, 337; Gunilla-Friederike Budde, *Frauen der Intelligenz: Akademikerinnen in der DDR 1945 bis 1975* (Göttingen: Vandenhoeck und Ruprecht, 2002), 257; and Karl-Heinz R., interview by author, August 2000.

109. Protokoll no. 3 Sitzung der Entnazifizierungskommission der Stadtkreises Brandenburg/Havel vom 23 October 1947, BLHA, Rep 203 Ministerium des Innern Entnazifizierung, no. 791, and Ritterakademie alumni newsletter *Der Kurier,* no. 10, 1 February 1948, and no. 16, 1 February 1949, DstA BRV 132/128, 1 and 2–3, respectively.

110. Nikitin, *Zwischen Dogma,* 23–24, 26–28, 47, and Geissler, *Geschichte des Schulwesens,* 66 and 186.

111. "Bericht über die pädagogische Tagung in Potsdam, vom 29.–31. August 45," BAB DR2/488, 1.

112. For a more complete discussion of this Zone-wide phenomenon, see Frank Biess, *Homecomings: Returning POWs and the Legacies of Defeat in Postwar Germany* (Princeton, NJ: Princeton University Press, 2006).

113. Hohlfeld, *Die Neulehrer,* 198. These inconsistencies grew partially out of and were sustained by the structural organization of the SMA, a chaotic system of institutions, agencies, and units not infrequently competing against each other for greater power; see Creuzberger, *Sowjetische Be-satzungsmacht,* 40–42, Nikitin, *Zwischen Dogma,* 32–33, and Geissler, *Geschichte des Schulwesens,* 66.

114. Hohlfeld, *Die Neulehrer,* 49–50.

115. Ibid., 53.

116. Minutes of meeting no. 9 of Commission for the Implementation of Directive no. 24, 19 February 1947, BLHA, Rep 203 Ministerium des Innern Entnazifizierung, no. 63, 50.

117. Vogt, *Denazification,* 77–78. For a masterful discussion of the relationship between democratic politics and the process of coming to terms with the Nazi past in West Germany, see Norbert Frei, *Adenauer's Germany and the Nazi Past: The Politics of Amnesty and Integration,* trans. Joel Golb (New York: Columbia University Press, 1997).

118. "Bericht über die 2. Tagung der Schulräte der Provinz Brandenburg vom 27. Februar bis 2. März 1946," 4 March 1946, BAB DR2/488, 18.

119. "Bericht über das Brandenburger Schulleben von Mai 1945 zum Mai 1948," StadtA Brandenburg, 2.0.12.17/241, 166.

120. Hohlfeld, *Die Neulehrer,* 71, and Circular from Central Committee of KPD to all KPD District Executives, 28 December 1945, SAPMO-BArch DY 30/IV 2/9.05/75, 10.

121. "Kurze Zusammenfassung eines Berichtes über die Lage in den Schulen des Kreises Brandenburg/Havel," SAPMO-BArch DY30/IV 2/9.05/77, 149.

122. Jessen, *Akademische Elite,* 13 and 51. It is hoped that scholars researching postwar transformations in the other eastern European "people's democracies" will someday take up the question of personnel changes in the schools of Poland, Czechoslovakia, or Hungary, for example; doing so would provide a broader comparative perspective that would help us better understand, among other things, the nature and efficacy of the denazification of Germany's schools.

5. The Creation of a Geniune Teachers' Union

1. Report from School Superintendent M., 20 December 1947, BLHA, Rep 205A Ministerium für Volksbildung, no. 433, 196–198.

2. See Ulrich Gill, *FDGB: Die DDR-Gewerkschaft von 1945 bis zu ihrer Auflösung 1990* (Köln: Bund Verlag, 1991) and Bundesministerium für innerdeutsche Beziehungen, ed., *DDR Handbuch* (Köln: Verlag Wissenschaft und Politik, 1985), 1:459–472.

3. SMA Order no. 2: Establishment of Anti-fascist Parties and Free Trade Unions in the Soviet Zone, 10 June 1945, reprinted in Beate Ruhm von Oppen, ed., *Documents on Germany under Occupation 1945–1954* (London: Oxford University Press, 1955), 37–38, and Gill, *FDGB*, 87–88.

4. Ruhm von Oppen, *Documents*, 87–88; Gill, *FDGB*, 23–25 and 88; Helke Stadtland, *Herrschaft nach Plan und Macht der Gewohnheit: Sozialgeschichte der Gewerkschaften in der SBZ/DDR 1945–1953* (Essen: Klartext Verlag, 2001), 55.

5. Gill, *FDGB*, 26, and Gert Geissler, *Geschichte des Schulwesens in der Sowjetischen Besatzungszone und in der Deutschen Demokratischen Republik 1945 bis 1962* (Frankfurt am Main: Peter Lang, 2000), 56–60.

6. Circular from Central Leadership of the Local Committee of the FDGB, 18 July 1945, StadtA Brandenburg, 2.0.2.110/583, 12.

7. "Bericht über die pädagogische Tagung in Potsdam, vom 29.–31. August 45," BAB DR2/488, 7; Gill, *FDGB*, 23–24; "Leitsätze zu dem Referat von Dr. Dembowski über die neue Lehrerorganisation" and "Organisation der neuen Schule," reports, StadtA Brandenburg, 2.0.12.26/250, 78–79, 85.

8. "Bericht von der am 5. Juni in Potsdam stattgefundenen Provinzial-Konferenz der Gewekschaft der Lehrer und Erzieher" and "Bericht über die Provinzial-Delegierten Konferenz der Lehrer und Erzieher der Mark Brandenburg am 5. Juni 1946," BLHA, Rep 347 FDGB Landesvorstand, no. 912, Potsdam Education Ministry to Colonel Warakin, Head of Political Department of Province Brandenburg SMA, 13 October 1945, BLHA, Rep 205a Ministerium für Volksbildung, no. 102, 1, and minutes of first meeting of Executive Committee of Regional Union Mark Brandenburg of Teachers and Educators in FDGB (Säule 18), 21 December 1945, BLHA, Rep 347 FDGB Landesvorstand, no. 914.

9. Although the statistical analysis refers to the teachers' memberships in the FDGB, we can safely assume they refer to the GLE, BLHA, Rep 205A Ministerium für Volksbildung, no. 346, 10; also "Mitgliederstand der Kreise im Jahre 1946," statistical analysis, BLHA, Rep 347 FDGB Landesvorstand, no. 1072.

10. Minutes of regional conference of Union of Teachers and Educators held on 5 June, Potsdam, BLHA, Rep 347 FDGB Landesvorstand, no. 912. Biographical information gathered from NSLB *Mitgliedskartei* for Gau Kurmark, BAB NS12, 2:82–88, Registry of All Teachers at Brandenburg (Havel) Schools, comp. 27 August 1945, Amt für Volksbildung, Abt. Schulamt, StadtA Brandenburg, 2.0.12.30/254, 42–58, and the city's registry of teachers, StadtA Brandenburg, 2.0.12.25/249, and List of Regional Executive Committee Members of Union for Teachers and Educators, BLHA, Rep 347 FDGB Landesvorstand, no. 1071.

11. "Report of the Regional Conference of Delegates of Mark Brandenburg Teachers and Educators on 5 June," BLHA, Rep 347 FDGB Landesvorstand, no. 912.

12. Minutes of regional conference of the delegates of Mark Brandenburg Teachers and Educators held on 5 June 1946, Potsdam, BLHA, Rep 347 FDGB Landesvorstand, no. 912, and minutes of first meeting of Full Regional Executive Committee *(Gesamtprovinzialvorstand)* of Union of Teachers and Educators Mark Brandenburg, 3 October 1946, BLHA, Rep 347 Landesvorstand Brandenburg FDGB, no. 914.

13. Report of the Regional Conference of Delegates of Mark Brandenburg Teachers and Educators on 5 June, BLHA, Rep 347 FDGB Landesvorstand, no. 912.

14. Ibid.

15. Gill, *FDGB*, 30–31.

16. Minutes of the first meeting of Executive Committee of Regional Union Mark Brandenburg of Teachers and Educators in FDGB (Säule 18), 21 December 1945, BLHA, Rep 347 FDGB Landesvorstand, no. 914.

17. "Bericht über die Überprüfung der Volksbildungsabteilung bei der Provinzialverwaltung in Potsdam und beim Oberlandrat in Brandenburg," 24 September 1946, BAB DR2/823, 96.

18. Ibid., 95–97.

19. Ibid.

20. Minutes of first meeting of Full Regional Executive Committee *(Gesamtprovinzialvorstand)* of Union of Teachers and Educators Mark Brandenburg, 3 October 1946, BLHA, Rep 347 Landesvorstand Brandenburg FDGB, no. 914.

21. "Material zur Lehrerbesoldung: Stand vom Oktober 1946," ed., Zonal Executive Committee of the Union of Teachers and Educators, BAB DR2/4717, 144.

22. Minutes of first meeting of Full Regional Executive Committee *(Gesamtprovinzialvorstand)* of Union of Teachers and Educators Mark Brandenburg, 3 October 1946, BLHA, Rep 347 Landesvorstand Brandenburg, FDGB, no. 914.

23. School Superintendent M. to Brandenburg Mayor and Education Ministry, 8 December 1947, StadtA Brandenburg, 2.0.12.24/248, 29.

24. Circular to Regional Organizations of the GLE, 5 December 1946, SAPMO-BArch DY51/18/339/3107. See also Bundesministerium für innerdeutsche Beziehungen, *DDR Handbuch*, 1:212.

25. Ibid.

26. Stadtland, *Herrschaft*, 118–127.

27. Minutes and attendance sheet of joint meeting of Regional Executive Committee of Teachers' Union Mark Brandenburg, of Teachers' Councils and of Chairmen of District Chapters of Teachers' Union Mark Brandenburg on 7 March 1947, and minutes of regional conference of Union of Teachers and Educators held on 5 June, Potsdam, BLHA, Rep 347 FDGB, no. 927 and FDGB Landesvorstand, no. 912, respectively; circular no. 121/46 sent to Regional Chapters of GLE, 5 December 1946, SAPMO-BArch DY51/18/339/3107, and letter from Ministry of the Interior, Information Department, Provincial Administration Mark Brandenburg, 14 January 1947, BLHA, Rep 332 Landesleitung SED Brandenburg no. 734, 20. Biographical information gathered from Registry of All Teachers at Brandenburg (Havel) Schools, comp. 27 August 1945, Amt für Volksbildung, Abt. Schulamt, StadtA Brandenburg, 2.0.12.30/254, 42–58, and the city's registry of teachers, StadtA Brandenburg, 2.0.12.25/249.

28. Minutes of first meeting of Teachers' Council, 26 June 1947, StadtA Brandenburg, 2.0.12.26/250, 141–142. Biographical information gathered from Registry of All Teachers at Brandenburg (Havel) Schools, comp. 27 August 1945, Amt für Volksbildung, Abt. Schulamt, StadtA Brandenburg, 2.0.12.30/254, 42–58, and the city's registry of teachers, StadtA Brandenburg, 2.0.12.25/249.

29. Minutes of first meeting of Teachers' Council, 26 June 1947, StadtA Brandenburg, 2.0.12.26/250, 141–142; minutes of Teachers' Council meeting of 30 August 1948, StadtA Brandenburg, 2.0.12.26/250, 176.

30. Brandenburg Province Education Ministry circular, copy, 30 September 1947, StadtA Brandenburg, 2.0.12.24/248, 22.

31. Letter from Chairman of the Union of Teachers and Educators, undated, copy, FDGB, SAPMO-BArch DY51/18/605/3207.

32. Ibid.

33. Directive no. 24, "Entfernung von Nationalsozialisten und Personen, die den Bestrebungen der Alliierten feindlich gegenüberstehen, aus Ämtern und verantwortlichen Stellungen," reprinted in Ruth-Kristin Rössler, ed., *Die Entnazifizierungspolitik der KPD/SED 1945–1948: Dokumente und Materialien* (Goldbach: Keip Verlag, 1994), 64–80; Timothy Vogt, *Denazification in Brandenburg* (Cambridge, Mass.: Harvard University Press, 2000), 83; GLE Executive Committee member Köhn to Paul Wandel, 4 January 1946, copy, BAB DR2/421, 9.

34. Minutes of first meeting of Full Regional Executive Committee *(Gesamtprovinzialvorstand)* of Union of Teachers and Educators Mark Brandenburg, 3 October 1946, BLHA, Rep 347 Landesvorstand Brandenburg FDGB, no. 914.

35. Minutes of meetings of Commission for Implementation of Directive no. 24, BLHA, Rep 203 Ministerium des Innern Entnazifizierung, no. 63, 1–235; minutes of meetings of Brandenburg Denazification Commission, BLHA, Rep 203 Ministerium des Innern Entnazifizierung, no. 791.

36. Report from School Superintendent M., 20 December 1947, BLHA, Rep 205A Ministerium für Volksbildung, no. 433, 196–198.

37. Minutes of meeting of Expanded Regional Executive Committee and District Executive Committees of Teachers' Union and of Chairmen of District Teachers' Councils, 20 November 1947, BLHA, Rep 347 Landesvorstand Brandenburg FDGB, no. 914; draft report from Professor Dr. Peters, 5 March 1948, BAB DR2/421, 130–131; Adolf Buchholz to GLE Central Committee, 6 August 1948, BLHA, Rep 347 Landesvorstand Brandenburg FDGB, no. 1061.

38. Report on GLE Executive Committee Meeting, 14 February 1948, and minutes of meeting of district Teachers' Council, 20 July 1948, StadtA Brandenburg, 2.0.12.26/250, 150–152 and 173, respectively. Biographical information from Registry of All Teachers at Brandenburg (Havel) Schools, comp. 27 August 1945, Amt für Volksbildung, Abt. Schulamt, StadtA Brandenburg, 2.0.12.30/254, 42–58, and the city's registry of teachers, StadtA Brandenburg, 2.0.12.25/249, and School-statistical Lists of School Supervision District Brandenburg (Havel) for 1939 to 1944, BLHA, Pr. Br. Rep 2A Regierung Potsdam II Brd., no. 198–203.

39. Ibid; minutes of meeting of *Betriebsgewerkschaftsleitung*, 28 January 1952, BLHA, Rep 548 Brandenburg-Stadt GUE, no. 35; minutes of 20 June 1951 and confidential letter, District Secretary of Brandenburg GLE chapter Günther S. to Province Brandenburg GLE, 21 August 1950, BLHA, Rep 347 FDGB GUE, no. 1031.

40. "Mitgliederstand der Kreise im Jahre 1946," "Mitgliederstand der Kreise im Jahre 1947," and "Mitgliederstand der Kreise im Jahre 1948," statistical analyses, BLHA, Rep 347 FDGB Landesvorstand, no. 1072.

41. Teachers' Registry for District of Brandenburg an der Havel, BLHA, Rep 205A Ministerium für Volksbildung, no. 352, 46.

42. "Mitgliederstand und Markenverkauf des FDGB Land Brandenburg in der IG/Gew Lehrer und Erzieher," statistical analysis, BLHA, Rep 347 FDGB Landesvorstand, no. 1072.

43. KPD City District Leadership to Brandenburg officials, 19 September 1945, StadtA Brandenburg, 2.0.2.74/74, 6; as Gareth Pritchard demonstrates, the KPD/SED's intention to transform itself from a cadre party to a *Volkspartei* failed at this time to change the attitudes and actions of many KPD/SED functionaries, *The Making of the GDR 1945–1953: From Antifascism to Stalinism* (Manchester, England: Manchester University Press,

2000), 56–78. See also the absence of KPD inquiries, policies, and positions regarding teachers in the late 1945 and early 1946 correspondence between the party and the Brandenburg city government, StadtA Brandenburg, 2.0.2.74/74, 1–115.

44. Statistical table, undated, BLHA, Rep 205A Ministerium für Volksbildung no. 346, 10; untitled statistical analysis, 1 March 1946, BLHA, Rep 205A Ministerium für Volksbildung, no. 215, 7, and "Politische Aufstellung aller Lehrkräfte," 22 June 1946, BLHA, Rep 205A Ministerium für Volksbildung, no. 346, 4.

45. Report for SED Secretariat meeting, 12 August 1946, and minutes of Executive Committee meeting, 14 October 1946, BLHA, Rep 334 SED Kreisleitung Brandenburg, no. 7, 25 and 42; statistical analysis comparing the teaching staff as of 1 March 1946 and 31 December 1946, BLHA, Rep 205A Ministerium für Volksbildung, no. 217, 14.

46. Brandenburg SED District Committee to SED Regional Executive Committee, 9 December 1946, BLHA, Rep 333 SED Landesvorstand Brandenburg, no. 735, 21, and "Auszug aus dem Arbeitsbericht des Kreisvorstandes Brandenburg, Abteilung Parteischulung, Monat Oktober 1947," 20 November 1947, BLHA, Rep 333 SED Landesvorstand Brandenburg, no. 1205, 45.

47. Correspondence, Cathedral Secondary School for Boys to City Superintendent, 12 March and 25 July 1947, StadtA Brandenburg, 2.0.12.118/960, 79 and 192.

48. SED Regional Executive Committee, Department of Training, Culture and Education, to SED Central Committee, Department of Culture and Education, 11 August 1947, copy, BLHA, Rep 333 SED Landesvorstand Brandenburg, no. 1205, 20; "Volksbildung 1947 in Brandenburg," report, 25 October 1947, and "Schulstatistische Erhebung am 15. Oktober 1948," Deutsche Verwaltung für Volksbildung, Statistische Zentralamt, StadtA Brandenburg, 2.0.12.1/225, 5 and 31.

49. Transcript of meeting with school superintendents, 9 March 1948, BLHA, Rep 205A Ministerium für Volksbildung, no. 433, 117.

50. Minutes of District Teachers' Conference, 11 June 1948, 12 June 1948, StadtA Brandenburg, 2.0.12.26/250, 161.

51. Report on Sekretariat meeting, 3 May 1949, BLHA, Rep 334 SED Kreisleitung Brandenburg, no. 8, 125.

52. Brandenburg Province SED to German Central Administration for Education, 15 June 1949, copy, BLHA, Rep 332 Landesleitung SED Brandenburg, no. 731, 25–27.

53. SED Regional Executive Committee, Department of Training, Culture and Education to Brandenburg SED District Committee, 3 December

1947, copy, BLHA, Rep 333 SED Landesvorstand Brandenburg, no. 1205, 44; SED Brandenburg Province Executive Committee, Training, Culture, and Education Department to Education Minister Rücker, 15 November 1947, BLHA, Rep 332 Landesleitung SED Brandenburg, no. 734, 65.

54. "Reisebericht, Dienstreise vom 29.4.–5.5.1947," BAB DR2/459, 15.

55. Chairman of the GLE Central Executive Richard Schallock to chairmen of GLE Regional Executive Committees, 31 December 1946, copy, SAPMO-BArch DY51, no. 371.

56. School Superintendent M., "Bericht über die Delegiertenkonferenz der Gewerkschaft Lehrer und Erzieher am 7. März 1950," 8 March 1950, BLHA, Rep 347 FDGB Landesvorstand Gewerkschaft Unterricht u. Erziehung, no. 1058.

57. Brandenburg GLE to Regional Executive Committee, 31 May 1949, "Bericht über den Ortsvorstande und die BGL der Lehrergewerkschaft in Brandenburg," 29 June 1949, and confidential letter, District Secretary of Brandenburg GLE chapter Günther S. to Province Brandenburg GLE, 21 August 1950, BLHA Rep 347 GUE, no. 1031, and Registry of All Teachers at Brandenburg (Havel) Schools, comp. 27 August 1945, Amt für Volksbildung, Abt. Schulamt, StadtA Brandenburg, 2.0.12.30/254, 42–58, and the city's registry of teachers, StadtA Brandenburg, 2.0.12.25/249.

58. Feiten, *NSLB*.

59. Regional education authorities to Colonel Varakin, head of Political Department of Brandenburg Province SMA, 13 October 1945, Rep 205a Ministerium für Volksbildung, no. 102 (Politische Schulung und Umschulung der Lehrer 1945), 1, and "Bericht zum Punkt 1 der Halleschen Tagesordnung über die Durchführung des Befehls des Marschalls Schukow über die Wiedereröffnung der Schulen," 3 November 1945, BAB DR2/280, 278.

60. Minutes of meetings of Provisional Executive Committee of GLE, Mark Brandenburg, 3 December 1946, 4 December 1946, 2 November 1948, and 5 November 1948, BLHA, Rep 347 FDGB Landesvorstand Brandenburg GLE, no. 918; meeting of Sekretariat, 7 May 1947, BLHA, Rep 334 SED Kreisleitung Brandenburg, no. 7, 92.

6. The Sovietization of Teachers and Their Union

1. "Bericht über die Kreisdelegiertenkonferenz in Brandenburg am 7.3.50," 27 March 1950, BLHA, Rep 347 FDGB Landesvorstand GUE, no. 990, 13–14. In March 1950 the SED failed to elect a number of BGL candidates proportional to the party's membership within the teaching staff

because the large majority of teachers who were *parteilos* almost exclusively supported non-SED candidates.

2. Ibid. In addition to the 20 teachers, the FDJ district chairman, and a kindergarten teachers' representative were appointed to serve on the BGL, BLHA, Rep 347 FDGB Landesvorstand GUE, no. 990; "Vorschläge für den Ortsvorstand der Lehrergewerkschaft," BLHA, Rep 334 SED Kreisleitung Brandenburg, no. 9. Biographical information gathered from NSLB *Mitgliedskartei* for Gau Kurmark, BAB NS12, 2:82–88, Brandenburg's registry of teachers, StadtA Brandenburg, 2.0.12.25/249, August 1945 Registry of All Teachers at Brandenburg (Havel) Schools, comp. 27 August 1945, StadtA Brandenburg, 2.0.12.30/254, 42–58, "Bericht von der Gewerkschafts-Vorstandssitzung—Lehrer u. Erzieher ," 14 February 1948, StadtA Brandenburg, 2.0.12.26/250, 150, and correspondence, Secondary School for Boys to Brandenburg School Superintendent, 12 May 1947, StadtA Brandenburg, 2.0.12.118/960, 140.

3. Activity report of Province Brandenburg Executive Committee for fourth quarter of 1950, BLHA, Rep 347 FDGB Landesvorstand GUE, no. 990, 33–34; confidential letter, District Secretary of Brandenburg GLE chapter Günther S. to Brandenburg Province GLE, 21 August 1950, BLHA, Rep 347 FDGB Landesvorstand GUE, no. 1031.

4. "Bericht über die Sitzung der Landesschulkommission vom 23. Mai 1949," SAPMO-BArch DY30/IV 2/9.05/38, 32–33, and "Protokoll Sitzung der Pädagogischen Kommissionen beim Landesvorstand Brandenburg der Gewerkschaft Lehrer und Erzieher im FDGB am 9.6.1950," BLHA, Rep 347 Landesvorstand Brandenburg FDGB, no. 927; "Protokoll der Geschäftsführende Vorstandssitzung des LV d. GLE, Potsdam am 4.4.50," BLHA, Rep 347 Landesvorstand Brandenburg FDGB, no. 918; Activity report of Province Brandenburg Executive Committee for fourth quarter of 1950, BLHA, Rep 347 FDGB Landesvorstand GUE, no. 990, 20, and "Die Prager Deutschland-Beschlüsse der Ostblockstaaten," 21 October 1950, reprinted in Christoph Klessmann, *Die doppelte Staatsgründung: Deutsche Geschichte 1945–1955* (Bonn: Bundeszentrale für politische Bildung, 1991), 463.

5. "Protokoll Ausserordentliche Geschäftsführende Vorstandssitzung am 1. Juni 1949 in Potsdam," BLHA, Rep 347 Landesvorstand Brandenburg FDGB, no. 918; Brandenburg GUE District Leader Willi S. to GUE Landesvorstand, 23 July 1949, BLHA, Rep 347 FDGB Landesvorstand GUE, no. 1031, and "Notiz zur Sekretariatssitzung," 20 April 1950, SAPMO-BArch DY51, no. 445.

6. The concept of democratic centralism lay at the heart of the structure and operation of both the Communist state and party. First institutionalized by

Lenin, the tenets of democratic centralism included a highly centralized hierarchy in which decisions made at an organization's highest level were binding on the lower levels. In the GDR, such a system theoretically guaranteed the frictionless implementation of Berlin's decisions by the local and regional chapters; see J. Wilczynski, *An Encyclopedic Dictionary of Marxism, Socialism, and Communism* (Berlin: de Gruyter, 1981), 139–140, and Bundesministerium für innerdeutsche Beziehungen, ed., *DDR Handbuch* (Köln: Verlag Wissenschaft und Politik, 1985), 1:268–269.

7. Ulrich Gill, *FDGB. Die DDR-Gewerkschaft von 1945 bis zu ihrer Auflösung 1990* (Köln: Bund Verlag, 1991), 34–39, Bundesministerium für innerdeutsche Beziehungen, *DDR Handbuch,* 1:461, and Friedrich-Ebert-Stiftung, ed., *Der FDGB von A–Z: Kleines Lexikon zum Gewerkschaftswesen in der DDR* (Bonn: Verlag Neue Gesellschaft, 1987), 14.

8. Constitution of the Union of Teachers and Educators of the FDGB, 15 December 1950, BLHA, Rep 347 FDGB Landesvorstand GUE, no. 934.

9. "Ziele und Aufgaben der Gewerkschaft Schule und Erziehung," undated, BLHA, Rep 347 FDGB Landesvorstand GUE, no. 934.

10. Confidential letter, District Secretary of Brandenburg GLE chapter Günther S. to Brandenburg Province GLE, 21 August 1950, BLHA, Rep 347 FDGB Landesvorstand GUE, no. 1031.

11. Ibid., and Brandenburg School Superintendent, "Bericht über die Delegiertenkonferenz der Gewerkschaft Lehrer und Erzieher am 7. März 1950," 8 March 1950, BLHA, Rep 347 FDGB Landesvorstand GUE, no. 1058; presentation for SED Sekretariat meeting, 22 March 1951, BLHA, Rep 334 SED Kreisleitung Brandenburg, no. 13.

12. See individual complaints from Goethe School (Boys and Girls), Heinrich Heine School (Boys and Girls), Jahn School, Görden School (Boys and Girls), Municipal Trade School, BBS Thälmann, Franz Ziegler School, and Joliot Curie School, BLHA Rep 347 FDGB Landesvorstand GUE, no. 1031. See also Presentation for SED Sekretariat meeting, 22 March 1951, BLHA, Rep 334 SED Kreisleitung Brandenburg, no. 13.

13. Resolution of SED Group Fontane School and Nicholas School, 9 March 1951, BLHA Rep 347 FDGB Landesvorstand GUE, no. 1031.

14. See letters, BLHA Rep 347 FDGB Landesvorstand GUE, no. 1031; presentation for SED Sekretariat meeting, 22 March 1951, BLHA, Rep 334 SED Kreisleitung Brandenburg, no. 13.

15. GLE Brandenburg Province Executive Committee to Brandenburg's School Union Groups, undated, copy, and Brandenburg Province Executive Committee to Brandenburg's School Union Groups, 15 March 1951, BLHA Rep 347 FDGB Landesvorstand GUE, no. 1031, and presentation

for SED Sekretariat meeting, 22 March 1951, BLHA, Rep 334 SED Kreisleitung Brandenburg, no. 13.

16. Presentation for SED Sekretariat meeting, 22 March 1951, BLHA, Rep 334 SED Kreisleitung Brandenburg, no. 13.

17. "Protokoll über die Kreisdelegiertenkonferenz der Gewerkschaft Lehrer und Erzieher am 14. April 1951," 14 April 1951, BLHA, Rep 347 FDGB Landesvorstand Gewerkschaft Unterricht und Erziehung, no. 1058.

18. Ibid., "Sekretariatsvorlage zur Verbesserung der Pionier- und Schularbeit im Stadtkreis Brandenburg (Havel)," 28 February 1951, BLHA, Rep 334 SED Kreisleitung Brandenburg, no. 13, and statistical analysis, 1 October 1950, BLHA, Rep 205A Ministerium für Volksbildung, no. 224, 45. Records for the school year 1953–1954 indicate that approximately half of the teaching staff were *parteilos*, see "Analyse des Schuljahres 1953/1954," StadtA Brandenburg, 2.0.12.24/248, 58. Membership data for the SED at this time reveal that the number of teachers belonging to it had increased to a third from slightly more than a fifth as of the fall of 1949; see "Bericht zur Organisationsstatistik für den Monat September 1949, Kreis Brandenburg an der Havel," BLHA, Rep 334 SED Kreisleitung Brandenburg, no. 9, and "Tätigkeitsbericht über das gesamte Aufgabengebiet des Dezernates für Volksbildung für die Zeit vom 1. Juli 1949 bis 30. November 1949," StadtA Brandenburg, 2.0.12.115/957, 52. For data on teachers' membership in the LDPD and the CDU since late 1946, see Chapter 5.

19. "Protokoll über die Kreisdelegiertenkonferenz der Gewerkschaft Lehrer und Erzieher am 14. April 1951," 14 April 1951, BLHA, Rep 347 FDGB Landesvorstand Gewerkschaft Unterricht und Erziehung, no. 1058.

20. Ibid.; transfer notice from Potsdam Regierungspräsident, 25 April 1938, copy, BLHA, Pr. Br. Rep 2A Regierung Potsdam II Brd., no. 125.

21. "Protokoll über die Kreisdelegiertenkonferenz der Gewerkschaft Lehrer und Erzieher am 14. April 1951," 14 April 1951, BLHA, Rep 347 FDGB Landesvorstand GUE, no. 1058. Biographical information collected from NSLB *Mitgliedskartei* for Gau Kurmark, BAB NS12, 2:82–88, Registry of All Teachers at Brandenburg (Havel) Schools, comp. 27 August 1945, Amt für Volksbildung, Abt. Schulamt, StadtA Brandenburg, 2.0.12.30/254, 42–58, the city's registry of teachers, StadtA Brandenburg, 2.0.12.25/249, School-statistical Lists of the School Supervision District Brandenburg (Havel) for 1939 to 1944, BLHA, Pr. Br. Rep 2A Regierung Potsdam II Brd., nos. 198–203, "Vorlage für die Sekretarait-Sitzung am 22.3.1951," BLHA, Rep 334 SED Kreisleitung Brandenburg, no. 13, and "Bericht über die Kreisdelegiertenkonferenz in Brandenburg am 7.3.50," 27 March 1950, BLHA, Rep 347 FDGB Landesvorstand GUE, no. 990, 13–14.

22. For an analysis of the state's inability to implement an effective denazification program for eastern Germany, see Timothy Vogt's excellent study *Denazification in Soviet-occupied Germany: Brandenburg, 1945–1948* (Cambridge, Mass.: Harvard University Press, 2000), especially 114–142. In his remarkable examination of the transformation of the East German labor movement, Gareth Pritchard depicts a movement in the late 1940s and early 1950s that was characterized by both a growing subservience to the party and state and at the same time a grassroots resistance within the trade unions to this sovietization process; *The Making of the GDR 1945–1953: From Antifascism to Stalinism* (Manchester, England: Manchester University Press, 2000), 140–205. See also Andrew I. Port, *Conflict and Stability in the German Democratic Republic* (New York: Cambridge University Press, 2007).

23. Brandenburg GLE chapter to GLE Regional Executive Committee, 21 June 1951, and Brandenburg GUE chapter to Regional Executive Committee GUE, 27 September 1951, BLHA, Rep 347 FDGB Landesvorstand, no. 1056. As of September 1951, the GLE had officially changed its name to the Union of Teaching and Education (Gewerkschaft Unterricht und Erziehung, GUE).

24. "Protokoll der Gewerkschaftskollektivtagung vom 26. Oktober 1951," Brandenburg GUE, 29 October 1951, BLHA, Rep 347 FDGB Landesvorstand Gewerkschaft Unterricht und Erziehung, no. 949.

25. Ibid., and "Bericht über die Tätgkeit der Gewerkschaft UuE BrH im III. Quartal 1951," 17 October 1951, BLHA Rep 347 FDGB Landesvorstand GUE, no. 1031.

26. Minutes of BGL meeting, 20 June 1951, and confidential letter, District Secretary of Brandenburg GLE chapter Günther S. to Province Brandenburg GLE, 21 August 1950, BLHA, Rep 347 FDGB Landesvorstand GUE, no. 1031.

27. Minutes of BGL meeting, 7 September 1951, BLHA, Rep 347 FDGB Landesvorstand GUE, no. 1031. Founded in 1948, the NDPD was charged with the integration of former Nazis and members of the middle classes into the eastern German political system for the benefit of the SED; see David Childs, *The GDR: Moscow's German Ally* (Boston: George Allen and Unwin, 1983), 24, and Bundesministerium für innerdeutsche Beziehungen, *DDR Handbuch*, 1:927.

28. Minutes of BGL meeting, 7 September 1951, BLHA, Rep 347 FDGB Landesvorstand GUE, no. 1031.

29. Minutes of BGL meeting, 16 November 1951, BLHA, Rep 347 FDGB Landesvorstand GUE, no. 1031.

30. See minutes of BGL meetings, 4 January 1952, 28 January 1952, and 22 February 1952, BLHA, Rep 548 Brandenburg-Stadt GUE, no. 35, for 9 November 1951, BLHA, Rep 347 FDGB Landesvorstand GUE, no. 949, and for 20 June 1951 and 7 September 1951, BLHA, Rep 347 FDGB Landesvorstand GUE, no. 1031.

31. "Protokoll der Gewerkschaftskollektivtagung vom 26. Oktober 1951," Brandenburg GUE, 29 October 1951, BLHA, Rep 347 FDGB Landesvorstand GUE, no. 949; minutes of BGL meeting, 11 January 1952, 12 January 1952, and 15 February 1952, 20 February 1952, BLHA, Rep 548 Brandenburg-Stadt GUE, no. 35.

32. See, for instance, "Protokoll der Gewerkschaftskollektivtagung vom 26. Oktober 1951," Brandenburg GUE, 29 October 1951, BLHA, Rep 347 FDGB Landesvorstand GUE, no. 949; minutes of BGL meetings, 20 June and 7 September 1951, BLHA, Rep 347 FDGB Landesvorstand GUE, no. 1031, and minutes of BGL meeting, 11 January 1952, 12 January 1952, and 15 February 1952, 20 February 1952, BLHA, Rep 548 Brandenburg-Stadt GUE, no. 35.

33. Minutes of BGL meeting, 14 March 1952, 21 March 1952, BLHA, Rep 548 Brandenburg-Stadt GUE, no. 35.

34. Burghard Ciesla, ed., *"Freiheit wollen wir": Der 17. Juni 1953 in Brandenburg* (Berlin: Ch. Links Verlag, 2003), 16–32, Arnulf Baring, *Uprising in East Germany: June 17, 1953* (Ithaca, N.Y.: Cornell University Press, 1972), 1–51, Mike Dennis, *The Rise and Fall of the German Democratic Republic, 1945–1990* (New York: Longman, 2000), 57–63; Peter Helmberger, *Blauhemd und Kugelkreuz: Konflikte zwischen der SED und den christlichen Kirchen um die Jugendlichen in der SBZ/DDR* (Munich: Martin Meidenbauer Verlagsbuchhandlung, 2008), and the essays in Gesellschaft zur Förderung vergleichender Staat-Kirche-Forschung e.V., ed., *Der 17. Juni 1953 und die Kirche* (Gesellschaft: Berlin, 2003). The 75 who were expelled from Brandenburg comprised more than a third of the total number of individuals in the Potsdam District who were punished in connection with the campaign against the Junge Gemeinde, Gert Geissler, *Geschichte des Schulwesens in der Sowjetischen Besatzungszone und in der Deutschen Demokratischen Republik 1945 bis 1962* (Frankfurt am Main: Peter Lang, 2000), 369.

35. Benita Blessing, *The Antifascist Classroom: Denazification in Soviet-occupied Germany, 1945–1949* (New York: Palgrave, 2006), 54–57.

36. "Umschau," *Pädagogik* 1:3 (October 1946), 191; "Die neuen Schulbücher," *Pädagogik* 2:2 (February 1947), 110.

37. "Die neuen Schulbücher," 112; "Die Schulbuchlieferung in der sowjeti-

schen Zone für das Schuljahr 1947/48," *Pädagogik*, 2:8 (August 1947), 491; Blessing, *Antifascist Classroom*, 54–59; Arthur Hearnden, *Education in the Two Germanies* (Oxford: Blackwell, 1974), 49; Hahn, *Education and Society*, 97–98; "Jahresbericht über die Entwicklung des Schulwesens im Jahre 1946 in der Mark Brandenburg," BAB DR2/280, 224, and "Bericht über das Brandenburger Schulleben von Mai 1945 zum Mai 1948," StadtA Brandenburg, 2.0.12.17/241, 167.

38. Otto Hermenau, "Zum Lehrplan für den Russischen Unterricht," *Pädagogik* 1:4 (November 1946), 233; "Berichte: Geschichtstagung in Wiesenburg," *Pädagogik* 1:4 (November 1946), 243; "Umschau: Gegenwartskunde an den Berufs- und Berufsfachschulen," *Pädagogik* 2:3 (March 1947), 183.

39. "Der Arbeitsplan des Ministerium für Volksbildung für Berufsschulen im Jahre 1950," *Pädagogik* 5:2 (1950), 38; "Eine neue Reifeprüfungsordnung für die Länder der Deutschen Demokratischen Republik," *Pädagogik* 5:3 (1950), 34; "Aus der Arbeit des Deutschen Pädagogischen Zentralinstituts: Der Friedensgedanke im Unterricht," *Pädagogik* 5:7 (1950), 51–53; "Umschau: Aus der Arbeit des Deutschen Pädagogischen Zentralinstituts," *Pädagogik* 5:11/12 (1950), 117.

40. "Verordnung über die Durchführung des Schuljahres 1950/51," *Pädagogik* 5:6 (1950), 23–24.

41. "Konferenzprotokoll Goetheschule für Mädchen (Oberschule) Brandenburg (Havel)," 20 May 1950, BAB DR2/5720, 225, and Eva-Maria B., interview by author, 3 August 2000.

42. "Arbeitsplan für das IV. Quartal 1952," Education Department, Rat des Bezirkes Potsdam, 17 September 1952, BLHA, Rep 401 Bezirkstag und Rat des Bezirkes Potsdam, no. 2057, 24, and Sonja Häder, "Von der 'demokratischen Schulreform' zur Stalinisierung des Bildungswesens— Der 17. Juni 1953 in Schulen und Schulverwaltung Ost-Berlins," in Jürgen Kocka, ed., *Historische DDR-Forschung: Aufsätze und Studien*, (Berlin: Akademie Verlag, 1993), 198.

43. Häder, "Von der 'demokratischen Schulreform'," 198–199 and 204–205, and Geissler, *Geschichte des Schulwesens*, 373–374 and 349–350.

44. Ciesla, *"Freiheit wollen wir,"* 16–32, Baring, *Uprising*, 1–51, Dennis, *Rise and Fall*, 57–63, Mary Fulbrook, *Anatomy of a Dictatorship: Inside the GDR* (New York: Oxford, 1995), 179–180, and Port, *Conflict and Stability*, 70–72.

45. Ciesla, *"Freiheit wollen wir,"* 24–27, Baring, *Uprising*, 19, Dennis, *Rise and Fall*, 62–63, and Eva-Maria B., interview by author, 3 August 2000.

46. Ciesla, *"Freiheit wollen wir,"* 30–32, Baring, *Uprising*, 22–49, Dennis, *Rise and Fall*, 62–63, and Fulbrook, *Anatomy*, 179–183.

47. Geissler, *Geschichte des Schulwesens*, 379–381.

48. "Kurzbericht über die Vorkommnisse in Brandenburg/Havel am 12. Juni 1953," BDVP Potsdam, 13 June 1953, report regarding the protest in front of the Kreisgericht Brandenburg/Havel on 12 June 1953, Volkspolizei-Kommandeur Marterer, and "Stimmungsbericht," VPKA Brandenburg/H, Department K, 13 June 1953, BLHA, Rep 471/15 Bezirksbehörde der Deutschen Volkspolizei Potsdam, no. 33, 56, 57–63, and 213.

49. Ciesla, *"Freiheit wollen wir,"* 30–32, Baring, *Uprising,* 22–49, Dennis, *Rise and Fall,* 62–63, and Fulbrook, *Anatomy,* 179–183.

50. Reports "Bericht über die Auswertung des volkspolizeilichen Einsatzes zur Niederschlagung der faschistischen Provokationen seit dem 16. Juni 1953 gemäss fernschriftlichen Anordnung—FS—Nr.: 581 vom 21. Juni 1953 der HVDVP," Bezirksbehörde Deutsche Volkspolizei Potsdam, 28 June 1953, "Bericht der Inspektionsgruppe Nr.: 32/53 über die Inspektionstätigkeit im Bereich des VPKA Brandenburg/H. am 25. und 26.6.1953," BDVP, 30 June 1953, and "Bericht über die Vorfälle im Gericht und Gefängnis in Brandenburg/H am 17. Juni 1953," Comrade Harry Benkendorff, 30 June 1953, copy, all in BLHA, Rep 471/15 Bezirksbehörde der Deutschen Volkspolizei Potsdam, no. 33, 1–6, 199–200, and 247.

51. See reports "Bericht über die Auswertung des volkspolizeilichen Einsatzes zur Niederschlagung der faschistischen Provokationen seit dem 16. Juni 1953," "Überprüfung der Vorkommnisse in der UHA Brandenburg," BDVP Potsdam, 21 June 1953, and "Bericht über die Vorfälle im Gericht und Gefängnis in Brandenburg/H am 17. Juni 1953," copy, all in BLHA, Rep 471/15 Bezirksbehörde der Deutschen Volkspolizei Potsdam, no. 33, 6 and 20, 221, and 249.

52. See reports "Bericht der Inspektionsgruppe Nr.: 32/53," "Bericht über die Vorfälle im Gericht und Gefängnis in Brandenburg/H am 17. Juni 1953," copy, both in BLHA, Rep 471/15 Bezirksbehörde der Deutschen Volkspolizei Potsdam, no. 33, 201, 247–251.

53. "Bericht über die Auswertung des volkspolizeilichen Einsatzes zur Niederschlagung der faschistischen Provokationen seit dem 16. Juni 1953," 6 and "Überfall auf das Volkspolizeikreisamt Brandenburg/H.," both in BLHA, Rep 471/15 Bezirksbehörde der Deutschen Volkspolizei Potsdam, no. 33, 6, 214.

54. "Bericht über die Auswertung des volkspolizeilichen Einsatzes zur Niederschlagung der faschistischen Provokationen seit dem 16. Juni 1953," BLHA, Rep 471/15 Bezirksbehörde der deutschen Volkspolizei Potsdam, no. 33, 7 and 10; "Befehl über den Ausnahmezustand der Stadt und des Bezirkes Potsdam," Militärkommandant des Bezirkes und der Stadt Potsdam, BLHA, Rep 471/15 Bezirksbehörde der Deutschen Volkspolizei Potsdam, no. 33, 53, and "Situation Report from Andrei Grechko and A.

Tarasov to Nikolai Bulganin, 17 June 1953, as of 11:00 p.m. Moscow Time," reprinted in Christian Ostermann, ed., *Uprising in East Germany 1953: The Cold War, the German Question and the First Major Upheaval behind the Iron Curtain* (New York: Central European University Press, 2001), 197.

55. "Information Nrs. 19–20, 22, 26–27," 18 June 1953, BLHA, Rep 471/15 Bezirksbehörde der Deutschen Volkspolizei Potsdam, no. 33, 39–41 and 46–47; "Bericht über die Unterstützung der Abt. K vom VPKA Brandenburg/Havel," BDVP, 25 June 1953, BLHA, Rep 471/15 Bezirksbehörde der Deutschen Volkspolizei Potsdam, no. 33, 232, and Ciesla, *"Freiheit wollen wir,"* 41–46.

56. Minutes of District Executive Committee meeting, 26 June 1953, in FDGB-Haus, BLHA, Rep 548 FBGB GUE Kreisvorstand Brandenburg Stadt, no. 25; Eva-Maria B. and Karl-Heinz R., interviews by author, August 2000; and "Zum Beschluss," GUE Central Committee Report, undated, SAPMO-BArch 51/706 (Previously DY51/18/654/3225).

57. "Bericht über die Auswertung des volkspolizeilichen Einsatzes zur Niederschlagung der faschistischen Provokationen seit dem 16. Juni 1953," BLHA, Rep 471/15 Bezirksbehörde der Deutschen Volkspolizei Potsdam, no. 33, 8–9, minutes of Twenty-seventh Sekretariat meeting, Thursday, 16 July 1953, SED Kreisleitung SED Brandenburg an der Havel, 17 July 1953, BLHA, Rep 531 SED-Kreisleitung Brandenburg, no. 77, 280–282, minutes of Twenty-ninth Sekretariat meeting, Thursday, 30 July 1953, SED Kreisleitung Brandenburg an der Havel, 30 July 1953, "Bericht über die Beschlüsse und Verordnungen des Ministerrates der DDR vom 11.6 und vom 25.6.1953 und Beschlussfassung über das Sonderbauprogram 1953," BLHA, Rep 531 SED Kreisleitung Brandenburg, no. 78, 29–30 and 39–48, and "Bericht über die Überprüfung der Durchführung der Anordnung des Ministers für Volksbildung vom 15.6.1953 in den Kreisen," 2 July 1953, BLHA, Rep 401 Bezirkstagung und Rat des Bezirkes Potsdam, no. 1030.

58. "Bericht über die Auswertung des volkspolizeilichen Einsatzes zur Niederschlagung der faschistischen Provokationen seit dem 16. Juni 1953," BLHA, Rep 471/15 Bezirksbehörde der Deutschen Volkspolizei Potsdam, no. 33, 10.

59. Jonathan Sperber, "17 June 1953: Revisiting a German Revolution," *German History* 22:4 (2004), 631; Häder, "Von der 'demokratischen Schulreform,'" 208; "Bericht über die Auswertung des volkspolizeilichen Einsatzes zur Niederschlagung der faschistischen Provokationen seit dem 16. Juni 1953," BLHA, Rep 471/15 Bezirksbehörde der Deutschen Volkspolizei Potsdam, no. 33, 7–8.

60. Report, SAPMO-BArch 51/706 (formerly DY51/18/654/3225); Häder, "Von der 'demokratischen Schulreform,'" 211; Geissler, *Geschichte des Schulwesens*, 383 and 385; Report, SAPMO-BArch 51/706 (formerly DY51/18/654/3225).

61. Sperber, "17 June 1953," 631–632.

62. "Bericht über die Überprüfung der Parteiarbeit in der Theodor-Neubauer-Schule," Kreisleitung-Mitglied, BLHA, Rep 531 SED-Kreisleitung Brandenburg, no. 770, 25; Geissler, *Geschichte des Schulwesens*, 386.

63. Helke Stadtland reaches similar conclusions regarding East German industrial workers, see *Herrschaft nach Plan und Macht der Gewohnheit: Sozialgeschichte der Gewerkschaften in der SBZ/DDR 1945–1953* (Essen: Klartext Verlag, 2001), 20.

64. Minutes of Expanded BGL meeting, 28 March 1952, BLHA, Rep 548 Brandenburg-Stadt GUE, no. 35.

65. Minutes of Kreisvorstand meeting, 11 June 1953, BLHA, Rep 548 FBGB GUE Kreisvorstand Brandenburg Stadt, no. 25.

66. "Beschluss zu den Aufgaben unserer Gewerkschaft beim Aufbau des Sozialismus," Central Committee of GUE, Berlin, 20 August 1952, SAPMO-BArch DY 51/680 (formerly DY 51/18/614/3210); "Protokoll der Gewerkschaftskollektivtagung vom 26. Oktober 1951," Brandenburg an der Havel GUE, BLHA, Rep 347 FDGB Landesvorstand Gewerkschaft Unterricht und Erziehung, no. 949.

Conclusion

1. "Analyse des Schuljahres 1953/54," BLHA, Rep 531 SED-Kreisleitung Brandenburg, no. 770, 4, 7–9, 16–17.

2. "Bericht über den Stand des Schulwesens," 30 September 1948, School Superintendent Karl P., StadtA Brandenburg, 2.0.12.17/241, 198.

3. For biographical information regarding Johannes S., see the city's registry of teachers, StadtA Brandenburg, 2.0.12.25/249, "Nachweisung über die Zugehörigkeit von Beamten zu Freimaurerlogen, anderen Logen oder logenähnlichen Organisationen und deren Ersatzorganisationen" draft report from Regierungspräsident Potsdam to Education Ministry, 30 September 1935, BLHA, Pr. Br. Rep 2A Regierung Potsdam II Gen., no. 733, and Lehrer-Verband der Provinz Brandenburg, ed., *Lehrer-Verzeichnis für die Provinz Brandenburg* 13. Jahrgang, (Liegnitz: Carl Seyffarth, 1928), 32. Moreover, Johannes S. not only continued to work in the schools in the postwar era but also served as a principal as late as 1954, "Analyse des Schuljahres 1953/54," BLHA, Rep 531 SED-Kreisleitung Brandenburg, no. 770, 22.

4. "Personen die bei der Durchführung des Befehls 201 mit Zwangsmassnahmen belegt wurden," table, BLHA, Rep 203 Ministerium des Innern Entnazifizierung, no. 690, and "Bericht über die 11. Sekretariat-Sitzung am Dienstag, dem 20. Dez. 1949," BLHA, Rep 334 SED Kreisleitung Brandenburg, no. 9.

5. Minutes of BGL Meeting, 7 September 1951, Rep 347 FDGB Landesvorstand GUE, no. 1031.

6. Ritterakademie Director to Oberpräsident Kube, 27 September 1935, BLHA, Pr. Br. Rep 34 P.S.K., no. 5303.

Acknowledgments

Although this book began to take shape formally during my graduate studies at Yale University, I first developed an interest in the subject of how Germans experienced radical change in their society while working in 1993–1994 among teachers who had only a few years earlier taught under the East German dictatorship and who were still finding their way in a re-unified Germany. At Yale University, the late Henry Ashby Turner, Jr., and historians Ute Frevert, John Merriman, and Ivo Banac helped me shape, structure, and polish an inchoate interest into a feasible book project. For their steadfast support and guidance, I am deeply grateful. I would also like to thank Paul Bushkovitch, Laura Engelstein, James Heinzen, Paul Kennedy, Kevin Repp, Timothy Snyder, Frank M. Turner, and Jay Winter for their advice and encouragement. Participants in various conferences as well as in Yale's stimulating Russian and East European Reading Group offered constructive criticism of portions of this work. At the University of Connecticut, my colleagues John Davis, Michael Dintenfass, Brendan Kane, Shirley Roe, and Sylvia Schafer helped me revise this study into its final book form. I have benefited immeasurably at every stage of this project from the friends I made in seminars, libraries, and archives, including Pertti Ahonen, Christof Biggeleben, William Lee Blackwood, Rachel Chrastil, Alon Confino, Astrid Eckart, William Glenn Gray, Molly Wilkinson Johnson, Marcus Jones, Charles Keith, Kenneth Ledford, Susan Mc-Donough, Jon Berndt Olson, Lindsay O'Neill, Jared Poley, Andrew Port, David Posner, Brian Rohlik, Nick Rutters, David Shearer, David Tompkins, Helen Zoe Veit, Brian Vick, and Greg Witkowski. A special thanks goes to Jay Howard Geller for his peerless counsel, boundless assistance, and sustaining friendship. Finally, without the support of a wonderful group of friends in Germany, especially Norman Schmidt and his family, I would not have been able to complete this study. A special note of gratitude is also due to Jürgen, Christine, Anne, and Frank Michaelsen; much of what I learned about teachers' lives in the German Democratic Republic came from our many rewarding conversations. While the strengths of this study are in large part due to the efforts of such mentors, colleagues, and friends, any shortcomings are entirely my own.

Such generosity would have accomplished little had it not been matched by the assistance provided by many helpful archivists and librarians in Germany, Russia, and the United States. The men and women of the Bundesarchiv in Berlin, the Stiftung Archiv Parteien und Massenorganisationen der DDR in Berlin, the Staatsbibliothek zu Berlin, the Brandenburgisches Landeshauptarchiv in Potsdam, the Domstiftarchiv in Brandenburg an der Havel, the National Archives in Washington, D.C., and librarian Sue Roberts at Yale University facilitated my research greatly. I want to thank particularly archive director Klaus Hess and the wonderful staff of the Stadtarchiv Brandenburg an der Havel; their extraordinary assistance enabled me to complete my research in a timely manner. I am also indebted to the former teachers who shared with me their experiences as *Neulehrer* in Brandenburg an der Havel and to Helmut Silber, Wolfgang Panther, and Torsten Fried, who made introductions. My research trip to Moscow in the summer of 2000 would not have been as productive as it was without the assistance of Elena Sergeevna Drozdova, the staff of Praxis International, and the archivists at Gosudarstvennyi Arkhiv Rossiiskoi Federatsii and Rossiiskii Gosudarstvennyi Voennyi Arkhiv. Hopefully, Russian archival policies will one day grant scholars full access to the records of the Soviet Military Administration in Germany. None of the research in German and Russian archives and libraries would have been possible without the generous financial support provided by the Fox International Fellowship Program, the Smith Richardson Foundation, the Foreign Language Area Studies program, and Yale University in the form of University, George W. Darr, and Gilbert Kenney Memorial fellowships.

I would like to thank editors Kathleen McDermott and Joyce Seltzer and their staff at Harvard University Press; their support of the project helped ensure its publication. I am also indebted to the two anonymous readers whose detailed feedback greatly improved the manuscript.

Finally, I would like to thank my parents, siblings, and extended family for their love and support over the years. Most important, I want to thank my wife, Amy, to whom I dedicate this book; her wisdom, love, and encouragement accompanied me every step of the way.

Bibliography

Archival Collections

Berlin Document Center, National Archives, Washington, D.C.

NS Lehrerbund Kartei und Akten

Brandenburgisches Landeshauptarchiv, Potsdam

Abteilung II Bestände der Provinz Brandenburg (1815–1945)
Abteilung III Bestände der Land Brandenburg (since 1945)

Bundesarchiv, Berlin

Abteilung III   Deutsches Reich
R 58   Reichssicherheitshauptamt
R4901   Reichsministerium für Wissenschaft, Erziehung und Volksbildung
R1501   Reichsministerium des Innern
NS12   Hauptamt für Erzieher/Reichswaltung NSLB
Abteilung V   Deutsche Demokratische Republik
DO1   Ministerium des Innern
DR2   Ministerium für Volksbildung
DX1   Sammlung SMAD Befehle

Stiftung Archiv der Parteien and Massenorganisationen der DDR im Bundesarchiv

DY30   Sozialistische Einheitspartei Deutschlands
DY34   Freie Deutsche Gewerkschaftsbund

DY51   Gewerkschaft Unterricht und Erziehung

Domstiftarchiv, Brandenburg an der Havel

1.0   Organisation
2.0   Lehrer und Beamte
4.0   Das Schul- und Erziehungswesen

Gosudarstvennyi Arkhiv Rossiskoi Federatsii, Moscow

f. 7317—SVAG (Soviet Military Administration in Germany) General Correspondence

Rossiiskii Gosudarstvennyi Voennyi Arkhiv, Moscow

Osobyi Arkhiv (Special Archive)

Stadtarchiv Brandenburg an der Havel

21.1   Magistrat
21.2   Polizei
21.3   Gericht- und Rechtwesen
21.4   Schulen, Kultur, Bildung

Published Primary Sources

Amtliches Schulblatt für den Regierungs-Bezirk Potsdam. 1928–1940.

Anweiler, Oskar, Hans-Jürgen Fuchs, Martina Dorner, and Eberhard Petermann. *Bildungspolitik in Deutschland 1945–1990: Ein historisch-vergleichender Quellenband.* Bonn: Bundeszentrale für politische Bildung, 1992.

Arbeitskreis Stadtgeschichte im Brandenburgischen Kulturbund e.V. (ed.). *Das Jahr 1945 in der Stadt Brandenburg: Eine Anthologie mit Darstellungen, Tagebuchaufzeichnungen und Lebenserinnerungen an das Ende des Zweiten Weltkrieges in der Stadt Brandenburg.* Brandenburg an der Havel: Werbe-Profi Brandenburg, 2001.

Baske, Siegfried, and Martha Engelbett (eds). *Zwei Jahrzehnte Bildungspolitik in der Sowjetzone Deutschlands: Dokumente. Pt. 1. 1945 bis 1958.* Berlin: Osteuropa-Institut an der Freien Universität Berlin, 1966.

Berichte der Landes- und Provinzialverwaltungen zur antifaschistisch-demokratisch Umwälzung 1945/46: Quellenedition. Berlin: Akademie Verlag, 1989.

Bloch, Peter. *Zwischen Hoffnung und Resignation: Als CDU-Politker in Brandenburg 1945–1950.* Köln: Verlag Wissenschaft und Politik, 1986.

Brandenburger Anzeiger. 1933–1945.

Brandenburger Warte. "Der Deutsche Vorwärts" für die Stadt Brandenburg, für Rathenow, das Havelland und den Kreis Zauch-Belzig. 1933–1934.

Brandenburger Zeitung. 1933.

Bundesministerium für Gesamtdeutsche Fragen (ed.). *Das Schulbuch in der Sowjetzone: Lehrbücher im Dienst Totalitärer Propaganda.* Bonn: Deutscher Bundes-Verlag, 1966.

Cisela, Burghard (ed.). *Freiheit wollen wir! Der 17. Juni 1953 in Brandenburg.* Berlin: Ch. Links Verlag, 2003.

Der Deutsche Erzieher: Kampfblatt der im nationalsozialistischen Lehrerbund geeinten Eigenschaften des Gau Württemberg-Hohenzollern. 1937.

Der Deutsche Erzieher: Reichszeitung des NSLB. Gau Kurmark ed. 1939–1943.

Der Märker. 1945–1946.

Deutsche Wissenschaft Erziehung und Volksbildung: Amtsblatt des Reichsministeriums für Wissenschaft, Erziehung und Volksbildung und der Unterrichts-Verwaltungen der Länder. Berlin: Franz Eher (Zentral Verlag der NSDAP), 1933–1944.

Deutschlands Städtebau: Brandenburg (Havel). Edited by Magistrat der Stadt Brandenburg (Havel). 2nd ed. Berlin: Deutscher Architektur- und Industrie-Verlag, 1926.

Die Ersten Jahre: Erinnerungen an den Beginn der revolutionären Umgestaltungen. Berlin: Dietz Verlag, 1979.

Die Erzieher der Kurmark 1936, Verzeichnis der Parteidienststellen, Schulbehörden, Lehranstalten und Lehrkräfte. Berlin: Verlag "Nationalsozialistische Erziehung," 1936.

du Bois-Reymond, Manuela, and Bruno Schonig (eds.). *Lehrerlebensgeschichten: Lehrerinnen und Lehrer aus Berlin und Leiden (Holland) Erzählen.* Weinheim: Beltz Verlag, 1982.

Fricke-Finkenburg, Renate (ed.). *Nationalsozialismus und Schule: Amtliche Erlasse und Richtlinien 1933–1945.* Opladen: Leske und Budrich, 1989.

Geissler, Gert, Falk Blask, and Thomas Scholze (eds.) *Schule: Streng vertraulich! Die Volksbildung der DDR in Dokumenten. Eine Publikation des Ministeriums fürs Bildung, Jugend und Sport des Landes Brandenburg.* Berlin: Basisdruck, 1996.

Gniffke, Erich W. *Jahre Mit Ulbricht.* Köln: Verlag Wissenschaft und Politik, 1966.

Grasow, Friedrich. *Brandenburg die tausendjährige Stadt: Ein Gang durch Kultur und Baukunst vergangener Jahrhunderte.* Brandenburg (Havel): Buch- und Kunstdruckerei J. Wiesike, 1927.

Grotesend, G. A., and Dr. C. Cretschmar. *Das gesamte deutsche und preussische Gesetzgebungsmaterial: Die Gesetze und Verordnungen sowie die Ausführungs-Anweisungen, Erlasse, Verfügungen usw. der preussischen und deutschen Zentralbehörden.* Vol. 1. Düsseldorf: L. Schwann Verlag, 1933.

Hammerstein, Notker (ed.). *Deutsche Bildung? Briefwechsel zweier Schulmänner: Otto Schumann—Martin Havenstein 1930–1944.* Frankfurt am Main: Insel Verlag, 1988.

Historische Gedenkstätte des Potsdamer Abkommens (ed.). *The Potsdam Agreement: Selected Documents Concerning the German Question 1943–1949.* Berlin: Staatsverlag der Deutschen Demokratischen Republik, 1967.

Hohmann, Joachim S. (ed.). *Lehrerflucht aus SBZ und DDR 1945–1961: Dokumente zur Geschichte und Soziologie sozialistischer Bildung und Erziehung.* Frankfurt am Main: Peter Lang, 2000.

Huchthausen, Liselot. *Alltag in der DDR: (1945)–1975.* Kückenshagen: Scheunen-Verlag, 1998.

Inventar der Offenen Befehle der Sowjetischen Militäradministration des Landes Brandenburg. Edited by Klaus Gessner and Wladimir W. Sacharow. Frankfurt am Main: Peter Lang, 2002.

Just, Gustav. *Deutsch, Jahrgang 1921: Ein Lebensbericht.* Potsdam: Verlag für Berlin-Brandenburg, 2001.

Kahl-Futhman, Dr. Gertrud. *Hans Schemm Spricht: Seine Reden und sein Werk.* Rev. ed. Bayreuth: Gauverlag Bayerische Ostmark, 1936.

Klemperer, Victor. *Ich will Zeugnis ablegen bis zum letzten: Tagebücher 1933–1945.* Edited by Walter Nowojski. Berlin: Aufbau Verlag, 1997.

———. *So sitze ich denn zwischen allen Stühlen: Tagebücher 1945–1959.* Edited by Walter Nowojski. Berlin: Aufbau Verlag, 1999.

Lehrer-Verband der Provinz Brandenburg (ed.). *Lehrer-Verzeichnis für die Provinz Brandenburg.* 13. Jahrgang, Liegnitz: Carl Seyffarth, 1928.

Leonhard, Wolfgang. *Die Revolution Entlässt Ihre Kinder.* Köln: Kiepenheuer und Witsch, 1955.

Leschinsky, Achim, and Gerhard Kluchert. *Zwischen Zwei Diktaturen: Gespräche über die Schulzeit im Nationalsozialismus und in der SBZ/DDR.* Weinheim: Deutscher Studien Verlag, 1997.

Märkische Volksstimme. 1946–1947.

Mertens, Adolf. *Schulungslager und Lagererziehung.* Dortmund: Druck und Verlag von W. Crüwell, 1937.

Nationalsozialistische Erziehung: Kampf- und Mitteilungsblatt des Nationalsozialistischen Lehrerbunds für den Gau Kurmark. 1936–1938.

Nationalsozialistische Erziehung: Kampf- und Mitteilungsblatt des Nationalsozialistischen Lehrerbundes im Bereich Norddeutschlands. 1933–1936.

Nikitin, Piotr I. *Zwischen Dogma und gesunden Menschenverstand: Wie ich die Universitäten der deutschen Besatzungszone "sowjetisierte." Erinnerungen des Sektorleiters Hochschulen und Wissenschaft der Sowjetischen Militäradministration in Deutschland.* Berlin: Akademie Verlag, 1997.

Noakes, J., and G. Pridham (eds.). *Nazism 1919–1945.* vol. 2. *State, Economy and Society 1933–1939: A Documentary Reader.* Exeter, England: University of Exeter Press, 2000.

Ostermann, Christian F. *Uprising in East Germany 1953: The Cold War, the German Question, and the First Major Upheaval behind the Iron Curtain.* New York: Central European Press, 2001.

Pädagogik. Berlin: Volk und Wissen Verlag. 1946–1947, 1950–1952.

Pätzold, Horst. *Nischen im Gras: Ein Leben in zwei Diktaturen.* Hamburg: Krämer, 1997.

Petzina, Dietmar, Werner Abelshauser, and Anselm Faust. *Sozialgeschichtliches Arbeitsbuch. Vol. 3. Materialien zur Statistik des Deutschen Reiches 1914–1945.* Munich: C. H. Beck Verlag, 1978.

Reich-Ranicki, Marcel (ed.). *Meine Schulzeit im Dritten Reich: Erinnerungen deutscher Schriftsteller.* Erweiterte Neuausgabe. Köln: Kiepenheuer und Witsch, 1988.

The Reorganization of Education in Prussia: Based on Official Documents and Publications. Translated by I. L. Kandel and Thomas Alexander. New York: Bureau of Publications, Teachers College, Columbia University, 1927.

Ribbe, Wolfgang (ed.). *Die Lageberichte der Geheimen Staatspolizei über die Provinz Brandenburg und die Reichshauptstadt Berlin 1933 bis 1936. Vol. 1. Der Regierungsbezirk Potsdam.* Köln: Böhlau Verlag, 1998.

Röhrs, Hermann. *Nationalsozialismus, Krieg, Neubeginn: Eine autobiographische Vergegenwärtigung aus pädagogischer Sicht.* Frankfurt am Main: Peter Lang, 1990.

Rosner, Fanny (ed.). *Vereint sind wir alles: Erinnerungen an die Gründung der SED.* Berlin: Dietz Verlag, 1966.

Rössler, Ruth-Kristin (ed.). *Die Entnazifizierungspolitik der KPD/SED 1945–1948. Dokumente und Materialien.* Goldbach: Keip Verlag, 1994.

Rytlewski, Ralf, and Manfred Opp de Hipt. *Die Deutsche Demokratische Republik in Zahlen 1945/49–1980: Ein sozialgeschichtliches Arbeitsbuch.* Munich: C. H. Beck Verlag, 1987.

Sägebrecht, Willy. *Nicht Amboss, Sondern Hammer Sein: Erinnerungen.* Berlin: Dietz Verlag, 1968.

Schaffer, Gordon. *Russian Zone.* London: George Allen and Unwin, 1947.

Schulspiegel: Blätter des Oberlyzeums-Brandenburg/Havel. 1928–1937.

Statistisches Jahrbuch für Preussen. (ed.). Preussischen Statistischen Landesamt.
    Vol. 30. Berlin: Verlag des Preussischen Statistischen Landesamts, 1934.

————. (ed.). Preussischen Statistischen Landesamt. Vol. 29. Berlin: Verlag des
    Preussischen Statistischen Landesamts, 1933.

————. (ed.). Preussischen Statistischen Landesamt. Vol. 28. Berlin: Verlag des
    Preussischen Statistischen Landesamts, 1932.

Stern, Carola. *Doppelleben: Eine Autobiographie.* Köln: Kiepenheuer und
    Witsch, 2001.

Thiede, Olaf, and Jörg Wacher (ed.). *Chronologie Potsdam und Umgebung: Die
    Kulturlandschaft von 800 bis 1918. Brandenburg, Potsdam, Berlin.* 3 vols.
    Potsdam: Druckerei und Buchbinderei Christian und Cornelius Rüss, 2007.

Volkswille: Zeitung für die Provinz Brandenburg. 1945–1946.

von Oppen, Beate Ruhm (ed.). *Documents on Germany under Occupation
    1945–1954.* London: Oxford University Press, 1955.

Index

Adam Opel AG truck factory: opening of in Brandenburg, 19; Soviet dismantling of, 22; damaged in Second World War, 132

All German Female Teachers' Association, 32, 69

Augusta Intermediate School, 30, 52, 54, 57, 104, 105, 106, 115, 116, 127, 133

Becher, Johannes, 139, 213

Berufsbeamtentum: Brandenburg teachers' identification with, 10, 12, 213, 220

Bormann, Martin, 59, 122

Brandenburg an der Havel, 1, 2; reputation as bastion of socialism, 13, 15, 23; creation of Nazi dictatorship in, 13, 20–21, 25–26, 34; role in Nazi T4 program, 13, 20, 23; a representative and unique German community, 13, 22–23; description and early history of, 13–14; industrial base of, 14–15; early trade union and socialist activities in, 15; political developments in after the First World War and in the Weimar Republic, 15–19; effects of Great Depression in, 16–17; Nazi rearmament programs in, 19–20; population explosion in, 19–20, 57, 87, 106, 134; postwar transformation of, 21; Soviet occupation of, 21, 132–133; creation of SED dictatorship in, 22; role in Night of Long Knives, 23; school system of, 29–30, 134; composition of teaching staff of, 30–33; Jewish community in, 52; Kristallnacht pogrom in, 89; devastation of in Second World War, 132–133; reconstruction of school system in, 134–136

Brandenburger Anzeiger, 25, 61, 80

Brandenburger Warte, 17, 25; role in purge of teachers, 26, 33–34, 41, 42, 43, 44, 45, 55

Brandenburger Zeitung, 20, 44

Brandenburg Steel and Rolling Mill: early history of, 15; dismantling of by Soviets, 22; role in Uprising of 17 June, 209, 211

Brennabor Works: early history of, 14; bankruptcy of in Great Depression, 16; arms production in Third Reich, 19; dismantling of by Soviets, 22; damaged in Second World War, 132

Catholic Community School, 30, 54

Christian Democratic Union (CDU), 21, 22, 148, 149, 152, 169, 183, 197, 202; Brandenburg teachers' membership in, 5, 186, 188, 190–191, 198; membership statistics for Brandenburg teachers, 147, 165, 184–185; Communist Party (KPD), 16, 19, 21, 27, 36, 169; Brandenburg teachers' membership in, 31, 147, 183; support for postwar school reform, 153